AMERICAN MEN AND WOMEN

2nd EDITION

AMERICAN MEN AND WOMEN

Who They Are and How They Live

BY THE EDITORS OF NEW STRATEGIST PRESS

New Strategist Press, LLC
Amityville, New York

New Strategist Press, LLC
P.O. Box 635, Amityville, New York 11701
800/848-0842; 631/608-8795
www.newstrategist.com

Copyright 2013. NEW STRATEGIST PRESS, LLC

ISBN 978-1-940308-05-0 (paper)

Printed in the United States of America

Table of Contents

Chapter 4. Income

Chapter 5. Labor Force

Chapter 6. Living Arrangements

Chapter 7. Population

Chapter 8. Spending

Chapter 9. Time Use

Chapter 10. Wealth

List of Tables

Chapter 3. Health

Chapter 4. Income

Chapter 5. Labor Force

Chapter 8. Spending

Chapter 9. Time Use

Chapter 10. Wealth

List of Charts

Chapter 5. Labor Force

Chapter 6. Living Arrangements

Chapter 7. Population

Chapter 8. Spending

Chapter 9. Time Use

Chapter 10. Wealth

Introduction

American men and women are not the people they used to be, and businesses and policymakers are struggling to keep up. Over the past half-century, women moved out of the home and into the labor force. Men's roles expanded from breadwinner and handyman to nurturer and home manager. As women became more independent of husbands and children, men became more involved in home and family. The changing roles of men and women have been nothing short of revolutionary, affecting every institution in our society—from the family to the workplace, from politics to the consumer marketplace.

The lives of American men and women are a work in progress, their roles still fluid and evolving. Today's young adults are postponing marriage and childbearing, driving the median age at first marriage to a record high. A new baby bust is underway as fertility rates have plunged to record lows. Young women are now more educated than their male counterparts, and a growing share earn more as well. Tracking and understanding these changes has become more important than ever as the nation struggles to recover from the Great Recession and businesses compete for customers.

American Men and Women: Who They Are and How They Live examines the many dimensions of the lives of men and women as they make their way through the second decade of the 21st century. These pages contain all-important demographic data showing the number of males and females, their changing age distribution, rising educational attainment, and diversifying racial composition. The Attitudes chapter, based on data from the renowned General Social Survey, compares what men and women think about a variety of issues and examines how their attitudes differ by age. Also included in this book is a chapter comparing and contrasting time use based on the Bureau of Labor Statistics' invaluable American Time Use Survey. *American Men and Women* also provides the latest labor force projections from the Bureau of Labor Statistics, the latest population projections from the Census Bureau, and statistics on income, labor force, living arrangements, spending, and wealth.

Value Added

While the government collected most of the data in *American Men and Women*, the tables published here are not reprints of government reports. Instead, New Strategist's editors spent hundreds of hours scouring web sites, compiling numbers into meaningful statistics, and creating tables with calculations to reveal the trends. Those who want the spreadsheet versions of the tables in this book, visit www .newstrategist.com to download the PDF file with links to each table in Excel format.

Government web sites are useful for obtaining summary data and tapping into complex databases. But too often summary data are not enough, and those complex databases usually require analysis by statistical program. With this volume, New Strategist has done the work for you, delving into the data and providing analyses and comparisons, placing the important information about American men and women at your fingertips. The texts and charts accompanying most of the tables tell the story, placing trends into context and revealing what the future holds. Thumbing through these pages will give you more insight than an afternoon spent surfing databases on the Internet. With *American Men and Women* at hand, you can get answers to your questions even faster than you can online.

How to Use This Book

American Men and Women is designed for easy use. It is divided into 10 chapters, organized alphabetically: Attitudes, Education, Health, Income, Labor Force, Living Arrangements, Population, Spending, Time Use, and Wealth.

Most of the tables in the book are based on data collected and published by the federal government, in particular the Census Bureau, the Bureau of Labor Statistics, the National Center for Education Statistics, and the National Center for Health Statistics. The federal government continues to be the best source of up-to-date, reliable information on the changing characteristics of Americans.

Perhaps the most important source of data for *American Men and Women* is the Current Population Survey. The CPS is a nationally representative survey of the civilian noninstitutional population aged 15 or older. Taken monthly by the Census Bureau, it collects information from 60,000 households on employment and unemployment. Each year, the March survey includes a demographic supplement, which is the source of most national data on the characteristics of Americans such as their educational attainment, living arrangements, and incomes.

The American Community Survey is another important source of data for *American Men and Women*. The ACS is an ongoing nationwide survey of 250,000 households per month, providing detailed demographic data at the community level. Designed to replace the census long-form questionnaire, the ACS collects data not only for the nation as a whole, but also for regions, states, counties, and metropolitan areas.

To explore changes in attitudes, New Strategist extracted data from the 2012 General Social Survey of the University of Chicago's National Opinion Research Center. NORC conducts the biennial survey through face-to-face interviews with a nationally representative sample of people aged 18 or older in the United States. The GSS is one of the best sources of attitudinal data on Americans available today.

The spending data in *American Men and Women* are from the 2011 Consumer Expenditure Survey, an ongoing study of the day-to-day spending of American households administered by the Bureau of Labor Statistics. Because the BLS collects spending data from households rather than individuals, spending patterns must be gleaned by examining the spending of men and women who live alone, of married couples, and of single-parent families. The great majority of men and women live in one of these three types of households, and their spending is detailed in *American Men and Women*.

The American Time Use Survey is the source of the time use statistics presented in this book. This survey, administered by the Bureau of Labor Statistics, collects data from a nationally representative sample of Americans aged 15 or older by asking them what they did during the previous 24 hours, minute by minute. Time use data reveals the priorities of Americans, allowing marketers and policymakers to better understand how our economy works. Most of the time use data shown in this book are not available online. The unpublished tables are available only by special request.

American Men and Women contains a comprehensive table list to help readers locate the information they need. For a more detailed search, use the index at the back of the book. Also in the back of the book is a glossary, which defines most of the terms commonly used in the tables and text and describes the surveys used to gather the information. Researchers who want even more should use the web sites listed in the sources at the bottom of each table to explore original documents.

American Men and Women will help you track and understand today's evolving lifestyles. With that understanding, you will be better equipped to meet the wants and needs of our rapidly changing population.

Attitudes

Most men and women are pretty happy.

Men under age 45 are most likely to find life exciting (61 percent). Women aged 65 or older are least likely to feel this way (44 percent).

Most men and women still believe in the American Dream.

Younger adults are most optimistic. Among men and women aged 65 or older, fewer than half still believe their family can get ahead.

Women are much more likely than men to support gay marriage.

The 54 percent majority of women support gay marriage versus 43 percent of men. Among men aged 65 or older, only 26 percent support gay marriage.

Women are more religious than men.

Women are more likely to attend church weekly, pray daily, and believe in God without a doubt. Perhaps consequently, they are less likely than men to believe in evolution.

Men are more conservative than women.

Men are more likely to identify themselves as politically conservative, especially those aged 65 or older.

Few men or women own a gun.

But among men aged 65 or older, more than 60 percent are gun owners.

Most Men and Women Are Pretty Happy

There is little variation in happiness by sex.

When asked how happy they are, about a third of men and women report being very happy, and most describe themselves as "pretty" happy. There is little variation in happiness by age or sex.

There is more variation in the percentage of men and women who find life exciting. Men under age 45 are most likely to find life exciting (61 percent). Women aged 65 or older are least likely to feel this way (44 percent). The majority of men and women aged 65 or older say life is routine. Few describe life as dull.

There are substantial differences by age in the degree to which men and women trust others. Only 28 percent of men and an even smaller 23 percent of women under age 45 think most people can be trusted. Among men and women aged 65 or older, the figures are 41 and 37 percent, respectively. Not surprisingly, a larger percentage of women than men are afraid to walk alone at night in the area where they live—45 versus 20 percent. Nevertheless, most men and women regardless of age say they are not afraid.

■ Most men favor the legalization of marijuana, and most women do not.

Support for the legalization of marijuana peaks among younger men

(percent of men aged 18 or older who support the legalization of marijuana, by age, 2012)

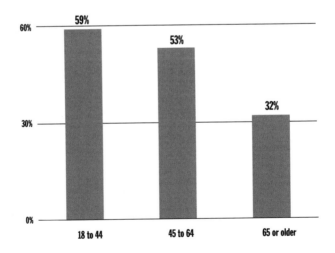

Table 1.1 General Happiness, 2012

"Taken all together, how would you say things are these days—would you say that you are very happy, pretty happy, or not too happy?"

(percent of people aged 18 or older responding by sex and age, 2012)

	very happy	pretty happy	not too happy
TOTAL PEOPLE	**32.9%**	**54.2%**	**12.9%**
Total men	**31.4**	**55.7**	**12.9**
Aged 18 to 44	29.8	58.9	11.3
Aged 45 to 64	31.9	52.9	15.2
Aged 65 or older	35.8	51.3	12.8
Total women	**34.2**	**52.9**	**12.9**
Aged 18 to 44	35.7	52.7	11.6
Aged 45 to 64	33.9	52.9	13.2
Aged 65 or older	31.1	54.3	14.6

Source: Survey Documentation and Analysis, Computer-assisted Survey Methods Program, University of California, Berkeley, General Social Survey, 1972–2012 Cumulative Data Files, Internet site http://sda.berkeley.edu/cgi-bin/hsda?harcsda+gss12; calculations by New Strategist

Table 1.2 Life Exciting or Dull, 2012

"In general, do you find life exciting, pretty routine, or dull?"

(percent of people aged 18 or older responding by sex and age, 2012)

	exciting	pretty routine	dull
TOTAL PEOPLE	**52.7%**	**42.6%**	**4.7%**
Total men	**55.9**	**39.4**	**4.7**
Aged 18 to 44	60.6	34.5	4.9
Aged 45 to 64	53.0	41.8	5.2
Aged 65 or older	46.7	50.3	3.0
Total women	**50.0**	**45.3**	**4.7**
Aged 18 to 44	50.2	45.1	4.6
Aged 45 to 64	52.0	42.3	5.7
Aged 65 or older	44.1	53.1	2.8

Source: Survey Documentation and Analysis, Computer-assisted Survey Methods Program, University of California, Berkeley, General Social Survey, 1972–2012 Cumulative Data Files, Internet site http://sda.berkeley.edu/cgi-bin/hsda?harcsda+gss12; calculations by New Strategist

Table 1.3 Trust in Others, 2012

"Generally speaking, would you say that most people can be trusted or that you can't be too careful in life?"

(percent of people aged 18 or older responding by sex and age, 2012)

	can trust	cannot trust	depends
TOTAL PEOPLE	**32.2%**	**64.2%**	**3.7%**
Total men	**34.5**	**62.5**	**3.0**
Aged 18 to 44	27.6	70.0	2.3
Aged 45 to 64	40.8	57.5	1.8
Aged 65 or older	40.7	52.2	7.1
Total women	**30.2**	**65.6**	**4.3**
Aged 18 to 44	22.6	72.8	4.6
Aged 45 to 64	36.6	59.8	3.6
Aged 65 or older	37.4	57.8	4.7

Source: Survey Documentation and Analysis, Computer-assisted Survey Methods Program, University of California, Berkeley, General Social Survey, 1972–2012 Cumulative Data Files, Internet site http://sda.berkeley.edu/cgi-bin/hsda?harcsda+gss12; calculations by New Strategist

Table 1.4 Afraid to Walk in Neighborhood at Night, 2012

"Is there any area right around here—that is, within a mile—where you would be afraid to walk alone at night?"

(percent of people aged 18 or older responding by sex and age, 2012)

	yes	no
TOTAL PEOPLE	**33.7%**	**66.3%**
Total men	**20.4**	**79.6**
Aged 18 to 44	19.5	80.5
Aged 45 to 64	23.8	76.2
Aged 65 or older	14.3	85.7
Total women	**45.0**	**55.0**
Aged 18 to 44	46.0	54.0
Aged 45 to 64	43.1	56.9
Aged 65 or older	45.9	54.1

Source: Survey Documentation and Analysis, Computer-assisted Survey Methods Program, University of California, Berkeley, General Social Survey, 1972–2012 Cumulative Data Files, Internet site http://sda.berkeley.edu/cgi-bin/hsda?harcsda+gss12; calculations by New Strategist

Table 1.5 Should Marijuana Be Made Legal, 2012

"Do you think the use of marijuana should be made legal or not?"

(percent of people aged 18 or older responding by sex and age, 2012)

	legal	not legal
TOTAL PEOPLE	**46.9%**	**53.1%**
Total men	**52.5**	**47.5**
Aged 18 to 44	59.3	40.7
Aged 45 to 64	53.2	46.8
Aged 65 or older	32.0	68.0
Total women	**42.3**	**57.7**
Aged 18 to 44	42.7	57.3
Aged 45 to 64	46.7	53.3
Aged 65 or older	33.1	66.9

Source: Survey Documentation and Analysis, Computer-assisted Survey Methods Program, University of California, Berkeley, General Social Survey, 1972–2012 Cumulative Data Files, Internet site http://sda.berkeley.edu/cgi-bin/hsda?harcsda+gss12; calculations by New Strategist

Most Still Have Faith in the American Dream

Older men and women have more doubts, however.

Despite the devastation of the Great Recession, the majority of men and women believe their families have the chance to improve their standard of living in the United States—perhaps the quintessential element of the American Dream. Men under age 45 are most likely to feel this way, with 66 percent believing their standard of living can improve. Older men and women are much more pessimistic. Fewer than half of those aged 65 or older believe their family can get ahead.

Although most men and women think their standard of living is higher than their parents' standard of living was at the same age, they are more uncertain about their children's standard of living in the future. Fewer than half of men aged 45 or older and women aged 65 or older think their children's standard of living will be better than theirs is now. The oldest men are particularly downbeat, with more than 40 percent saying their children's standard of living will be worse.

■ The Great Recession undermined the economic confidence of middle-aged and older Americans, but younger adults remain optimistic.

Younger women are most likely to think their children will be better off

(percent of women aged 18 or older who think their children's standard of living will be better than theirs is now, by age, 2012)

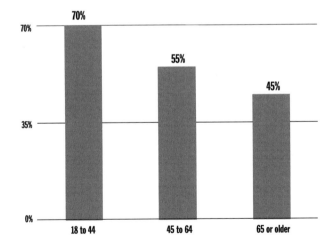

Table 1.6 Standard of Living Will Improve, 2012

"The way things are in America, people like me and my family have a good chance of improving our standard of living. Do you agree or disagree?"

(percent of people aged 18 or older responding by sex and age, 2012)

	agree	neither	disagree
TOTAL PEOPLE	**54.8%**	**17.9%**	**27.4%**
Total men	**58.3**	**17.5**	**24.2**
Aged 18 to 44	66.1	17.1	16.8
Aged 45 to 64	54.0	19.0	27.1
Aged 65 or older	46.0	15.8	38.2
Total women	**51.7**	**18.2**	**30.1**
Aged 18 to 44	59.3	19.1	21.5
Aged 45 to 64	47.8	17.2	35.1
Aged 65 or older	39.9	18.1	42.1

Source: Survey Documentation and Analysis, Computer-assisted Survey Methods Program, University of California, Berkeley, General Social Survey, 1972–2012 Cumulative Data Files, Internet site http://sda.berkeley.edu/cgi-bin/hsda?harcsda+gss12; calculations by New Strategist

Table 1.7 Parents' Standard of Living, 2012

"Compared to your parents when they were the age you are now, do you think your own standard of living now is much better, somewhat better, about the same, somewhat worse, or much worse than theirs was?"

(percent of people aged 18 or older responding by sex and age, 2012)

	better	same	worse
TOTAL PEOPLE	**62.1%**	**21.2%**	**16.6%**
Total men	**65.3**	**20.8**	**13.9**
Aged 18 to 44	69.0	19.7	11.3
Aged 45 to 64	56.2	23.2	20.7
Aged 65 or older	73.7	19.0	7.3
Total women	**59.3**	**21.6**	**19.1**
Aged 18 to 44	56.3	22.7	21.0
Aged 45 to 64	61.4	20.4	18.3
Aged 65 or older	63.0	21.5	15.6

Source: Survey Documentation and Analysis, Computer-assisted Survey Methods Program, University of California, Berkeley, General Social Survey, 1972–2012 Cumulative Data Files, Internet site http://sda.berkeley.edu/cgi-bin/hsda?harcsda+gss12; calculations by New Strategist

Table 1.8 Children's Standard of Living, 2012

"When your children are at the age you are now, do you think their standard of living will be much better, somewhat better, about the same, somewhat worse, or much worse than yours is now?"

(percent of people aged 18 or older with children responding by sex and age, 2012)

	better	same	worse
TOTAL PEOPLE WITH CHILDREN	**57.0%**	**20.5%**	**22.5%**
Total men with children	**52.9**	**20.4**	**26.7**
Aged 18 to 44	64.6	18.0	17.5
Aged 45 to 64	42.2	25.8	31.9
Aged 65 or older	42.9	16.5	40.5
Total women with children	**60.4**	**20.5**	**19.2**
Aged 18 to 44	70.2	19.2	10.7
Aged 45 to 64	55.2	20.1	24.7
Aged 65 or older	44.8	25.4	29.9

Source: Survey Documentation and Analysis, Computer-assisted Survey Methods Program, University of California, Berkeley, General Social Survey, 1972–2012 Cumulative Data Files, Internet site http://sda.berkeley.edu/cgi-bin/hsda?harcsda+gss12; calculations by New Strategist

Middle Class Identification Is Highest among Elderly Women

It is lowest among men and women under age 45.

Americans as a whole are about evenly split on whether they are "working" class or "middle" class, 44 percent identifying with each term. But there are sharp differences in middle class identification by age among both men and women. People under age 45 are more likely to call themselves working than middle class. The opposite is true among the elderly, with 54 percent of men and 62 percent of women aged 65 or older identifying themselves as middle class.

When asked to compare their family income with other families, the plurality of men and women say their income is average. Women under age 45 are most likely to think their family income is average (50 percent). Men aged 45 to 64 are most likely to think their family income is above average (26 percent).

Younger men and women are much more likely than their elders to report improving finances over the past few years, with 39 percent of men and 34 percent of women under age 45 saying things have gotten better. This is not surprising, since many in the age group are advancing in their career. Among men aged 45 to 64, only 18 percent say their finances have gotten better, and twice as many say their finances have gotten worse.

■ Older men and women are most likely to be satisfied with their financial situation because the majority are retirees with stable incomes.

Fewer than one-third of men and women are satisfied with their finances

(percent of people aged 18 or older who are satisfied with their present financial situation, by sex, 2012)

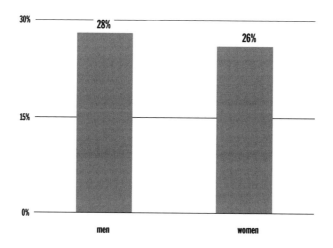

Table 1.9 Social Class Membership, 2012

"If you were asked to use one of four names for your social class,
which would you say you belong in: the lower class,
the working class, the middle class, or the upper class?"

(percent of people aged 18 or older responding by sex and age, 2012)

	lower	working	middle	upper
TOTAL PEOPLE	**8.4%**	**44.3%**	**43.7%**	**3.6%**
Total men	**8.3**	**43.1**	**44.1**	**4.5**
Aged 18 to 44	7.8	47.6	39.8	4.8
Aged 45 to 64	7.4	42.5	45.9	4.2
Aged 65 or older	12.3	29.7	54.1	4.0
Total women	**8.5**	**45.3**	**43.3**	**2.8**
Aged 18 to 44	8.5	55.1	35.0	1.5
Aged 45 to 64	9.1	40.9	45.5	4.5
Aged 65 or older	7.8	27.3	62.1	2.8

Source: Survey Documentation and Analysis, Computer-assisted Survey Methods Program, University of California, Berkeley, General Social Survey, 1972–2012 Cumulative Data Files, Internet site http://sda.berkeley.edu/cgi-bin/hsda?harcsda+gss12; calculations by New Strategist

Table 1.10 Family Income Relative to Others, 2012

"Compared with American families in general, would you say your family income is far below average, below average, average, above average, or far above average?"

(percent of people aged 18 or older responding by sex and age, 2012)

	far below average	below average	average	above average	far above average
TOTAL PEOPLE	6.8%	25.9%	45.5%	19.0%	2.7%
Total men	**6.2**	**25.7**	**43.7**	**21.5**	**2.9**
Aged 18 to 44	5.9	25.5	43.1	23.1	2.4
Aged 45 to 64	7.5	23.6	42.6	22.3	4.0
Aged 65 or older	4.1	31.1	48.1	14.7	2.1
Total women	**7.4**	**26.1**	**47.1**	**16.8**	**2.6**
Aged 18 to 44	7.4	26.8	50.4	13.1	2.3
Aged 45 to 64	8.9	24.6	42.5	21.0	3.1
Aged 65 or older	4.4	27.4	48.1	17.7	2.3

Source: Survey Documentation and Analysis, Computer-assisted Survey Methods Program, University of California, Berkeley, General Social Survey, 1972–2012 Cumulative Data Files, Internet site http://sda.berkeley.edu/cgi-bin/hsda?harcsda+gss12; calculations by New Strategist

Table 1.11 Change in Financial Situation, 2012

"During the last few years, has your financial situation been
getting better, worse, or has it stayed the same?"

(percent of people aged 18 or older responding by sex and age, 2012)

	better	worse	stayed same
TOTAL PEOPLE	**28.2%**	**30.2%**	**41.6%**
Total men	**27.6**	**28.6**	**43.8**
Aged 18 to 44	38.6	22.5	38.8
Aged 45 to 64	18.1	35.9	46.0
Aged 65 or older	13.1	32.1	54.7
Total women	**28.7**	**31.5**	**39.8**
Aged 18 to 44	33.5	26.8	39.7
Aged 45 to 64	30.0	36.0	34.0
Aged 65 or older	13.6	35.5	50.8

Source: Survey Documentation and Analysis, Computer-assisted Survey Methods Program, University of California, Berkeley, General Social Survey, 1972–2012 Cumulative Data Files, Internet site http://sda.berkeley.edu/cgi-bin/hsda?harcsda+gss12; calculations by New Strategist

Table 1.12 Satisfaction with Financial Situation, 2012

"So far as you and your family are concerned, would you say that you are
pretty well satisfied with your present financial situation, more
or less satisfied, or not satisfied at all?"

(percent of people aged 18 or older responding by sex and age, 2012)

	satisfied	more or less satisfied	not at all sarisfied
TOTAL PEOPLE	**27.0%**	**45.0%**	**28.0%**
Total men	**27.8**	**45.8**	**26.4**
Aged 18 to 44	26.2	45.5	28.3
Aged 45 to 64	26.0	46.3	27.7
Aged 65 or older	37.2	45.9	16.8
Total women	**26.2**	**44.3**	**29.5**
Aged 18 to 44	19.1	51.0	29.8
Aged 45 to 64	27.5	39.6	32.9
Aged 65 or older	43.2	34.8	22.0

Source: Survey Documentation and Analysis, Computer-assisted Survey Methods Program, University of California, Berkeley, General Social Survey, 1972–2012 Cumulative Data Files, Internet site http://sda.berkeley.edu/cgi-bin/hsda?harcsda+gss12; calculations by New Strategist

Older Men Do Not Support Gay Marriage

Most younger men and women think gays and lesbians should have the right to marry.

Premarital sex seems like a nonissue these days, but in fact many older men and women still object. Although the majority of adults under age 65 say premarital sex is not wrong at all, only about one-third of those aged 65 or older agree.

The older generation is even less accepting of gays and lesbians. When asked how they feel about sexual relations between two adults of the same sex, only 17 percent of men aged 65 or older say it is not wrong at all and an enormous 75 percent say it is always wrong. Elderly women are somewhat more accepting, but even so the 60 percent majority thinks such relations are always wrong.

On the issue of gay marriage, most men and women under age 45 think gays and lesbians should have the right to marry. But 70 percent of men aged 65 or older disagree. Older women are more tolerant than their male counterparts, with 41 percent for and 48 percent against the right of gays and lesbians to marry.

■ American attitudes toward gays and lesbians have become increasingly tolerant over the past few decades because of generational replacement and changing attitudes. Elderly men have been resistant to change, however.

Most women support gay marriage

(percent of people aged 18 or older who agree that gays and lesbians should have the right to marry, by sex, 2012)

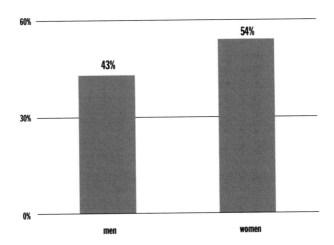

Table 1.13 Premarital Sex, 2012

"If a man and woman have sex relations before marriage, do you
think it is always wrong, almost always wrong, wrong
only sometimes, or not wrong at all?"

(percent of people aged 18 or older responding by sex and age, 2012)

	always wrong	almost always or sometimes wrong	not wrong at all
TOTAL PEOPLE	**21.9%**	**20.6%**	**57.5%**
Total men	**20.1**	**19.8**	**60.1**
Aged 18 to 44	16.8	17.4	65.9
Aged 45 to 64	18.7	19.9	61.4
Aged 65 or older	35.5	28.7	35.8
Total women	**23.5**	**21.3**	**55.2**
Aged 18 to 44	18.8	21.6	59.6
Aged 45 to 64	23.6	18.6	57.8
Aged 65 or older	37.0	26.1	36.9

Source: Survey Documentation and Analysis, Computer-assisted Survey Methods Program, University of California, Berkeley, General Social Survey, 1972–2012 Cumulative Data Files, Internet site http://sda.berkeley.edu/cgi-bin/hsda?harcsda+gss12; calculations by New Strategist

Table 1.14 Homosexual Relations, 2012

"What about sexual relations between two adults of the same sex?"

(percent of people aged 18 or older responding by sex and age, 2012)

	always wrong	almost always or sometimes wrong	not wrong at all
TOTAL PEOPLE	**45.7%**	**10.6%**	**43.8%**
Total men	**50.9**	**13.9**	**35.3**
Aged 18 to 44	42.0	15.5	42.6
Aged 45 to 64	53.3	14.1	32.6
Aged 65 or older	75.3	8.1	16.7
Total women	**41.2**	**7.8**	**51.0**
Aged 18 to 44	32.6	9.0	58.4
Aged 45 to 64	44.7	7.0	48.3
Aged 65 or older	60.3	5.8	34.0

Source: Survey Documentation and Analysis, Computer-assisted Survey Methods Program, University of California, Berkeley, General Social Survey, 1972–2012 Cumulative Data Files, Internet site http://sda.berkeley.edu/cgi-bin/hsda?harcsda+gss12; calculations by New Strategist

Table 1.15 Gay Marriage, 2012

"Do you agree or disagree that homosexual couples should have the right to marry one another?"

(percent of people aged 18 or older responding by sex and age, 2012)

	agree	neither agree nor disagree	disagree
TOTAL PEOPLE	**48.9%**	**12.0%**	**39.1%**
Total men	**43.0**	**12.2**	**44.9**
Aged 18 to 44	51.4	13.3	35.3
Aged 45 to 64	38.3	13.8	47.9
Aged 65 or older	26.3	4.0	69.7
Total women	**53.9**	**11.8**	**34.2**
Aged 18 to 44	63.6	10.7	25.6
Aged 45 to 64	47.2	14.0	38.8
Aged 65 or older	41.3	11.1	47.6

Source: Survey Documentation and Analysis, Computer-assisted Survey Methods Program, University of California, Berkeley, General Social Survey, 1972–2012 Cumulative Data Files, Internet site http://sda.berkeley.edu/cgi-bin/hsda?harcsda+gss12; calculations by New Strategist

Table 1.16 Sexual Orientation, 2012

"Which of the following best describes you?"

(percent of people aged 18 or older responding by sex and age, 2012)

	gay, lesbian or homosexual	bisexual	heterosexual or straight
TOTAL PEOPLE	**1.5%**	**2.2%**	**96.3%**
Total men	**2.2**	**1.8**	**96.0**
Aged 18 to 44	2.7	2.9	94.5
Aged 45 to 64	2.1	0.6	97.3
Aged 65 or older	1.1	0.4	98.5
Total women	**0.8**	**2.6**	**96.6**
Aged 18 to 44	0.5	4.3	95.1
Aged 45 to 64	1.3	0.9	97.8
Aged 65 or older	0.6	1.0	98.3

Source: Survey Documentation and Analysis, Computer-assisted Survey Methods Program, University of California, Berkeley, General Social Survey, 1972–2012 Cumulative Data Files, Internet site http://sda.berkeley.edu/cgi-bin/hsda?harcsda+gss12; calculations by New Strategist

Americans Still Struggle to Balance Work and Family

Most no longer believe working mothers harm children, however.

Support for traditional sex roles—where the husband works and the wife takes care of home and family—has all but disappeared in the United States, except among older men. Most Americans, regardless of age or sex, think a working mother can have just as warm a relationship with her children as a mother who does not work. But most women and men still struggle with the best way to organize modern family life.

When asked how families with preschoolers can best organize family life, the 42 percent plurality of Americans aged 18 or older agrees that the mother working part-time and the father working full-time is best. But a larger share of some demographic segments thinks it would be best if mother stayed home, including men aged 45 or older and women aged 65 or older. There is more agreement about the worst way to organize family life, with two arrangements singled out: mother working full-time and father at home, and both parents working full-time.

■ The great majority of men and women under age 65 were raised by a mother who worked for pay.

Older men still support traditional sex roles

(percent of people aged 18 or older who agree it is better for the man to be the achiever outside the home while the woman takes care of home and family, by sex and age, 2012)

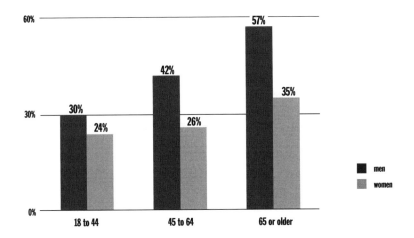

Table 1.17 Better for Man to Work, Woman to Tend Home, 2012

"Do you agree or disagree that it is much better for everyone involved
if the man is the achiever outside the home and the woman
takes care of the home and family?"

(percent of people aged 18 or older responding by sex and age, 2012)

	agree	disagree
TOTAL PEOPLE	**31.7%**	**68.3%**
Total men	**37.7**	**62.2**
Aged 18 to 44	30.3	69.8
Aged 45 to 64	41.7	58.2
Aged 65 or older	57.3	42.7
Total women	**26.3**	**73.6**
Aged 18 to 44	23.6	76.4
Aged 45 to 64	26.2	73.8
Aged 65 or older	35.3	64.8

Source: Survey Documentation and Analysis, Computer-assisted Survey Methods Program, University of California, Berkeley, General Social Survey, 1972–2012 Cumulative Data Files, Internet site http://sda.berkeley.edu/cgi-bin/hsda?harcsda+gss12; calculations by New Strategist

Table 1.18 Working Mother Doesn't Hurt Children, 2012

"A working mother can establish just as warm and secure a relationship
with her children as a mother who does not work."

(percent of people aged 18 or older responding by sex and age, 2012)

	agree	disagree
TOTAL PEOPLE	**71.7%**	**28.3%**
Total men	**64.7**	**35.2**
Aged 18 to 44	67.2	32.9
Aged 45 to 64	62.0	37.9
Aged 65 or older	61.5	38.5
Total women	**77.9**	**22.1**
Aged 18 to 44	79.3	20.7
Aged 45 to 64	77.1	22.9
Aged 65 or older	74.9	25.1

Source: Survey Documentation and Analysis, Computer-assisted Survey Methods Program, University of California, Berkeley, General Social Survey, 1972–2012 Cumulative Data Files, Internet site http://sda.berkeley.edu/cgi-bin/hsda?harcsda+gss12; calculations by New Strategist

Table 1.19 Best Way to Organize Family Life, 2012

"Consider a family with a child under school age. What, in your opinion, is the best way for them to organize their family and work life?"

(percent of people aged 18 or older responding by sex and age, 2012)

	mother stays home, father works full-time	mother works part-time, father works full-time	both work full-time	both work part-time	father works part-time, mother works full-time	father stays home, mother works full-time
TOTAL PEOPLE	**39.7%**	**41.6%**	**11.3%**	**6.8%**	**0.2%**	**0.5%**
Total men	**46.4**	**37.0**	**10.9**	**4.9**	**0.2**	**0.7**
Aged 18 to 44	34.9	42.3	14.3	7.5	0.3	0.6
Aged 45 to 64	59.7	28.2	8.9	2.6	0.0	0.6
Aged 65 or older	60.1	35.9	2.3	0.6	0.0	1.1
Total women	**33.6**	**45.7**	**11.7**	**8.5**	**0.2**	**0.3**
Aged 18 to 44	30.0	46.8	11.0	11.9	0.0	0.3
Aged 45 to 64	33.8	45.7	14.7	5.3	0.0	0.5
Aged 65 or older	45.5	43.2	7.5	2.7	0.0	1.1

Source: Survey Documentation and Analysis, Computer-assisted Survey Methods Program, University of California, Berkeley, General Social Survey, 1972–2012 Cumulative Data Files, Internet site http://sda.berkeley.edu/cgi-bin/hsda?harcsda+gss12; calculations by New Strategist

Table 1.20 Worst Way to Organize Family Life, 2012

"Consider a family with a child under school age. What, in your opinion, is the least desirable way for them to organize their family and work life?"

(percent of people aged 18 or older responding by sex and age, 2012)

	mother stays home, father works full-time	mother works part-time, father works full-time	both work full-time	both work part-time	father works part-time, mother works full-time	father stays home, mother works full-time
TOTAL PEOPLE	**5.4%**	**1.7%**	**36.3%**	**12.9%**	**4.9%**	**38.8%**
Total men	**3.5**	**1.5**	**37.7**	**14.0**	**5.2**	**38.1**
Aged 18 to 44	4.0	1.5	38.0	15.1	5.4	36.0
Aged 45 to 64	2.4	2.1	36.8	14.4	5.1	39.3
Aged 65 or older	4.0	0.5	38.7	8.8	4.6	43.4
Total women	**7.2**	**1.9**	**35.0**	**11.9**	**4.6**	**39.4**
Aged 18 to 44	5.3	2.0	37.9	10.4	3.5	40.9
Aged 45 to 64	8.0	0.1	31.4	12.7	6.3	40.7
Aged 65 or older	11.9	3.8	31.3	15.6	5.2	32.3

Source: Survey Documentation and Analysis, Computer-assisted Survey Methods Program, University of California, Berkeley, General Social Survey, 1972–2012 Cumulative Data Files, Internet site http://sda.berkeley.edu/cgi-bin/hsda?harcsda+gss12; calculations by New Strategist

Table 1.21 Mother Worked while You Were Growing Up, 2012

"Did your mother ever work for pay for as long as a year while you were growing up?"

(percent of people aged 18 or older responding by sex and age, 2012)

	yes	no
TOTAL PEOPLE	**72.5%**	**27.5%**
Total men	**71.7**	**28.3**
Aged 18 to 44	79.8	20.2
Aged 45 to 64	69.8	30.2
Aged 65 or older	49.7	50.3
Total women	**73.2**	**26.8**
Aged 18 to 44	82.9	17.1
Aged 45 to 64	69.7	30.3
Aged 65 or older	53.1	46.9

Source: Survey Documentation and Analysis, Computer-assisted Survey Methods Program, University of California, Berkeley, General Social Survey, 1972–2012 Cumulative Data Files, Internet site http://sda.berkeley.edu/cgi-bin/hsda?harcsda+gss12; calculations by New Strategist

Most Describe Their Marriage as Very Happy

Two out of three women say they always or usually do the household cleaning.

Two-thirds of married men and women describe their marriage as "very" happy. Another one-third says their marriage is "pretty" happy. Women aged 45 to 64 are most likely to say their marriage is not too happy (6 percent).

Traditional sex roles emerge when men and women are asked who does the household cleaning. Among women living with a spouse or partner, the largest share say they always do the household cleaning, the figure peaking at 57 percent among women aged 65 or older. Men are more likely than women to say they share cleaning chores about equally (35 percent of men say this versus 24 percent of women).

Both men and women are more likely to socialize frequently with relatives than with friends. Among men, 34 percent socialize with relatives at least once a week. Among women, 40 percent socialize with relatives on a weekly basis. Twenty-four percent of men and women say they socialize with friends at least once a week.

■ Younger Americans are more likely than older adults to socialize frequently with family and friends.

Young adults are twice as likely to socialize with friends at least once a week

(percent of people aged 18 or older who socialize with friends at least once a week, by sex and age, 2012)

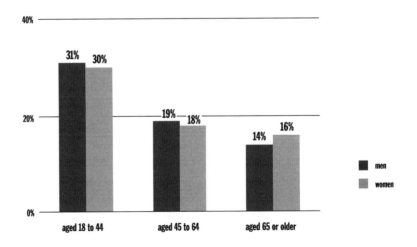

Table 1.22 Happiness of Marriage, 2012

"Taking all things together, how would you describe your marriage?"

(percent of married people aged 18 or older responding by sex and age, 2012)

	very happy	pretty happy	not too happy
TOTAL MARRIED PEOPLE	**65.4%**	**32.2%**	**2.3%**
Total married men	**66.4**	**32.7**	**0.9**
Aged 18 to 44	69.8	29.7	0.4
Aged 45 to 64	63.1	35.1	1.7
Aged 65 or older	66.6	33.4	0.0
Total married women	**64.6**	**31.8**	**3.6**
Aged 18 to 44	73.3	24.5	2.3
Aged 45 to 64	56.9	37.0	6.1
Aged 65 or older	59.7	39.3	0.9

Source: Survey Documentation and Analysis, Computer-assisted Survey Methods Program, University of California, Berkeley, General Social Survey, 1972–2012 Cumulative Data Files, Internet site http://sda.berkeley.edu/cgi-bin/hsda?harcsda+gss12; calculations by New Strategist

Table 1.23 Who Does the Household Cleaning, 2012

"In your household, who does the household cleaning?"

(percent of people aged 18 or older living with a spouse/partner responding by sex and age, 2012)

	always me	usually me	about equal or together	usually my spouse/ partner	always my spouse/ partner	done by a third party
TOTAL PEOPLE LIVING WITH SPOUSE/PARTNER	**23.1%**	**17.3%**	**28.7%**	**16.9%**	**8.5%**	**5.4%**
Total men living with spouse/partner	**4.6**	**4.9**	**34.6**	**33.5**	**16.5**	**5.8**
Aged 18 to 44	3.6	6.4	32.6	43.3	10.7	3.4
Aged 45 to 64	2.1	3.3	38.8	26.7	22.5	6.5
Aged 65 or older	12.2	4.8	30.5	24.5	18.0	10.1
Total women living with spouse/partner	**39.1**	**28.0**	**23.7**	**2.5**	**1.6**	**5.1**
Aged 18 to 44	36.3	29.8	28.9	2.1	0.0	2.9
Aged 45 to 64	36.0	30.1	21.8	3.9	2.7	5.5
Aged 65 or older	57.4	14.7	12.6	0.0	4.1	11.2

Source: Survey Documentation and Analysis, Computer-assisted Survey Methods Program, University of California, Berkeley, General Social Survey, 1972–2012 Cumulative Data Files, Internet site http://sda.berkeley.edu/cgi-bin/hsda?harcsda+gss12; calculations by New Strategist

Table 1.24 Spend Evening with Relatives, 2012

"How often do you spend a social evening with relatives?"

(percent of people aged 18 or older responding by sex and age, 2012)

	almost daily	several times a week	several times a month	once a month	several times a year	once a year	never
TOTAL PEOPLE	**13.6%**	**23.5%**	**22.4%**	**13.6%**	**15.8%**	**6.7%**	**4.4%**
Total men	**11.8**	**22.5**	**22.3**	**13.5**	**18.3**	**7.0**	**4.6**
Aged 18 to 44	16.8	25.2	21.6	12.3	15.0	5.6	3.4
Aged 45 to 64	5.7	19.9	25.5	15.6	19.3	8.4	5.5
Aged 65 or older	6.4	17.6	17.6	13.2	28.9	9.2	7.2
Total women	**15.2**	**24.5**	**22.5**	**13.7**	**13.6**	**6.4**	**4.2**
Aged 18 to 44	19.1	23.0	24.8	11.9	11.2	5.2	4.9
Aged 45 to 64	13.0	26.0	20.0	14.9	16.1	8.1	1.9
Aged 65 or older	8.5	25.6	19.5	17.1	16.1	6.6	6.6

Source: Survey Documentation and Analysis, Computer-assisted Survey Methods Program, University of California, Berkeley, General Social Survey, 1972–2012 Cumulative Data Files, Internet site http://sda.berkeley.edu/cgi-bin/hsda?harcsda+gss12; calculations by New Strategist

Table 1.25 Spend Evening with Friends, 2012

"How often do you spend a social evening with friends
who live outside the neighborhood?"

(percent of people aged 18 or older responding by sex and age, 2012)

	almost daily	several times a week	several times a month	once a month	several times a year	once a year	never
TOTAL PEOPLE	**4.5%**	**19.6%**	**21.0%**	**21.0%**	**16.2%**	**8.3%**	**9.5%**
Total men	**5.7**	**18.9**	**18.9**	**22.8**	**17.1**	**8.2**	**8.4**
Aged 18 to 44	8.2	22.6	24.0	19.0	12.9	7.3	6.1
Aged 45 to 64	3.4	15.2	15.8	30.3	19.4	7.1	8.6
Aged 65 or older	1.4	12.7	6.3	20.2	28.0	14.3	17.0
Total women	**3.4**	**20.2**	**22.8**	**19.4**	**15.4**	**8.3**	**10.5**
Aged 18 to 44	6.1	23.7	27.9	16.0	15.2	5.1	6.1
Aged 45 to 64	1.1	17.0	19.0	23.7	15.5	12.6	11.1
Aged 65 or older	0.0	16.5	14.8	20.4	16.3	9.8	22.2

Source: Survey Documentation and Analysis, Computer-assisted Survey Methods Program, University of California, Berkeley, General Social Survey, 1972–2012 Cumulative Data Files, Internet site http://sda.berkeley.edu/cgi-bin/hsda?harcsda+gss12; calculations by New Strategist

Women Are More Religious than Men

Older women are the most religious of all.

On many issues, there is little difference between the attitudes of men and women. On religious matters, however, there are significant differences. Men are less likely than women to regard themselves as "very" religious, for example. Only 16 percent of men regard themselves as very religious compared with 21 percent of women. A substantial 47 percent of men say they are only slightly or not religious versus 37 percent of women.

Given these numbers, it is not surprising that men are more likely than women to have no religious affiliation (24 versus 16 percent) and never go to church (29 versus 22 percent). Men are less likely than women to believe in God without a doubt (54 versus 64 percent), believe the Bible is the word of God (28 versus 35 percent), and pray at least once a day (50 versus 67 percent).

The fact that men are less religious than women may explain why men are more likely to believe in evolution. Sixty-four percent of men agree that humans developed from earlier species of animals compared with just 49 percent of women.

■ Men and women are about equally likely to agree that science makes our way of life change too fast.

Most men under age 65 believe in evolution

(percent of people aged 18 or older who agree with the statement, "Human beings, as we know them today, developed from earlier species of animals," by sex and age, 2012)

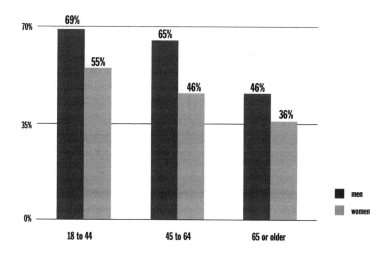

Table 1.26 Degree of Religiosity, 2012

"To what extent do you consider yourself a religious person?"

(percent of people aged 18 or older responding by sex and age, 2012)

	very religious	moderately religious	slightly religious	not religious
TOTAL PEOPLE	**18.8%**	**39.5%**	**21.6%**	**20.1%**
Total men	**16.1**	**37.1**	**24.1**	**22.7**
Aged 18 to 44	12.1	34.2	27.6	26.2
Aged 45 to 64	20.1	38.5	19.6	21.8
Aged 65 or older	20.2	43.5	23.1	13.2
Total women	**21.2**	**41.5**	**19.5**	**17.8**
Aged 18 to 44	15.1	37.3	21.8	25.8
Aged 45 to 64	28.0	42.6	17.1	12.2
Aged 65 or older	23.7	50.8	18.2	7.3

Source: Survey Documentation and Analysis, Computer-assisted Survey Methods Program, University of California, Berkeley, General Social Survey, 1972–2012 Cumulative Data Files, Internet site http://sda.berkeley.edu/cgi-bin/hsda?harcsda+gss12; calculations by New Strategist

Table 1.27 Religious Preference, 2012

"What is your religious preference?"

(percent of people aged 18 or older responding by sex and age, 2012)

	Protestant	Catholic	none	Christian	Jewish	Moslem/ Islam	other
TOTAL PEOPLE	**44.3%**	**24.2%**	**19.7%**	**6.0%**	**1.5%**	**1.1%**	**3.2%**
Total men	**39.4**	**24.9**	**23.6**	**4.9**	**1.3**	**2.0**	**3.9**
Aged 18 to 44	33.2	25.6	27.7	5.1	1.0	1.7	5.7
Aged 45 to 64	41.1	25.1	21.0	6.1	1.5	3.4	1.8
Aged 65 or older	55.6	21.9	16.1	1.3	2.1	0.0	3.0
Total women	**48.5**	**23.7**	**16.4**	**6.9**	**1.6**	**0.2**	**2.7**
Aged 18 to 44	36.6	24.3	24.1	9.8	1.7	0.3	3.2
Aged 45 to 64	56.7	23.2	11.6	5.0	1.0	0.0	2.5
Aged 65 or older	66.6	22.2	5.3	2.8	2.7	0.4	0.0

Source: Survey Documentation and Analysis, Computer-assisted Survey Methods Program, University of California, Berkeley, General Social Survey, 1972–2012 Cumulative Data Files, Internet site http://sda.berkeley.edu/cgi-bin/hsda?harcsda+gss12; calculations by New Strategist

Table 1.28 Attendance at Religious Services, 2012

"How often do you attend religious services?"

(percent of people aged 18 or older responding by sex and age, 2012)

	more than once a week	every week	nearly every week	two or three times a month	once a month	several times a year	once a year	less than once a year	never
TOTAL PEOPLE	**6.5%**	**19.7%**	**4.0%**	**8.9%**	**6.8%**	**10.8%**	**13.0%**	**5.0%**	**25.3%**
Total men	**4.8**	**19.0**	**3.3**	**6.5**	**7.1**	**11.8**	**13.7**	**5.1**	**28.7**
Aged 18 to 44	4.7	12.4	2.8	8.1	7.3	12.2	16.6	5.7	30.2
Aged 45 to 64	3.9	23.6	4.3	5.1	8.6	11.7	12.0	3.2	27.6
Aged 65 or older	7.5	29.9	3.0	4.3	3.0	10.6	8.1	7.5	26.1
Total women	**7.9**	**20.4**	**4.6**	**10.9**	**6.5**	**10.0**	**12.4**	**4.8**	**22.3**
Aged 18 to 44	5.9	19.1	3.4	8.6	8.6	9.6	14.1	4.7	25.8
Aged 45 to 64	8.5	19.5	4.7	15.7	4.5	9.5	13.2	5.8	18.7
Aged 65 or older	12.8	25.6	7.4	8.1	4.8	11.9	6.3	2.7	20.4

Source: Survey Documentation and Analysis, Computer-assisted Survey Methods Program, University of California, Berkeley, General Social Survey, 1972–2012 Cumulative Data Files, Internet site http://sda.berkeley.edu/cgi-bin/hsda?harcsda+gss12; calculations by New Strategist

Table 1.29 Confidence in the Existence of God, 2012

"The statement which comes closest to expressing what you believe about God is:
1) I don't believe in God. 2) I don't know whether there is a God and I don't believe
there is any way to find out. 3) I don't believe in a personal God, but I do believe
in a Higher Power of some kind. 4) I find myself believing in God some of
the time, but not at others. 5) While I have doubts, I feel that I do believe
in God. 6) I know God really exists and I have no doubts about it."

(percent of people aged 18 or older responding by sex and age, 2012)

	1 don't believe	2 no way to find out	3 higher power	4 believe sometimes	5 believe but doubts	6 know God exists
TOTAL PEOPLE	**3.1%**	**5.6%**	**11.6%**	**4.2%**	**16.5%**	**59.1%**
Total men	**4.8**	**7.3**	**11.9**	**4.4**	**18.0**	**53.6**
Aged 18 to 44	5.9	7.7	14.0	5.1	20.0	47.3
Aged 45 to 64	3.9	7.3	11.0	3.2	17.3	57.2
Aged 65 or older	3.1	5.6	6.7	5.2	13.2	66.2
Total women	**1.6**	**4.2**	**11.4**	**4.0**	**15.2**	**63.7**
Aged 18 to 44	1.5	6.0	15.6	4.5	15.0	57.5
Aged 45 to 64	2.0	2.5	7.6	3.7	15.1	69.0
Aged 65 or older	1.2	2.5	7.2	2.8	16.2	70.2

Source: Survey Documentation and Analysis, Computer-assisted Survey Methods Program, University of California, Berkeley, General Social Survey, 1972–2012 Cumulative Data Files, Internet site http://sda.berkeley.edu/cgi-bin/hsda?harcsda+gss12; calculations by New Strategist

Table 1.30 Feelings about the Bible, 2012

"The statement which comes closest to describing your feelings about the Bible is:
1) The Bible is the actual word of God and is to be taken literally. 2) The Bible is
the inspired word of God but not everything in it should be taken literally,
word for word. 3) The Bible is an ancient book of fables, legends,
history, and moral precepts recorded by men."

(percent of people aged 18 or older responding by sex and age, 2012)

	word of God	inspired word	book of fables	other
TOTAL PEOPLE	**32.1%**	**44.6%**	**21.8%**	**1.5%**
Total men	**28.3**	**44.1**	**25.5**	**2.0**
Aged 18 to 44	25.8	44.4	28.5	1.3
Aged 45 to 64	28.3	45.0	23.7	3.0
Aged 65 or older	37.3	41.0	19.4	2.3
Total women	**35.3**	**45.1**	**18.6**	**1.0**
Aged 18 to 44	30.5	45.4	23.2	0.8
Aged 45 to 64	38.8	46.6	13.9	0.7
Aged 65 or older	41.9	39.9	15.8	2.4

*Source: Survey Documentation and Analysis, Computer-assisted Survey Methods Program, University of California, Berkeley,
General Social Survey, 1972–2012 Cumulative Data Files, Internet site http://sda.berkeley.edu/cgi-bin/hsda?harcsda+gss12;
calculations by New Strategist*

Table 1.31 Frequency of Prayer, 2012

"About how often do you pray?"

(percent of people aged 18 or older responding by sex and age, 2012)

	at least once a day	once to several times a week	less than once a week	never
TOTAL PEOPLE	**59.4%**	**16.8%**	**10.1%**	**13.8%**
Total men	**50.0**	**18.8**	**12.3**	**18.8**
Aged 18 to 44	45.3	19.2	11.9	23.7
Aged 45 to 64	54.4	19.4	10.4	15.7
Aged 65 or older	55.6	16.4	18.2	9.8
Total women	**67.3**	**15.0**	**8.1**	**9.6**
Aged 18 to 44	57.3	18.4	10.7	13.7
Aged 45 to 64	75.4	13.1	5.4	6.1
Aged 65 or older	79.0	9.0	6.6	5.4

Source: Survey Documentation and Analysis, Computer-assisted Survey Methods Program, University of California, Berkeley, General Social Survey, 1972–2012 Cumulative Data Files, Internet site http://sda.berkeley.edu/cgi-bin/hsda?harcsda+gss12; calculations by New Strategist

Table 1.32 Scientific Knowledge: Human Beings Developed from Animals, 2012

"Human beings, as we know them today, developed from earlier species of animals. Is that true or false?"

(percent of people aged 18 or older responding by sex and age, 2012)

	true	false
TOTAL PEOPLE	**55.8%**	**44.2%**
Total men	**63.6**	**36.4**
Aged 18 to 44	69.4	30.6
Aged 45 to 64	64.5	35.5
Aged 65 or older	46.5	53.5
Total women	**48.7**	**51.3**
Aged 18 to 44	54.8	45.2
Aged 45 to 64	46.4	53.6
Aged 65 or older	35.9	64.1

Source: Survey Documentation and Analysis, Computer-assisted Survey Methods Program, University of California, Berkeley, General Social Survey, 1972–2012 Cumulative Data Files, Internet site http://sda.berkeley.edu/cgi-bin/hsda?harcsda+gss12; calculations by New Strategist

Table 1.33 Science Makes Our Way of Life Change Too Fast, 2012

"Do you agree or disagree that science makes our way of life change too fast?"

(percent of people aged 18 or older responding by sex and age, 2012)

	agree	disagree
TOTAL PEOPLE	**43.5%**	**56.5%**
Total men	**44.5**	**55.5**
Aged 18 to 44	41.3	58.7
Aged 45 to 64	46.1	53.8
Aged 65 or older	48.3	51.7
Total women	**42.6**	**57.4**
Aged 18 to 44	40.1	59.9
Aged 45 to 64	46.3	53.8
Aged 65 or older	41.1	58.9

Source: Survey Documentation and Analysis, Computer-assisted Survey Methods Program, University of California, Berkeley, General Social Survey, 1972–2012 Cumulative Data Files, Internet site http://sda.berkeley.edu/cgi-bin/hsda?harcsda+gss12; calculations by New Strategist

Few Younger Adults Read a Daily Newspaper

Most men and women get their news from television.

The Internet is in the process of transforming the way people get their news about current events. Readership of printed newspapers is in decline, with few young adults reading a daily paper. Only 26 to 28 percent of men and women read a newspaper every day. The percentage who never read a newspaper is almost as large, at 24 to 25 percent. Among adults under age 45, those who never read a newspaper greatly outnumber those who read a paper every day.

Half of women and 45 percent of men say they get most of their information about current events from television. The Internet ranks second, being the primary source of news for 31 percent of women and 30 percent of men. Among adults under age 45, the Internet is the dominant source of news, outstripping television.

■ Men and women are equally likely to get most of their news from the Internet.

Internet use differs by age

(percent of people aged 18 or older who get most of their information about current events from the Internet, by sex and age, 2012)

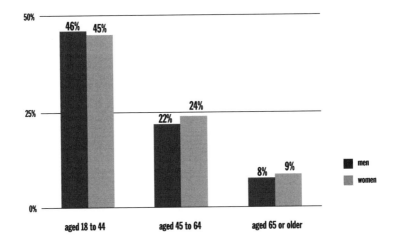

Table 1.34 Frequency of Reading the Newspaper, 2012

"How often do you read the newspaper—every day, a few times
a week, less than once a week, or never?"

(percent of people aged 18 or older responding by sex and age, 2012)

	every day	not every day, but at least once a week	less than once a week	never
TOTAL PEOPLE	**26.7%**	**32.0%**	**16.5%**	**24.8%**
Total men	**27.8**	**31.4**	**16.6**	**24.3**
Aged 18 to 44	16.7	33.5	22.3	27.5
Aged 45 to 64	31.7	30.3	13.8	24.3
Aged 65 or older	61.0	25.7	1.4	11.9
Total women	**25.8**	**32.7**	**16.3**	**25.2**
Aged 18 to 44	18.8	36.0	18.0	27.2
Aged 45 to 64	22.8	31.8	20.5	24.9
Aged 65 or older	51.2	24.0	4.2	20.6

*Source: Survey Documentation and Analysis, Computer-assisted Survey Methods Program, University of California, Berkeley,
General Social Survey, 1972–2012 Cumulative Data Files, Internet site http://sda.berkeley.edu/cgi-bin/hsda?harcsda+gss12;
calculations by New Strategist*

Table 1.35 Main Source of Information about Events in the News, 2012

"Where do you get most of your information about current news events?"

(percent of people aged 18 or older responding by sex and age, 2012)

	television	Internet	newspapers	radio	other
TOTAL PEOPLE	**47.9%**	**30.0%**	**12.4%**	**4.7%**	**5.0%**
Total men	**45.3**	**29.5**	**14.3**	**6.7**	**4.2**
Aged 18 to 44	34.7	46.4	7.2	6.3	5.4
Aged 45 to 64	50.0	21.7	17.5	7.5	3.3
Aged 65 or older	59.1	8.4	23.2	6.0	3.3
Total women	**50.3**	**30.5**	**10.7**	**2.8**	**5.7**
Aged 18 to 44	42.0	45.1	5.8	1.4	5.7
Aged 45 to 64	55.6	23.7	11.2	3.1	6.4
Aged 65 or older	59.1	9.3	21.9	5.5	4.2

*Source: Survey Documentation and Analysis, Computer-assisted Survey Methods Program, University of California, Berkeley,
General Social Survey, 1972–2012 Cumulative Data Files, Internet site http://sda.berkeley.edu/cgi-bin/hsda?harcsda+gss12;
calculations by New Strategist*

Men Are More Likely than Women to Identify Themselves as Republicans

Men are more conservative than women, and older men are the most conservative of all.

The percentage of Americans who identify themselves as politically conservative peaks among men aged 65 or older at 47 percent. The figure is lowest among women aged 18 to 44, at 26 percent. Conversely, the percentage of Americans who identify themselves as liberal is highest (31 percent) among women under age 45 and lowest (19 percent) among men aged 65 or older.

Although self-identified conservatives outnumber liberals, Democrats outnumber Republicans among both men and women in every age group. Those most likely to identify themselves as Republican are men aged 65 or older. Nevertheless, Democrats outnumber Republicans even among the oldest men (45 versus 42 percent).

■ When asked whether the federal government should help people with their medical bills, men aged 65 or older—universally covered by the government's Medicare program—are most likely to say no.

Liberal identification is greater among women than men

(percent of people aged 18 or older who identify themselves as political liberal or conservative, by sex, 2012)

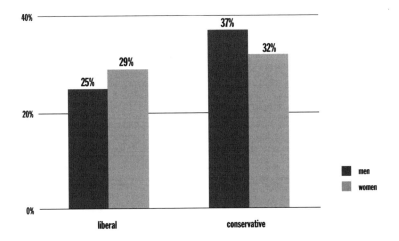

Table 1.36 Political Leanings, 2012

"We hear a lot of talk these days about liberals and conservatives. On a seven-point scale from extremely liberal (1) to extremely conservative (7), where would you place yourself?"

(percent of people aged 18 or older responding by sex and age, 2012)

	liberal	moderate	conservative
TOTAL PEOPLE	**27.0%**	**38.5%**	**34.6%**
Total men	**24.9**	**38.2**	**37.0**
Aged 18 to 44	25.4	39.6	35.1
Aged 45 to 64	26.7	37.9	35.3
Aged 65 or older	19.0	34.2	46.8
Total women	**28.8**	**38.7**	**32.5**
Aged 18 to 44	31.4	42.2	26.3
Aged 45 to 64	27.6	34.5	37.9
Aged 65 or older	23.5	38.5	38.0

Source: Survey Documentation and Analysis, Computer-assisted Survey Methods Program, University of California, Berkeley, General Social Survey, 1972–2012 Cumulative Data Files, Internet site http://sda.berkeley.edu/cgi-bin/hsda?harcsda+gss12; calculations by New Strategist

Table 1.37 Political Party Affiliation, 2012

"Generally speaking, do you usually think of yourself as a Republican, Democrat, Independent, or what?"

(percent of people aged 18 or older responding by sex and age, 2012)

	Democrat	independent	Republican	other
TOTAL PEOPLE	**46.1%**	**19.8%**	**31.7%**	**2.3%**
Total men	**45.0**	**17.6**	**34.2**	**3.3**
Aged 18 to 44	43.7	22.7	31.2	2.5
Aged 45 to 64	46.8	13.3	34.7	5.2
Aged 65 or older	45.2	10.7	42.4	1.8
Total women	**47.0**	**21.8**	**29.8**	**1.5**
Aged 18 to 44	46.1	25.9	26.2	1.7
Aged 45 to 64	46.3	20.9	31.8	0.9
Aged 65 or older	50.9	11.1	35.9	2.1

Source: Survey Documentation and Analysis, Computer-assisted Survey Methods Program, University of California, Berkeley, General Social Survey, 1972–2012 Cumulative Data Files, Internet site http://sda.berkeley.edu/cgi-bin/hsda?harcsda+gss12; calculations by New Strategist

Table 1.38 Government Should Help Pay for Medical Care, 2012

"In general, some people think that it is the responsibility of the government in Washington to see to it that people have help in paying for doctors and hospital bills; they are at point 1. Others think that these matters are not the responsibility of the federal government and that people should take care of these things themselves; they are at point 5. Where would you place yourself on the scale?"

(percent of people aged 18 or older responding by sex and age, 2012)

	1 government should help	2	3 agree with both	4	5 people should help themselves
TOTAL PEOPLE	**28.4%**	**18.1%**	**31.4%**	**12.4%**	**9.7%**
Total men	**22.2**	**19.5**	**33.5**	**16.1**	**8.8**
Aged 18 to 44	19.8	21.9	34.4	18.6	5.4
Aged 45 to 64	28.4	21.4	28.2	13.2	8.8
Aged 65 or older	16.9	9.2	41.3	14.7	17.9
Total women	**33.6**	**17.0**	**29.6**	**9.3**	**10.5**
Aged 18 to 44	35.4	21.2	27.3	9.0	7.1
Aged 45 to 64	32.1	15.4	29.4	9.7	13.3
Aged 65 or older	31.4	8.9	36.6	9.2	13.9

Source: Survey Documentation and Analysis, Computer-assisted Survey Methods Program, University of California, Berkeley, General Social Survey, 1972–2012 Cumulative Data Files, Internet site http://sda.berkeley.edu/cgi-bin/hsda?harcsda+gss12; calculations by New Strategist

A Minority of Americans Owns a Gun

Most support gun control.

Only 34 percent of Americans own a gun, with men more likely than women to say they have a gun at home (39 versus 31 percent). Only 30 percent of men under age 45 own a gun compared with the 61 percent majority of men aged 65 or older.

The great majority of men and women support gun control. Sixty-seven percent of men and 80 percent of women think there should be a law that requires people to have a police permit before they can buy a gun.

■ As the United States becomes increasingly urban, gun ownership is declining.

Men and women support capital punishment

(percent of people aged 18 or older who favor the death penalty for people convicted of murder, by sex, 2012)

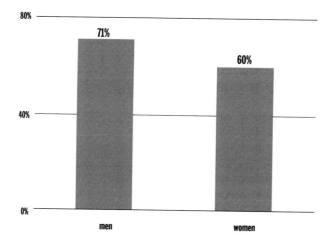

Table 1.39 Have Gun in Home, 2012

"Do you happen to have in your home (or garage) any guns or revolvers?"

(percent of people aged 18 or older responding by sex and age, 2012)

	yes	no	refused
TOTAL PEOPLE	**34.4%**	**63.6%**	**2.0%**
Total men	**38.8**	**59.1**	**2.1**
Aged 18 to 44	30.0	68.5	1.6
Aged 45 to 64	41.9	56.5	1.5
Aged 65 or older	60.9	33.4	5.7
Total women	**30.8**	**67.3**	**1.9**
Aged 18 to 44	26.9	72.4	0.6
Aged 45 to 64	34.6	61.6	3.8
Aged 65 or older	34.9	63.8	1.4

Source: Survey Documentation and Analysis, Computer-assisted Survey Methods Program, University of California, Berkeley, General Social Survey, 1972–2012 Cumulative Data Files, Internet site http://sda.berkeley.edu/cgi-bin/hsda?harcsda+gss12; calculations by New Strategist

Table 1.40 Favor or Oppose Gun Permits, 2012

"Would you favor or oppose a law which would require a person to obtain a police permit before he or she could buy a gun?"

(percent of people aged 18 or older responding by sex and age, 2012)

	favor	oppose
TOTAL PEOPLE	**73.7%**	**26.3%**
Total men	**66.9**	**33.1**
Aged 18 to 44	62.2	37.8
Aged 45 to 64	72.9	27.1
Aged 65 or older	66.5	33.5
Total women	**79.5**	**20.5**
Aged 18 to 44	79.0	21.0
Aged 45 to 64	77.5	22.5
Aged 65 or older	85.4	14.6

Source: Survey Documentation and Analysis, Computer-assisted Survey Methods Program, University of California, Berkeley, General Social Survey, 1972–2012 Cumulative Data Files, Internet site http://sda.berkeley.edu/cgi-bin/hsda?harcsda+gss12; calculations by New Strategist

Table 1.41 Favor or Oppose Death Penalty for Murder, 2012

"Do you favor or oppose the death penalty for persons convicted of murder?"

(percent of people aged 18 or older responding by sex and age, 2012)

	favor	oppose
TOTAL PEOPLE	**65.1%**	**34.9%**
Total men	**70.6**	**29.4**
Aged 18 to 44	66.0	34.0
Aged 45 to 64	76.2	23.8
Aged 65 or older	72.0	28.0
Total women	**60.3**	**39.7**
Aged 18 to 44	63.3	36.7
Aged 45 to 64	58.3	41.7
Aged 65 or older	56.8	43.2

Source: Survey Documentation and Analysis, Computer-assisted Survey Methods Program, University of California, Berkeley, General Social Survey, 1972–2012 Cumulative Data Files, Internet site http://sda.berkeley.edu/cgi-bin/hsda?harcsda+gss12; calculations by New Strategist

Attitudes toward Abortion Depend on the Reason

In the case of rape, both men and women say abortion should be legal.

In many ways, abortion is not a controversial issue. Seventy-six percent of both men and women, with few differences by age, agree that abortion should be legal for women who have been raped. An even larger 85 percent of men and 88 percent of women think abortion should be legal if a woman's health is endangered by pregnancy.

The controversy regarding abortion arises when people are asked whether women should be able to obtain a legal abortion for any reason. Only 41 percent of men and 44 percent of women agree. Men aged 65 or older are least likely to agree, with only 26 percent saying a woman should be able to obtain a legal abortion for any reason.

■ Men and women aged 65 or older are less likely than younger adults to support abortion for any reason.

Most support abortion if a woman's health is endangered

(percent of people aged 18 or older who think a pregnant woman should be able to obtain a legal abortion if her health is seriously endangered by pregnancy, by sex, 2012)

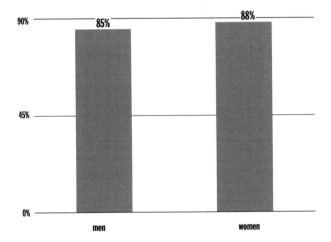

Table 1.42 Abortion if a Woman Is Pregnant as a Result of Rape, 2012

"Please tell me whether or not you think it should be possible for a pregnant woman to obtain a legal abortion if she became pregnant as a result of rape?"

(percent of people aged 18 or older responding by sex and age, 2012)

	yes	no
TOTAL PEOPLE	**75.8%**	**24.2%**
Total men	**75.5**	**24.5**
Aged 18 to 44	73.6	26.4
Aged 45 to 64	78.3	21.7
Aged 65 or older	75.6	24.4
Total women	**76.0**	**24.0**
Aged 18 to 44	79.0	21.0
Aged 45 to 64	73.0	27.0
Aged 65 or older	74.0	25.9

Source: Survey Documentation and Analysis, Computer-assisted Survey Methods Program, University of California, Berkeley, General Social Survey, 1972–2012 Cumulative Data Files, Internet site http://sda.berkeley.edu/cgi-bin/hsda?harcsda+gss12; calculations by New Strategist

Table 1.43 Abortion if Woman's Health Is Seriously Endangered, 2012

"Please tell me whether or not you think it should be possible for a pregnant woman to obtain a legal abortion if the woman's own health is seriously endangered by the pregnancy?"

(percent of people aged 18 or older responding by sex and age, 2012)

	yes	no
TOTAL PEOPLE	**86.7%**	**13.3%**
Total men	**85.5**	**14.5**
Aged 18 to 44	83.4	16.6
Aged 45 to 64	89.2	10.8
Aged 65 or older	82.6	17.4
Total women	**87.7**	**12.3**
Aged 18 to 44	86.5	13.5
Aged 45 to 64	89.5	10.5
Aged 65 or older	89.3	10.7

Source: Survey Documentation and Analysis, Computer-assisted Survey Methods Program, University of California, Berkeley, General Social Survey, 1972–2012 Cumulative Data Files, Internet site http://sda.berkeley.edu/cgi-bin/hsda?harcsda+gss12; calculations by New Strategist

Table 1.44 Abortion for Any Reason, 2012

"Please tell me whether or not you think it should be possible for a pregnant woman to obtain a legal abortion if the woman wants it for any reason?"

(percent of people aged 18 or older responding by sex and age, 2012)

	yes	no
TOTAL PEOPLE	**42.7%**	**57.3%**
Total men	**40.9**	**59.1**
Aged 18 to 44	43.6	56.4
Aged 45 to 64	42.7	57.3
Aged 65 or older	25.8	74.2
Total women	**44.3**	**55.7**
Aged 18 to 44	44.2	55.8
Aged 45 to 64	47.4	52.6
Aged 65 or older	39.6	60.4

Source: Survey Documentation and Analysis, Computer-assisted Survey Methods Program, University of California, Berkeley, General Social Survey, 1972–2012 Cumulative Data Files, Internet site http://sda.berkeley.edu/cgi-bin/hsda?harcsda+gss12; calculations by New Strategist

2

Education

Men and women are better educated.

Between 1950 and 2012, the proportion of men and women with a high school diploma climbed from about one-third to nearly 90 percent. The proportion with a college degree rose from the single digits to 31 percent.

There are differences in educational attainment by generation.

Among men, boomers aged 60 to 64 are most likely to be college graduates. Among women, those under age 40 are most likely to have a bachelor's degree.

Asian men and women are better educated than others.

Hispanic men and women are the least educated.

The majority of college students are female.

Women account for the 55 percent majority of college students, but male college enrollment has grown faster than female since 2000.

More than one-third of college students are minorities.

Blacks are the largest minority among female students, Hispanics among male.

Women earn most college degrees.

Men account for most degrees in a number of fields including computer science and engineering.

Educational Attainment Has Soared

Men and women are much more likely to be high school or college graduates today than even a few decades ago.

The educational attainment of Americans has increased over the decades as boomers and younger generations replaced older, less-educated adults. In 1950, barely one-third of men and women had graduated from high school. By 2012, nearly nine out of 10 were high school graduates.

The proportion of people aged 25 or older with a college degree has also climbed sharply. In 1950, just 5 and 7 percent of women and men, respectively, were college graduates. By 2012, the figure had reached 31 percent among both men and women. The gap in the percentage of men and women with a college degree was widest in 1980, when 20.9 percent of men but only 13.6 percent of women were college graduates.

■ Men were much more likely than women to have a college degree in 1980 because many men had gone to college in the 1960s and 1970s to avoid the Vietnam War draft.

Today, women are as likely as men to be college graduates

(percentage of people aged 25 or older who are college graduates, by sex, 1950, 1980, and 2012)

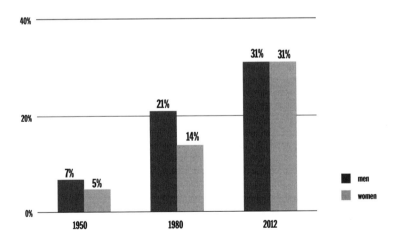

Table 2.1 Educational Attainment of Women, 1950 to 2012

(percent of women aged 25 or older who are high school or college graduates, 1950 to 2012, percentage point change, 1950–2012)

	high school graduate	college graduate
2012	88.0%	30.6%
2011	88.0	30.1
2010	87.6	29.6
2009	87.1	29.1
2008	87.2	28.8
2007	86.4	28.0
2005	85.5	26.5
2000	84.0	23.6
1995	81.6	20.2
1990	77.5	18.4
1985	73.5	16.0
1980	68.1	13.6
1975	62.1	10.6
1970	55.4	8.2
1965	49.9	7.1
1959	45.2	6.0
1950	36.0	5.2
PERCENTAGE POINT CHANGE		
1950 to 2012	52.0	25.4

Source: Bureau of the Census, Educational Attainment, CPS Historical Time Series Tables, Internet site http://www.census .gov/hhes/socdemo/education/data/cps/historical/index.html; calculations by New Strategist

Table 2.2 Educational Attainment of Men, 1950 to 2012

(percent of men aged 25 or older who are high school or college graduates, 1950 to 2012, percentage point change, 1950–2012)

	high school graduate	college graduate
2012	87.3%	31.4%
2011	87.1	30.8
2010	86.6	30.3
2009	86.2	30.1
2008	85.9	30.1
2007	85.0	29.5
2005	84.9	28.9
2000	84.2	27.8
1995	81.7	26.0
1990	77.7	24.4
1985	74.4	23.1
1980	69.2	20.9
1975	63.1	17.6
1970	55.0	14.1
1965	48.0	12.0
1959	42.2	10.3
1950	32.6	7.3
PERCENTAGE POINT CHANGE		
1950 to 2012	54.7	24.1

Source: Bureau of the Census, Educational Attainment, CPS Historical Time Series Tables, Internet site http://www.census .gov/hhes/socdemo/education/data/cps/historical/index.html; calculations by New Strategist

Most Men and Women Have College Experience

In every age group, most men have at least some college education.

Fifty-six percent of men and 58 percent of women aged 25 or older have at least some college education. Women aged 65 or older are the only group in which the majority has not been a college student.

The percentage of women with a bachelor's degree peaks at 37 to 38 percent among those aged 25 to 39. The pattern is different among men, with those aged 60 to 64 most likely to have a bachelor's degree. Behind this statistic is the Vietnam War, which drove many young men onto college campuses in the 1960s and 1970s to avoid the draft. This also explains why older men are more likely than their female counterparts to have a bachelor's degree.

Among adults under age 50, women are more likely than men to have a bachelor's degree. The gap is greatest in the 25-to-29 age group where 37.2 percent of women but only 29.8 percent of men have a degree.

■ As well-educated baby-boom and younger generations fill the older age groups, educational attainment is showing less variation by age.

More than one in 10 men and women have a graduate degree

(percentage of people aged 25 or older with a master's or higher degree, by sex, 2012)

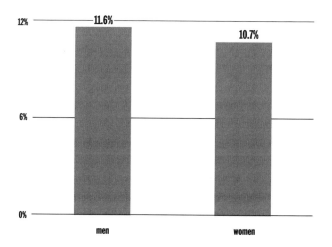

Table 2.3 Educational Attainment of Women by Age, 2012

(number and percent distribution of women aged 25 or older by educational attainment and age, 2012; numbers in thousands)

	total	25 to 29	30 to 34	35 to 39	40 to 44	45 to 49	50 to 54	55 to 59	60 to 64	65+
TOTAL WOMEN	**106,460**	**10,464**	**10,292**	**9,719**	**10,532**	**11,000**	**11,466**	**10,592**	**9,223**	**23,175**
Not a high school graduate	12,771	934	1,034	1,037	1,010	1,082	1,151	1,055	928	4,544
High school graduate only	31,898	2,443	2,405	2,211	2,666	3,228	3,635	3,340	2,825	9,147
Some college, no degree	18,091	2,127	1,791	1,683	1,761	1,886	1,998	1,718	1,752	3,376
Associate's degree	11,176	1,067	1,160	1,187	1,287	1,256	1,295	1,287	1,059	1,579
Bachelor's degree	21,146	2,976	2,466	2,293	2,498	2,379	2,207	1,947	1,609	2,771
Master's degree	9,062	730	1,100	998	1,082	929	934	1,006	861	1,421
Professional degree	1,155	107	187	147	126	116	134	114	85	140
Doctoral degree	1,162	80	149	162	104	122	113	126	105	200
High school graduate or more	93,690	9,530	9,258	8,681	9,524	9,916	10,316	9,538	8,296	18,634
Some college or more	61,792	7,087	6,853	6,470	6,858	6,688	6,681	6,198	5,471	9,487
Associate's degree or more	43,701	4,960	5,062	4,787	5,097	4,802	4,683	4,480	3,719	6,111
Bachelor's degree or more	32,525	3,893	3,902	3,600	3,810	3,546	3,388	3,193	2,660	4,532
TOTAL WOMEN	**100.0%**	**100.0%**	**100.0 %**	**100.0%**	**100.0%**	**100.0%**	**100.0%**	**100.0%**	**100.0%**	**100.0%**
Not a high school graduate	12.0	8.9	10.0	10.7	9.6	9.8	10.0	10.0	10.1	19.6
High school graduate only	30.0	23.3	23.4	22.7	25.3	29.3	31.7	31.5	30.6	39.5
Some college, no degree	17.0	20.3	17.4	17.3	16.7	17.1	17.4	16.2	19.0	14.6
Associate's degree	10.5	10.2	11.3	12.2	12.2	11.4	11.3	12.2	11.5	6.8
Bachelor's degree	19.9	28.4	24.0	23.6	23.7	21.6	19.2	18.4	17.4	12.0
Master's degree	8.5	7.0	10.7	10.3	10.3	8.4	8.1	9.5	9.3	6.1
Professional degree	1.1	1.0	1.8	1.5	1.2	1.1	1.2	1.1	0.9	0.6
Doctoral degree	1.1	0.8	1.4	1.7	1.0	1.1	1.0	1.2	1.1	0.9
High school graduate or more	88.0	91.1	90.0	89.3	90.4	90.1	90.0	90.0	89.9	80.4
Some college or more	58.0	67.7	66.6	66.6	65.1	60.8	58.3	58.5	59.3	40.9
Associate's degree or more	41.0	47.4	49.2	49.3	48.4	43.7	40.8	42.3	40.3	26.4
Bachelor's degree or more	30.6	37.2	37.9	37.0	36.2	32.2	29.5	30.1	28.8	19.6

Source: Bureau of the Census, Educational Attainment in the United States: 2012, Internet site http://www.census.gov/hhes/ socdemo/education/data/cps/2012/tables.html; calculations by New Strategist

Table 2.4 Educational Attainment of Men by Age, 2012

(number and percent distribution of men aged 25 or older by educational attainment and age, 2012; numbers in thousands)

	total	25 to 29	30 to 34	35 to 39	40 to 44	45 to 49	50 to 54	55 to 59	60 to 64	65+
TOTAL MEN	**98,119**	**10,430**	**10,034**	**9,421**	**10,255**	**10,584**	**10,906**	**9,879**	**8,278**	**18,333**
Not a high school graduate	12,504	1,209	1,238	1,107	1,235	1,289	1,283	1,039	806	3,299
High school graduate only	30,216	3,200	2,926	2,688	3,117	3,393	3,671	3,206	2,402	5,612
Some college, no degree	16,072	2,034	1,724	1,603	1,641	1,661	1,673	1,637	1,388	2,713
Associate's degree	8,560	882	980	876	951	1,028	1,008	863	806	1,166
Bachelor's degree	19,415	2,525	2,178	2,029	2,066	2,085	2,056	1,891	1,652	2,933
Master's degree	7,397	417	659	811	865	757	789	829	781	1,490
Professional degree	1,938	117	198	144	179	209	226	203	197	465
Doctoral degree	2,016	46	130	164	202	163	201	211	246	653
High school graduate or more	85,614	9,221	8,795	8,315	9,021	9,296	9,624	8,840	7,472	15,032
Some college or more	55,398	6,021	5,869	5,627	5,904	5,903	5,953	5,634	5,070	9,420
Associate's degree or more	39,326	3,987	4,145	4,024	4,263	4,242	4,280	3,997	3,682	6,707
Bachelor's degree or more	30,766	3,105	3,165	3,148	3,312	3,214	3,272	3,134	2,876	5,541
TOTAL MEN	**100.0%**	**100.0%**	**100.0 %**	**100.0%**	**100.0%**	**100.0%**	**100.0%**	**100.0%**	**100.0%**	**100.0%**
Not a high school graduate	12.7	11.6	12.3	11.8	12.0	12.2	11.8	10.5	9.7	18.0
High school graduate only	30.8	30.7	29.2	28.5	30.4	32.1	33.7	32.5	29.0	30.6
Some college, no degree	16.4	19.5	17.2	17.0	16.0	15.7	15.3	16.6	16.8	14.8
Associate's degree	8.7	8.5	9.8	9.3	9.3	9.7	9.2	8.7	9.7	6.4
Bachelor's degree	19.8	24.2	21.7	21.5	20.1	19.7	18.9	19.1	20.0	16.0
Master's degree	7.5	4.0	6.6	8.6	8.4	7.2	7.2	8.4	9.4	8.1
Professional degree	2.0	1.1	2.0	1.5	1.7	2.0	2.1	2.1	2.4	2.5
Doctoral degree	2.1	0.4	1.3	1.7	2.0	1.5	1.8	2.1	3.0	3.6
High school graduate or more	87.3	88.4	87.7	88.3	88.0	87.8	88.2	89.5	90.3	82.0
Some college or more	56.5	57.7	58.5	59.7	57.6	55.8	54.6	57.0	61.2	51.4
Associate's degree or more	40.1	38.2	41.3	42.7	41.6	40.1	39.2	40.5	44.5	36.6
Bachelor's degree or more	31.4	29.8	31.5	33.4	32.3	30.4	30.0	31.7	34.7	30.2

Source: Bureau of the Census, Educational Attainment in the United States: 2012, Internet site http://www.census.gov/hhes/ socdemo/education/data/cps/2012/tables.html; calculations by New Strategist

Non-Hispanic Whites Are Most Likely to Be High School Graduates

Asians are most likely to be college graduates.

From 92 to 93 percent of non-Hispanic white men and women aged 25 or older are high school graduates, a higher share than any other racial or ethnic group. Those least likely to have a high school diploma are Hispanics, with only 64 percent of men and 66 percent of women being high school graduates. Asian men and women are most likely to be college graduates. The 53 percent majority of Asian men and 49 percent of Asian women have a bachelor's degree.

Regardless of race or Hispanic origin, young women are better educated than older women. Among Asian women, for example, the 63 percent majority of 25-to-29-year-olds has a college degree versus only 26 percent of those aged 65 or older. Among black, Hispanic, and non-Hispanic white men, there is little variation in the percentage with a bachelor's degree by age. Among Asian men, however, the figure varies from a high of more than 60 percent among 35-to-44-year-olds to a low of 40 percent among those aged 65 or older.

■ The educational attainment of Hispanics is relatively low because many are recent immigrants from countries with poorly educated populations.

Among blacks and Hispanics, women are more likely than men to have a bachelor's degree

*(percent of men and women aged 25 or older with a college degree,
by race and Hispanic origin, 2012)*

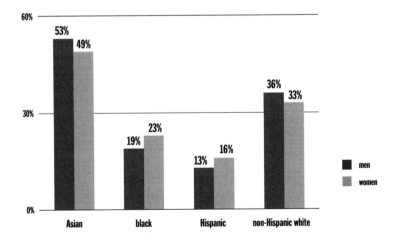

Table 2.5 Female High School and College Graduates by Race and Hispanic Origin, 2012

(percent of women aged 25 or older who have a high school diploma or a bachelor's degree, by race and Hispanic origin, and index of race/Hispanic origin group to total, 2012)

	high school graduate	college graduate
TOTAL WOMEN	**88.0%**	**30.6%**
Asian	87.8	48.6
Black	85.6	22.9
Hispanic	66.0	15.8
Non-Hispanic white	92.7	33.5
Index of race/Hispanic origin group to total		
TOTAL WOMEN	**100**	**100**
Asian	100	159
Black	97	75
Hispanic	75	52
Non-Hispanic white	105	110

Note: Asians and blacks are those who identify themselves as being of the race alone and those who identify themselves as being of the race in combination with other races. Hispanics may be of any race. Non-Hispanic whites are those who identify themselves as being white alone and not Hispanic.
Source: Bureau of the Census, Educational Attainment in the United States: 2012, Internet site http://www.census.gov/hhes/socdemo/education/data/cps/2012/tables.html; calculations by New Strategist

Table 2.6 Male High School and College Graduates by Race and Hispanic Origin, 2012

(percent of men aged 25 or older who have a high school diploma or a bachelor's degree, by race and Hispanic origin, and index of race/Hispanic origin group to total, 2012)

	high school graduate	college graduate
TOTAL MEN	**87.3%**	**31.4%**
Asian	90.5	52.6
Black	84.5	19.4
Hispanic	64.0	13.3
Non-Hispanic white	92.2	35.5
Index of race/Hispanic origin group to total		
TOTAL MEN	**100**	**100**
Asian	104	168
Black	97	62
Hispanic	73	42
Non-Hispanic white	106	113

Note: Asians and blacks are those who identify themselves as being of the race alone and those who identify themselves as being of the race in combination with other races. Hispanics may be of any race. Non-Hispanic whites are those who identify themselves as being white alone and not Hispanic.
Source: Bureau of the Census, Educational Attainment in the United States: 2012, Internet site http://www.census.gov/hhes/socdemo/education/data/cps/2012/tables.html; calculations by New Strategist

Table 2.7 Female High School and College Graduates by Age, Race, and Hispanic Origin, 2012

(percent of women aged 25 or older with a high school diploma or a bachelor's degree, by age, race, and Hispanic origin, 2012)

	total	Asian	black	Hispanic	non-Hispanic white
High school diploma or more					
TOTAL WOMEN	**88.0%**	**87.8%**	**85.6%**	**66.0%**	**92.7%**
Aged 25 to 29	91.1	94.7	89.7	77.0	95.3
Aged 30 to 34	90.0	94.1	88.1	71.1	95.9
Aged 35 to 39	89.3	94.0	89.7	66.7	95.9
Aged 40 to 44	90.4	88.9	91.9	67.3	96.4
Aged 45 to 49	90.1	92.6	87.5	69.6	94.8
Aged 50 to 54	90.0	87.9	87.1	66.2	94.6
Aged 55 to 59	90.0	86.6	86.0	62.5	94.7
Aged 60 to 64	89.9	83.8	87.8	58.7	94.5
Aged 65 or older	80.4	69.0	70.2	47.3	85.3
Bachelor's degree or more					
TOTAL WOMEN	**30.6%**	**48.6%**	**22.9%**	**15.8%**	**33.5%**
Aged 25 to 29	37.2	63.2	26.9	17.5	43.6
Aged 30 to 34	37.9	57.5	24.3	18.2	45.8
Aged 35 to 39	37.0	61.9	25.0	17.6	43.6
Aged 40 to 44	36.2	54.8	27.4	16.6	41.4
Aged 45 to 49	32.2	50.5	22.8	18.3	35.7
Aged 50 to 54	29.5	42.1	21.9	14.4	32.7
Aged 55 to 59	30.1	38.4	23.2	16.0	32.8
Aged 60 to 64	28.8	37.6	21.3	10.8	31.7
Aged 65 or older	19.6	26.0	16.0	9.3	20.6

Note: Asians and blacks are those who identify themselves as being of the race alone and those who identify themselves as being of the race in combination with other races. Hispanics may be of any race. Non-Hispanic whites are those who identify themselves as being white alone and not Hispanic.
Source: Bureau of the Census, Educational Attainment in the United States: 2012, Internet site http://www.census.gov/hhes/socdemo/education/data/cps/2012/tables.html; calculations by New Strategist

Table 2.8 Male High School and College Graduates by Age, Race, and Hispanic Origin, 2012

(percent of men aged 25 or older with a high school diploma or a bachelor's degree, by age, race, and Hispanic origin, 2012)

	total	Asian	black	Hispanic	non-Hispanic white
High school diploma or more					
TOTAL MEN	**87.3%**	**90.5%**	**84.5%**	**64.0%**	**92.2%**
Aged 25 to 29	88.4	96.0	86.8	73.3	93.8
Aged 30 to 34	87.7	93.7	87.1	64.8	94.5
Aged 35 to 39	88.3	94.5	89.1	64.3	95.3
Aged 40 to 44	88.0	89.7	89.2	64.8	94.0
Aged 45 to 49	87.8	90.4	88.3	61.8	93.4
Aged 50 to 54	88.2	90.9	86.3	61.4	92.8
Aged 55 to 59	89.5	91.8	83.6	64.4	93.5
Aged 60 to 64	90.3	84.3	84.3	62.9	94.3
Aged 65 or older	82.0	80.2	68.6	50.0	86.3
Bachelor's degree or more					
TOTAL MEN	**31.4%**	**52.6%**	**19.4%**	**13.3%**	**35.5%**
Aged 25 to 29	29.8	55.6	18.1	12.5	36.0
Aged 30 to 34	31.5	57.6	21.7	12.9	37.2
Aged 35 to 39	33.4	62.1	20.4	12.9	39.6
Aged 40 to 44	32.3	61.1	22.9	13.4	36.9
Aged 45 to 49	30.4	51.9	19.0	12.7	34.9
Aged 50 to 54	30.0	44.3	20.1	14.7	33.4
Aged 55 to 59	31.7	48.7	18.5	14.4	35.1
Aged 60 to 64	34.7	46.7	18.0	12.2	38.8
Aged 65 or older	30.2	39.8	16.3	14.4	32.7

Note: Asians and blacks are those who identify themselves as being of the race alone and those who identify themselves as being of the race in combination with other races. Hispanics may be of any race. Non-Hispanic whites are those who identify themselves as being white alone and not Hispanic.
Source: Bureau of the Census, Educational Attainment in the United States: 2012, Internet site http://www.census.gov/hhes/ socdemo/education/data/cps/2012/tables.html; calculations by New Strategist

Nearly 2 Million Women Aged 35 or Older Are in School

More than 90 percent of girls and boys aged 5 to 17 are in school.

The value Americans place on education is apparent in school enrollment statistics. Virtually all children aged 5 to 17 are enrolled in school. Although it was once rare for children to be in preschool, today more than half of 3-to-4-year-olds are in school. School enrollment falls below the 90 percent threshold in the 18-to-19 age group as some young adults go to work rather than college. In the 20-to-21 age group more than half of women and 49 percent of men are still in school.

With advancing age, women account for a growing share of students. Nearly 2 million women aged 35 or older are enrolled in school, accounting for more than 60 percent of older students.

■ The number of older students has been growing as middle-aged men and women return to school to update their credentials.

School is the norm for many young adults

(percent of men and women aged 18 to 24 enrolled in school, 2012)

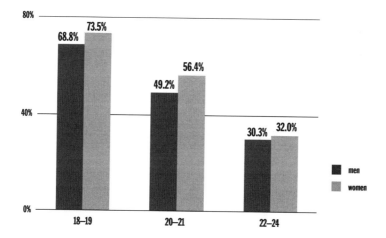

Table 2.9 School Enrollment of Females by Age, 2011

(total number of people aged 3 or older enrolled in school, number and percent of females enrolled in school and female share of total, by age, 2011; numbers in thousands)

		females enrolled		
	total	number	percent	share of total
Total enrolled	**79,043**	**39,798**	**26.5%**	**50.3%**
Aged 3 to 4	4,597	2,239	52.1	48.7
Aged 5 to 6	8,009	3,866	95.2	48.3
Aged 7 to 9	12,319	6,066	97.9	49.2
Aged 10 to 13	15,941	7,780	98.4	48.8
Aged 14 to 15	7,825	3,836	98.9	49.0
Aged 16 to 17	7,906	3,882	96.0	49.1
Aged 18 to 19	6,017	3,029	73.5	50.3
Aged 20 to 21	4,618	2,406	56.4	52.1
Aged 22 to 24	3,961	2,031	32.0	51.3
Aged 25 to 29	3,139	1,761	16.8	56.1
Aged 30 to 34	1,571	919	8.9	58.5
Aged 35 to 44	1,688	1,032	5.2	61.1
Aged 45 to 54	1012	669	3.0	66.1
Aged 55 or older	438	283	0.7	64.6

Source: Bureau of the Census, School Enrollment, CPS October 2011—Detailed Tables, Internet site http://www.census.gov/ hhes/school/data/cps/2011/tables.html; calculations by New Strategist

Table 2.10 School Enrollment of Males by Age, 2011

(total number of people aged 3 or older enrolled in school, number and percent of males enrolled in school and male share of total, by age, 2011; numbers in thousands)

	total	males enrolled number	males enrolled percent	males enrolled share of total
Total enrolled	**79,043**	**39,245**	**27.2%**	**49.7%**
Aged 3 to 4	4,597	2,358	52.8	51.3
Aged 5 to 6	8,009	4,143	95.1	51.7
Aged 7 to 9	12,319	6,253	98.1	50.8
Aged 10 to 13	15,941	8,161	98.6	51.2
Aged 14 to 15	7,825	3,990	98.4	51.0
Aged 16 to 17	7,906	4,025	95.4	50.9
Aged 18 to 19	6,017	2,987	68.8	49.6
Aged 20 to 21	4,618	2,213	49.2	47.9
Aged 22 to 24	3,961	1,931	30.3	48.8
Aged 25 to 29	3,139	1,378	12.9	43.9
Aged 30 to 34	1,571	653	6.4	41.6
Aged 35 to 44	1,688	656	3.4	38.9
Aged 45 to 54	1012	343	1.6	33.9
Aged 55 or older	438	155	0.4	35.4

Source: Bureau of the Census, School Enrollment, CPS October 2011—Detailed Tables, Internet site http://www.census.gov/ hhes/school/data/cps/2011/tables.html; calculations by New Strategist

College Enrollment Rate May Have Peaked

The number of students enrolled in college is at an all-time high, however.

In 2011, fully 72 percent of girls who graduated from high school continued their education by enrolling in college, up from 66 percent in 2000. Among boys, the proportion climbed from 60 percent in 2000 to 65 percent in 2011. Women's college enrollment rate was lower in 2011 than in the previous two years, perhaps reflecting the difficulty many families are facing in affording ever-higher college costs. Men's enrollment rate in 2011 was somewhat below the level of the mid-2000s.

The number of college students climbed 12 percent between 1990 and 2000 and by a much larger 33 percent between 2000 and 2011. Women's college enrollment grew faster than average in the 1990-to-2000 time period, but more slowly than average between 2000 and 2011. Men's enrollment shows the opposite pattern and has grown faster than women's since 2000.

■ College enrollment is growing in every age group.

More than 11 million women are enrolled in college

(number of students enrolled in college by sex, 2011)

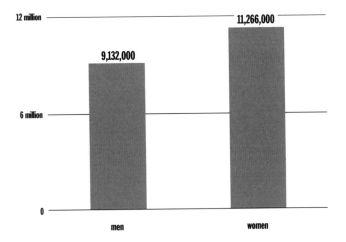

Table 2.11 College Enrollment Rate by Sex, 1960 to 2011

(percentage of people aged 16 to 24 who graduated from high school in the previous 12 months and were enrolled in college as of October, by sex, and difference between men and women, 1960 to 2011; percentage point change in enrollment rate for selected years)

	total	men	women	difference between men and women
2011	68.2%	64.7%	72.2%	−7.5
2010	68.1	62.8	74.0	−11.2
2009	70.1	66.0	73.8	−7.8
2008	68.6	65.9	71.6	−5.7
2007	67.2	66.1	68.3	−2.2
2006	66.0	65.8	66.1	−0.3
2005	68.6	66.5	70.4	−3.9
2004	66.7	61.4	71.5	−10.1
2003	63.9	61.2	66.5	−5.3
2002	65.2	62.1	68.3	−6.2
2001	61.7	59.7	63.6	−3.9
2000	63.3	59.9	66.2	−6.3
1999	62.9	61.4	64.4	−3.0
1998	65.6	62.4	69.1	−6.7
1997	67.0	63.6	70.3	−6.7
1996	65.0	60.1	69.7	−9.6
1995	61.9	62.6	61.3	1.3
1994	61.9	60.6	63.2	−2.6
1993	62.6	59.9	65.2	−5.3
1992	61.9	60.0	63.8	−3.8
1991	62.5	57.9	67.1	−9.2
1990	60.1	58.0	62.2	−4.2
1989	59.6	57.6	61.6	−4.0
1988	58.9	57.1	60.7	−3.6
1987	56.8	58.3	55.3	3.0
1986	53.8	55.8	51.9	3.9
1985	57.7	58.6	56.8	1.8
1984	55.2	56.0	54.5	1.5
1983	52.7	51.9	53.4	−1.5
1982	50.6	49.1	52.0	−2.9
1981	53.9	54.8	53.1	1.7
1980	49.3	46.7	51.8	−5.1
1979	49.3	50.4	48.4	2.0
1978	50.1	51.1	49.3	1.8
1977	50.6	52.1	49.3	2.8
1976	48.8	47.2	50.3	−3.1
1975	50.7	52.6	49.0	3.6
1974	47.6	49.4	45.9	3.5
1973	46.6	50.0	43.4	6.6

	total	men	women	difference between men and women
1972	49.2%	52.7%	46.0%	6.7
1971	53.5	57.6	49.8	7.8
1970	51.7	55.2	48.5	6.7
1969	53.3	60.1	47.2	12.9
1968	55.4	63.2	48.9	14.3
1967	51.9	57.6	47.2	10.4
1966	50.1	58.7	42.7	16.0
1965	50.9	57.3	45.3	12.0
1964	48.3	57.2	40.7	16.5
1963	45.0	52.3	39.0	13.3
1962	49.0	55.0	43.5	11.5
1961	48.0	56.3	41.3	15.0
1960	45.1	54.0	37.9	16.1
Percentage point change				
2000 to 2011	4.9	4.8	6.0	–
1960 to 2011	23.1	10.7	34.3	–

Note: "–" means not applicable.
Source: National Center for Education Statistics, Digest of Education Statistics 2012, Internet site http://nces.ed.gov/programs/digest/2012menu_tables.asp; calculations by New Strategist

Table 2.12 College Enrollment of Women, 1990 to 2011

(total number of people aged 14 or older enrolled in college, number of women enrolled and female share of total, 1990 to 2011; percent change for selected years; numbers in thousands)

	total in college	women in college	
		number	share of total
2011	20,398	11,266	55.2%
2010	20,275	11,268	55.6
2009	19,764	11,123	56.3
2008	18,631	10,321	55.4
2007	17,956	10,130	56.4
2006	17,232	9,726	56.4
2005	17,473	9,934	56.9
2004	17,382	9,807	56.4
2003	16,638	9,320	56.0
2002	16,498	9,258	56.1
2001	15,873	8,998	56.7
2000	15,314	8,631	56.4
1999	15,203	8,247	54.2
1998	15,546	8,641	55.6
1997	15,436	8,593	55.7
1996	15,227	8,406	55.2
1995	14,715	8,013	54.5
1994	15,023	8,258	55.0
1993	13,898	7,574	54.5
1992	14,035	7,844	55.9
1991	14,057	7,618	54.2
1990	13,622	7,429	54.5
Percent change			
2000 to 2011	33.2%	30.5%	–
1990 to 2000	12.4	16.2	–

Note: "–" means not applicable.
Source: Bureau of the Census, School Enrollment, Historical Tables, Internet site http://www.census.gov/hhes/school/data/cps/historical/index.html; calculations by New Strategist

Table 2.13 College Enrollment of Men, 1990 to 2011

(total number of people aged 14 or older enrolled in college, number of men enrolled and male share of total, 1990 to 2011; percent change for selected years; numbers in thousands)

	total in college	men in college	
		number	share of total
2011	20,398	9,132	44.8%
2010	20,275	9,008	44.4
2009	19,764	8,642	43.7
2008	18,631	8,311	44.6
2007	17,956	7,825	43.6
2006	17,232	7,506	43.6
2005	17,473	7,538	43.1
2004	17,382	7,575	43.6
2003	16,638	7,318	44.0
2002	16,498	7,240	43.9
2001	15,873	6,875	43.3
2000	15,314	6,682	43.6
1999	15,203	6,957	45.8
1998	15,546	6,905	44.4
1997	15,436	6,843	44.3
1996	15,227	6,821	44.8
1995	14,715	6,703	45.6
1994	15,023	6,764	45.0
1993	13,898	6,324	45.5
1992	14,035	6,193	44.1
1991	14,057	6,440	45.8
1990	13,622	6,192	45.5
Percent change			
2000 to 2011	33.2%	36.7%	–
1990 to 2000	12.4	7.9	–

Note: "–" means not applicable.
Source: Bureau of the Census, School Enrollment, Historical Tables, Internet site http://www.census.gov/hhes/school/data/cps/historical/index.html; calculations by New Strategist

Table 2.14 Women in College by Age, 2000 to 2011

(number and percent distribution of women aged 14 or older enrolled in college by age; 2000 to 2011; percent change in number and percentage point change in distribution, 2000–11; numbers in thousands)

	2011	2010	2000	percent change, 2000–11
Total women in college	11,266	11,268	8,631	30.5%
Under age 20	2,388	2,490	2,117	12.8
Aged 20 to 21	2,333	2,240	1,697	37.5
Aged 22 to 24	1,992	1,920	1,383	44.0
Aged 25 to 29	1,722	1,596	1,118	54.0
Aged 30 to 34	908	973	728	24.7
Aged 35 or older	1,923	2,049	1,589	21.0

PERCENT DISTRIBUTION BY AGE				percentage point change, 2000–11
Total women in college	100.0%	100.0%	100.0%	–
Under age 20	21.2	22.1	24.5	–3.3
Aged 20 to 21	20.7	19.9	19.7	1.0
Aged 22 to 24	17.7	17.0	16.0	1.7
Aged 25 to 29	15.3	14.2	13.0	2.3
Aged 30 to 34	8.1	8.6	8.4	–0.4
Aged 35 or older	17.1	18.2	18.4	–1.3

Note: "–" means not applicable.
Source: Bureau of the Census, School Enrollment, Historical Tables, Internet site http://www.census.gov/hhes/school/data/cps/historical/index.html; calculations by New Strategist

Table 2.15 Men in College by Age, 2000 to 2011

(number and percent distribution of men aged 14 or older enrolled in college by age; 2000 to 2011; percent change in number and percentage point change in distribution, 2000–11; numbers in thousands)

	2011	2010	2000	percent change, 2000–11
Total men in college	**9,132**	**9,007**	**6,682**	**36.7%**
Under age 20	2,057	2,103	1,631	26.1
Aged 20 to 21	2,127	2,108	1,472	44.5
Aged 22 to 24	1,877	1,580	1,300	44.4
Aged 25 to 29	1,343	1,396	844	59.1
Aged 30 to 34	643	659	517	24.4
Aged 35 or older	1,084	1,160	918	18.1

				percentage point change, 2000–11
PERCENT DISTRIBUTION BY AGE				
Total men in college	**100.0%**	**100.0%**	**100.0%**	–
Under age 20	22.5	23.3	24.4	–1.9
Aged 20 to 21	23.3	23.4	22.0	1.3
Aged 22 to 24	20.6	17.5	19.5	1.1
Aged 25 to 29	14.7	15.5	12.6	2.1
Aged 30 to 34	7.0	7.3	7.7	–0.7
Aged 35 or older	11.9	12.9	13.7	–1.9

Note: "–" means not applicable.
Source: Bureau of the Census, School Enrollment, Historical Tables, Internet site http://www.census.gov/hhes/school/data/cps/historical/index.html; calculations by New Strategist

More than One-Third of College Students Are Minorities

Hispanic enrollment has grown most rapidly since 2000.

Non-Hispanic whites accounted for 62 percent of the women and 63 percent of the men enrolled in college in 2011, down from 69 and 71 percent, respectively, in 2000. Among male college students, Hispanics are the largest minority (16 percent), followed by blacks (14 percent) and Asians (7 percent). Among female college students, blacks are the largest minority (18 percent), followed by Hispanics (13 percent) and Asians (6 percent).

Enrollment increased in every racial and ethnic group between 2000 and 2011, the fastest growth occurring among Hispanics. The number of Hispanic men enrolled in college more than doubled, and the number of Hispanic women in college climbed by 88 percent. Black college enrollment also grew rapidly, by more than 50 percent.

■ Among non-Hispanic whites, women's college enrollment grew only 18 percent between 2000 and 2011 and men's increased by a larger 22 percent.

Blacks are the largest minority among female college students

(percent distribution of female college students by race and Hispanic origin, 2011)

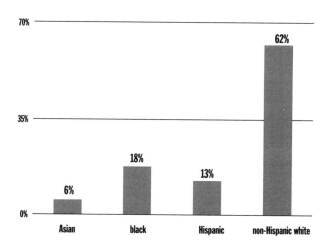

Table 2.16 Women in College by Race and Hispanic Origin, 2000 to 2011

(number and percent distribution of women aged 14 or older enrolled in college by race and Hispanic origin, 2000 to 2011; percent change in number and percentage point change in distribution, 2000–11; numbers in thousands)

	2011	2010	2000	percent change, 2000–11
Total women in college	**11,266**	**11,268**	**8,631**	**30.5%**
Asian	697	727	532	31.0
Black	2,037	2,009	1,349	51.0
Hispanic	1,515	1,576	807	87.7
Non-Hispanic white	6,972	6,940	5,921	17.8

				percentage point change, 2000–11
PERCENT DISTRIBUTION BY RACE AND HISPANIC ORIGIN				
Total women in college	**100.0%**	**100.0%**	**100.0%**	–
Asian	6.2	6.5	6.2	0.0
Black	18.1	17.8	15.6	2.5
Hispanic	13.4	14.0	9.4	4.1
Non-Hispanic white	61.9	61.6	68.6	–6.7

Note: Numbers do not add to total because not all races are shown and Hispanics may be of any race. In 2010 and 2011, Asians and blacks are those who identify themselves as being of the race alone and those who identify themselves as being of the race in combination with other races. Non-Hispanic whites are those who identify themselves as being white alone and not Hispanic. "–" means not applicable.
Source: Bureau of the Census, School Enrollment, Historical Tables, Internet site http://www.census.gov/population/www/ socdemo/school.html; calculations by New Strategist

Table 2.17 Men in College by Race and Hispanic Origin, 2000 to 2011

(number and percent distribution of men aged 14 or older enrolled in college by race and Hispanic origin, 2000 to 2011; percent change in number and percentage point change in distribution, 2000–11; numbers in thousands)

	2011	2010	2000	percent change, 2000–11
Total men in college	**9,132**	**9,007**	**6,682**	**36.7%**
Asian	658	740	517	27.3
Black	1,279	1,241	815	56.9
Hispanic	1,438	1,302	619	132.3
Non-Hispanic white	5,731	5,673	4,716	21.5

PERCENT DISTRIBUTION BY RACE AND HISPANIC ORIGIN				percentage point change, 2000–11
Total men in college	**100.0%**	**100.0%**	**100.0%**	–
Asian	7.2	8.2	7.7	–0.5
Black	14.0	13.8	12.2	1.8
Hispanic	15.7	14.5	9.3	6.5
Non-Hispanic white	62.8	63.0	70.6	–7.8

Note: Numbers do not add to total because not all races are shown and Hispanics may be of any race. In 2010 and 2011, Asians and blacks are those who identify themselves as being of the race alone and those who identify themselves as being of the race in combination with other races. Non-Hispanic whites are those who identify themselves as being white alone and not Hispanic. "–" means not applicable.

Source: Bureau of the Census, School Enrollment, Historical Tables, Internet site http://www.census.gov/population/www/socdemo/school.html; calculations by New Strategist

Most Students Are Full-Timers

Even in graduate school, most students attend school full-time.

Among men and women who attend four-year colleges, more than 80 percent are full-time students. The proportion of male students at four-year schools who attend full-time falls from a high of 94 percent among those under age 20 to a low of 44 percent among those aged 35 or older. Regardless of age, most women at four-year schools are full-time students.

At two-year schools the majority of students under age 35 are full-timers, and most of those aged 35 or older—both men and women—are part-timers. In graduate school as well, part-timers are more numerous than full-timers only among students aged 35 or older.

■ When jobs become more plentiful, not only might college enrollment fall but a growing share of students may attend part-time rather than full-time.

Most men under age 35 who attend four-year colleges are full-time students

(percentage of men enrolled in four-year colleges who attend school full-time, by age, 2011)

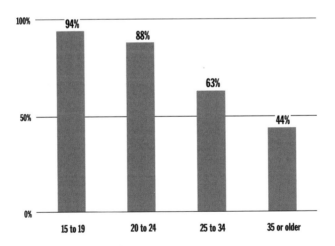

Table 2.18 Women in College by Age and Attendance Status, 2011

(number and percent distribution of women aged 15 or older enrolled in college by age and attendance status, 2011; numbers in thousands)

| | | undergraduate | | | | | | graduate school | | |
| | | two-year college | | | four-year college | | | | | |
	total	total	full-time	part-time	total	full-time	part-time	total	full-time	part-time
Total women in college	**11,266**	**3,252**	**2,053**	**1,199**	**5,858**	**4,855**	**1,003**	**2,155**	**1,261**	**895**
Aged 15 to 19	2,388	849	700	150	1,534	1,488	46	5	5	0
Aged 20 to 24	4,325	1,029	670	359	2,774	2,490	284	522	419	102
Aged 25 to 34	2,631	756	415	340	979	581	397	896	544	352
Aged 35 or older	1,923	617	267	350	572	297	275	733	293	440

PERCENT DISTRIBUTION BY ATTENDANCE STATUS

Total women in college	–	**100.0%**	**63.1%**	**36.9%**	**100.0%**	**82.9%**	**17.1%**	**100.0%**	**58.5%**	**41.5%**
Aged 15 to 19	–	100.0	82.4	17.7	100.0	97.0	3.0	100.0	100.0	0.0
Aged 20 to 24	–	100.0	65.1	34.9	100.0	89.8	10.2	100.0	80.3	19.5
Aged 25 to 34	–	100.0	54.9	45.0	100.0	59.3	40.6	100.0	60.7	39.3
Aged 35 or older	–	100.0	43.3	56.7	100.0	51.9	48.1	100.0	40.0	60.0

PERCENT DISTRIBUTION BY AGE

Total women in college	**100.0**	**100.0**	**100.0**	**100.0**	**100.0**	**100.0**	**100.0**	**100.0**	**100.0**	**100.0**
Aged 15 to 19	21.2	26.1	34.1	12.5	26.2	30.6	4.6	0.2	0.4	0.0
Aged 20 to 24	38.4	31.6	32.6	29.9	47.4	51.3	28.3	24.2	33.2	11.4
Aged 25 to 34	23.4	23.2	20.2	28.4	16.7	12.0	39.6	41.6	43.1	39.3
Aged 35 or older	17.1	19.0	13.0	29.2	9.8	6.1	27.4	34.0	23.2	49.2

Note: "–" means not applicable.
Source: Bureau of the Census, School Enrollment, CPS October 2011—Detailed Tables, Internet site http://www.census.gov/ hhes/school/data/cps/2011/tables.html; calculations by New Strategist

Table 2.19 Men in College by Age and Attendance Status, 2011

(number and percent distribution of men aged 15 or older enrolled in college by age and attendance status, 2011; numbers in thousands)

| | | undergraduate | | | | | | graduate school | | |
| | | two-year college | | | four-year college | | | | | |
	total	total	full-time	part-time	total	full-time	part-time	total	full-time	part-time
Total men in college	**9,132**	**2,453**	**1,664**	**789**	**5,061**	**4,166**	**896**	**1617**	**905**	**712**
Aged 15 to 19	2,058	747	641	106	1,304	1,230	74	6	1	5
Aged 20 to 24	4,003	1,003	670	333	2,563	2,260	303	437	342	96
Aged 25 to 34	1,987	480	257	224	804	505	300	702	411	291
Aged 35 or older	1,084	222	95	127	390	172	218	472	150	321

PERCENT DISTRIBUTION BY ATTENDANCE STATUS

Total men in college	–	**100.0%**	**67.8%**	**32.2%**	**100.0%**	**82.3%**	**17.7%**	**100.0%**	**56.0%**	**44.0%**
Aged 15 to 19	–	100.0	85.8	14.2	100.0	94.3	5.7	100.0	16.7	83.3
Aged 20 to 24	–	100.0	66.8	33.2	100.0	88.2	11.8	100.0	78.3	22.0
Aged 25 to 34	–	100.0	53.5	46.7	100.0	62.8	37.3	100.0	58.5	41.5
Aged 35 or older	–	100.0	42.8	57.2	100.0	44.1	55.9	100.0	31.8	68.0

PERCENT DISTRIBUTION BY AGE

Total men in college	**100.0**	**100.0**	**100.0**	**100.0**	**100.0**	**100.0**	**100.0**	**100.0**	**100.0**	**100.0**
Aged 15 to 19	22.5	30.5	38.5	13.4	25.8	29.5	8.3	0.4	0.1	0.7
Aged 20 to 24	43.8	40.9	40.3	42.2	50.6	54.2	33.8	27.0	37.8	13.5
Aged 25 to 34	21.8	19.6	15.4	28.4	15.9	12.1	33.5	43.4	45.4	40.9
Aged 35 or older	11.9	9.1	5.7	16.1	7.7	4.1	24.3	29.2	16.6	45.1

Note: "–" means not applicable.
Source: Bureau of the Census, School Enrollment, CPS October 2011—Detailed Tables, Internet site http://www.census.gov/ hhes/school/data/cps/2011/tables.html; calculations by New Strategist

Women Earn Most College Degrees

Even at the doctoral level, women are awarded the majority of degrees.

Of the 3.6 million degrees awarded by institutions of higher education in 2010–11, women earned the 59 percent majority. Among blacks, women earned 67 percent of degrees awarded that year, while the figure was 61 percent among Hispanics. Only among foreign students (called nonresident aliens) did women earn fewer than half of degrees in 2010–11 (46 percent).

Women earned 62 percent of associate's degrees awarded in 2010–11. They earned 57 percent of bachelor's degrees, 60 percent of master's degrees, and 51 percent of doctoral and first-professional degrees. In every racial and ethnic group, women earned the majority of associates, bachelor's, master's, doctoral, and first-professional degrees. Among foreign students, however, men accounted for the majority of degrees at the master's and doctoral level.

■ As today's highly educated women enter the workforce, the earnings gap between men and women should continue to shrink.

Women's share of bachelor's degrees varies by race and Hispanic origin

(women's share of bachelor's degrees awarded by race and Hispanic origin, 2010–11)

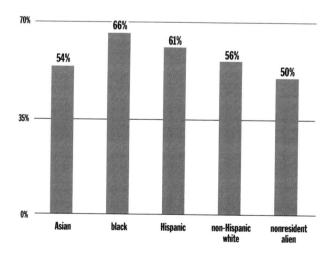

Table 2.20 Degrees Earned by Women by Level of Degree, Race, and Hispanic Origin, 2010–11

(total number of degrees conferred by institutions of higher education, number and percent distribution of degrees earned by women, and female share of total, by level of degree, race, and Hispanic origin, 2010–11)

	total	degrees earned by women		
		number	percent	share of total
Total degrees	**3,552,640**	**2,085,993**	**100.0%**	**58.7%**
Asian	227,748	125,682	6.0	55.2
Black	393,351	265,059	12.7	67.4
Hispanic	335,116	205,494	9.9	61.3
White, non-Hispanic	2,355,350	1,367,943	65.6	58.1
Nonresident alien	174,024	80,694	3.9	46.4
Associate's degrees	**942,327**	**581,018**	**100.0**	**61.7**
Asian	45,876	26,695	4.6	58.2
Black	128,703	87,107	15.0	67.7
Hispanic	125,616	77,934	13.4	62.0
White, non-Hispanic	604,110	366,032	63.0	60.6
Nonresident alien	16,574	9,783	1.7	59.0
Bachelor's degrees	**1,715,913**	**981,780**	**100.0**	**57.2**
Asian	121,066	65,776	6.7	54.3
Black	173,017	113,898	11.6	65.8
Hispanic	154,063	93,321	9.5	60.6
White, non-Hispanic	1,182,405	662,522	67.5	56.0
Nonresident alien	52,625	26,447	2.7	50.3
Master's degrees	**730,635**	**439,084**	**100.0**	**60.1**
Asian	43,728	23,678	5.4	54.1
Black	80,706	56,965	13.0	70.6
Hispanic	46,787	29,574	6.7	63.2
White, non-Hispanic	462,903	285,123	64.9	61.6
Nonresident alien	85,863	37,099	8.4	43.2
Doctoral and first-professional degrees	**163,765**	**84,111**	**100.0**	**51.4**
Asian	17,078	9,533	11.3	55.8
Black	10,925	7,089	8.4	64.9
Hispanic	8,650	4,665	5.5	53.9
White, non-Hispanic	105,932	54,266	64.5	51.2
Nonresident alien	18,962	7,365	8.8	38.8

Note: Numbers do not add to total because not all races are shown.
Source: National Center for Education Statistics, Digest of Education Statistics 2012, Internet site http://nces.ed.gov/programs/digest/2012menu_tables.asp; calculations by New Strategist

Table 2.21 Degrees Earned by Men by Level of Degree, Race, and Hispanic Origin, 2010–11

(total number of degrees conferred by institutions of higher education, number and percent distribution of degrees earned by men, and male share of total, by level of degree, race, and Hispanic origin, 2010–11)

	total	degrees earned by men		
		number	percent	share of total
Total degrees	**3,552,640**	**1,466,647**	**100.0%**	**41.3%**
Asian	227,748	102,066	7.0	44.8
Black	393,351	128,292	8.7	32.6
Hispanic	335,116	129,622	8.8	38.7
White, non-Hispanic	2,355,350	987,407	67.3	41.9
Nonresident alien	174,024	93,330	6.4	53.6
Associate's degrees	**942,327**	**361,309**	**100.0**	**38.3**
Asian	45,876	19,181	5.3	41.8
Black	128,703	41,596	11.5	32.3
Hispanic	125,616	47,682	13.2	38.0
White, non-Hispanic	604,110	238,078	65.9	39.4
Nonresident alien	16,574	6,791	1.9	41.0
Bachelor's degrees	**1,715,913**	**734,133**	**100.0**	**42.8**
Asian	121,066	55,290	7.5	45.7
Black	173,017	59,119	8.1	34.2
Hispanic	154,063	60,742	8.3	39.4
White, non-Hispanic	1,182,405	519,883	70.8	44.0
Nonresident alien	52,625	26,178	3.6	49.7
Master's degrees	**730,635**	**291,551**	**100.0**	**39.9**
Asian	43,728	20,050	6.9	45.9
Black	80,706	23,741	8.1	29.4
Hispanic	46,787	17,213	5.9	36.8
White, non-Hispanic	462,903	177,780	61.0	38.4
Nonresident alien	85,863	48,764	16.7	56.8
Doctoral and first-professional degrees	**163,765**	**79,654**	**100.0**	**48.6**
Asian	17,078	7,545	9.5	44.2
Black	10,925	3,836	4.8	35.1
Hispanic	8,650	3,985	5.0	46.1
White, non-Hispanic	105,932	51,666	64.9	48.8
Nonresident alien	18,962	11,597	14.6	61.2

Note: Numbers do not add to total because not all races are shown.
Source: National Center for Education Statistics, Digest of Education Statistics 2012, Internet site http://nces.ed.gov/programs/digest/2012menu_tables.asp; calculations by New Strategist

Men Earn Most Engineering Degrees

The percentage of degrees awarded to men varies greatly by field.

Women earn most of the associate's, bachelor's, master's, and doctoral degrees awarded each year, but in many fields of study men outnumber women.

The share of associate's degrees awarded to men in 2010–11 ranged from a low of 4 percent in family and consumer sciences to a high of 95 percent in mechanic and repair technologies. Among bachelor's degrees awarded in 2010–11, men earned more than 80 percent of those in computer science and engineering and only 18 percent of those in public administration and social services. At the master's level, men earned two-thirds of the degrees awarded in theology but only 19 percent of degrees in library science.

Women earned slightly more than half the doctoral and first-professional degrees awarded in 2010–11. But men earned most of the degrees in business, philosophy, and law.

■ Because men and women choose different fields of study in college, their career paths diverge upon graduation.

Men earn most computer science degrees

(men's share of selected bachelor's degrees awarded in 2010–11)

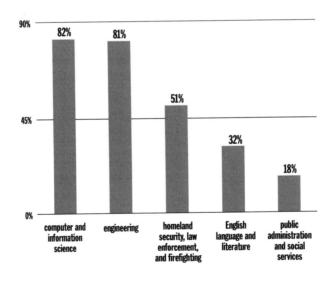

Table 2.22 Associate's Degrees Earned by Women by Field of Study, 2010–11

(total number of associate's degrees conferred and number and percent earned by women, by field of study, 2010–11)

		degrees earned by women	
	total	number	percent of total
Total associate's degrees	**942,327**	**361,309**	**38.3%**
Agriculture and natural resources	6,425	4,089	63.6
Architecture and related programs	569	310	54.5
Area, ethnic, and cultural studies	209	60	28.7
Biological and biomedical sciences	3,245	1,116	34.4
Business	139,986	51,171	36.6
Communication, journalism, and related programs	3,051	1,411	46.2
Communications technologies	4,209	2,774	65.9
Computer and information sciences	37,677	29,060	77.1
Construction trades	5,402	5,105	94.5
Education	20,459	2,733	13.4
Engineering	2,825	2,426	85.9
Engineering technologies	35,521	31,094	87.5
English language and literature/letters	2,019	647	32.0
Family and consumer sciences	8,532	358	4.2
Foreign languages and literatures	1,876	377	20.1
Health professions and related sciences	201,831	30,073	14.9
Homeland security, law enforcement, and firefighting	44,923	23,931	53.3
Legal professions and studies	11,620	1,835	15.8
Liberal arts and sciences, general studies, and humanities	306,670	118,556	38.7
Library science	160	21	13.1
Mathematics and statistics	1,644	1,024	62.3
Mechanic and repair technologies	19,969	18,998	95.1
Military technologies	856	693	81.0
Multi-/interdisciplinary studies	23,729	8,905	37.5
Parks, recreation, leisure, and fitness	2,366	1,432	60.5
Philosophy and religion	283	177	62.5
Physical sciences	5,078	2,958	58.3
Precision production trades	3,254	3,024	92.9
Psychology	3,866	896	23.2
Public administration and social services	7,472	1,025	13.7
Social sciences and history	12,767	4,511	35.3
Theology and religious vocations	758	395	52.1
Transportation and material moving	1,697	1,418	83.6
Visual and performing arts	21,379	8,706	40.7

Source: National Center for Education Statistics, Digest of Education Statistics 2012, Internet site http://nces.ed.gov/programs/digest/2012menu_tables.asp; calculations by New Strategist

Table 2.23 Associate's Degrees Earned by Men by Field of Study, 2010–11

(total number of associate's degrees conferred and number and percent earned by men, by field of study, 2010–11)

	total	degrees earned by men number	degrees earned by men percent of total
Total associate's degrees	**942,327**	**581,018**	**61.7%**
Agriculture and natural resources	6,425	2,336	36.4
Architecture and related programs	569	259	45.5
Area, ethnic, and cultural studies	209	149	71.3
Biological and biomedical sciences	3,245	2,129	65.6
Business	139,986	88,815	63.4
Communication, journalism, and related programs	3,051	1,640	53.8
Communications technologies	4,209	1,435	34.1
Computer and information sciences	37,677	8,617	22.9
Construction trades	5,402	297	5.5
Education	20,459	17,726	86.6
Engineering	2,825	399	14.1
Engineering technologies	35,521	4,427	12.5
English language and literature/letters	2,019	1,372	68.0
Family and consumer sciences	8,532	8,174	95.8
Foreign languages and literatures	1,876	1,499	79.9
Health professions and related sciences	201,831	171,758	85.1
Homeland security, law enforcement, and firefighting	44,923	20,992	46.7
Legal professions and studies	11,620	9,785	84.2
Liberal arts and sciences, general studies, and humanities	306,670	188,114	61.3
Library science	160	139	86.9
Mathematics and statistics	1,644	620	37.7
Mechanic and repair technologies	19,969	971	4.9
Military technologies	856	163	19.0
Multi-/interdisciplinary studies	23,729	14,824	62.5
Parks, recreation, leisure, and fitness	2,366	934	39.5
Philosophy and religion	283	106	37.5
Physical sciences	5,078	2,120	41.7
Precision production trades	3,254	230	7.1
Psychology	3,866	2,970	76.8
Public administration and social services	7,472	6,447	86.3
Social sciences and history	12,767	8,256	64.7
Theology and religious vocations	758	363	47.9
Transportation and material moving	1,697	279	16.4
Visual and performing arts	21,379	12,673	59.3

Source: National Center for Education Statistics, Digest of Education Statistics 2012, Internet site http://nces.ed.gov/programs/digest/2012menu_tables.asp; calculations by New Strategist

Table 2.24 Bachelor's Degrees Earned by Women by Field of Study, 2010–11

(total number of bachelor's degrees conferred and number and percent earned by women, by field of study, 2010–11)

		degrees earned by women	
	total	number	percent of total
Total bachelor's degrees	**1,715,913**	**981,780**	**57.2%**
Agriculture and natural resources	28,623	13,948	48.7
Architecture and related programs	9,832	4,136	42.1
Area, ethnic, and cultural studies	9,100	6,299	69.2
Biological and biomedical sciences	90,003	53,111	59.0
Business	365,093	178,012	48.8
Communication, journalism, and related programs	83,274	53,759	64.6
Communications technologies	4,858	1,350	27.8
Computer and information sciences	43,072	7,594	17.6
Construction trades	328	25	7.6
Education	103,992	82,797	79.6
Engineering	76,376	14,257	18.7
Engineering technologies	16,187	1,718	10.6
English language and literature/letters	52,744	35,828	67.9
Family and consumer sciences	22,444	19,682	87.7
Foreign languages, literatures, and linguistics	21,706	14,986	69.0
Health professions and related sciences	143,430	121,894	85.0
Homeland security, law enforcement, and firefighting	47,602	23,241	48.8
Legal professions and studies	4,429	3,112	70.3
Liberal arts and sciences, general studies, and humanities	46,727	30,239	64.7
Library science	96	83	86.5
Mathematics and statistics	17,182	7,399	43.1
Mechanic and repair technologies	226	17	7.5
Military technologies	64	14	21.9
Multi-/interdisciplinary studies	42,228	28,626	67.8
Parks, recreation, leisure, and fitness	35,924	16,988	47.3
Philosophy and religion	12,836	4,687	36.5
Physical sciences	24,712	9,930	40.2
Precision production trades	43	21	48.8
Psychology	100,893	77,664	77.0
Public administration and social services	26,774	21,866	81.7
Social sciences and history	177,144	87,330	49.3
Theology and religious vocations	9,074	2,956	32.6
Transportation and material moving	4,941	596	12.1
Visual and performing arts	93,956	57,615	61.3

Source: National Center for Education Statistics, Digest of Education Statistics 2012, Internet site http://nces.ed.gov/programs/digest/2012menu_tables.asp; calculations by New Strategist

Table 2.25 Bachelor's Degrees Earned by Men by Field of Study, 2010–11

(total number of bachelor's degrees conferred and number and percent earned by men, by field of study, 2010–11)

		degrees earned by men	
	total	number	percent of total
Total bachelor's degrees	**1,715,913**	**734,133**	**42.8%**
Agriculture and natural resources	28,623	14,675	51.3
Architecture and related programs	9,832	5,696	57.9
Area, ethnic, and cultural studies	9,100	2,801	30.8
Biological and biomedical sciences	90,003	36,892	41.0
Business	365,093	187,081	51.2
Communication, journalism, and related programs	83,274	29,515	35.4
Communications technologies	4,858	3,508	72.2
Computer and information sciences	43,072	35,478	82.4
Construction trades	328	303	92.4
Education	103,992	21,195	20.4
Engineering	76,376	62,119	81.3
Engineering technologies	16,187	14,469	89.4
English language and literature/letters	52,744	16,916	32.1
Family and consumer sciences	22,444	2,762	12.3
Foreign languages, literatures, and linguistics	21,706	6,720	31.0
Health professions and related sciences	143,430	21,536	15.0
Homeland security, law enforcement, and firefighting	47,602	24,361	51.2
Legal professions and studies	4,429	1,317	29.7
Liberal arts and sciences, general studies, and humanities	46,727	16,488	35.3
Library science	96	13	13.5
Mathematics and statistics	17,182	9,783	56.9
Mechanic and repair technologies	226	209	92.5
Military technologies	64	50	78.1
Multi-/interdisciplinary studies	42,228	13,602	32.2
Parks, recreation, leisure, and fitness	35,924	18,936	52.7
Philosophy and religion	12,836	8,149	63.5
Physical sciences	24,712	14,782	59.8
Precision production trades	43	22	51.2
Psychology	100,893	23,229	23.0
Public administration and social services	26,774	4,908	18.3
Social sciences and history	177,144	89,814	50.7
Theology and religious vocations	9,074	6,118	67.4
Transportation and material moving	4,941	4,345	87.9
Visual and performing arts	93,956	36,341	38.7

Source: National Center for Education Statistics, Digest of Education Statistics 2012, Internet site http://nces.ed.gov/programs/digest/2012menu_tables.asp; calculations by New Strategist

Table 2.26 Master's Degrees Earned by Women by Field of Study, 2010–11

(total number of master's degrees conferred and number and percent earned by women, by field of study, 2010–11)

		degrees earned by women	
	total	number	percent of total
Total master's degrees	**730,635**	**439,084**	**60.1%**
Agriculture and natural resources	5,773	3,023	52.4
Architecture and related programs	7,788	3,523	45.2
Area, ethnic, and cultural studies	1,914	1,191	62.2
Biological and biomedical sciences	11,327	6,456	57.0
Business	187,213	85,763	45.8
Communication, journalism, and related programs	8,303	5,783	69.6
Communications technologies	502	202	40.2
Computer and information sciences	19,446	5,490	28.2
Education	185,009	142,987	77.3
Engineering	38,719	8,629	22.3
Engineering technologies	4,515	1,187	26.3
English language and literature/letters	9,476	6,339	66.9
Family and consumer sciences	2,918	2,523	86.5
Foreign languages, literatures, and linguistics	3,727	2,471	66.3
Health professions and related sciences	75,579	61,538	81.4
Homeland security, law enforcement, and firefighting	7,433	4,017	54.0
Legal professions and studies	6,300	3,246	51.5
Liberal arts and sciences, general studies, and humanities	3,971	2,352	59.2
Library science	7,727	6,244	80.8
Mathematics and statistics	5,843	2,390	40.9
Multi-/interdisciplinary studies	6,748	4,187	62.0
Parks, recreation, leisure, and fitness	6,553	2,968	45.3
Philosophy and religion	1,833	667	36.4
Physical sciences	6,386	2,479	38.8
Precision production trades	5	2	40.0
Psychology	25,051	19,933	79.6
Public administration and social services	38,634	28,841	74.7
Social sciences and history	21,084	10,506	49.8
Theology and religious vocations	13,191	4,523	34.3
Transportation and material moving	1,390	229	16.5
Visual and performing arts	16,277	9,395	57.7

Source: National Center for Education Statistics, Digest of Education Statistics 2012, Internet site http://nces.ed.gov/programs/digest/2012menu_tables.asp; calculations by New Strategist

Table 2.27 Master's Degrees Earned by Men by Field of Study, 2010–11

(total number of master's degrees conferred and number and percent earned by men, by field of study, 2010–11)

	total	degrees earned by men	
		number	percent of total
Total master's degrees	**730,635**	**291,551**	**39.9%**
Agriculture and natural resources	5,773	2,750	47.6
Architecture and related programs	7,788	4,265	54.8
Area, ethnic, and cultural studies	1,914	723	37.8
Biological and biomedical sciences	11,327	4,871	43.0
Business	187,213	101,450	54.2
Communication, journalism, and related programs	8,303	2,520	30.4
Communications technologies	502	300	59.8
Computer and information sciences	19,446	13,956	71.8
Education	185,009	42,022	22.7
Engineering	38,719	30,090	77.7
Engineering technologies	4,515	3,328	73.7
English language and literature/letters	9,476	3,137	33.1
Family and consumer sciences	2,918	395	13.5
Foreign languages, literatures, and linguistics	3,727	1,256	33.7
Health professions and related sciences	75,579	14,041	18.6
Homeland security, law enforcement, and firefighting	7,433	3,416	46.0
Legal professions and studies	6,300	3,054	48.5
Liberal arts and sciences, general studies, and humanities	3,971	1,619	40.8
Library science	7,727	1,483	19.2
Mathematics and statistics	5,843	3,453	59.1
Multi-/interdisciplinary studies	6,748	2,561	38.0
Parks, recreation, leisure, and fitness	6,553	3,585	54.7
Philosophy and religion	1,833	1,166	63.6
Physical sciences	6,386	3,907	61.2
Precision production trades	5	3	60.0
Psychology	25,051	5,118	20.4
Public administration and social services	38,634	9,793	25.3
Social sciences and history	21,084	10,578	50.2
Theology and religious vocations	13,191	8,668	65.7
Transportation and material moving	1,390	1,161	83.5
Visual and performing arts	16,277	6,882	42.3

Source: National Center for Education Statistics, Digest of Education Statistics 2012, Internet site http://nces.ed.gov/programs/digest/2012menu_tables.asp; calculations by New Strategist

Table 2.28 Doctoral and First-Professional Degrees Earned by Women by Field of Study, 2010–11

(total number of doctoral and first-professional degrees conferred and number and percent earned by women, by field of study, 2010–11)

	total	degrees earned by women	
		number	percent of total
Total doctoral and first-professional degrees	**163,765**	**84,111**	**51.4%**
Agriculture and natural resources	1,246	571	45.8
Architecture and related programs	205	95	46.3
Area, ethnic, and cultural studies	278	162	58.3
Biological and biomedical sciences	7,693	4,045	52.6
Business	2,286	929	40.6
Communication, journalism, and related programs	577	370	64.1
Communications technologies	1	1	100.0
Computer and information sciences	1,588	321	20.2
Education	9,623	6,559	68.2
Engineering	8,369	1,859	22.2
Engineering technologies	56	18	32.1
English language and literature/letters	1,344	815	60.6
Family and consumer sciences	320	261	81.6
Foreign languages, literatures, and linguistics	1,158	681	58.8
Health professions and related sciences	60,153	34,792	57.8
Homeland security, law enforcement, and firefighting	131	69	52.7
Legal professions and studies	44,877	21,157	47.1
Liberal arts and sciences, general studies, and humanities	95	55	57.9
Library science	50	32	64.0
Mathematics and statistics	1,586	454	28.6
Multi-/interdisciplinary studies	660	384	58.2
Parks, recreation, leisure, and fitness	257	117	45.5
Philosophy and religion	805	275	34.2
Physical sciences	5,295	1,687	31.9
Psychology	5,851	4,370	74.7
Public administration and social services	851	524	61.6
Social sciences and history	4,390	2,059	46.9
Theology and religious vocations	2,374	573	24.1
Visual and performing arts	1,646	876	53.2

Source: National Center for Education Statistics, Digest of Education Statistics 2012, Internet site http://nces.ed.gov/programs/digest/2012menu_tables.asp; calculations by New Strategist

Table 2.29 Doctoral and First-Professional Degrees Earned by Men by Field of Study, 2010–11

(total number of doctoral and first-professional degrees conferred and number and percent earned by men, by field of study, 2010–11)

		degrees earned by men	
	total	number	percent of total
Total doctoral and first-professional degrees	**163,765**	**79,654**	**48.6%**
Agriculture and natural resources	1,246	675	54.2
Architecture and related programs	205	110	53.7
Area, ethnic, and cultural studies	278	116	41.7
Biological and biomedical sciences	7,693	3,648	47.4
Business	2,286	1,357	59.4
Communication, journalism, and related programs	577	207	35.9
Communications technologies	1	0	0.0
Computer and information sciences	1,588	1,267	79.8
Education	9,623	3,064	31.8
Engineering	8,369	6,510	77.8
Engineering technologies	56	38	67.9
English language and literature/letters	1,344	529	39.4
Family and consumer sciences	320	59	18.4
Foreign languages, literatures, and linguistics	1,158	477	41.2
Health professions and related sciences	60,153	25,361	42.2
Homeland security, law enforcement, and firefighting	131	62	47.3
Legal professions and studies	44,877	23,720	52.9
Liberal arts and sciences, general studies, and humanities	95	40	42.1
Library science	50	18	36.0
Mathematics and statistics	1,586	1,132	71.4
Multi-/interdisciplinary studies	660	276	41.8
Parks, recreation, leisure, and fitness	257	140	54.5
Philosophy and religion	805	530	65.8
Physical sciences	5,295	3,608	68.1
Psychology	5,851	1,481	25.3
Public administration and social services	851	327	38.4
Social sciences and history	4,390	2,331	53.1
Theology and religious vocations	2,374	1,801	75.9
Visual and performing arts	1,646	770	46.8

Source: National Center for Education Statistics, Digest of Education Statistics 2012, Internet site http://nces.ed.gov/programs/ digest/2012menu_tables.asp; calculations by New Strategist

3

Health

Many health problems among Americans stem from being overweight.

Seventy-three percent of men and nearly 65 percent of women are overweight.

The Great Recession has created a new baby bust.

The fertility rate among women under age 25 has plunged since 2007.

Most babies are born to women in their twenties.

Only 8 percent of babies are born to women younger than 20, and just 15 percent are born to women aged 35 or older.

Males are the majority of the nation's uninsured.

More than 25 million males and 23 million females do not have health insurance.

Women are the 59 percent majority of adults with arthritis.

Women dominate many health conditions because of their older average age.

Most females have taken a prescription drug in the past month.

Among men and women aged 65 or older, most have taken at least three prescription drugs in the past month.

Men are less likely than women to go to a health care provider.

Among adults who have not seen a health care provider in the past year, 65 percent are men.

Heart disease is the biggest killer of males and females.

Male life expectancy at birth is about five years less than female life expectancy.

Most Men and Women Are Overweight

Over the past few decades, the average woman has gained 21 pounds.

The average man weighed 22 pounds more in 2007–10 than in 1976–80. The average woman gained 21 pounds during those years. These weight gains mean that most men and women are overweight. In 2007–10, fully 73.2 percent of men and 64.5 percent of women were overweight, according to height and weight measurements of a representative sample of the population. More than one-third of men and women are obese.

One reason why so many are overweight is that about half do not get enough exercise. The 51 percent majority of women and a substantial 43 percent of men met neither the muscle-strengthening nor the aerobic-activity guidelines recommended by the federal government. Only 24 percent of men and 16 percent of women met both guidelines.

■ If Americans took the advice of health professionals by eating less and exercising more, fewer would be overweight.

Men are more likely than women to be overweight

(percent of people aged 20 or older who are overweight, by sex, 2007–10)

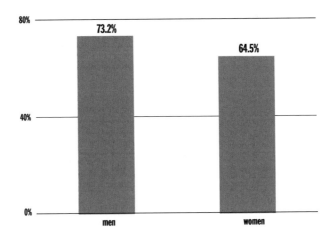

Table 3.1 Average Measured Weight of Women by Age, 1976–80 and 2007–10

(average weight in pounds of women aged 20 or older, by age, 1976–80 and 2007–10; change in pounds, 1976–80 to 2007–10)

	2007–10	1976–80*	change in pounds
Women aged 20 or older	**166.2 lbs**	**145.4 lbs.**	**20.8 lbs.**
Aged 20 to 29	161.9	135.7	26.2
Aged 30 to 39	169.1	145.5	23.6
Aged 40 to 49	168.0	148.8	19.2
Aged 50 to 59	170.0	150.4	19.6
Aged 60 to 69	170.5	146.9**	–
Aged 70 to 79	164.9	–	–
Aged 80 or older	143.1	–	–

* Women aged 20 to 74.
** Women aged 60 to 74.
Note: Data are based on the measured weight of a sample of the civilian noninstitutionalized population. "–" means data are not available.
Source: National Center for Health Statistics, National Health and Nutrition Examination Surveys, Internet site http://www.cdc.gov/nchs/nhanes.htm; calculations by New Strategist

Table 3.2 Average Measured Weight of Men by Age, 1976–80 and 2007–10

(average weight in pounds of men aged 20 or older, by age, 1976–80 and 2007–10; change in pounds, 1976–80 to 2007–10)

	2007–10	1976–80*	change in pounds
Men aged 20 or older	**195.5 lbs.**	**173.8 lbs.**	**21.7 lbs.**
Aged 20 to 29	183.9	167.9	16.0
Aged 30 to 39	199.5	175.5	24.0
Aged 40 to 49	200.6	179.7	20.9
Aged 50 to 59	201.3	176.0	25.3
Aged 60 to 69	199.4	167.5**	–
Aged 70 to 79	190.6	–	–
Aged 80 or older	174.9	–	–

* Men aged 20 to 74.
** Men aged 60 to 74.
Note: Data are based on the measured weight of a sample of the civilian noninstitutionalized population. "–" means data are not available.
Source: National Center for Health Statistics, National Health and Nutrition Examination Surveys, Internet site http://www.cdc.gov/nchs/nhanes.htm; calculations by New Strategist

Table 3.3 Adults Measured as Overweight by Sex and Age, 1976–80 and 2007–10

(percent of people aged 20 or older who are overweight, by sex and age, 1976–80 and 2007–10; percentage point change, 1976–80 to 2007–10)

OVERWEIGHT	2007–10	1976–80	percentage point change
Total men	**73.2%**	**52.9%**	**20.3**
Aged 20 to 34	61.1	41.2	19.9
Aged 35 to 44	80.2	57.2	23.0
Aged 45 to 54	76.8	60.2	16.6
Aged 55 to 64	79.8	60.2	19.6
Aged 65 to 74	77.5	54.2	23.3
Aged 75 or older	73.2	–	–
Total women	**64.5**	**42.0**	**22.5**
Aged 20 to 34	55.4	27.9	27.5
Aged 35 to 44	63.9	40.7	23.2
Aged 45 to 54	66.2	48.7	17.5
Aged 55 to 64	72.2	53.7	18.5
Aged 65 to 74	74.2	59.5	14.7
Aged 75 or older	28.7	–	–

Note: "Overweight" is defined as a body mass index of 25 or higher. Body mass index is calculated by dividing weight in kilograms by height in meters squared. Data are based on measured height and weight of a representative sample of the civilian noninstitutionalized population. "–" means data are not available.
Source: National Center for Health Statistics, Health United States 2012, Internet site http://www.cdc.gov/nchs/hus.htm; calculations by New Strategist

Table 3.4 Adults Measured as Obese by Sex and Age, 1976–80 and 2007–10

(percent of people aged 20 or older who are obese, by sex and age, 1976–80 and 2007–10; percentage point change, 1976–80 to 2007–10)

OBESE	2007–10	1976–80	percentage point change
Total men	**33.9%**	**12.8%**	**21.1**
Aged 20 to 34	27.1	8.9	18.2
Aged 35 to 44	37.2	13.5	23.7
Aged 45 to 54	36.6	16.7	19.9
Aged 55 to 64	37.3	14.1	23.2
Aged 65 to 74	41.5	13.2	28.3
Aged 75 or older	26.6	–	–
Total women	**35.9**	**17.1**	**18.8**
Aged 20 to 34	30.4	11.0	19.4
Aged 35 to 44	37.1	17.8	19.3
Aged 45 to 54	36.9	19.6	17.3
Aged 55 to 64	43.4	22.9	20.5
Aged 65 to 74	40.3	21.5	18.8
Aged 75 or older	63.2	–	–

Note: "Obese" is defined as a body mass index of 30 or higher. Body mass index is calculated by dividing weight in kilograms by height in meters squared. Data are based on measured height and weight of a representative sample of the civilian noninstitutionalized population. "–" means data are not available.
Source: National Center for Health Statistics, Health United States 2012, Internet site http://www.cdc.gov/nchs/hus.htm; calculations by New Strategist

Table 3.5 Physical Activity Status of People Aged 18 or Older by Sex, 2011

(number and percent distribution of people aged 18 or older by muscle-strengthening and aerobic-activity federal guideline status, by sex, 2011; numbers in thousands)

			met at least one guideline			
	total	met neither guideline	total	met muscle-strengthening guideline only	met aerobic guideline only	met both guidelines
NUMBER						
Total people	231,376	109,188	117,611	7,928	63,064	46,619
Men	112,093	48,063	61,614	4,201	30,443	26,970
Women	119,283	61,124	55,996	3,727	32,620	19,649
PERCENT DISTRIBUTION BY GUIDELINE STATUS						
Total people	100.0%	47.2%	50.8%	3.4%	27.3%	20.1%
Men	100.0	42.9	55.0	3.7	27.2	24.1
Women	100.0	51.2	46.9	3.1	27.3	16.5
PERCENT DISTRIBUTION BY SEX						
Total people	100.0	100.0	100.0	100.0	100.0	100.0
Men	48.4	44.0	52.4	53.0	48.3	57.9
Women	51.6	56.0	47.6	47.0	51.7	42.1

Note: Federal aerobic guideline recommends that adults perform at least 150 minutes per week of moderate-intensity or 75 minutes per week of vigorous-intensity aerobic physical activity or equivalent combination. Federal muscle-strengthening guidelines recommend muscle-strengthening activities of moderate or high intensity involving all major muscle groups on two or more days per week.
Source: National Center for Health Statistics, Summary Health Statistics for U.S. Adults: National Health Interview Survey, 2011, Vital and Health Statistics, Series 10, No. 256, 2012, Internet site http://www.cdc.gov/nchs/nhis.htm; calculations by New Strategist

Among Men and Women, Former Smokers Outnumber Current Smokers

Drinking is more popular than smoking among both men and women.

Public health campaigns against cigarette smoking have had an impact. In 2011, only 22 percent of men and 17 percent of women aged 18 or older smoked cigarettes. Former smokers outnumber current smokers: 25 percent of men and 19 percent of women once smoked but gave it up. Both current and former smokers are greatly outnumbered by the 53 percent of men and 64 percent of women who have never smoked. Those most likely to smoke today are the less educated, while few college graduates smoke.

Seventy percent of men and 59 percent of women currently drink alcohol, which is defined as having had at least 12 drinks in their lifetime and at least one drink in the past year. About 15 percent of men and women are former drinkers (no drinks in the past year). Among women, a substantial 25 percent are lifetime abstainers (fewer than 12 drinks in their lifetime and none in the past year).

■ Cigarette smoking should continue to decline as prices rise and smoking is increasingly restricted.

College graduates are much less likely to smoke cigarettes

(percent of people aged 25 or older who currently smoke cigarettes by sex and educational attainment, 2011)

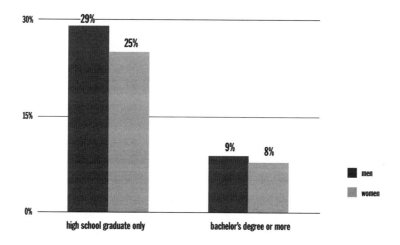

Table 3.6 Cigarette Smoking Status by Sex, 2011

(number and percent distribution of people aged 18 or older by cigarette smoking status, by sex, 2011; numbers in thousands)

	men	women
Total people	**112,093**	**119,283**
Current smokers	24,138	19,683
Every-day smokers	18,320	15,769
Some-day smokers	5,817	3,914
Former smokers	27,860	22,556
Nonsmokers	59,761	76,767
PERCENT DISTRIBUTION		
Total people	**100.0%**	**100.0%**
Current smokers	21.5	16.5
Every-day smokers	16.3	13.2
Some-day smokers	5.2	3.3
Former smokers	24.9	18.9
Nonsmokers	53.3	64.4

Note: "Current smokers" have smoked at least 100 cigarettes in lifetime and still smoke; "every-day smokers" are current smokers who smoke every day; "some-day smokers" are current smokers who smoke on some days; "former smokers" have smoked at least 100 cigarettes in lifetime but currently do not smoke; "nonsmokers" have smoked less than 100 cigarettes in lifetime. Numbers may not add to total because "unknown" is not shown.
Source: National Center for Health Statistics, Summary Health Statistics for U.S. Adults: National Health Interview Survey, 2011, Vital and Health Statistics, Series 10, No. 256, 2012, Internet site http://www.cdc.gov/nchs/nhis.htm; calculations by New Strategist

Table 3.7 Current Cigarette Smoking among Women by Age, Race, and Educational Attainment, 2010

(percent of women who currently smoke cigarettes by age, race, and educational attainment, 2010)

AGE	total	black	white
Total women aged 18 or older	**17.3%**	**17.0%**	**17.9%**
Aged 18 to 24	17.4	14.2	18.4
Aged 25 to 44	20.6	19.3	22.0
Aged 45 to 54	19.0	17.2	20.5
Aged 55 to 64	21.3	20.4	22.4
Aged 65 or older	16.5	18.9	15.9
EDUCATIONAL ATTAINMENT			
Total women aged 25 or older	**17.5%**	**17.0%**	**18.3%**
Not a high school graduate	23.7	25.8	24.0
High school graduate or GED	24.9	22.9	25.8
Some college, no degree	19.6	15.0	21.0
Bachelor's degree or more	7.9	6.6	8.7

Note: Current smokers are those who have smoked at least 100 cigarettes in lifetime and currently smoke some days or every day. Blacks and whites include Hispanics.
Source: National Center for Health Statistics, Health United States 2011, Internet site http://www.cdc.gov/nchs/hus.htm; calculations by New Strategist

Table 3.8 Current Cigarette Smoking among Men by Age, Race, and Educational Attainment, 2010

(percent of men who currently smoke cigarettes by age, race, and educational attainment, 2010)

AGE	total	black	white
Total men aged 18 or older	**21.5%**	**24.3%**	**21.4%**
Aged 18 to 24	22.8	18.8	23.8
Aged 25 to 44	26.1	25.7	26.6
Aged 45 to 54	22.5	22.6	23.1
Aged 55 to 64	25.2	33.2	24.5
Aged 65 or older	20.7	29.6	20.1
EDUCATIONAL ATTAINMENT			
Total men aged 25 or older	**21.0%**	**23.9%**	**21.0%**
Not a high school graduate	29.7	34.4	29.4
High school graduate or GED	29.3	28.8	29.6
Some college, no degree	23.2	24.2	23.4
Bachelor's degree or more	8.7	8.1	8.8

Note: Current smokers are those who have smoked at least 100 cigarettes in lifetime and currently smoke some days or every day. Blacks and whites include Hispanics.
Source: National Center for Health Statistics, Health United States 2011, Internet site http://www.cdc.gov/nchs/hus.htm; calculations by New Strategist

Table 3.9 Alcohol Drinking Status by Sex, 2011

(number and percent distribution of people aged 18 or older by alcohol drinking status, by sex, 2011; numbers in thousands)

	men	women
Total people	**112,093**	**119,283**
Current drinker	78,269	70,702
Current regular drinker	66,847	50,965
Current infrequent drinker	11,422	19,737
Former drinker	16,345	17,318
Lifetime abstainer	15,653	29,715
PERCENT DISTRIBUTION		
Total people	**100.0%**	**100.0%**
Current drinker	69.8	59.3
Current regular drinker	59.6	42.7
Current infrequent drinker	10.2	16.5
Former drinker	14.6	14.5
Lifetime abstainer	14.0	24.9

Note: "Current drinker" had more than 12 drinks in lifetime and drinks in past year; "regular drinker" had more than 12 drinks in one year; "infrequent drinker" had fewer than 12 drinks in one year; "former drinker" had more than 12 drinks in lifetime, no drinks in past year; "lifetime abstainer" had fewer than 12 drinks in lifetime, no drinks in past year. Numbers may not add to total because "unknown" is not shown.
Source: National Center for Health Statistics, Summary Health Statistics for U.S. Adults: National Health Interview Survey, 2011, Vital and Health Statistics, Series 10, No. 256, 2012, Internet site http://www.cdc.gov/nchs/nhis.htm; calculations by New Strategist

Most Women of Childbearing Age Use Contraceptives

The pill and female sterilization are the most popular contraceptives.

Among the nation's women of childbearing age—15 to 44—the 62 percent majority uses contraceptives. The pill is most popular, with 17.1 percent of women taking it, according to the federal government's National Survey of Family Growth. Female sterilization is the contraceptive choice of 16.5 percent of women, while condoms rank third at 10.2 percent. Use of the pill peaks at 27 percent among women aged 20 to 24, while women aged 30 or older are more likely to have been sterilized than to be on the pill.

More than one-third of women aged 15 to 44 are not using contraceptives. Most of them are not using birth control because they are not sexually active. Nine percent of women in the age group are pregnant or trying to get pregnant.

■ Only 8 percent of women aged 15 to 44 are sexually active, not currently pregnant or trying to become pregnant, and not using birth control.

The pill is popular among young women

(percent of women aged 15 to 44 who are using the contraceptive pill, 2006–10)

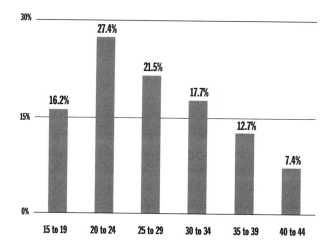

Table 3.10 Contraceptive Use by Age, 2006–10

(total number of women aged 15 to 44 and percent distribution by contraceptive status and age, 2006–10; numbers in thousands)

	total	15 to 19	20 to 24	25 to 29	30 to 34	35 to 39	40 to 44
TOTAL WOMEN AGED 15 TO 44 (NUMBER)	61,755	10,478	10,365	10,535	9,188	10,538	10,652
TOTAL WOMEN AGED 15 TO 44 (PERCENT)	100.0%	100.0%	100.0%	100.0%	100.0%	100.0%	100.0%
Using contraception	62.2	30.5	58.3	65.3	69.7	74.6	75.3
Female sterilization	16.5	–	1.5	10.7	20.9	27.9	38.1
Male sterilization	6.2	–	0.5	2.7	6.6	12.4	15.1
Pill	17.1	16.2	27.4	21.5	17.7	12.7	7.4
Other hormonal methods	4.5	4.9	7.1	7.4	3.9	2.0	1.4
Implant, Lunelle, or Patch	0.9	0.7	1.1	1.5	0.9	0.5	–
Three-month injectable (Depo-Provera)	2.3	3.5	3.3	3.4	1.7	1.0	0.6
Contraceptive ring	1.3	0.7	2.7	2.4	1.4	0.5	0.4
Intrauterine device (IUD)	3.5	0.8	3.3	4.7	4.9	4.8	2.4
Condom	10.2	6.1	14.9	13.6	10.8	9.0	6.8
Periodic abstinence— calendar rhythm method	0.6	–	0.2	0.5	0.8	1.0	1.1
Periodic abstinence— natural family planning	0.1	0.0	0.0	0.0	0.4	–	–
Withdrawal	3.2	2.1	3.3	4.1	3.2	4.1	2.6
Other methods	0.3	0.2	–	0.3	0.5	0.6	0.4
Not using contraception	37.8	69.5	41.7	34.7	30.3	25.4	24.7
Surgically sterile-female (noncontraceptive)	0.4	–	–	0.2	–	0.4	1.5
Nonsurgically sterile, female or male	1.7	0.5	1.4	1.4	1.8	2.0	3.1
Pregnant or postpartum	5.0	3.2	8.1	8.4	7.2	2.3	1.4
Seeking pregnancy	4.0	0.6	4.0	6.3	6.0	4.8	2.4
Never had intercourse	11.8	51.4	11.6	3.1	1.9	1.1	0.6
No intercourse in past three months	7.3	7.1	7.9	7.0	6.6	6.5	8.6
Had intercourse during past three months	7.7	6.7	8.7	8.4	6.7	8.4	7.1

Note: "Other methods" includes diaphragm, emergency contraceptive, Today sponge, cervical cap, female condom, and other methods. "–" means sample is too small to make a reliable estimate.
Source: National Center for Health Statistics, Current Contraceptive Use in the United States, 2006–2010, and Changes in Patterns of Use since 1995, National Health Statistics Reports, No. 60, 2012, Internet site http://www.cdc.gov/nchs/nsfg.htm; calculations by New Strategist

Many Women Have Not Had Children

Postponing pregnancy sometimes results in no pregnancy.

A growing proportion of women are childless. Among women aged 15 to 44, a larger share (47 percent) is childless today than in 2000 (43 percent).

Among women aged 20 to 24, the childless proportion climbed from 64 to 70 percent between 2000 and 2010. Among women aged 25 to 29, the figure increased from 44 to 48 percent during those years. Most of the childless in these age groups will eventually have children. In the 40-to-44 age group, 19 percent of women were childless in 2010, about the same as in 2000. Most of these women will never have children.

■ Some of today's younger women who are postponing childbearing because of the economy will end up childless.

Most women under age 25 are childless

(percent of women who have had no live births, by age, 2010)

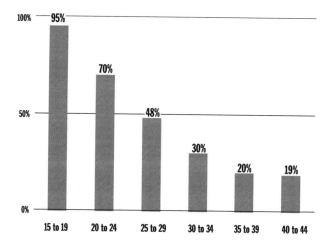

Table 3.11 Childless Women by Age, 2000 and 2010

(percent of women aged 15 to 44 who have not had a live birth, by age, 2000 and 2010; percentage point change, 2000–10)

	2010	2000	percentage point change
Total women	**47.1%**	**42.8%**	**4.3**
Aged 15 to 19	94.6	90.5	4.1
Aged 20 to 24	70.5	63.6	6.9
Aged 25 to 29	47.6	44.2	3.4
Aged 30 to 34	29.7	28.1	1.6
Aged 35 to 39	19.7	20.1	−0.4
Aged 40 to 44	18.8	19.0	−0.2

Source: Bureau of the Census, Fertility of American Women, Historical Time Series Tables, Internet site http://www.census.gov/hhes/fertility/data/cps/historical.html

Fertility Rate Is Falling

The decline has been especially pronounced among women under age 25.

The Great Recession has created a new baby bust. Between 2007 and 2011, the fertility rate (the number of live births per 1,000 women aged 15 to 44) fell from 69.3 to 63.2—a substantial 9 percent decline.

Among women aged 15 to 19, the fertility rate plunged by a stunning 25 percent between 2007 and 2011. Among women aged 20 to 24, the rate fell 19 percent during those years. The decline was smaller among women in their late twenties and thirties. Consequently, in an unprecedented turn of events, women aged 30 to 34 now have a higher fertility rate than women aged 20 to 24.

■ The fertility rate among women aged 40 or older is rising as those who postponed childbearing hurry to catch up.

The fertility rate of women aged 30 to 34 now exceeds that of women aged 20 to 24

(number of births per 1,000 women in selected age groups, 2007 and 2011)

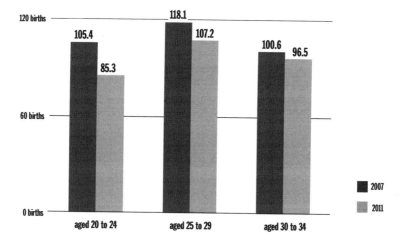

Table 3.12 Fertility Rate by Age, 2000 to 2011

(number of live births per 1,000 women aged 15 to 44 by age, 2000 to 2011; percent change in rate for selected years)

	total *	15 to 19	20 to 24	25 to 29	30 to 34	35 to 39	40 to 44	45 or older
2011	63.2	31.3	85.3	107.2	96.5	47.2	10.3	0.7
2010	64.1	34.2	90.0	108.3	96.5	45.9	10.2	0.7
2009	66.2	37.9	96.2	111.5	97.5	46.1	10.0	0.7
2008	68.1	40.2	101.8	115.0	99.4	46.8	9.9	0.7
2007	69.3	41.5	105.4	118.1	100.6	47.6	9.6	0.6
2006	68.6	41.1	105.5	118.0	98.9	47.5	9.4	0.6
2005	66.7	39.7	101.8	116.5	96.7	46.4	9.1	0.6
2004	66.4	40.5	101.5	116.5	96.2	45.5	9.0	0.5
2003	66.1	41.1	102.3	116.7	95.7	43.9	8.7	0.5
2002	65.0	42.6	103.1	114.7	92.6	41.6	8.3	0.5
2001	65.1	45.0	105.6	113.8	91.8	40.5	8.1	0.5
2000	65.9	47.7	109.7	113.5	91.2	39.7	8.0	0.5

PERCENT CHANGE

	total *	15 to 19	20 to 24	25 to 29	30 to 34	35 to 39	40 to 44	45 or older
2007 to 2011	−8.8%	−24.6%	−19.1%	−9.2%	−4.1%	−0.8%	7.3%	16.7%
2000 to 2011	−4.1	−34.4	−22.2	−5.6	5.8	18.9	28.8	40.0

* Total is the number of births per 1,000 women aged 15 to 44.
Source: National Center for Health Statistics, Births Data, Internet site http://www.cdc.gov/nchs/births.htm; calculations by New Strategist

Most New Mothers Are in Their Twenties

More than half of women giving birth in 2011 were aged 20 to 29.

Births to teenagers and older women receive a lot of media attention, but they are not the norm. Three-quarters of all births in 2011 were to women aged 20 to 34. The 52 percent majority were to women in their twenties. Only 15 percent of births in 2011 were to women aged 35 or older, and just 8 percent were to women under age 20.

Although many women wait until their thirties to begin a family, most 30-to-39-year-olds who gave birth in 2011 already had children. Only 29 percent of babies born to women aged 30 to 34 and 22 percent of those born to women aged 35 to 39 were first births.

■ As young women postpone childbearing, the number of births to women aged 30 to 34 has surpassed the number born to women aged 20 to 24.

Few babies are born to women aged 35 or older

(percent distribution of births by age of mother, 2011)

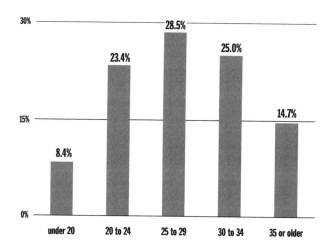

Table 3.13 Births by Age of Mother, 2011

(number and percent distribution of births, by age of mother, 2011)

	number	percent distribution
Total births	**3,953,593**	**100.0%**
Under age 15	3,974	0.1
Aged 15 to 19	329,797	8.3
Aged 20 to 24	925,213	23.4
Aged 25 to 29	1,127,592	28.5
Aged 30 to 34	986,661	25.0
Aged 35 to 39	463,815	11.7
Aged 40 to 44	108,891	2.8
Aged 45 to 54	7,651	0.2
Under age 20	333,771	8.4%
Aged 20 to 29	2,052,805	51.9
Aged 30 to 39	1,450,476	36.7
Aged 40 or older	116,542	2.9

Source: National Center for Health Statistics, Births: Preliminary Data for 2011, National Vital Statistics Report, Vol. 61, No. 5, 2012, Internet site http://www.cdc.gov/nchs/births.htm; calculations by New Strategist

Table 3.14 Births by Age of Mother and Birth Order, 2011

(number and percent distribution of births by age of mother and birth order, 2011)

	total	first child	second child	third child	fourth or later child
Total births	**3,953,593**	**1,577,344**	**1,239,136**	**648,124**	**458,777**
Under age 15	3,974	3,875	64	8	2
Aged 15 to 19	329,797	269,075	50,343	7,234	885
Aged 20 to 24	925,213	463,161	300,390	113,409	41,647
Aged 25 to 29	1,127,592	423,123	369,740	201,235	125,114
Aged 30 to 34	986,661	287,506	337,124	198,407	155,799
Aged 35 to 39	463,815	104,337	149,135	103,940	102,437
Aged 40 to 44	108,891	24,204	30,420	22,592	30,633
Aged 45 to 54	7,651	2,063	1,920	1,298	2,260

PERCENT DISTRIBUTION BY BIRTH ORDER

	total	first child	second child	third child	fourth or later child
Total births	**100.0%**	**39.9%**	**31.3%**	**16.4%**	**11.6%**
Under age 15	100.0	97.5	1.6	0.2	0.0
Aged 15 to 19	100.0	81.6	15.3	2.2	0.3
Aged 20 to 24	100.0	50.1	32.5	12.3	4.5
Aged 25 to 29	100.0	37.5	32.8	17.8	11.1
Aged 30 to 34	100.0	29.1	34.2	20.1	15.8
Aged 35 to 39	100.0	22.5	32.2	22.4	22.1
Aged 40 to 44	100.0	22.2	27.9	20.7	28.1
Aged 45 to 54	100.0	27.0	25.1	17.0	29.5

PERCENT DISTRIBUTION BY AGE

	total	first child	second child	third child	fourth or later child
Total births	**100.0**	**100.0**	**100.0**	**100.0**	**100.0**
Under age 15	0.1	0.2	0.0	0.0	0.0
Aged 15 to 19	8.3	17.1	4.1	1.1	0.2
Aged 20 to 24	23.4	29.4	24.2	17.5	9.1
Aged 25 to 29	28.5	26.8	29.8	31.0	27.3
Aged 30 to 34	25.0	18.2	27.2	30.6	34.0
Aged 35 to 39	11.7	6.6	12.0	16.0	22.3
Aged 40 to 44	2.8	1.5	2.5	3.5	6.7
Aged 45 to 54	0.2	0.1	0.2	0.2	0.5

Note: Numbers do not add to total because "not stated" is not shown.
Source: National Center for Health Statistics, Births: Preliminary Data for 2011, National Vital Statistics Report, Vol. 61, No. 5, 2012, Internet site http://www.cdc.gov/nchs/births.htm; calculations by New Strategist

Minorities Account for a Large Share of Births

The share is greatest among women under age 25.

Of the 3,953,593 babies born in 2011, only 54 percent were born to non-Hispanic whites. Twenty-three percent were born to Hispanics, 15 percent to blacks, and 6 percent to Asians. Among births to women under age 25, however, minorities were the majority.

Asian women have children at an older age than black, Hispanic, or non-Hispanic white women. Among babies born to Asians, the 59 percent majority was born to mothers aged 30 or older in 2011. The proportion was 43 percent among non-Hispanic whites, 34 percent among Hispanics, and 29 percent among blacks.

■ Variation in the timing of childbearing creates lifestyle differences by race and Hispanic origin.

Births to Hispanics outnumber births to blacks

(number of births by race and Hispanic origin of mother, 2011)

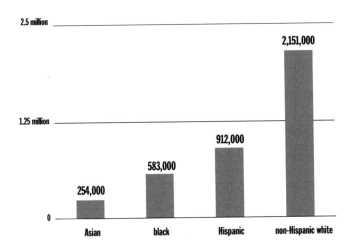

Table 3.15 Births by Age, Race, and Hispanic Origin, 2011

(number and percent distribution of births by age, race, and Hispanic origin of the mother, 2011)

	total	American Indian	Asian	non-Hispanic black	Hispanic	non-Hispanic white
Total births	**3,953,593**	**46,536**	**253,864**	**583,079**	**912,290**	**2,150,926**
Under age 15	3,974	95	66	1,379	1,570	875
Aged 15 to 19	329,797	6,818	5,721	78,637	109,218	129,693
Aged 20 to 24	925,213	15,610	27,796	186,443	242,411	453,006
Aged 25 to 29	1,127,592	12,500	70,404	147,886	246,635	648,883
Aged 30 to 34	986,661	7,401	88,621	104,460	191,047	592,239
Aged 35 to 39	463,815	3,305	49,495	50,305	97,538	261,098
Aged 40 to 44	108,891	774	10,950	12,960	22,635	60,807
Aged 45 to 54	7,651	32	812	1,008	1,236	4,325

PERCENT DISTRIBUTION BY RACE AND HISPANIC ORIGIN

Total births	**100.0%**	**1.2%**	**6.4%**	**14.7%**	**23.1%**	**54.4%**
Under age 15	100.0	2.4	1.7	34.7	39.5	22.0
Aged 15 to 19	100.0	2.1	1.7	23.8	33.1	39.3
Aged 20 to 24	100.0	1.7	3.0	20.2	26.2	49.0
Aged 25 to 29	100.0	1.1	6.2	13.1	21.9	57.5
Aged 30 to 34	100.0	0.8	9.0	10.6	19.4	60.0
Aged 35 to 39	100.0	0.7	10.7	10.8	21.0	56.3
Aged 40 to 44	100.0	0.7	10.1	11.9	20.8	55.8
Aged 45 to 54	100.0	0.4	10.6	13.2	16.2	56.5

PERCENT DISTRIBUTION BY AGE

Total births	**100.0**	**100.0**	**100.0**	**100.0**	**100.0**	**100.0**
Under age 15	0.1	0.2	0.0	0.2	0.2	0.0
Aged 15 to 19	8.3	14.7	2.3	13.5	12.0	6.0
Aged 20 to 24	23.4	33.5	10.9	32.0	26.6	21.1
Aged 25 to 29	28.5	26.9	27.7	25.4	27.0	30.2
Aged 30 to 34	25.0	15.9	34.9	17.9	20.9	27.5
Aged 35 to 39	11.7	7.1	19.5	8.6	10.7	12.1
Aged 40 to 44	2.8	1.7	4.3	2.2	2.5	2.8
Aged 45 to 54	0.2	0.1	0.3	0.2	0.1	0.2

Note: Births by race and Hispanic origin do not add to total because Hispanics may be of any race and "not stated" is not shown.

Source: National Center for Health Statistics, Births: Preliminary Data for 2011, National Vital Statistics Report, Vol. 61, No. 5, 2012, Internet site http://www.cdc.gov/nchs/births.htm; calculations by New Strategist

Unmarried Mothers Are Common

More than 40 percent of births in 2011 were out-of-wedlock.

In 2011, a substantial 41 percent of the nation's births were to unmarried women, up from just 11 percent in 1970. More than 1.6 million single women gave birth in 2011. Most new mothers under age 25 are unmarried. The unmarried proportion bottoms out at 20 percent among women aged 35 to 39.

The percentage of babies born to unmarried women varies by race and Hispanic origin. Among black women, 72 percent of births are out-of-wedlock. The proportion is 53 percent among Hispanics, 29 percent among non-Hispanic whites, and just 17 percent among Asians.

■ The average Hispanic woman will have 2.2 children in her lifetime—the largest number among racial and ethnic groups.

Most black and Hispanic children are born to unmarried mothers

(percent of babies born to unmarried mothers, by race and Hispanic origin of mother, 2011)

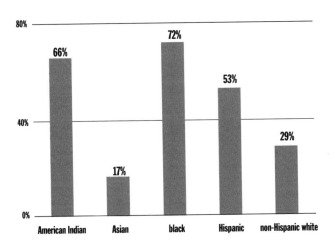

Table 3.16 Births to Unmarried Women by Age, 2011

(total number of births, number and percent to unmarried women, and unmarried share of total, by age, 2011)

		unmarried women		
	total	number	percent distribution	share of total
Total births	**3,953,593**	**1,608,087**	**100.0%**	**40.7%**
Under age 15	3,974	3,940	0.2	99.1
Aged 15 to 19	329,797	291,778	18.1	88.5
Aged 20 to 24	925,213	592,647	36.9	64.1
Aged 25 to 29	1,127,592	387,452	24.1	34.4
Aged 30 to 34	986,661	213,032	13.2	21.6
Aged 35 to 39	463,815	93,167	5.8	20.1
Aged 40 to 54	116,542	26,072	1.6	22.4

Source: National Center for Health Statistics, Births: Preliminary Data for 2011, National Vital Statistics Report, Vol. 61, No. 5, 2012, Internet site http://www.cdc.gov/nchs/births.htm; calculations by New Strategist

Table 3.17 Fertility Characteristics by Race and Hispanic Origin, 2011

(total number of births, birth rate, lifetime births, and percent of births to unmarried women, by race and Hispanic origin, 2011)

	number	birth rate	births in lifetime	percent of births to unmarried women
Total births	**3,953,593**	**12.7**	**1.89**	**40.7%**
American Indian	46,536	10.7	1.38	66.2
Asian	253,864	14.5	1.71	17.2
Black, non-Hispanic	583,079	14.7	1.92	72.3
Hispanic	912,290	17.5	2.20	53.3
White, non-Hispanic	2,150,926	10.8	1.78	29.1

Note: The "birth rate" is the number of births per 1,000 population of the specified race/Hispanic origin. Births by race and Hispanic origin do not add to total because Hispanics may be of any race and "not stated" is not shown.
Source: National Center for Health Statistics, Births: Preliminary Data for 2011, National Vital Statistics Report, Vol. 61, No. 5, 2012, Internet site http://www.cdc.gov/nchs/births.htm; calculations by New Strategist

Many Do Not Have Health Insurance

More than 25 million males are not covered.

Most Americans have health insurance coverage, but many do not. In 2011, nearly 17 percent of males and 15 percent of females were uninsured, according to Census Bureau estimates. Males account for the 53 percent majority of the nation's uninsured. The National Center for Health Statistics finds that fully 40 percent of men aged 25 to 34 have been without insurance for a portion of the past 12 months.

Most males and females have employment-based health insurance coverage, but only 32 percent of males and 25 percent of females have employment-based coverage in their own name. The others depend on the benefits provided by the employer of a parent or spouse. Seventeen percent of females and 15 percent of males are covered by Medicaid—the health insurance program for the poor. Another 16 percent of females and 14 percent of males have Medicare coverage, which is the federal health insurance program for people aged 65 or older.

■ With millions of Americans covered by health insurance benefits provided by the employer of a parent or spouse, many are only a birthday, divorce, or job loss away from no coverage at all.

Nearly 50 million Americans do not have health insurance

(number without health insurance by sex, 2011)

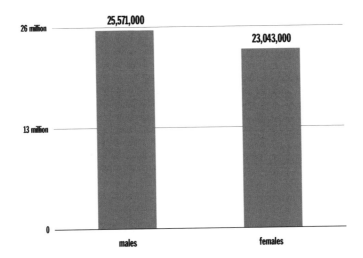

Table 3.18 Health Insurance Coverage of Females by Type, 2011

(number of total people, number and percent distribution of females by health insurance coverage status, and female share of total, 2011; numbers in thousands)

	total	female		
		number	percent distribution	share of total
Total population	**308,827**	**157,653**	**100.0%**	**51.0%**
No health insurance at any time during the year	48,613	23,043	14.6	47.4
With health insurance during the year	260,214	134,610	85.4	51.7
Private insurance	197,323	100,620	63.8	51.0
Employment-based	170,102	85,698	54.4	50.4
Own employment-based	88,237	40,008	25.4	45.3
Direct purchase	30,244	16,157	10.2	53.4
Government insurance	99,497	53,541	34.0	53.8
Medicaid	50,835	27,473	17.4	54.0
Medicare	46,922	25,985	16.5	55.4
Military	13,712	6,369	4.0	46.4

Note: Numbers do not add to total because some people have more than one type of health insurance coverage.
Source: Bureau of the Census, Health Insurance, Internet site http://www.census.gov/hhes/www/cpstables/032012/health/toc .htm; calculations by New Strategist

Table 3.19 Health Insurance Coverage of Males by Type, 2011

(number of total people, number and percent distribution of males by health insurance coverage status, and male share of total, 2011; numbers in thousands)

	total	male		
		number	percent distribution	share of total
Total population	**308,827**	**151,175**	**100.0%**	**49.0%**
No health insurance at any time during the year	48,613	25,571	16.9	52.6
With health insurance during the year	260,214	125,604	83.1	48.3
Private insurance	197,323	96,703	64.0	49.0
Employment-based	170,102	84,404	55.8	49.6
Own employment-based	88,237	48,229	31.9	54.7
Direct purchase	30,244	14,087	9.3	46.6
Government insurance	99,497	45,956	30.4	46.2
Medicaid	50,835	23,362	15.5	46.0
Medicare	46,922	20,936	13.8	44.6
Military	13,712	7,343	4.9	53.6

Note: Numbers do not add to total because some people have more than one type of health insurance coverage.
Source: Bureau of the Census, Health Insurance, Internet site http://www.census.gov/hhes/www/cpstables/032012/health/toc .htm; calculations by New Strategist

Table 3.20 People without Health Insurance by Sex and Age, 2011

(percent of people without health insurance for selected time periods, by sex and age, 2011)

	uninsured at time of interview	uninsured for part of past 12 months	uninsured for entire past 12 months
Total females	**13.5%**	**17.6%**	**9.4%**
Under age 18	6.9	11.0	3.6
Aged 18 to 24	23.4	31.2	14.6
Aged 25 to 34	23.6	30.5	16.7
Aged 35 to 44	19.6	24.6	14.7
Aged 45 to 64	14.6	17.4	11.4
Aged 65 or older	1.0	2.0	0.8
Total males	**16.8**	**20.8**	**13.0**
Under age 18	7.1	10.9	3.8
Aged 18 to 24	28.3	35.1	21.6
Aged 25 to 34	32.8	40.0	26.8
Aged 35 to 44	25.2	29.1	20.2
Aged 45 to 54	16.4	19.2	13.3
Aged 65 or older	1.2	2.0	1.0

Source: National Center for Health Statistics, Health Insurance Coverage: Early Release of Estimates from the National Health Interview Survey, 2011, Internet site http://www.cdc.gov/nchs/nhis.htm

Women Dominate Many Health Problems

Women's longer life leads to more health conditions.

Chronic joint symptoms, back pain, arthritis, high blood pressure, and headaches top the list of female health conditions. From 22 to 31 percent of women aged 18 or older reported experiencing these conditions in 2011, according to the National Center for Health Statistics. Except for headaches, the same conditions top men's most common problems.

Women account for large majorities of those experiencing a number of conditions such as arthritis (59 percent) and stroke (57 percent). Women also account for more than half of those with hypertension or cancer. Women's dominance of certain conditions occurs because many illnesses are more common among older people, and women live longer than men.

Women account for the 62 percent majority of people with difficulties in physical functioning. Nineteen percent of women have such difficulties compared with 13 percent of men. Nine percent of women would find it difficult or impossible to walk a quarter of a mile versus 6 percent of men.

Women are in the minority among people who have been diagnosed with AIDS. In 2009, women accounted for only 20 percent of Americans ever diagnosed with the disease.

■ Many Americans have difficulties in physical functioning because of weight problems.

Women are the majority of the 37 million Americans with physical difficulties

(number of people aged 18 or older with difficulties in physical functioning, by sex, 2011)

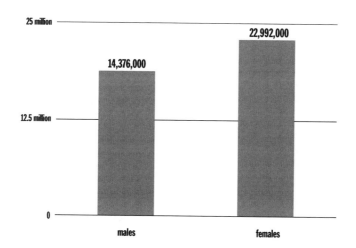

Table 3.21 Health Conditions among Women, 2011

(total number of people aged 18 or older with selected health conditions, number and percent of women with condition, and women's share of total, by type of condition, 2011; numbers in thousands)

	total	women number	percent with condition	share of total
TOTAL PEOPLE	**231,376**	**119,283**	**100.0%**	**51.6%**
Selected circulatory diseases				
Heart disease, all types	26,485	12718	10.7	48.0
Coronary	15,300	6097	5.1	39.8
Hypertension	58,959	30,277	25.4	51.4
Stroke	6,171	3,517	2.9	57.0
Selected respiratory conditions				
Emphysema	4,680	2,552	2.1	54.5
Asthma, ever	29,041	16,759	14.0	57.7
Asthma, still	18,869	11,946	10.0	63.3
Hay fever	16,869	9,986	8.4	59.2
Sinusitis	29,611	19,495	16.3	65.8
Chronic bronchitis	10,071	6,754	5.7	67.1
Cancer				
Any cancer	19,025	10,803	9.1	56.8
Breast cancer	3,195	3,195	2.7	100.0
Cervical cancer	1,188	1,188	1.0	100.0
Other selected diseases and conditions				
Diabetes	20,589	10,247	8.6	49.8
Ulcers	15,502	8,481	7.1	54.7
Kidney disease	4,381	2,484	2.1	56.7
Liver disease	3,016	1,568	1.3	52.0
Arthritis	53,782	31,534	26.4	58.6
Chronic joint symptoms	68,749	37,207	31.2	54.1
Migraines or severe headaches	37,904	25,807	21.6	68.1
Pain in neck	35,798	21,355	17.9	59.7
Pain in lower back	66,917	36,306	30.4	54.3
Pain in face or jaw	11,436	7,627	6.4	66.7
Selected sensory problems				
Hearing	37,122	15,759	13.2	42.5
Vision	21,232	12,524	10.5	59.0
Absence of all natural teeth	18,038	9,561	8.0	53.0

Note: The conditions shown are those that have ever been diagnosed by a doctor, except as noted. Hay fever, sinusitis, and chronic bronchitis have been diagnosed in the past 12 months. Kidney and liver disease have been diagnosed in the past 12 months and exclude kidney stones, bladder infections, and incontinence. Chronic joint symptoms are shown if respondent had pain, aching, or stiffness in or around a joint (excluding back and neck) and the condition began more than three months ago. Migraines, pain in neck, lower back, face, or jaw are shown only if pain lasted a whole day or more.
Source: National Center for Health Statistics, Summary Health Statistics for U.S. Adults: National Health Interview Survey, 2011, Vital and Health Statistics, Series 10, No. 256, 2012, Internet site http://www.cdc.gov/nchs/nhis.htm; calculations by New Strategist

Table 3.22 Health Conditions among Men, 2011

(total number of people aged 18 or older with selected health conditions, number and percent of men with condition, and men's share of total, by type of condition, 2011; numbers in thousands)

	total	men number	men percent with condition	men share of total
TOTAL PEOPLE	231,376	112,093	100.0%	48.4%
Selected circulatory diseases				
Heart disease, all types	26,485	13,767	12.3	52.0
Coronary	15,300	9,203	8.2	60.2
Hypertension	58,959	28,683	25.6	48.6
Stroke	6,171	2,654	2.4	43.0
Selected respiratory conditions				
Emphysema	4,680	2,129	1.9	45.5
Asthma, ever	29,041	12,282	11.0	42.3
Asthma, still	18,869	6,923	6.2	36.7
Hay fever	16,869	6,882	6.1	40.8
Sinusitis	29,611	10,116	9.0	34.2
Chronic bronchitis	10,071	3,316	3.0	32.9
Cancer				
Any cancer	19,025	8,222	7.3	43.2
Prostate cancer	2,280	2,280	2.0	100.0
Other selected diseases and conditions				
Diabetes	20,589	10,342	9.2	50.2
Ulcers	15,502	7,021	6.3	45.3
Kidney disease	4,381	1,897	1.7	43.3
Liver disease	3,016	1,449	1.3	48.0
Arthritis	53,782	22,248	19.8	41.4
Chronic joint symptoms	68,749	31,542	28.1	45.9
Migraines or severe headaches	37,904	12,097	10.8	31.9
Pain in neck	35,798	14,442	12.9	40.3
Pain in lower back	66,917	30,611	27.3	45.7
Pain in face or jaw	11,436	3,809	3.4	33.3
Selected sensory problems				
Hearing	37,122	21,363	19.1	57.5
Vision	21,232	8,708	7.8	41.0
Absence of all natural teeth	18,038	8,478	7.6	47.0

Note: The conditions shown are those that have ever been diagnosed by a doctor, except as noted. Hay fever, sinusitis, and chronic bronchitis have been diagnosed in the past 12 months. Kidney and liver disease have been diagnosed in the past 12 months and exclude kidney stones, bladder infections, and incontinence. Chronic joint symptoms are shown if respondent had pain, aching, or stiffness in or around a joint (excluding back and neck) and the condition began more than three months ago. Migraines, pain in neck, lower back, face, or jaw are shown only if pain lasted a whole day or more.

Source: National Center for Health Statistics, Summary Health Statistics for U.S. Adults: National Health Interview Survey, 2011, Vital and Health Statistics, Series 10, No. 256, 2012, Internet site http://www.cdc.gov/nchs/nhis.htm; calculations by New Strategist

Table 3.23 Difficulties in Physical Functioning among Women, 2011

(total number of people aged 18 or older with difficulties in physical functioning, number and percent of women with difficulties, and women's share of total, by type of difficulty, 2011; numbers in thousands)

		women		
	total	number	percent with difficulty	share of total
TOTAL PEOPLE	**231,376**	**119,283**	–	**51.6%**
Total with any physical difficulty	**37,368**	**22,992**	**19.3**	**61.5**
Walk quarter of a mile	17,597	10,783	9.0	61.3
Climb 10 steps without resting	12,887	8,366	7.0	64.9
Stand for two hours	22,369	13,425	11.3	60.0
Sit for two hours	7,724	4,649	3.9	60.2
Stoop, bend, or kneel	21,677	13,300	11.1	61.4
Reach over head	6,550	3,948	3.3	60.3
Grasp or handle small objects	4,329	2,588	2.2	59.8
Lift or carry 10 pounds	10,677	7,508	6.3	70.3
Push or pull large objects	15,998	10,758	9.0	67.2

Note: Respondents were classified as having difficulties if they said a task would be very difficult or they could not do it at all.
"–" means not applicable.
Source: National Center for Health Statistics, Summary Health Statistics for U.S. Adults: National Health Interview Survey, 2011, Vital and Health Statistics, Series 10, No. 256, 2012, Internet site http://www.cdc.gov/nchs/nhis.htm; calculations by New Strategist

Table 3.24 Difficulties in Physical Functioning among Men, 2011

(total number of people aged 18 or older with difficulties in physical functioning, number and percent of men with difficulties, and men's share of total, by type of difficulty, 2011; numbers in thousands)

	total	men number	men percent with difficulty	men share of total
TOTAL PEOPLE	**231,376**	**112,093**	–	**48.4%**
Total with any physical difficulty	**37,368**	**14,376**	**12.8**	**38.5**
Walk quarter of a mile	17,597	6,814	6.1	38.7
Climb 10 steps without resting	12,887	4,521	4.0	35.1
Stand for two hours	22,369	8,943	8.0	40.0
Sit for two hours	7,724	3,075	2.7	39.8
Stoop, bend, or kneel	21,677	8,377	7.5	38.6
Reach over head	6,550	2,603	2.3	39.7
Grasp or handle small objects	4,329	1,742	1.6	40.2
Lift or carry 10 pounds	10,677	3,169	2.8	29.7
Push or pull large objects	15,998	5,240	4.7	32.8

Note: Respondents were classified as having difficulties if they said a task would be very difficult or they could not do it at all. "–" means not applicable.
Source: National Center for Health Statistics, Summary Health Statistics for U.S. Adults: National Health Interview Survey, 2011, Vital and Health Statistics, Series 10, No. 256, 2012, Internet site http://www.cdc.gov/nchs/nhis.htm; calculations by New Strategist

Table 3.25 AIDS Diagnoses by Sex through 2009

(cumulative number of AIDS cases diagnosed among people aged 13 or older by age, race, Hispanic origin, and sex, and male share of total, through 2009)

			men	
	total	females	number	share of total
Total cases, aged 13 or older	**1,099,161**	**220,795**	**878,366**	**79.9%**
Aged 13 to 14	1,321	609	712	53.9
Aged 15 to 24	50,134	15,185	34,949	69.7
Aged 25 to 34	343,787	71,302	272,485	79.3
Aged 35 to 44	427,811	81,013	346,798	81.1
Aged 45 to 54	198,707	37,042	161,665	81.4
Aged 55 to 64	59,656	11,518	48,138	80.7
Aged 65 or older	17,743	4,125	13,618	76.8
Race and Hispanic origin				
American Indian	3,668	789	2,879	78.5
Asian	8,276	1,208	7,068	85.4
Black	460,562	136,690	323,872	70.3
Hispanic	188,401	36,091	152,310	80.8
Non-Hispanic white	424,500	42,602	381,898	90.0

Source: National Center for Health Statistics, Health United States 2011, Internet site http://www.cdc.gov/nchs/hus.htm; calculations by New Strategist

Prescription Drug Use Is Widespread

Most females have taken a prescription drug in the past month.

The use of prescription drugs to treat a variety of illnesses, particularly chronic conditions, is commonplace in the United States. The percentage of females having taken at least one prescription drug during the past month stood at 54 percent in 2005–08. Twenty-five percent of females had taken three or more prescription drugs in the past month.

Prescription drug use is lower among males. Forty-two percent of males have taken at least one prescription drug in the past month and 18 percent have taken three or more. Among men and women aged 65 or older, the proportion having taken three or more prescription drugs in the past month is a nearly identical 65 percent.

Non-Hispanic whites are most likely to have taken at least one prescription medication during the past month. Hispanics are least likely to have taken prescription drugs, in part because so many lack health insurance.

■ Behind the increase in the use of prescription drugs is the introduction and marketing of new drugs to treat chronic health problems.

One in four females has taken at least three prescription drugs during the past month

(percent having taken at least one or three or more prescription drugs in the past month, by sex, 2005–08)

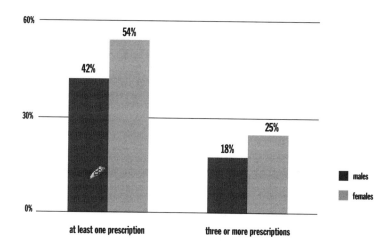

Table 3.26 Prescription Drug Use among Females by Age, Race, and Hispanic Origin, 2005–08

(percent of females who took at least one or three or more prescription drugs in the past month, by age, race, and Hispanic origin, 2005–08)

	total	black	Hispanic (Mexican)	non-Hispanic white
AT LEAST ONE				
Total females	**53.9%**	**44.4%**	**27.9%**	**61.5%**
Under age 18	25.2	18.1	16.7	30.7
Aged 18 to 44	47.9	36.6	22.0	56.6
Aged 45 to 64	70.2	69.1	54.1	73.0
Aged 65 or older	90.5	91.7	83.9	90.7
THREE OR MORE				
Total females	**24.8**	**20.2**	**9.7**	**29.1**
Under age 18	3.8	1.9	1.8	4.8
Aged 18 to 44	13.3	9.4	4.1	16.1
Aged 45 to 64	39.4	39.1	29.0	41.8
Aged 65 or older	65.3	70.6	58.6	65.3

Source: National Center for Health Statistics, Health United States 2011, Internet site http://www.cdc.gov/nchs/hus.htm; calculations by New Strategist

Table 3.27 Prescription Drug Use among Males by Age, Race, and Hispanic Origin, 2005–08

(percent of males who have taken at least one or three or more prescription drugs in the past month, by age, race, and Hispanic origin, 2005–08)

	total	black	Hispanic (Mexican)	non-Hispanic white
AT LEAST ONE				
Total males	**41.7%**	**33.9%**	**21.4%**	**48.4%**
Under age 18	25.3	23.4	17.3	29.2
Aged 18 to 44	27.5	20.9	14.2	33.3
Aged 45 to 64	59.3	54.7	46.0	62.3
Aged 65 or older	89.7	85.1	67.8	91.6
THREE OR MORE				
Total males	**17.8**	**14.4**	**6.1**	**21.3**
Under age 18	5.0	5.3	3.5	5.7
Aged 18 to 44	6.2	4.9	1.5	8.0
Aged 45 to 64	28.6	29.0	19.7	29.4
Aged 65 or older	64.6	61.5	45.0	66.3

Source: National Center for Health Statistics, Health United States 2011, Internet site http://www.cdc.gov/nchs/hus.htm; calculations by New Strategist

Women Account for Most Health Care Visits

Men account for two-thirds of those without health care visit in the past year.

Among people aged 18 or older who have visited a health care provider in the past 12 months, only 45 percent are men. In part, women's dominance in the waiting room is due to their older average age, but childbearing also boosts women's health care visits. Among adults who have not seen a health care provider in the past year, 65 percent are men. Among those who have seen a health care provider 10 or more times, 64 percent are women.

Females are more likely than males to have been hospitalized in the past year, again because of women's older average age. In 2011, 9.5 percent of women and 6.3 percent of men spent at least one night in a hospital.

■ Men are less likely than women to see a health care provider in part because they are less likely to seek medical help for their problems.

Males are a minority of those with a health care visit in the past year

(percent distribution of people aged 18 or older who have visited a health care provider at least once in the past 12 months, by sex, 2011)

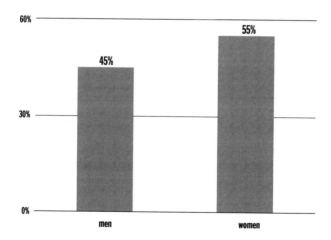

Table 3.28 Health Care Office Visits by Sex, 2011

(number and percent distribution of people aged 18 or older by number of office visits to a health care provider in past 12 months, by sex, 2011; numbers in thousands)

			one or more visits				
	total	no visits	total	one	two to three	four to nine	10 or more
Total people	**231,376**	**43,578**	**185,321**	**39,552**	**59,226**	**55,721**	**30,822**
Men	112,093	28,215	82,697	21,854	27,317	22,547	10,979
Women	119,283	15,363	102,624	17,698	31,909	33,174	19,843
PERCENT DISTRIBUTION BY NUMBER OF VISITS							
Total people	**100.0%**	**18.8%**	**80.1%**	**17.1%**	**25.6%**	**24.1%**	**13.3%**
Men	100.0	25.2	73.8	19.5	24.4	20.1	9.8
Women	100.0	12.9	86.0	14.8	26.8	27.8	16.6
PERCENT DISTRIBUTION BY SEX							
Total people	**100.0**	**100.0**	**100.0**	**100.0**	**100.0**	**100.0**	**100.0**
Men	48.4	64.7	44.6	55.3	46.1	40.5	35.6
Women	51.6	35.3	55.4	44.7	53.9	59.5	64.4

Note: Health care visits exclude overnight hospitalizations, visits to emergency rooms, home visits, dental visits, and telephone calls.
Source: National Center for Health Statistics, Summary Health Statistics for U.S. Adults: National Health Interview Survey, 2011, Vital and Health Statistics, Series 10, No. 256, 2012, Internet site http://www.cdc.gov/nchs/nhis.htm; calculations by New Strategist

Table 3.29 Overnight Hospital Stays by Sex, 2011

(number and percent distribution of people with an overnight hospital stay in past 12 months, by sex and number of stays, 2011; numbers in thousands)

			one or more nights			
	total	none	total	one	two	three or more
Total people	**305,088**	**281,040**	**24,254**	**18,042**	**3,652**	**2,560**
Males	150,193	140,469	9,421	6,897	1,450	1,074
Females	155,695	140,571	14,833	11,145	2,202	1,486
PERCENT DISTRIBUTION BY NUMBER OF STAYS						
Total people	**100.0%**	**92.1%**	**7.9%**	**5.9%**	**1.2%**	**0.8%**
Males	100.0	93.5	6.3	4.6	1.0	0.7
Females	100.0	90.3	9.5	7.2	1.4	1.0
PERCENT DISTRIBUTION BY SEX						
Total people	**100.0**	**100.0**	**100.0**	**100.0**	**100.0**	**100.0**
Males	49.2	50.0	38.8	38.2	39.7	42.0
Females	51.0	50.0	61.2	61.8	60.3	58.0

Source: National Center for Health Statistics, Summary Health Statistics for the U.S. Population: National Health Interview Survey, 2011, Series 10, No. 255, 2012, Internet site http://www.cdc.gov/nchs/nhis.htm; calculations by New Strategist

Heart Disease Is the Leading Killer

Heart disease accounts for the largest share of deaths among males and females.

One in four deaths among males and females in 2009 was due to heart disease, according to the National Center for Health Statistics. Among all deaths due to heart disease, males account for 51 percent of the total. They account for 52 percent of all deaths due to cancer. Accidents are the fifth leading cause of death, with males accounting for 64 percent of all accidental deaths. Females far surpass males in deaths from Alzheimer's disease—70 to 30 percent.

At birth, the average male can expect to live about five fewer years than the average female—76.3 years for males versus 81.1 years for females. At age 65, some of the gap has closed and men are expected to live 2.6 fewer years than their female counterparts—17.8 more years for men versus 20.4 more years for women.

■ Death rates from heart disease have fallen over the past few decades, boosting life expectancy for males and females.

Females live longer than males

(average number of expected years of life remaining at birth and at age 65, by sex, 2011)

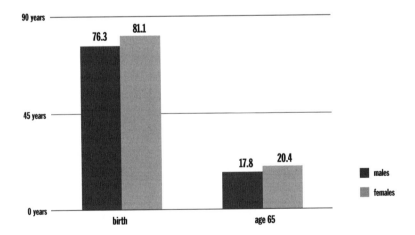

Table 3.30 Leading Causes of Death among Females, 2009

(number of total deaths, number and percent distribution of deaths to females, and female share of total, for the 10 leading causes of death among females, 2009)

	total	females number	females percent distribution	females share of total
Total deaths	**2,437,163**	**1,219,784**	**100.0%**	**50.0%**
1. Diseases of the heart (1)	599,413	292,188	24.0	48.7
2. Malignant neoplasms (cancer) (2)	567,628	270,865	22.2	47.7
3. Cerebrovascular diseases (4)	128,842	76,769	6.3	59.6
4. Chronic lower respiratory disease (3)	137,353	72,234	5.9	52.6
5. Alzheimer's disease (6)	79,003	55,103	4.5	69.7
6. Accidents (unintentional injuries) (5)	118,021	42,999	3.5	36.4
7. Diabetes mellitus (7)	68,705	33,651	2.8	49.0
8. Influenza and pneumonia (8)	53,692	28,564	2.3	53.2
9. Nephritis, nephrotic syndrome, and nephrosis (9)	48,935	25,005	2.0	51.1
10. Septicemia	35,639	19,268	1.6	54.1
All other causes	598,662	303,138	24.9	50.6

Note: Number in parentheses shows rank for all Americans if the cause of death is in top 10.
Source: National Center for Health Statistics, Deaths: Leading Causes for 2009, National Vital Statistics Report, Vol. 61, No. 7, 2009, Internet site http://www.cdc.gov/nchs/deaths.htm; calculations by New Strategist

Table 3.31 Leading Causes of Death among Males, 2009

(number of total deaths, number and percent distribution of deaths to males, and male share of total, for the 10 leading causes of death among males, 2009)

		total	males number	males percent distribution	males share of total
	Total deaths	**2,437,163**	**1,217,379**	**100.0%**	**50.0%**
1.	Diseases of the heart (1)	599,413	307,225	25.2	51.3
2.	Malignant neoplasms (cancer) (2)	567,628	296,763	24.4	52.3
3.	Accidents (unintentional injuries) (5)	118,021	75,022	6.2	63.6
4.	Chronic lower respiratory disease (3)	137,353	65,119	5.3	47.4
5.	Cerebrovascular diseases (4)	128,842	52,073	4.3	40.4
6.	Diabetes mellitus (7)	68,705	35,054	2.9	51.0
7.	Suicide (10)	36,909	29,089	2.4	78.8
8.	Influenza and pneumonia (8)	53,692	25,128	2.1	46.8
9.	Nephritis, nephrotic syndrome, and nephrosis (9)	48,935	23,930	2.0	48.9
10.	Alzheimer's disease (6)	79,003	23,900	2.0	30.3
	All other causes	598,662	284,076	23.3	47.5

Note: Number in parentheses shows rank for all Americans if the cause of death is in top 10.
Source: National Center for Health Statistics, Deaths: Leading Causes for 2009, National Vital Statistics Report, Vol. 61, No. 7, 2009, Internet site http://www.cdc.gov/nchs/deaths.htm; calculations by New Strategist

Table 3.32 Life Expectancy by Age and Sex, 2011

(expected years of life remaining at selected ages by sex, and difference between female and male life expectancy, 2011)

	total	female	male	female minus male
At birth	78.7 yrs.	81.1 yrs.	76.3 yrs.	4.8 yrs.
Aged 1	78.2	80.5	75.8	4.7
Aged 5	74.3	76.6	71.9	4.7
Aged 10	69.3	71.6	66.9	4.7
Aged 15	64.4	66.7	62.0	4.7
Aged 20	59.5	61.8	57.2	4.6
Aged 25	54.8	56.9	52.5	4.4
Aged 30	50.0	52.0	47.9	4.1
Aged 35	45.3	47.2	43.2	4.0
Aged 40	40.6	42.5	38.6	3.9
Aged 45	36.0	37.8	34.0	3.8
Aged 50	31.5	33.2	29.6	3.6
Aged 55	27.2	28.8	25.5	3.3
Aged 60	23.1	24.5	21.5	3.0
Aged 65	19.2	20.4	17.8	2.6
Aged 70	15.5	16.5	14.3	2.2
Aged 75	12.1	12.9	11.0	1.9
Aged 80	9.1	9.7	8.2	1.5
Aged 85	6.5	6.9	5.9	1.0
Aged 90	4.6	4.8	4.1	0.7
Aged 95	3.2	3.3	2.9	0.4
Aged 100	2.3	2.3	2.1	0.2

Source: National Center for Health Statistics, Deaths: Preliminary Data for 2011, National Vital Statistics Report, Vol. 61, No. 6, 2012, Internet site http://www.cdc.gov/nchs/deaths.htm; calculations by New Strategist

4

Income

Men's median income in 2011 was lower than their median income in 1990.

The median income of men aged 35 to 54 fell 11 percent between 1990 and 2011, after adjusting for inflation.

The historic rise in women's income has come to an end.

In almost every age group, women's median income was lower in 2011 than in 2007, after adjusting for inflation.

Incomes peak among men aged 45 to 54 and women aged 35 to 44.

Men aged 45 to 54 had a median income of $45,950 in 2011; women aged 35 to 44 had a median income of $29,095.

Among full-time workers, women earn 77 percent as much as men.

This figure is up from 71 percent in 1990, but down from 79 percent in 2005.

Every household type lost ground between 2000 and 2011.

Men who live alone experienced the largest income loss during those years, a 14 percent decline after adjusting for inflation.

The poverty rate among men is close to a record high.

Female-headed families with children under age 18 are most likely to be poor, with a poverty rate of 40.9 percent in 2011.

Men's Incomes Are Falling

Most men have lower incomes today than they did in 2000.

Men under age 65 had lower incomes in 2011 than they did in 2000, thanks in part to the Great Recession. The median income of men under age 55 fell by double-digit percentages during those years, after adjusting for inflation. In contrast, men aged 65 or older saw their median income rise as Social Security payments—indexed to inflation—continued to grow.

Even going back to 1990, most men have lower incomes today than their counterparts did more than two decades ago. The median income of men aged 35 to 54 fell by a substantial 11 percent between 1990 and 2011, after adjusting for inflation. In 1990, the median income of men aged 65 or older was just 70 percent as high as the median for all men. By 2011, the median income of older men was 84 percent as high as the overall median.

■ Today's older men were the beneficiaries of generous government and employer handouts that have been eliminated or sharply reduced for middle-aged and younger men.

Only older men have gained ground since the Great Recession

(percent change in median income of men aged 15 or older, by age, 2007 to 2011; in 2011 dollars)

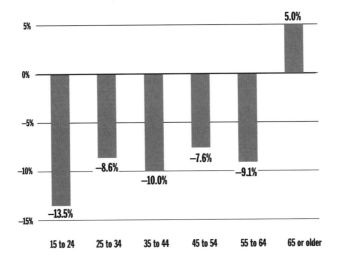

Table 4.1 Median Income of Men by Age, 1990 to 2011

(median income of men aged 15 or older with income by age, 1990 to 2011; percent change in income for selected years; index of men's income by age to total, 1990 to 2011; in 2011 dollars)

	total men	under age 25	aged 25 to 34	aged 35 to 44	aged 45 to 54	aged 55 to 64	aged 65 or older
2011	$32,986	$10,518	$32,581	$43,967	$45,950	$41,550	$27,707
2010	33,221	10,219	32,949	43,564	46,882	42,543	26,542
2009	33,747	10,523	33,464	44,275	46,904	43,302	27,134
2008	34,640	11,259	34,905	46,159	47,571	43,619	26,640
2007	36,009	12,159	35,660	48,832	49,734	45,699	26,384
2006	35,992	12,230	35,842	47,562	50,971	46,268	26,214
2005	36,031	12,061	35,900	47,194	50,262	46,836	25,097
2004	36,335	12,005	36,902	48,264	49,849	46,780	25,161
2003	36,602	12,181	37,374	47,931	51,458	47,588	24,902
2002	36,553	12,054	38,352	47,372	51,219	45,353	24,299
2001	36,969	11,816	38,759	48,707	52,218	45,273	25,011
2000	37,017	12,468	39,513	49,528	53,599	44,653	25,352
1999	36,841	11,271	39,654	49,129	55,078	45,199	26,051
1998	36,505	11,286	38,744	48,473	53,633	45,164	25,032
1997	35,226	10,434	36,322	45,900	52,569	43,533	24,826
1996	34,021	9,935	35,940	45,915	51,718	42,145	23,815
1995	33,062	10,130	34,597	46,043	52,148	42,467	24,156
1994	32,595	10,577	33,924	46,081	52,423	40,631	22,885
1993	32,343	9,854	33,608	46,506	50,816	38,531	22,965
1992	32,127	9,890	33,763	46,319	50,544	40,231	22,926
1991	32,964	10,115	34,777	47,187	51,178	41,002	23,121
1990	33,852	10,541	35,687	49,667	51,725	41,378	23,660
PERCENT CHANGE							
2007 to 2011	−8.4%	−13.5%	−8.6%	−10.0%	−7.6%	−9.1%	5.0%
2000 to 2011	−10.9	−15.6	−17.5	−11.2	−14.3	−6.9	9.3
1990 to 2011	−2.6	−0.2	−8.7	−11.5	−11.2	0.4	17.1

	total men	under age 25	aged 25 to 34	aged 35 to 44	aged 45 to 54	aged 55 to 64	aged 65 or older
INDEX OF MEDIAN INCOME BY AGE TO TOTAL							
2011	100	32	99	133	139	126	84
2010	100	31	99	131	141	128	80
2009	100	31	99	131	139	128	80
2008	100	33	101	133	137	126	77
2007	100	34	99	136	138	127	73
2006	100	34	100	132	142	129	73
2005	100	33	100	131	139	130	70
2004	100	33	102	133	137	129	69
2003	100	33	102	131	141	130	68
2002	100	33	105	130	140	124	66
2001	100	32	105	132	141	122	68
2000	100	34	107	134	145	121	68
1999	100	31	108	133	150	123	71
1998	100	31	106	133	147	124	69
1997	100	30	103	130	149	124	70
1996	100	29	106	135	152	124	70
1995	100	31	105	139	158	128	73
1994	100	32	104	141	161	125	70
1993	100	30	104	144	157	119	71
1992	100	31	105	144	157	125	71
1991	100	31	106	143	155	124	70
1990	100	31	105	147	153	122	70

Note: The index is calculated by dividing the median income of each age group by the median income of all men and multiplying by 100.
Source: Bureau of the Census, Current Population Survey, Historical Tables, Internet site http://www.census.gov/hhes/www/income/data/historical/people/; calculations by New Strategist

Many Women Are Losing Ground

The rapid growth in women's incomes has come to an end.

As better-educated and career-oriented baby-boom women entered the labor force, they boosted women's incomes. Generation X and millennial women followed in their footsteps, with a growing percentage of women committed to full-time jobs. With more women working full-time, women's median income increased substantially over the years, climbing 26 percent between 1990 and 2011, to $21,102, after adjusting for inflation. Women's median income remains far below men's largely because women are less likely to work full-time.

Since 2000, the growth in women's median has come to a halt because of the Great Recession. The overall median income of women fell 7 percent between 2007 and 2011, after adjusting for inflation. Most age groups lost ground. Nevertheless, women aged 65 or older continued to make gains.

■ Expect to see the incomes of women aged 65 or older climb in the years ahead as career-oriented boomer women enter the age group.

For most women, income growth came to a halt with the Great Recession

(percent change in median income of women aged 15 or older, by age, 2007 to 2011; in 2011 dollars)

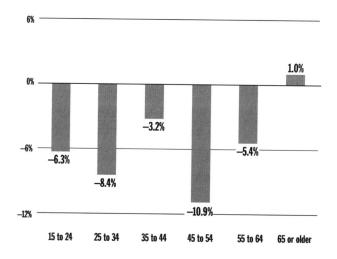

Table 4.2 Median Income of Women by Age, 1990 to 2011

(median income of women aged 15 or older with income by age, 1990 to 2011; percent change in income for selected years; index of women's income by age to total, 1990 to 2011; in 2011 dollars)

	total women	under age 25	aged 25 to 34	aged 35 to 44	aged 45 to 54	aged 55 to 64	aged 65 or older
2011	$21,102	$9,107	$25,723	$29,095	$28,460	$25,923	$15,362
2010	21,430	8,971	26,368	30,195	28,546	26,268	15,563
2009	21,975	9,385	26,462	29,249	30,007	26,332	16,024
2008	21,798	9,298	26,692	28,592	29,495	26,653	15,208
2007	22,695	9,718	28,077	30,049	31,949	27,402	15,209
2006	22,326	9,652	26,972	29,414	31,060	26,980	15,174
2005	21,401	9,470	26,285	29,303	30,502	25,486	14,395
2004	21,036	9,172	26,275	29,055	31,234	24,769	14,385
2003	21,106	9,092	26,894	28,703	31,631	24,908	14,485
2002	21,018	9,479	27,065	27,907	31,461	23,960	14,260
2001	21,106	9,486	27,279	28,547	30,661	22,642	14,372
2000	20,979	9,613	27,491	28,834	30,995	22,098	14,397
1999	20,658	9,014	26,062	27,887	30,463	21,519	14,791
1998	19,884	9,004	25,158	27,952	29,748	20,222	14,474
1997	19,146	8,861	24,657	26,136	28,690	20,086	14,059
1996	18,292	8,395	23,386	26,331	27,186	19,007	13,740
1995	17,775	7,781	22,797	25,493	25,971	18,143	13,709
1994	17,207	8,266	22,336	24,295	25,588	16,308	13,431
1993	16,930	8,202	21,440	24,284	25,020	16,598	13,027
1992	16,828	8,120	21,409	24,214	24,897	15,915	12,852
1991	16,871	8,369	20,878	24,358	23,712	15,947	13,188
1990	16,799	8,177	21,001	24,195	23,738	15,681	13,419
PERCENT CHANGE							
2007 to 2011	−7.0%	−6.3%	−8.4%	−3.2%	−10.9%	−5.4%	1.0%
2000 to 2011	0.6	−5.3	−6.4	0.9	−8.2	17.3	6.7
1990 to 2011	25.6	11.4	22.5	20.3	19.9	65.3	14.5

	total women	under age 25	aged 25 to 34	aged 35 to 44	aged 45 to 54	aged 55 to 64	aged 65 or older

INDEX OF MEDIAN INCOME BY AGE TO TOTAL

	total women	under age 25	aged 25 to 34	aged 35 to 44	aged 45 to 54	aged 55 to 64	aged 65 or older
2011	100	43	122	138	135	123	73
2010	100	42	123	141	133	123	73
2009	100	43	120	133	137	120	73
2008	100	43	122	131	135	122	70
2007	100	43	124	132	141	121	67
2006	100	43	121	132	139	121	68
2005	100	44	123	137	143	119	67
2004	100	44	125	138	148	118	68
2003	100	43	127	136	150	118	69
2002	100	45	129	133	150	114	68
2001	100	45	129	135	145	107	68
2000	100	46	131	137	148	105	69
1999	100	44	126	135	147	104	72
1998	100	45	127	141	150	102	73
1997	100	46	129	137	150	105	73
1996	100	46	128	144	149	104	75
1995	100	44	128	143	146	102	77
1994	100	48	130	141	149	95	78
1993	100	48	127	143	148	98	77
1992	100	48	127	144	148	95	76
1991	100	50	124	144	141	95	78
1990	100	49	125	144	141	93	80

Note: The index is calculated by dividing the median income of each age group by the median income of all women and multiplying by 100.

Source: Bureau of the Census, Current Population Survey, Historical Tables, Internet site http://www.census.gov/hhes/www/income/data/historical/people/; calculations by New Strategist

Incomes Fell Regardless of Race or Hispanic Origin

The Great Recession reduced the incomes of Asian, black, Hispanic, and non-Hispanic white men and women.

The median income of men fell 8 percent between 2007 and 2011, after adjusting for inflation. The losses ranged from a high of 16 percent among black men to a 6 percent decline among non-Hispanic whites. The losses were similar among women, with Asian women seeing the biggest loss during those years (16 percent) and non-Hispanic white women experiencing the smallest (6 percent).

Despite the Great Recession, Hispanic and non-Hispanic white women had higher incomes in 2011 than in 2000. Among men, however, every racial and ethnic group lost ground during those years.

■ Women's incomes were far higher in 2011 than in 1990 because a growing share of women have full-time jobs.

Non-Hispanic white men lost the least

(percent change in median income of men aged 15 or older with income, by race and Hispanic origin, 2007 to 2011; in 2011 dollars)

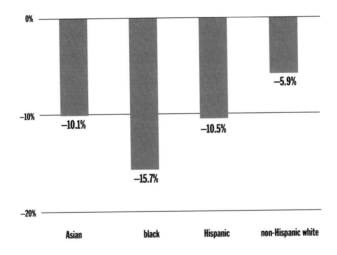

Table 4.3 Median Income of Men by Race and Hispanic Origin, 1990 to 2011

(median income of men aged 15 or older with income by race and Hispanic origin, 1990 to 2011; percent change in income for selected years; index of men's income by race/Hispanic origin group to total, 1990–2011; in 2011 dollars)

	total men	Asian	black	Hispanic	non-Hispanic white
2011	$32,986	$35,835	$23,584	$23,731	$38,148
2010	33,221	36,229	23,814	23,127	38,326
2009	33,747	38,678	24,824	23,337	38,572
2008	34,640	37,818	26,238	25,073	39,077
2007	36,009	39,841	27,977	26,523	40,540
2006	35,992	41,391	27,971	26,161	40,787
2005	36,031	38,060	26,047	25,448	40,720
2004	36,335	38,657	27,044	25,667	40,100
2003	36,602	38,811	26,824	25,745	39,537
2002	36,553	38,555	26,890	25,881	40,049
2001	36,969	39,504	27,270	25,648	40,387
2000	37,017	40,269	27,875	25,465	41,151
1999	36,841	37,630	27,592	24,117	41,667
1998	36,505	34,620	26,624	23,780	41,149
1997	35,226	34,994	25,284	22,657	38,506
1996	34,021	33,364	23,539	22,035	37,526
1995	33,062	32,476	23,455	21,746	37,340
1994	32,595	34,351	22,483	21,760	36,199
1993	32,343	33,169	22,385	20,981	35,515
1992	32,127	31,240	20,518	21,059	35,180
1991	32,964	31,610	20,874	22,253	35,710
1990	33,852	32,353	21,466	22,470	36,630
PERCENT CHANGE					
2007 to 2011	−8.4%	−10.1%	−15.7%	−10.5%	−5.9%
2000 to 2011	−10.9	−11.0	−15.4	−6.8	−7.3
1990 to 2011	−2.6	10.8	9.9	5.6	4.1

	total men	Asian	black	Hispanic	non-Hispanic white
INDEX OF MEDIAN INCOME OF RACE/ HISPANIC ORIGIN GROUP TO TOTAL					
2011	100	109	71	72	116
2010	100	109	72	70	115
2009	100	115	74	69	114
2008	100	109	76	72	113
2007	100	111	78	74	113
2006	100	115	78	73	113
2005	100	106	72	71	113
2004	100	106	74	71	110
2003	100	106	73	70	108
2002	100	105	74	71	110
2001	100	107	74	69	109
2000	100	109	75	69	111
1999	100	102	75	65	113
1998	100	95	73	65	113
1997	100	99	72	64	109
1996	100	98	69	65	110
1995	100	98	71	66	113
1994	100	105	69	67	111
1993	100	103	69	65	110
1992	100	97	64	66	110
1991	100	96	63	68	108
1990	100	96	63	66	108

Note: Beginning in 2002, data for Asians and blacks are for those who identify themselves as being of the race alone and those who identify themselves as being of the race in combination with one or more other races. Hispanics may be of any race. Beginning in 2002, data for non-Hispanic whites are for those who identify themselves as white alone and not Hispanic. The index is calculated by dividing the median income of each race/Hispanic origin group by the median income of all men and multiplying by 100.
Source: Bureau of the Census, Current Population Survey, Historical Tables, Internet site http://www.census.gov/hhes/www/ income/data/historical/people/; calculations by New Strategist

Table 4.4 Median Income of Women by Race and Hispanic Origin, 1990 to 2011

(median income of women aged 15 or older with income by race and Hispanic origin, 1990 to 2011; percent change in income for selected years; index of women's income by race/Hispanic origin group to total, 1990–2011; in 2011 dollars)

	total women	Asian	black	Hispanic	non-Hispanic white
2011	$21,102	$22,013	$19,561	$16,829	$22,226
2010	21,430	24,295	20,165	16,806	22,400
2009	21,975	25,344	20,356	16,997	23,005
2008	21,798	24,041	21,104	17,149	22,719
2007	22,695	26,137	21,382	18,167	23,525
2006	22,326	24,633	21,267	17,578	23,121
2005	21,401	24,911	20,271	17,323	22,409
2004	21,036	24,547	20,655	17,208	21,951
2003	21,106	21,864	20,226	16,683	22,380
2002	21,018	22,376	20,842	16,708	21,740
2001	21,106	23,534	20,684	15,985	21,887
2000	20,979	22,668	20,741	15,996	21,765
1999	20,658	22,673	19,945	15,356	21,477
1998	19,884	20,984	18,102	14,968	20,969
1997	19,146	19,997	18,231	14,335	20,104
1996	18,292	20,889	16,803	13,537	19,290
1995	17,775	18,848	16,062	13,083	18,767
1994	17,207	18,551	15,823	12,925	17,926
1993	16,930	18,952	14,573	12,415	17,778
1992	16,828	18,645	13,958	13,049	17,673
1991	16,871	17,757	14,198	12,904	17,715
1990	16,799	18,493	13,893	12,565	17,651
Percent change					
2007 to 2011	−7.0%	−15.8%	−8.5%	−7.4%	−5.5%
2000 to 2011	0.6	−2.9	−5.7	5.2	2.1
1990 to 2011	25.6	19.0	40.8	33.9	25.9

	total women	Asian	black	Hispanic	non-Hispanic white
INDEX OF MEDIAN INCOME OF RACE/ HISPANIC ORIGIN GROUP TO TOTAL					
2011	100	104	93	80	105
2010	100	113	94	78	105
2009	100	115	93	77	105
2008	100	110	97	79	104
2007	100	115	94	80	104
2006	100	110	95	79	104
2005	100	116	95	81	105
2004	100	117	98	82	104
2003	100	104	96	79	106
2002	100	106	99	79	103
2001	100	112	98	76	104
2000	100	108	99	76	104
1999	100	110	97	74	104
1998	100	106	91	75	105
1997	100	104	95	75	105
1996	100	114	92	74	105
1995	100	106	90	74	106
1994	100	108	92	75	104
1993	100	112	86	73	105
1992	100	111	83	78	105
1991	100	105	84	76	105
1990	100	110	83	75	105

Note: Beginning in 2002, data for Asians and blacks are for those who identify themselves as being of the race alone and those who identify themselves as being of the race in combination with one or more other races. Hispanics may be of any race. Beginning in 2002, data for non-Hispanic whites are for those who identify themselves as white alone and not Hispanic. The index is calculated by dividing the median income of each race/Hispanic origin group by the median income of all women and multiplying by 100.
Source: Bureau of the Census, Current Population Survey, Historical Tables, Internet site http://www.census.gov/hhes/www/ income/data/historical/people/; calculations by New Strategist

In Every Region, Incomes of Men and Women Declined

Those in the West lost the most between 2007 and 2011.

The median income of men fell 8 percent overall between 2007 and 2011, after adjusting for inflation. In the West, men's median income fell by a larger 14 percent during those years—from $37,541 to $32,211. Among women, those in the West also experienced the biggest drop in median income between 2007 and 2011—a 10 percent decline.

The median income of men is higher in the Northeast than in the other regions. In 2011, men in the Northeast had a median income 8 percent above average. Men in the South and West had below-average median incomes. Women's median income varies less by region.

■ Among men in the West, median income was lower in 2011 than in 1990, after adjusting for inflation.

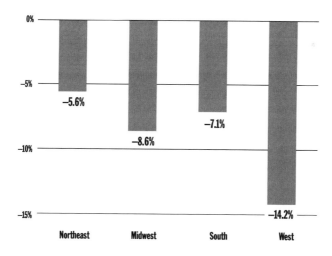

Men in the Northeast experienced the smallest loss

(percent change in median income of men aged 15 or older with income, by region, 2007 to 2011; in 2011 dollars)

Table 4.5 Median Income of Men by Region, 1990 to 2011

(median income of men aged 15 or older with income by region, 1990 to 2011; percent change in income for selected years; index of men's income by region to total, 1990–2011; in 2011 dollars)

	total men	Northeast	Midwest	South	West
2011	$32,986	$35,752	$34,034	$32,116	$32,211
2010	33,221	36,576	33,304	32,276	33,451
2009	33,747	37,134	33,617	32,555	34,803
2008	34,640	37,363	34,746	33,087	36,620
2007	36,009	37,880	37,232	34,589	37,541
2006	35,992	39,288	36,659	34,748	36,573
2005	36,031	37,584	36,853	34,544	36,389
2004	36,335	38,039	37,081	34,270	36,506
2003	36,602	38,413	37,040	33,767	37,207
2002	36,553	38,317	37,803	34,410	36,373
2001	36,969	38,920	38,470	34,739	36,438
2000	37,017	39,623	39,324	34,749	36,896
1999	36,841	39,016	39,830	34,985	36,517
1998	36,505	37,923	38,126	34,859	36,321
1997	35,226	36,856	36,726	33,388	34,695
1996	34,021	36,087	36,264	31,737	33,394
1995	33,062	36,063	35,606	31,011	32,699
1994	32,595	35,580	33,428	30,528	33,059
1993	32,343	34,153	33,254	30,216	33,009
1992	32,127	34,695	32,937	29,198	32,981
1991	32,964	35,992	33,128	29,751	34,740
1990	33,852	36,545	34,486	30,743	35,013
PERCENT CHANGE					
2007 to 2011	−8.4%	−5.6%	−8.6%	−7.1%	−14.2%
2000 to 2011	−10.9	−9.8	−13.5	−7.6	−12.7
1990 to 2011	−2.6	−2.2	−1.3	4.5	−8.0

	total men	Northeast	Midwest	South	West
INDEX OF MEDIAN INCOME BY REGION TO TOTAL					
2011	100	108	103	97	98
2010	100	110	100	97	101
2009	100	110	100	96	103
2008	100	108	100	96	106
2007	100	105	103	96	104
2006	100	109	102	97	102
2005	100	104	102	96	101
2004	100	105	102	94	100
2003	100	105	101	92	102
2002	100	105	103	94	100
2001	100	105	104	94	99
2000	100	107	106	94	100
1999	100	106	108	95	99
1998	100	104	104	95	99
1997	100	105	104	95	98
1996	100	106	107	93	98
1995	100	109	108	94	99
1994	100	109	103	94	101
1993	100	106	103	93	102
1992	100	108	103	91	103
1991	100	109	100	90	105
1990	100	108	102	91	103

Note: The index is calculated by dividing the median income of each region by the median income of all men and multiplying by 100.
Source: Bureau of the Census, Current Population Survey, Historical Tables, Internet site http://www.census.gov/hhes/www/income/data/historical/people/; calculations by New Strategist

Table 4.6 Median Income of Women by Region, 1990 to 2011

(median income of women aged 15 or older with income by region, 1990 to 2011; percent change in income for selected years; index of women's income by region to total, 1990–2011; in 2011 dollars)

	total women	Northeast	Midwest	South	West
2011	$21,102	$21,871	$20,860	$20,830	$21,209
2010	21,430	22,095	21,373	21,158	21,422
2009	21,975	23,139	22,006	21,245	22,157
2008	21,798	22,908	21,745	21,023	22,363
2007	22,695	23,529	22,299	22,060	23,509
2006	22,326	22,627	22,472	21,511	22,951
2005	21,401	22,427	21,725	20,750	21,393
2004	21,036	21,786	21,305	20,442	21,381
2003	21,106	21,952	21,398	20,377	21,399
2002	21,018	21,557	21,154	20,282	21,607
2001	21,106	21,683	21,452	20,233	21,571
2000	21,000	21,290	21,528	20,280	21,397
1999	20,658	21,274	20,933	19,875	20,987
1998	19,884	20,409	20,012	19,260	20,218
1997	19,146	20,026	19,420	18,214	19,564
1996	18,292	19,200	18,629	17,638	18,315
1995	17,775	18,291	18,142	16,982	18,254
1994	17,207	17,953	17,366	16,416	17,704
1993	16,930	17,435	16,907	16,181	17,730
1992	16,828	17,748	16,550	15,935	17,819
1991	16,871	17,790	16,425	16,190	17,676
1990	16,799	17,903	16,880	15,709	17,461

PERCENT CHANGE

	total women	Northeast	Midwest	South	West
2007 to 2011	−7.0%	−7.0%	−6.5%	−5.6%	−9.8%
2000 to 2011	0.5	2.7	−3.1	2.7	−0.9
1990 to 2011	25.6	22.2	23.6	32.6	21.5

	total women	Northeast	Midwest	South	West
INDEX OF MEDIAN INCOME BY REGION TO TOTAL					
2011	100	104	99	99	101
2010	100	103	100	99	100
2009	100	105	100	97	101
2008	100	105	100	96	103
2007	100	104	98	97	104
2006	100	101	101	96	103
2005	100	105	102	97	100
2004	100	104	101	97	102
2003	100	104	101	97	101
2002	100	103	101	96	103
2001	100	103	102	96	102
2000	100	101	103	97	102
1999	100	103	101	96	102
1998	100	103	101	97	102
1997	100	105	101	95	102
1996	100	105	102	96	100
1995	100	103	102	96	103
1994	100	104	101	95	103
1993	100	103	100	96	105
1992	100	105	98	95	106
1991	100	105	97	96	105
1990	100	107	100	94	104

Note: The index is calculated by dividing the median income of each region by the median income of all women and multiplying by 100.
Source: Bureau of the Census, Current Population Survey, Historical Tables, Internet site http://www.census.gov/hhes/www/income/data/historical/people/; calculations by New Strategist

Incomes Are Highest for Men Aged 45 to 54

Among full-time workers, however, income peaks in older age groups.

In 2011, the median income of men stood at $32,986. Men's income rises with age to a peak of $45,950 in the 45-to-54 age group, a figure 39 percent greater than men's overall median. Women's median income peaks in the 35-to-44 age group at $29,095—38 percent greater than women's overall median of $21,102. Women's median income is far below men's because men are more likely to work full-time.

Forty-eight percent of men aged 15 or older work full-time. Those who do had a median income of $50,316 in 2011. The median income of men who work full-time peaks in the oldest age groups at more than $60,000. Among women, 34 percent work full-time, and their median income was $38,685 in 2011. The median income of women who work full-time peaks in the older age groups at more than $40,000.

■ The incomes of older men and women should rise in the years ahead as baby boomers postpone retirement.

Men's income peaks in middle age

(median income of men aged 15 or older with income, by age, 2011)

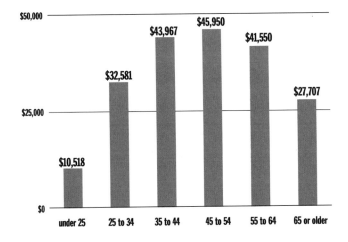

Table 4.7 Income Distribution of Men by Age, 2011

(number and percent distribution of men aged 15 or older by income and age, 2011; median income of men with income and of men working full-time, year-round; percent working full-time, year-round; men in thousands as of 2012)

	total	15–24	25–34	35–44	45–54	55–64	65 or older total	65–74	75+
TOTAL MEN	119,946	21,826	20,464	19,677	21,490	18,157	18,332	10,980	7,353
Without income	13,718	8,740	1,581	1,065	1,169	749	414	231	184
With income	106,228	13,086	18,883	18,612	20,320	17,408	17,918	10,749	7,169
Under $5,000	7,090	3,798	952	589	646	744	362	207	155
$5,000 to $9,999	7,441	2,490	1,182	754	951	1,034	1,030	575	455
$10,000 to $14,999	9,020	1,801	1,331	1,045	1,272	1,274	2,296	1,172	1,124
$15,000 to $19,999	8,537	1,350	1,483	1,065	1,129	1,084	2,427	1,222	1,205
$20,000 to $24,999	8,522	1,181	1,708	1,273	1,284	1,132	1,945	1,067	878
$25,000 to $29,999	7,054	726	1,522	1,102	1,094	1,001	1,610	912	698
$30,000 to $34,999	7,019	560	1,625	1,264	1,149	1,083	1,337	796	541
$35,000 to $39,999	6,010	380	1,350	1,169	1,204	935	972	568	404
$40,000 to $44,999	5,672	256	1,292	1,151	1,164	973	835	570	266
$45,000 to $49,999	4,567	131	978	983	1,053	730	692	475	216
$50,000 to $54,999	4,903	106	1,039	1,041	1,120	901	697	476	221
$55,000 to $59,999	3,066	51	601	682	673	590	468	301	167
$60,000 to $64,999	3,646	90	702	858	858	708	429	304	125
$65,000 to $69,999	2,339	18	456	536	535	509	285	203	82
$70,000 to $74,999	2,472	20	421	604	601	526	299	201	98
$75,000 to $79,999	2,058	12	346	483	544	431	242	180	61
$80,000 to $84,999	2,125	27	309	524	602	428	235	173	61
$85,000 to $89,999	1,271	3	193	308	337	271	157	105	52
$90,000 to $94,999	1,375	11	219	320	377	274	175	137	38
$95,000 to $99,999	917	10	129	193	241	218	126	114	12
$100,000 or more	11,123	66	1,044	2,666	3,486	2,562	1,300	992	308
MEDIAN INCOME									
Men with income	$32,986	$10,518	$32,581	$43,967	$45,950	$41,550	$27,707	$31,235	$23,622
Working full-time	50,316	24,423	41,433	51,926	56,675	60,388	64,655	64,748	63,839
Percent full-time	48.4%	17.1%	63.7%	71.7%	68.5%	54.4%	14.0%	19.6%	5.5%
PERCENT DISTRIBUTION									
TOTAL MEN	100.0%	100.0%	100.0%	100.0%	100.0%	100.0%	100.0%	100.0%	100.0%
Without income	11.4	40.0	7.7	5.4	5.4	4.1	2.3	2.1	2.5
With income	88.6	60.0	92.3	94.6	94.6	95.9	97.7	97.9	97.5
Under $15,000	19.6	37.1	16.9	12.1	13.4	16.8	20.1	17.8	23.6
$15,000 to $24,999	14.2	11.6	15.6	11.9	11.2	12.2	23.8	20.8	28.3
$25,000 to $34,999	11.7	5.9	15.4	12.0	10.4	11.5	16.1	15.6	16.9
$35,000 to $49,999	13.5	3.5	17.7	16.8	15.9	14.5	13.6	14.7	12.1
$50,000 to $74,999	13.7	1.3	15.7	18.9	17.6	17.8	11.9	13.5	9.4
$75,000 or more	15.7	0.6	10.9	22.8	26.0	23.0	12.2	15.5	7.2

Source: Bureau of the Census, 2012 Current Population Survey Annual Social and Economic Supplement, Internet site http:// www.census.gov/hhes/www/cpstables/032012/perinc/toc.htm; calculations by New Strategist

Table 4.8 Income Distribution of Women by Age, 2011

(number and percent distribution of women aged 15 or older by income and age, 2011; median income of women with income and of women working full-time, year-round; percent working full-time, year-round; women in thousands as of 2012)

	total	15–24	25–34	35–44	45–54	55–64	65 or older total	65–74	75+
TOTAL WOMEN	127,751	21,291	20,755	20,251	22,465	19,814	23,174	12,404	10,771
Without income	19,419	8,363	3,120	2,578	2,512	1,948	898	518	380
With income	108,332	12,927	17,635	17,672	19,954	17,867	22,276	11,886	10,391
Under $5,000	12,472	4,152	1,971	1,830	1,847	1,656	1,016	592	424
$5,000 to $9,999	14,270	2,740	1,698	1,335	1,802	1,950	4,744	2,412	2,331
$10,000 to $14,999	14,043	1,909	1,662	1,595	1,748	2,006	5,123	2,471	2,652
$15,000 to $19,999	10,865	1,318	1,605	1,482	1,755	1,540	3,164	1,411	1,753
$20,000 to $24,999	9,218	1,018	1,596	1,485	1,630	1,502	1,988	1,033	956
$25,000 to $29,999	7,341	537	1,422	1,283	1,498	1,173	1,429	747	682
$30,000 to $34,999	6,908	429	1,632	1,302	1,378	1,144	1,022	634	388
$35,000 to $39,999	5,785	313	1,223	1,197	1,219	1,079	753	445	308
$40,000 to $44,999	4,809	181	1,042	996	1,088	897	605	395	210
$45,000 to $49,999	3,537	74	754	744	889	623	452	304	148
$50,000 to $54,999	3,677	69	695	771	918	795	430	290	140
$55,000 to $59,999	2,144	50	416	503	558	383	233	165	68
$60,000 to $64,999	2,365	43	406	554	601	545	217	155	62
$65,000 to $69,999	1,647	19	270	420	382	386	170	126	43
$70,000 to $74,999	1,430	18	244	347	383	292	146	122	25
$75,000 to $79,999	1,186	8	182	278	347	225	146	99	47
$80,000 to $84,999	1,053	11	161	255	289	247	89	70	19
$85,000 to $89,999	636	2	82	144	180	171	55	48	7
$90,000 to $94,999	690	10	77	145	188	212	59	49	10
$95,000 to $99,999	451	10	48	98	129	101	65	44	21
$100,000 or more	3,807	16	449	907	1,125	938	372	275	97
MEDIAN INCOME									
Women with income	$21,102	$9,107	$25,723	$29,095	$28,460	$25,923	$15,362	$16,474	$14,590
Working full-time	38,685	22,360	36,199	40,868	41,274	41,888	44,893	45,960	40,409
Percent full-time	34.2%	13.1%	46.2%	50.4%	51.5%	40.2%	6.8%	10.7%	2.4%
PERCENT DISTRIBUTION									
TOTAL WOMEN	100.0%	100.0%	100.0%	100.0%	100.0%	100.0%	100.0%	100.0%	100.0%
Without income	15.2	39.3	15.0	12.7	11.2	9.8	3.9	4.2	3.5
With income	84.8	60.7	85.0	87.3	88.8	90.2	96.1	95.8	96.5
Under $15,000	31.9	41.3	25.7	23.5	24.0	28.3	47.0	44.1	50.2
$15,000 to $24,999	15.7	11.0	15.4	14.7	15.1	15.4	22.2	19.7	25.1
$25,000 to $34,999	11.2	4.5	14.7	12.8	12.8	11.7	10.6	11.1	9.9
$35,000 to $49,999	11.1	2.7	14.5	14.5	14.2	13.1	7.8	9.2	6.2
$50,000 to $74,999	8.8	0.9	9.8	12.8	12.6	12.1	5.2	6.9	3.1
$75,000 or more	6.1	0.3	4.8	9.0	10.1	9.6	3.4	4.7	1.9

Source: Bureau of the Census, 2012 Current Population Survey Annual Social and Economic Supplement, Internet site http:// www.census.gov/hhes/www/cpstables/032012/perinc/toc.htm; calculations by New Strategist

Non-Hispanic White Men Have the Highest Incomes

Hispanic women have the lowest incomes.

Non-Hispanic white men had a median income of $38,148 in 2011. More than one-third had an income of $50,000 or more. Asian men had a median income of $35,835. Median income was below $24,000 for both black and Hispanic men in 2011. The pattern changes when looking at the incomes of full-time workers. Black men have a much higher median income than Hispanic men ($40,136 versus $32,088), and Asian men have the highest median of all—$56,088 versus $55,763 for non-Hispanic white men.

Hispanic women have the lowest median income, just $16,829 in 2011. Non-Hispanic white women have the highest median—$22,226 and slightly above the $22,013 of Asian women and $19,561 of black women. About one-third of women work full-time. Among full-time workers, Asians and non-Hispanic whites have the highest median income (over $41,000), followed by blacks ($35,090) and Hispanics ($30,102).

■ The incomes of Hispanics are well below those of non-Hispanic whites, Asians, and blacks because many are recent immigrants with little education or earning power.

Among men, blacks have higher incomes than Hispanics

(median income of men aged 15 or older working full-time
year-round, by race and Hispanic origin, 2011)

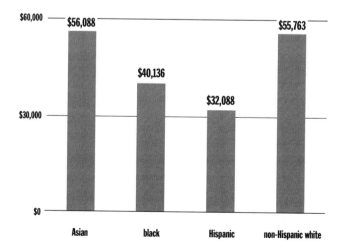

Table 4.9 Income Distribution of Men by Race and Hispanic Origin, 2011

(number and percent distribution of men aged 15 or older by income, race, and Hispanic origin, 2011; median income of men with income and of men working full-time, year-round; percent working full-time, year-round; men in thousands as of 2012)

	total	Asian	black	Hispanic	non-Hispanic white
TOTAL MEN	**119,946**	**6,578**	**14,499**	**18,867**	**79,468**
Without income	**13,718**	**1,022**	**2,937**	**3,202**	**6,566**
With income	**106,228**	**5,556**	**11,562**	**15,665**	**72,902**
Under $5,000	7,090	397	1,063	1,144	4,410
$5,000 to $9,999	7,441	479	1,469	1,501	3,913
$10,000 to $14,999	9,020	394	1,397	1,925	5,229
$15,000 to $19,999	8,537	396	1,007	1,822	5,306
$20,000 to $24,999	8,522	451	1,058	1,749	5,251
$25,000 to $29,999	7,054	266	806	1,332	4,612
$30,000 to $34,999	7,019	332	751	1,210	4,697
$35,000 to $39,999	6,010	257	647	946	4,147
$40,000 to $44,999	5,672	211	589	834	4,021
$45,000 to $49,999	4,567	196	436	544	3,360
$50,000 to $54,999	4,903	246	446	560	3,636
$55,000 to $59,999	3,066	149	211	280	2,417
$60,000 to $64,999	3,646	201	279	370	2,780
$65,000 to $69,999	2,339	100	207	174	1,855
$70,000 to $74,999	2,472	160	195	203	1,900
$75,000 to $79,999	2,058	129	130	162	1,631
$80,000 to $84,999	2,125	158	169	148	1,636
$85,000 to $89,999	1,271	76	70	74	1,034
$90,000 to $94,999	1,375	99	103	87	1,075
$95,000 to $99,999	917	81	34	50	737
$100,000 or more	11,123	776	493	551	9,254
MEDIAN INCOME					
Men with income	**$32,986**	**$35,835**	**$23,584**	**$23,731**	**$38,148**
Working full-time	50,316	56,088	40,136	32,088	55,763
Percent full-time	48.4%	52.2%	38.3%	48.2%	50.1%

PERCENT DISTRIBUTION	total	Asian	black	Hispanic	non-Hispanic white
TOTAL MEN	**100.0%**	**100.0%**	**100.0%**	**100.0%**	**100.0%**
Without income	**11.4**	**15.5**	**20.3**	**17.0**	**8.3**
With income	**88.6**	**84.5**	**79.7**	**83.0**	**91.7**
Under $15,000	19.6	19.3	27.1	24.2	17.1
$15,000 to $24,999	14.2	12.9	14.2	18.9	13.3
$25,000 to $34,999	11.7	9.1	10.7	13.5	11.7
$35,000 to $49,999	13.5	10.1	11.5	12.3	14.5
$50,000 to $74,999	13.7	13.0	9.2	8.4	15.8
$75,000 or more	15.7	20.1	6.9	5.7	19.3

Note: Asians and blacks are those who identify themselves as being of the race alone and those who identify themselves as being of the race in combination with other races. Non-Hispanic whites are those who identify themselves as white alone and not Hispanic. Numbers do not add to total because some people identify themselves as being of more than one race, not all races are shown, and Hispanics may be of any race.
Source: Bureau of the Census, 2012 Current Population Survey Annual Social and Economic Supplement, Internet site http://www.census.gov/hhes/www/cpstables/032012/perinc/toc.htm; calculations by New Strategist

Table 4.10 Income Distribution of Women by Race and Hispanic Origin, 2011

(number and percent distribution of women aged 15 or older by income, race, and Hispanic origin, 2011; median income of women with income and of women working full-time, year-round; percent working full-time, year-round; women in thousands as of 2012)

	total	Asian	black	Hispanic	non-Hispanic white
TOTAL WOMEN	**127,751**	**7,397**	**17,426**	**18,633**	**83,747**
Without income	**19,419**	**1,576**	**3,015**	**5,355**	**9,541**
With income	**108,332**	**5,820**	**14,411**	**13,278**	**74,206**
Under $5,000	12,472	844	1,567	1,779	8,196
$5,000 to $9,999	14,270	738	2,155	2,188	9,048
$10,000 to $14,999	14,043	601	2,002	1,906	9,448
$15,000 to $19,999	10,865	466	1,598	1,650	7,129
$20,000 to $24,999	9,218	489	1,285	1,319	6,083
$25,000 to $29,999	7,341	351	990	888	5,042
$30,000 to $34,999	6,908	359	971	821	4,716
$35,000 to $39,999	5,785	254	803	629	4,084
$40,000 to $44,999	4,809	261	564	463	3,479
$45,000 to $49,999	3,537	171	419	309	2,637
$50,000 to $54,999	3,677	192	479	314	2,669
$55,000 to $59,999	2,144	98	279	149	1,610
$60,000 to $64,999	2,365	153	259	207	1,742
$65,000 to $69,999	1,647	74	156	101	1,307
$70,000 to $74,999	1,430	85	148	124	1,078
$75,000 to $79,999	1,186	102	131	83	860
$80,000 to $84,999	1,053	87	124	65	758
$85,000 to $89,999	636	45	52	45	491
$90,000 to $94,999	690	59	62	29	539
$95,000 to $99,999	451	28	48	23	350
$100,000 or more	3,807	364	318	187	2,941
MEDIAN INCOME					
Women with income	**$21,102**	**$22,013**	**$19,561**	**$16,829**	**$22,226**
Working full-time	38,685	41,687	35,090	30,102	41,373
Percent full-time	34.2%	35.2%	35.8%	31.6%	34.4%

	total	Asian	black	Hispanic	non-Hispanic white
PERCENT DISTRIBUTION					
TOTAL WOMEN	**100.0%**	**100.0%**	**100.0%**	**100.0%**	**100.0%**
Without income	**15.2**	**21.3**	**17.3**	**28.7**	**11.4**
With income	**84.8**	**78.7**	**82.7**	**71.3**	**88.6**
Under $15,000	31.9	29.5	32.8	31.5	31.9
$15,000 to $24,999	15.7	12.9	16.5	15.9	15.8
$25,000 to $34,999	11.2	9.6	11.3	9.2	11.7
$35,000 to $49,999	11.1	9.3	10.3	7.5	12.2
$50,000 to $74,999	8.8	8.1	7.6	4.8	10.0
$75,000 or more	6.1	9.3	4.2	2.3	7.1

Note: Asians and blacks are those who identify themselves as being of the race alone and those who identify themselves as being of the race in combination with other races. Non-Hispanic whites are those who identify themselves as white alone and not Hispanic. Numbers do not add to total because some people identify themselves as being of more than one race, not all races are shown, and Hispanics may be of any race.
Source: Bureau of the Census, 2012 Current Population Survey Annual Social and Economic Supplement, Internet site http:// www.census.gov/hhes/www/cpstables/032012/perinc/toc.htm; calculations by New Strategist

Men's Earnings Are Higher than Women's

Until the Great Recession, the earnings gap had been shrinking.

The median income of women was only 64 percent as high as the median income of men in 2011, but much of the gap stems from different employment patterns. Men are more likely than women to have full-time jobs, boosting their median income. Among full-time workers, women earn 77 percent as much as men—up from 71 percent in 1990 and 75 percent in 2000. In 2011, the median income of men who worked full-time stood at $50,316 versus women's $38,685.

Among full-time workers, the median earnings of women had been approaching those of men because women's earnings were growing faster. But since the Great Recession, women who work full-time have lost ground while men have made some gains. Consequently, women's earnings have slipped as a percentage of men's since peaking in 2005.

■ The earnings gap between men and women should begin to shrink again as younger, well-educated women replace older women in the labor force.

Since 2005, women have lost some ground relative to men

(median earnings of people aged 15 or older who work full-time year-round, by sex, 2005 and 2011; in 2011 dollars)

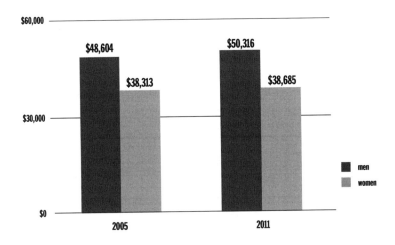

Table 4.11 Women's Earnings as a Percentage of Men's Earnings, 1990 to 2011

(median earnings of people aged 15 or older who work full-time, year-round, by sex, and index of men's earnings to women's, 1990 to 2011; percent change in earnings for selected years; in 2011 dollars)

	men	women	index of women's earnings to men's
2011	$50,316	$38,685	77
2010	51,733	39,651	77
2009	51,552	39,043	76
2008	49,910	38,324	77
2007	50,141	39,231	78
2006	50,151	39,030	78
2005	48,604	38,313	79
2004	49,613	38,241	77
2003	50,753	38,708	76
2002	50,641	38,718	76
2001	50,988	38,645	76
2000	50,794	38,036	75
1999	50,551	36,939	73
1998	49,954	37,005	74
1997	49,249	36,368	74
1996	47,872	35,592	74
1995	47,184	34,843	74
1994	47,440	34,913	74
1993	47,632	34,439	72
1992	48,425	34,700	72
1991	48,846	34,214	70
1990	48,342	34,350	71
PERCENT CHANGE			
2007 to 2011	0.3%	−1.4%	–
2000 to 2011	−0.9	1.7	–
1990 to 2011	4.1	12.6	–

Note: The index is calculated by dividing the median earnings of women by the median earnings of men and multiplying by 100. "–" means not applicable.
Source: Bureau of the Census, Current Population Survey, Historical Tables, Internet site http://www.census.gov/hhes/www/income/data/historical/people/; calculations by New Strategist

Men's and Women's Earnings Rise with Education

Those with professional degrees earn the most.

Earnings rise in lock step with education. Among men who work full-time, those with no more than a high school diploma earned a median of $40,447 in 2011. Those with a bachelor's degree earned a median of $66,196, and median earnings climbed to $83,027 for those with a master's degree. Men with a doctoral or professional degree had median earnings above $100,000.

The pattern is the same for women who work full-time. Among those who went no further than high school, median earnings were $30,011 in 2011. Among those with a bachelor's degree, median earnings were a larger $49,108. Women with master's degree earned a median of $60,304.

■ The higher earnings of college graduates has been the driving force behind the rise in college enrollment over the past few decades.

More education means higher earnings

(median earnings of men aged 25 or older who work full-time year-round, by educational attainment, 2011)

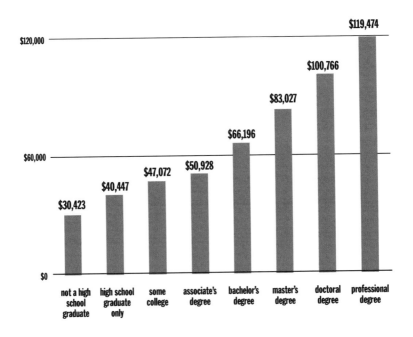

Table 4.12 Earnings of Men Who Work Full-Time by Education, 2011

(number and percent distribution of men aged 25 or older working full-time, year-round by earnings and educational attainment, and median earnings of those with earnings, 2011; men in thousands as of 2012)

	total	less than 9th grade	9th to 12th grade, no degree	high school graduate including GED	some college, no degree	associate's degree	bachelor's degree or more				
							total	bachelor's degree	master's degree	professional degree	doctoral degree
Total men with earnings	54,279	1,848	2,715	15,335	8,752	5,206	20,423	13,013	4,839	1,300	1,271
Under $10,000	692	63	89	230	90	38	182	133	38	1	10
$10,000 to $19,999	3,454	530	473	1,333	445	216	457	340	72	31	13
$20,000 to $29,999	6,765	576	746	2,760	1,257	517	907	694	155	35	25
$30,000 to $39,999	8,064	333	592	3,125	1,473	845	1,697	1,350	254	54	39
$40,000 to $49,999	7,326	187	336	2,593	1,378	834	2,000	1,538	339	57	66
$50,000 to $59,999	5,962	63	174	1,809	1,094	761	2,062	1,453	443	72	96
$60,000 to $69,999	4,865	42	101	1,208	965	545	2,006	1,352	483	61	109
$70,000 to $79,999	3,690	15	59	748	597	449	1,821	1,227	417	66	108
$80,000 to $89,999	2,735	8	37	497	353	295	1,542	994	383	88	76
$90,000 to $99,999	1,738	3	22	237	240	200	1,036	648	283	50	55
$100,000 or more	8,991	28	88	797	859	504	6,714	3,283	1,971	787	673
Median earnings	**$50,655**	**$25,223**	**$30,423**	**$40,447**	**$47,072**	**$50,928**	**$73,854**	**$66,196**	**$83,027**	**$119,474**	**$100,766**
Total men with earnings	100.0%	100.0%	100.0%	100.0%	100.0%	100.0%	100.0%	100.0%	100.0%	100.0%	100.0%
Under $10,000	1.3	3.4	3.3	1.5	1.0	0.7	0.9	1.0	0.8	0.1	0.8
$10,000 to $19,999	6.4	28.7	17.4	8.7	5.1	4.1	2.2	2.6	1.5	2.4	1.0
$20,000 to $29,999	12.5	31.2	27.5	18.0	14.4	9.9	4.4	5.3	3.2	2.7	2.0
$30,000 to $39,999	14.9	18.0	21.8	20.4	16.8	16.2	8.3	10.4	5.2	4.2	3.1
$40,000 to $49,999	13.5	10.1	12.4	16.9	15.7	16.0	9.8	11.8	7.0	4.4	5.2
$50,000 to $59,999	11.0	3.4	6.4	11.8	12.5	14.6	10.1	11.2	9.2	5.5	7.6
$60,000 to $69,999	9.0	2.3	3.7	7.9	11.0	10.5	9.8	10.4	10.0	4.7	8.6
$70,000 to $79,999	6.8	0.8	2.2	4.9	6.8	8.6	8.9	9.4	8.6	5.1	8.5
$80,000 to $89,999	5.0	0.4	1.4	3.2	4.0	5.7	7.6	7.6	7.9	6.8	6.0
$90,000 to $99,999	3.2	0.2	0.8	1.5	2.7	3.8	5.1	5.0	5.8	3.8	4.3
$100,000 or more	16.6	1.5	3.2	5.2	9.8	9.7	32.9	25.2	40.7	60.5	53.0

Source: Bureau of the Census, 2012 Current Population Survey Annual Social and Economic Supplement, Internet site http://www.census.gov/hhes/www/cpstables/032012/perinc/toc.htm; calculations by New Strategist

Table 4.13 Earnings of Women Who Work Full-Time by Education, 2011

(number and percent distribution of women aged 25 or older working full-time, year-round by earnings and educational attainment, and median earnings of those with earnings, 2011; women in thousands as of 2012)

	total	less than 9th grade	9th to 12th grade, no degree	high school graduate including GED	some college, no degree	associate's degree	bachelor's degree or more total	bachelor's degree	master's degree	professional degree	doctoral degree
Total women with earnings	40,885	779	1,380	10,040	6,989	5,131	16,566	10,537	4,700	635	694
Under $10,000	756	41	67	297	166	66	119	80	32	5	0
$10,000 to $19,999	4,380	343	532	1,766	760	405	576	442	109	11	11
$20,000 to $29,999	7,804	282	465	2,954	1,682	1,057	1,363	1,140	188	14	21
$30,000 to $39,999	7,992	76	204	2,393	1,814	1,079	2,427	1,870	484	41	31
$40,000 to $49,999	5,949	22	64	1,258	1,010	855	2,739	1,828	801	45	65
$50,000 to $59,999	4,317	5	26	620	629	659	2,380	1,520	701	77	82
$60,000 to $69,999	2,958	4	5	287	396	422	1,842	1,060	667	51	65
$70,000 to $79,999	1,983	3	4	175	190	254	1,357	762	451	68	76
$80,000 to $89,999	1,189	0	1	101	105	117	865	441	318	41	63
$90,000 to $99,999	784	1	6	57	83	81	556	316	193	15	32
$100,000 or more	2,775	2	5	135	153	135	2,345	1,074	758	267	245
Median earnings	$38,909	$20,102	$21,113	$30,011	$34,592	$39,286	$52,136	$49,108	$60,304	$80,718	$77,458
Total women with earnings	100.0%	100.0%	100.0%	100.0%	100.0%	100.0%	100.0%	100.0%	100.0%	100.0%	100.0%
Under $10,000	1.8	5.3	4.9	3.0	2.4	1.3	0.7	0.8	0.7	0.8	0.0
$10,000 to $19,999	10.7	44.0	38.6	17.6	10.9	7.9	3.5	4.2	2.3	1.7	1.6
$20,000 to $29,999	19.1	36.2	33.7	29.4	24.1	20.6	8.2	10.8	4.0	2.2	3.0
$30,000 to $39,999	19.5	9.8	14.8	23.8	26.0	21.0	14.7	17.7	10.3	6.5	4.5
$40,000 to $49,999	14.6	2.8	4.6	12.5	14.5	16.7	16.5	17.3	17.0	7.1	9.4
$50,000 to $59,999	10.6	0.6	1.9	6.2	9.0	12.8	14.4	14.4	14.9	12.1	11.8
$60,000 to $69,999	7.2	0.5	0.4	2.9	5.7	8.2	11.1	10.1	14.2	8.0	9.4
$70,000 to $79,999	4.9	0.4	0.3	1.7	2.7	5.0	8.2	7.2	9.6	10.7	11.0
$80,000 to $89,999	2.9	0.0	0.1	1.0	1.5	2.3	5.2	4.2	6.8	6.5	9.1
$90,000 to $99,999	1.9	0.1	0.4	0.6	1.2	1.6	3.4	3.0	4.1	2.4	4.6
$100,000 or more	6.8	0.3	0.4	1.3	2.2	2.6	14.2	10.2	16.1	42.0	35.3

Source: Bureau of the Census, 2012 Current Population Survey Annual Social and Economic Supplement, Internet site http://www.census.gov/hhes/www/cpstables/032012/perinc/toc.htm; calculations by New Strategist

Physicians Have the Highest Earnings

Among men and women who work full-time, cashiers earn the least.

Male physicians earned an annual median of $150,449 in 2011. Their female counterparts earned $120,136, putting both at the top of the pay scale. Male physicians earn 20 percent more than female physicians in part because male doctors are older and more experienced than female doctors and also because of the different medical specialties chosen by men and women. Also at the top of the pay scale for men and women are lawyers, CEOs, engineers, and computer scientists.

Cashiers are at the bottom of the pay scale. Male cashiers earned a median of only $20,249 in 2011, and their female counterparts earned an even lower $19,780. Also at the bottom of the pay scale for men and women are chefs and cooks, building maintenance workers, farmers, and personal care attendants.

■ Although it is assumed that sex discrimination explains the pay gap between men and women, a more important reason is the older age and higher educational attainment of the average male worker.

There is a big gap between the top and bottom earners

(median annual earnings of full-time workers who earn the most and least, by sex, 2011)

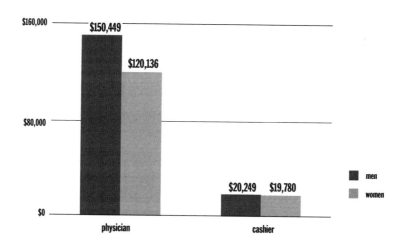

Table 4.14 Median Earnings of Full-time Workers by Occupation and Sex, 2011

(median earnings of full-time, year-round workers aged 15 or older by occupation and sex, and index of women's to men's earnings, 2011)

	men	women	index of women's earnings to men's
TOTAL FULL-TIME WORKERS AGED 15 OR OLDER	**$48,202**	**$37,118**	77
Management, science, and arts occupations	**71,495**	**50,829**	71
Management, business, and financial operations occupations	75,147	51,959	69
Management occupations	76,538	54,902	72
Chief executives, general and operations managers	102,304	75,147	73
All other managers	70,915	52,189	74
Business and financial operations occupations	67,457	50,624	75
Business operations specialists	65,024	49,498	76
Financial specialists	71,927	51,577	72
Professional and related occupations	70,157	50,194	72
Computer and mathematical occupations	78,177	66,163	85
Computer scientists, analysts, programmers, engineers, and administrators	77,006	66,070	86
Mathematicians, statisticians, operations research and other math occupations	94,272	–	–
Architecture and engineering occupations	76,511	65,007	85
Architects, except naval	93,809	–	–
Engineers	81,972	74,399	91
Drafters, engineering technicians, and surveying and mapping technicians	54,337	–	–
Life, physical, and social science occupations	66,465	55,961	84
Psychologists and sociologists	–	65,458	–
All other scientists	69,350	57,366	83
Science technicians	49,001	45,179	92
Community and social services occupations	41,771	40,307	96
Legal occupations	115,422	51,291	44
Lawyers, judges, and magistrates	122,471	91,544	75
Paralegals, legal assistants, and legal support workers	–	41,798	–
Education, training, and library occupations	55,605	45,102	81
Postsecondary teachers	71,371	60,260	84
All other teachers	51,284	45,505	89
Archivists, curators, museum technicians, librarians, and other technicians and assistants	46,984	26,470	56
Arts, design, entertainment, sports, and media occupations	51,797	41,567	80
Health care practitioner and technical occupations	78,464	53,480	68
Doctors	150,449	120,136	80
Nurses	69,709	56,072	80
All other health and technical occupations	57,605	46,654	81

	men	women	index of women's earnings to men's
Service occupations	$30,955	$23,367	75
Health care support occupations	29,084	26,567	91
Protective service occupations	51,812	41,740	81
Supervisors	66,963	–	–
Firefighters and police	66,699	60,590	91
All other protective service occupations	35,855	37,214	104
Food preparation and serving related occupations	23,128	20,411	88
Supervisors	28,680	22,258	78
Chefs and cooks	22,363	20,311	91
All other food preparation occupations	23,194	20,094	87
Building and grounds cleaning and maintenance occupations	27,078	20,996	78
Supervisors	38,982	30,744	79
All other maintenance occupations	26,271	20,498	78
Personal care and service occupations	33,901	22,461	66
Supervisors	47,695	30,684	64
All other personal care and service occupations	30,938	22,189	72
Sales and office occupations	42,366	33,254	78
Sales and related occupations	48,638	30,406	63
Supervisors	49,813	35,067	70
Cashiers	20,249	19,780	98
Insurance sales agents	60,767	38,305	63
Real estate brokers and sales agents	53,915	36,714	68
All other sales and related occupations	50,558	31,988	63
Office and administrative support occupations	37,340	34,772	93
Supervisors	51,144	42,039	82
Postal workers	55,977	51,718	92
All other office and administrative support occupations	35,233	32,564	92
Natural resources, construction, and maintenance occupations	40,480	30,182	75
Farming, fishing, and forestry occupations	25,249	21,019	83
Construction and extraction occupations	38,256	29,845	78
Construction	37,404	29,474	79
Supervisors	61,428	–	–
Carpenters	32,402	–	–
Electricians	49,294	–	–
Painters and paperhangers	26,816	–	–
All other construction trades	36,014	–	–
Extraction workers	68,473	–	–
Installation, maintenance, and repair occupations	43,645	35,601	82
Supervisors	49,733	–	–
Aircraft mechanics and service workers	56,636	–	–
Auto, bus, truck, heavy equipment mechanics	41,249	–	–

	men	women	index of women's earnings to men's
Heating, air conditioning, and refrigeration mechanics and installers	$39,861	–	–
Electrical power-line and telecommunications line installers and repairers	55,751	–	–
All other installation, maintenance, and repair occupations	42,442	$37,493	88
Production, transportation, and material-moving occupations	**39,266**	**25,851**	**66**
Production occupations	40,137	25,846	64
Supervisors	52,237	37,409	72
All other production occupations	37,394	25,152	67
Transportation and material-moving occupations	37,871	25,862	68
Supervisors	53,387	–	–
Aircraft pilots and flight engineers	141,305	–	–
Auto, bus, truck, ambulance, taxi drivers	41,485	26,175	63
All other transportation occupations	31,322	25,498	81
Armed Forces	**46,818**	–	–

Note: The index is calculated by dividing women's median earnings by men's median earnings and multiplying by 100.
"–" means sample is too small to make a reliable estimate.
Source: Bureau of the Census, 2012 Current Population Survey Annual Social and Economic Supplement, Internet site http:// www.census.gov/hhes/www/cpstables/032012/perinc/toc.htm; calculations by New Strategist

Every Household Type Has Seen Its Income Decline

Even married couples lost ground between 2000 and 2011.

The median income of American households fell 9 percent between 2000 and 2011, from $54,841 to $50,054 after adjusting for inflation. No household type escaped the economic decline. Among married couples, median income fell 4 percent during those years. Women who live alone also experienced a 4 percent loss. Median income fell 9 to 10 percent for female- and male-headed families. Men who live alone saw the biggest loss, their median income falling by 14 percent.

The median income of male-headed households, except married couples, was lower in 2011 than in 1990, after adjusting for inflation. Male-headed families saw their median income fall 6 percent during those years, and the median income of men who live alone fell 8 percent. In contrast, female-headed families saw their median income rise 12 percent between 1990 and 2011, and the median income of women who live alone climbed 6 percent. The median income of married couples grew 11 percent during those years.

■ The rise of dual-earner couples is behind the growing incomes of married couples since 1990—until the Great Recession intervened.

Men who live alone lost the most since the start of the Great Recession in 2007

(percent change in median household income by household type, 2007 to 2011; in 2011 dollars)

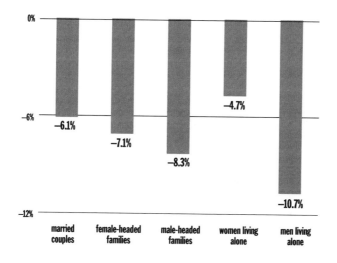

Table 4.15 Median Income of Households Headed by Men, 1990 to 2011

(median income of households headed by men by household type, 1990 to 2011; percent change for selected years; in 2011 dollars)

	total households	married couples	male-headed families, no spouse present	men living alone
2011	$50,054	$74,130	$49,567	$30,623
2010	50,830	74,782	51,384	31,181
2009	52,195	75,319	50,420	33,130
2008	52,546	76,266	51,379	32,096
2007	54,489	78,952	54,062	34,284
2006	53,768	77,768	52,516	34,880
2005	53,371	76,114	53,866	34,585
2004	52,788	75,981	53,605	32,641
2003	52,973	76,314	51,311	33,553
2002	53,019	76,579	52,147	33,515
2001	53,646	76,821	51,724	35,930
2000	54,841	77,412	55,057	35,462
1999	54,932	76,471	56,382	36,140
1998	53,582	74,791	54,311	35,856
1997	51,704	72,209	51,185	33,353
1996	50,661	71,167	50,898	34,329
1995	49,935	69,063	49,141	33,097
1994	48,418	67,592	45,729	31,838
1993	47,884	66,104	45,750	32,757
1992	48,117	65,912	47,605	31,379
1991	48,516	66,149	49,940	32,626
1990	49,950	66,721	52,634	33,304
Percent change				
2007 to 2011	−8.1%	−6.1%	−8.3%	−10.7%
2000 to 2011	−8.7	−4.2	−10.0	−13.6
1990 to 2011	0.2	11.1	−5.8	−8.0

Source: Bureau of the Census, Current Population Surveys, Annual Social and Economic Supplement, Internet site http://www .census.gov/hhes/www/income/data/historical/household/index.html; calculations by New Strategist

Table 4.16 Median Income of Households Headed by Women, 1990 to 2011

(median income of households headed by women by household type, 1990 to 2011; percent change for selected years; in 2011 dollars)

	total households	married couples	female-headed families, no spouse present	women living alone
2011	$50,054	$74,130	$33,637	$22,262
2010	50,830	74,782	32,978	22,828
2009	52,195	75,319	34,180	23,408
2008	52,546	76,266	34,548	23,000
2007	54,489	78,952	36,197	23,372
2006	53,768	77,768	35,493	23,811
2005	53,371	76,114	35,311	23,233
2004	52,788	75,981	35,514	23,234
2003	52,973	76,314	35,839	22,839
2002	53,019	76,579	36,257	22,363
2001	53,646	76,821	35,751	22,699
2000	54,841	77,412	36,914	23,283
1999	54,932	76,471	35,357	23,326
1998	53,582	74,791	33,613	22,607
1997	51,704	72,209	32,192	21,699
1996	50,661	71,167	30,780	20,877
1995	49,935	69,063	31,283	21,001
1994	48,418	67,592	29,822	20,156
1993	47,884	66,104	28,424	19,918
1992	48,117	65,912	28,846	20,313
1991	48,516	66,149	28,931	20,668
1990	49,950	66,721	30,142	20,932
Percent change				
2007 to 2011	–8.1%	–6.1%	–7.1%	–4.7%
2000 to 2011	–8.7	–4.2	–8.9	–4.4
1990 to 2011	0.2	11.1	11.6	6.4

Source: Bureau of the Census, Current Population Surveys, Annual Social and Economic Supplement, Internet site http://www .census.gov/hhes/www/income/data/historical/household/index.html; calculations by New Strategist

Male-Headed Families Have Average Incomes

Female-headed families have below-average incomes

Married couples are the only household type with a median income that exceeds the national median of $50,054. The median income of male-headed families is just below the national median, at $49,567. Female-headed families have a much lower median of $33,637. Among people who live alone, men have a substantially higher median income than their female counterparts—$30,623 versus $22,262.

Behind the higher incomes of married couples is the likelihood that there are at least two earners in the household. More earners also explain why male-headed families have higher incomes than female-headed families. Male- and female-headed families include not only single parents but also men and women living with adult relatives such as grown children, siblings, or parents who may be in the labor force. Male-headed families are more likely than female-headed families to have these additional earners in the household.

■ Every household type has seen its median household income fall because of the Great Recession.

Nearly half of male-headed families have incomes of $50,000 or more

(income distribution of male-headed families, 2011)

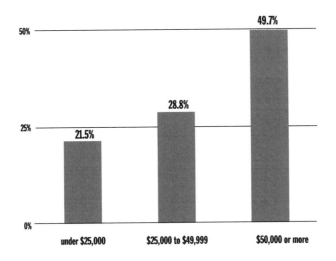

Table 4.17 Income Distribution of Households Headed by Men, 2011

(number and percent distribution of households headed by men by income and household type, 2011; households in thousands as of 2012)

	total	family households headed by men		nonfamily households headed by men	
		married couples	male householder, no spouse present	male householder total	living alone
Total households	**121,084**	**58,949**	**5,888**	**19,195**	**14,835**
Under $5,000	4,261	712	150	1,051	924
$5,000 to $9,999	4,972	552	140	1,149	1,058
$10,000 to $14,999	7,127	985	263	1,677	1,556
$15,000 to $19,999	6,882	1,528	322	1,410	1,266
$20,000 to $24,999	7,095	2,157	390	1,537	1,308
$25,000 to $29,999	6,591	2,255	352	1,340	1,118
$30,000 to $34,999	6,667	2,500	408	1,308	1,087
$35,000 to $39,999	6,136	2,617	354	1,025	831
$40,000 to $44,999	5,795	2,538	309	1,017	797
$45,000 to $49,999	4,945	2,369	273	799	608
$50,000 to $54,999	5,170	2,536	291	869	674
$55,000 to $59,999	4,250	2,264	295	635	436
$60,000 to $64,999	4,432	2,376	286	687	517
$65,000 to $69,999	3,836	2,211	222	498	303
$70,000 to $74,999	3,606	2,170	209	473	301
$75,000 to $79,999	3,452	2,310	176	355	229
$80,000 to $84,999	3,036	1,990	155	411	249
$85,000 to $89,999	2,566	1,737	146	281	176
$90,000 to $94,999	2,594	1,826	106	285	157
$95,000 to $99,999	2,251	1,565	137	187	98
$100,000 to $124,999	9,129	6,773	385	849	479
$125,000 to $149,999	5,311	4,176	217	421	186
$150,000 to $174,999	3,829	2,955	133	347	205
$175,000 to $199,999	2,046	1,646	49	173	57
$200,000 or more	5,106	4,200	121	413	214
Median income	**$50,054**	**$74,130**	**$49,567**	**$35,482**	**$30,623**
PERCENT DISTRIBUTION					
Total households	**100.0%**	**100.0%**	**100.0%**	**100.0%**	**100.0%**
Under $25,000	25.1	10.1	21.5	35.5	41.2
$25,000 to $49,999	24.9	20.8	28.8	28.6	29.9
$50,000 to $74,999	17.6	19.6	22.1	16.5	15.0
$75,000 to $99,999	11.5	16.0	12.2	7.9	6.1
$100,000 or more	21.0	33.5	15.4	11.5	7.7

Source: Bureau of the Census, 2012 Current Population Survey, Internet site http://www.census.gov/hhes/www/income/data/incpovhlth/2011/dtables.html; calculations by New Strategist

Table 4.18 Income Distribution of Households Headed by Women, 2011

(number and percent distribution of households headed by women by income and household type, 2011; households in thousands as of 2012)

| | total | family households headed by women | | nonfamily households headed by women | |
| | | married couples | female householder, no spouse present | female householder | |
				total	living alone
Total households	**121,084**	**58,949**	**15,669**	**21,383**	**18,354**
Under $5,000	4,261	712	1,087	1,262	1,154
$5,000 to $9,999	4,972	552	1,022	2,109	2,038
$10,000 to $14,999	7,127	985	1,208	2,993	2,874
$15,000 to $19,999	6,882	1,528	1,227	2,397	2,289
$20,000 to $24,999	7,095	2,157	1,258	1,753	1,599
$25,000 to $29,999	6,591	2,255	1,186	1,458	1,300
$30,000 to $34,999	6,667	2,500	1,096	1,356	1,223
$35,000 to $39,999	6,136	2,617	985	1,156	1,021
$40,000 to $44,999	5,795	2,538	943	988	812
$45,000 to $49,999	4,945	2,369	717	787	613
$50,000 to $54,999	5,170	2,536	676	799	633
$55,000 to $59,999	4,250	2,264	553	504	371
$60,000 to $64,999	4,432	2,376	502	581	453
$65,000 to $69,999	3,836	2,211	422	482	367
$70,000 to $74,999	3,606	2,170	350	404	268
$75,000 to $79,999	3,452	2,310	289	322	219
$80,000 to $84,999	3,036	1,990	241	239	163
$85,000 to $89,999	2,566	1,737	222	179	116
$90,000 to $94,999	2,594	1,826	193	183	115
$95,000 to $99,999	2,251	1,565	178	183	93
$100,000 to $124,999	9,129	6,773	590	531	291
$125,000 to $149,999	5,311	4,176	249	247	114
$150,000 to $174,999	3,829	2,955	189	205	110
$175,000 to $199,999	2,046	1,646	106	72	32
$200,000 or more	5,106	4,200	178	193	86
Median income	**$50,054**	**$74,130**	**$33,637**	**$25,492**	**$22,262**

PERCENT DISTRIBUTION

	total	married couples	female householder, no spouse present	female householder total	living alone
Total households	**100.0%**	**100.0%**	**100.0%**	**100.0%**	**100.0%**
Under $25,000	25.1	10.1	37.0	49.2	54.2
$25,000 to $49,999	24.9	20.8	31.4	26.9	27.1
$50,000 to $74,999	17.6	19.6	16.0	13.0	11.4
$75,000 to $99,999	11.5	16.0	7.2	5.2	3.8
$100,000 or more	21.0	33.5	8.4	5.8	3.4

Source: Bureau of the Census, 2012 Current Population Survey, Internet site http://www.census.gov/hhes/www/income/data/incpovhlth/2011/dtables.html; calculations by New Strategist

Married Couples Are the Nation's Income Elite

Dual-earner couples make the most money.

Married couples account for 78 percent of households with incomes of $100,000 or more. Most couples achieve this affluence only because both husband and wife are in the labor force. Among all couples, median household income stood at $74,130 in 2011. Among couples in which both husband and wife work, median income is a higher $95,234. When both husband and wife work full-time, median income is a substantial $107,141. Fifty-six percent of these couples make $100,000 or more.

Most husbands earn more than their wives. Fifty-five percent of husbands earn at least $5,000 more their wives. Twenty-eight percent of wives earned more than their husbands in 2011, up from 18 percent in 1990.

■ Until the Great Recession hit, the dual-income couples of the baby-boom generation had created record levels of affluence.

Single-earner couples make much less

*(median income of households headed by married couples,
by work status of husband and wife, 2011)*

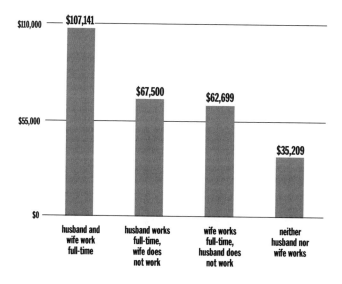

Table 4.19 Income Distribution of Married Couples by Age of Householder, 2011

(number and percent distribution of married couples by household income and age of householder, 2011; married couples in thousands as of 2012)

	total	15 to 24	25 to 34	35 to 44	45 to 54	55 to 64	65 or older total	65 to 74	75 or older
Total married couples	**58,949**	**1,058**	**8,658**	**11,954**	**13,299**	**12,093**	**11,886**	**7,596**	**4,290**
Under $5,000	712	38	124	119	119	192	120	51	69
$5,000 to $9,999	552	24	95	103	105	145	81	37	44
$10,000 to $14,999	985	64	151	151	177	198	244	136	108
$15,000 to $19,999	1,528	53	267	212	234	242	521	301	219
$20,000 to $24,999	2,157	76	321	309	303	349	799	386	413
$25,000 to $29,999	2,255	92	273	302	321	353	915	487	427
$30,000 to $34,999	2,500	99	403	353	340	396	909	451	458
$35,000 to $39,999	2,617	108	428	371	359	454	896	557	339
$40,000 to $44,999	2,538	79	395	435	414	500	716	418	298
$45,000 to $49,999	2,369	77	417	423	435	404	612	363	249
$50,000 to $54,999	2,536	61	440	472	497	470	596	393	204
$55,000 to $59,999	2,264	42	431	429	449	384	529	372	157
$60,000 to $64,999	2,376	62	416	532	482	440	444	312	132
$65,000 to $69,999	2,211	33	366	427	422	468	494	321	173
$70,000 to $74,999	2,170	27	380	449	520	445	349	230	118
$75,000 to $79,999	2,310	21	408	480	482	510	409	292	117
$80,000 to $84,999	1,990	21	350	462	449	405	304	205	99
$85,000 to $89,999	1,737	10	270	398	411	374	274	197	78
$90,000 to $94,999	1,826	7	258	413	491	406	252	188	64
$95,000 to $99,999	1,565	11	215	377	431	302	230	177	53
$100,000 to $124,999	6,774	26	954	1,691	1,784	1,462	859	675	184
$125,000 to $149,999	4,176	18	531	994	1,206	990	439	342	98
$150,000 to $174,999	2,956	7	299	709	954	692	291	238	55
$175,000 to $199,999	1,646	2	145	375	541	419	165	115	50
$200,000 or more	4,200	2	322	971	1,374	1,094	437	351	86
Median income	**$74,130**	**$38,491**	**$66,879**	**$84,246**	**$91,019**	**$81,006**	**$50,957**	**$57,913**	**$41,076**

PERCENT DISTRIBUTION

	total	15 to 24	25 to 34	35 to 44	45 to 54	55 to 64	65 or older total	65 to 74	75 or older
Total married couples	**100.0%**	**100.0%**	**100.0%**	**100.0%**	**100.0%**	**100.0%**	**100.0%**	**100.0%**	**100.0%**
Under $25,000	10.1	24.1	11.1	7.5	7.1	9.3	14.8	12.0	19.9
$25,000 to $49,999	20.8	43.0	22.1	15.8	14.1	17.4	34.1	30.0	41.3
$50,000 to $74,999	19.6	21.3	23.5	19.3	17.8	18.3	20.3	21.4	18.3
$75,000 to $99,999	16.0	6.6	17.3	17.8	17.0	16.5	12.4	13.9	9.6
$100,000 or more	33.5	5.2	26.0	39.7	44.1	38.5	18.4	22.7	11.0

Source: Bureau of the Census, 2012 Current Population Survey, Internet site http://www.census.gov/hhes/www/income/data/incpovhlth/2011/dtables.html; calculations by New Strategist

Table 4.20 Income Distribution of Married Couples by Work Status of Husband and Wife, 2011

(number and percent distribution of households headed by men by income and household type, 2011; households in thousands as of 2012)

	total	husband and wife work		husband works, wife does not		wife works, husband does not		neither husband nor wife works
		total	both work full-time	total	husband works full-time	total	wife works full-time	
Total married couples	58,949	31,241	16,591	13,038	10,161	4,731	3,023	9,954
Under $5,000	712	34	4	71	24	28	4	591
$5,000 to $9,999	552	44	3	143	32	75	14	301
$10,000 to $14,999	985	118	16	273	126	144	45	474
$15,000 to $19,999	1,528	214	35	450	262	169	67	716
$20,000 to $24,999	2,157	347	44	593	399	218	93	1,002
$25,000 to $29,999	2,255	437	43	597	392	261	138	970
$30,000 to $34,999	2,500	577	129	757	560	288	172	887
$35,000 to $39,999	2,617	733	173	740	538	328	178	827
$40,000 to $44,999	2,538	911	263	709	520	275	185	643
$45,000 to $49,999	2,369	1,011	338	664	514	246	158	463
$50,000 to $54,999	2,536	1,129	400	655	534	302	205	464
$55,000 to $59,999	2,264	1,165	484	510	404	228	144	349
$60,000 to $64,999	2,376	1,248	600	609	504	248	170	285
$65,000 to $69,999	2,211	1,207	592	517	432	183	143	295
$70,000 to $74,999	2,170	1,290	678	470	383	180	139	232
$75,000 to $79,999	2,310	1,413	807	463	404	185	135	242
$80,000 to $84,999	1,990	1,290	730	396	323	192	125	128
$85,000 to $89,999	1,737	1,158	611	314	257	127	97	137
$90,000 to $94,999	1,826	1,234	710	340	291	120	92	131
$95,000 to $99,999	1,565	1,081	634	261	215	88	64	125
$100,000 to $124,999	6,774	4,822	2,936	1,238	1,053	367	282	318
$125,000 to $149,999	4,176	3,198	2,136	576	481	202	157	187
$150,000 to $174,999	2,956	2,159	1,360	574	519	113	76	90
$175,000 to $199,999	1,646	1,304	838	243	206	44	35	47
$200,000 or more	4,200	3,119	2,030	875	789	120	102	54
Median income	$74,130	$95,234	$107,141	$62,195	$67,500	$55,636	$62,699	$35,209
PERCENT DISTRIBUTION								
Total married couples	100.0%	100.0%	100.0%	100.0%	100.0%	100.0%	100.0%	100.0%
Under $25,000	10.1	2.4	0.6	11.7	8.3	13.4	7.4	31.0
$25,000 to $49,999	20.8	11.7	5.7	26.6	24.8	29.5	27.5	38.1
$50,000 to $74,999	19.6	19.3	16.6	21.2	22.2	24.1	26.5	16.3
$75,000 to $99,999	16.0	19.8	21.0	13.6	14.7	15.0	17.0	7.7
$100,000 or more	33.5	46.7	56.1	26.9	30.0	17.9	21.6	7.0

Source: Bureau of the Census, 2012 Current Population Survey, Internet site http://www.census.gov/hhes/www/income/data/incpovhlth/2011/dtables.html; calculations by New Strategist

Table 4.21 Earnings Difference between Husbands and Wives, 2012

(number and percent distribution of married-couple family groups by earnings difference between husbands and wives, 2012; numbers in thousands)

	number	percent distribution
Total married couples	**61,047**	**100.0%**
Husband earns at least $50,000 more than wife	13,232	21.7
Husband earns $30,000 to $49,999 more than wife	7,495	12.3
Husband earns $10,000 to $29,999 more than wife	10,126	16.6
Husband earns $5,000 to $9,999 more than wife	2,458	4.0
Husband earns within $4,999 of wife	15,495	25.4
Wife earns $5,000 to $9,999 more than husband	1,780	2.9
Wife earns $10,000 to $29,999 more than husband	5,230	8.6
Wife earns $30,000 to $49,999 more than husband	2,508	4.1
Wife earns at least $50,000 more than husband	2,723	4.5

Note: Married-couple family groups include married-couple householders and married couples living in households headed by others.
Source: Bureau of the Census, America's Families and Living Arrangements: 2012, Current Population Survey Annual Social and Economic Supplement, Internet site http://www.census.gov/hhes/families/data/cps2012.html; calculations by New Strategist

Table 4.22 Wives Who Earn More than Their Husbands, 1990 to 2011

(number of married couples in which both husband and wife have earnings, number in which wives earn more than husbands, and percent of wives earning more than husbands, 1990 to 2011; couples in thousands as of the following year)

	total married couples	husbands and wives both have earnings	wife earns more than husband	
			number	percent
2011	58,963	31,165	8,755	28.1%
2010	58,667	31,573	9,215	29.2
2009	58,428	32,285	9,291	28.8
2008	59,137	33,905	9,002	26.6
2007	58,395	33,678	8,700	25.8
2006	58,964	33,838	8,688	25.7
2005	58,189	33,364	8,521	25.5
2004	57,983	33,110	8,387	25.3
2003	57,725	33,189	8,355	25.2
2002	57,327	33,531	8,394	25.0
2001	56,755	33,666	8,109	24.1
2000	56,598	33,876	7,906	23.3
1999	55,315	33,344	7,420	22.3
1998	54,778	32,783	7,435	22.7
1997	54,321	32,745	7,446	22.7
1996	53,604	32,390	7,327	22.6
1995	53,570	32,030	7,028	21.9
1994	53,865	32,093	7,218	22.5
1993	53,181	31,267	6,960	22.3
1992	53,090	31,224	6,979	22.4
1991	52,457	31,003	6,499	21.0
1990	51,675	29,079	5,266	18.1

Source: Bureau of the Census, Historical Income Tables—Families, Internet site http://www.census.gov/hhes/www/income/data/historical/families/

Female-Headed Families Have Below-Average Incomes

Among male-headed families, there is little variation in median household income by age of householder.

Female-headed families had a median income of $33,637 in 2011. Those headed by householders under age 35 have the lowest incomes, a median of only $24,000 to $25,000. The median income of female-headed families rises above $40,000 for those headed by women ranging in age from 45 to 74.

Male-headed families had a median income of $49,567 in 2011—almost equal to the $50,054 national median. Among families headed by men, there is little variation in income by age of householder and almost no decline in income in the older age groups.

Male- and female-headed families include not only single parents, but also men and women living with adult relatives such as grown children, siblings, or parents. Families headed by young women are most likely to include children and have only one earner, which accounts for their low incomes.

■ Both male- and female-headed families have lost ground because of the Great Recession.

Less than one-third of female-headed families have incomes of $50,000 or more

(percent distribution of female-headed families by income, 2011)

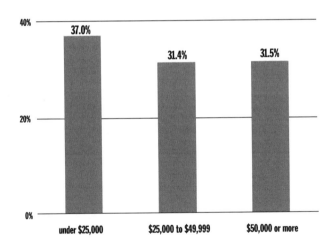

Table 4.23 Income Distribution of Male-Headed Families by Age of Householder, 2011

(number and percent distribution of male-headed families by household income and age of householder, 2011; male-headed families in thousands as of 2012)

	total	15 to 24	25 to 34	35 to 44	45 to 54	55 to 64	65 or older total	65 to 74	75 or older
Total male-headed families	5,888	819	1,432	1,157	1,112	795	573	317	256
Under $5,000	150	30	33	34	23	29	0	0	0
$5,000 to $9,999	140	32	28	33	21	25	3	2	1
$10,000 to $14,999	263	40	57	56	56	34	19	8	11
$15,000 to $19,999	322	64	72	45	53	49	37	13	24
$20,000 to $24,999	390	59	89	62	85	46	48	33	15
$25,000 to $29,999	352	34	115	48	56	38	62	34	28
$30,000 to $34,999	408	63	83	84	80	57	41	25	16
$35,000 to $39,999	354	50	81	78	71	44	31	15	16
$40,000 to $44,999	309	62	65	73	54	29	27	18	9
$45,000 to $49,999	273	32	58	70	46	41	26	13	12
$50,000 to $54,999	291	30	86	71	50	32	22	15	7
$55,000 to $59,999	295	29	72	58	49	44	42	29	13
$60,000 to $64,999	286	49	86	40	50	38	22	17	5
$65,000 to $69,999	222	30	47	38	42	39	26	10	16
$70,000 to $74,999	209	30	37	66	33	28	14	5	9
$75,000 to $79,999	176	9	49	41	32	29	16	4	11
$80,000 to $84,999	155	16	33	31	29	28	19	9	9
$85,000 to $89,999	146	13	43	38	28	18	6	3	2
$90,000 to $94,999	106	9	35	11	33	8	10	0	10
$95,000 to $99,999	137	31	42	24	15	23	3	1	1
$100,000 to $124,999	385	51	95	65	90	47	39	21	18
$125,000 to $149,999	218	10	57	36	53	31	29	12	17
$150,000 to $174,999	133	15	27	28	26	15	21	18	2
$175,000 to $199,999	49	10	12	4	12	5	5	5	0
$200,000 or more	121	18	32	22	22	21	6	6	1
Median income	**$49,567**	**$42,382**	**$51,968**	**$49,450**	**$50,719**	**$50,740**	**$47,295**	**$48,912**	**$46,663**
PERCENT DISTRIBUTION									
Total male-headed families	100.0%	100.0%	100.0%	100.0%	100.0%	100.0%	100.0%	100.0%	100.0%
Under $25,000	21.5	27.5	19.5	19.9	21.4	23.0	18.7	17.7	19.9
$25,000 to $49,999	28.8	29.4	28.1	30.5	27.6	26.3	32.6	33.1	31.6
$50,000 to $74,999	22.1	20.5	22.9	23.6	20.1	22.8	22.0	24.0	19.5
$75,000 to $99,999	12.2	9.5	14.1	12.5	12.3	13.3	9.4	5.4	12.9
$100,000 or more	15.4	12.7	15.6	13.4	18.3	15.0	17.5	19.6	14.8

Source: Bureau of the Census, 2012 Current Population Survey, Internet site http://www.census.gov/hhes/www/income/data/ incpovhlth/2011/dtables.html; calculations by New Strategist

Table 4.24 Income Distribution of Female-Headed Families by Age of Householder, 2011

(number and percent distribution of female-headed families by household income and age of householder, 2011; female-headed families in thousands as of 2012)

	total	15 to 24	25 to 34	35 to 44	45 to 54	55 to 64	65 or older total	65 to 74	75 or older
Total female-headed families	15,669	1,455	3,420	3,672	3,137	2,013	1,972	1,010	962
Under $5,000	1,087	205	354	235	169	84	41	18	23
$5,000 to $9,999	1,022	153	377	211	135	77	68	38	30
$10,000 to $14,999	1,208	145	346	257	202	129	128	56	72
$15,000 to $19,999	1,227	114	345	297	170	130	170	82	88
$20,000 to $24,999	1,258	126	285	313	209	159	167	64	103
$25,000 to $29,999	1,186	104	248	329	212	126	166	85	81
$30,000 to $34,999	1,096	101	227	280	206	120	161	76	85
$35,000 to $39,999	985	75	250	251	169	112	128	67	61
$40,000 to $44,999	943	70	180	211	219	133	130	68	62
$45,000 to $49,999	717	40	112	186	165	110	104	48	56
$50,000 to $54,999	676	52	114	150	154	102	104	61	43
$55,000 to $59,999	553	40	94	148	128	86	57	26	31
$60,000 to $64,999	502	36	75	124	113	90	64	38	26
$65,000 to $69,999	422	25	55	104	103	64	72	45	27
$70,000 to $74,999	350	30	44	74	106	52	43	24	19
$75,000 to $79,999	289	18	39	70	75	39	49	32	17
$80,000 to $84,999	241	17	34	53	58	37	42	21	20
$85,000 to $89,999	222	12	37	39	66	37	32	20	12
$90,000 to $94,999	193	7	26	37	49	49	25	16	9
$95,000 to $99,999	178	7	28	39	39	27	39	17	22
$100,000 to $124,999	591	27	71	124	175	103	91	55	34
$125,000 to $149,999	249	13	32	44	72	51	39	26	11
$150,000 to $174,999	189	5	15	42	58	41	27	19	8
$175,000 to $199,999	106	18	7	18	37	21	5	1	4
$200,000 or more	178	15	22	35	51	35	20	7	13
Median income	**$33,637**	**$24,410**	**$25,038**	**$33,251**	**$41,697**	**$42,134**	**$38,622**	**$41,450**	**$34,872**

PERCENT DISTRIBUTION

	total	15 to 24	25 to 34	35 to 44	45 to 54	55 to 64	65 or older total	65 to 74	75 or older
Total female-headed families	100.0%	100.0%	100.0%	100.0%	100.0%	100.0%	100.0%	100.0%	100.0%
Under $25,000	37.0	51.1	49.9	35.8	28.2	28.8	29.1	25.5	32.8
$25,000 to $49,999	31.4	26.8	29.7	34.2	31.0	29.9	34.9	34.1	35.9
$50,000 to $74,999	16.0	12.6	11.2	16.3	19.3	19.6	17.2	19.2	15.2
$75,000 to $99,999	7.2	4.2	4.8	6.5	9.1	9.4	9.5	10.5	8.3
$100,000 or more	8.4	5.4	4.3	7.2	12.5	12.5	9.2	10.7	7.3

Source: Bureau of the Census, 2012 Current Population Survey, Internet site http://www.census.gov/hhes/www/income/data/incpovhlth/2011/dtables.html; calculations by New Strategist

Older Women Who Live Alone Have the Lowest Incomes

Among 35-to-44-year-olds who live alone, the median incomes of men and women are almost identical.

The median income of the 18 million women who live alone stood at $22,262 in 2011, well below the $30,623 median of men who live alone. Behind the income gap is the differing age of men and women who live alone. Most men who live alone are of working age and in the labor force. Nearly half (46 percent) of women who live alone are aged 65 or older and most are not in the labor force. Their median income is just $18,179.

Incomes are more similar for men and women of working age who live alone. Among those aged 35 to 44, median income is almost identical—$38,924 for men and $38,155 for women.

■ The incomes of older women who live alone should rise in the years ahead as career-oriented boomer women age.

Men and women of working age who live alone have similar incomes

(median income of men and women who live alone, for selected age groups, 2011)

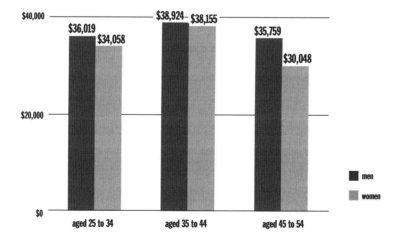

Table 4.25 Income Distribution of Men Who Live Alone by Age of Householder, 2011

(number and percent distribution of men who live alone by household income and age of householder, 2011; men who live alone in thousands as of 2012)

	total	15 to 24	25 to 34	35 to 44	45 to 54	55 to 64	65 or older total	65 to 74	75 or older
Total men who live alone	**14,835**	**654**	**2,323**	**2,137**	**3,052**	**3,206**	**3,462**	**1,829**	**1,633**
Under $5,000	924	115	146	98	260	205	100	55	44
$5,000 to $9,999	1,058	88	92	131	222	288	237	137	100
$10,000 to $14,999	1,556	84	120	122	278	375	577	279	298
$15,000 to $19,999	1,266	82	152	142	168	243	478	202	276
$20,000 to $24,999	1,308	75	208	174	198	243	410	198	212
$25,000 to $29,999	1,118	37	187	152	200	219	323	184	140
$30,000 to $34,999	1,087	69	207	156	167	218	270	128	142
$35,000 to $39,999	831	26	167	103	153	192	188	99	89
$40,000 to $44,999	797	25	171	134	167	168	133	72	61
$45,000 to $49,999	608	12	102	99	169	139	87	52	34
$50,000 to $54,999	674	12	124	134	135	150	119	80	39
$55,000 to $59,999	436	4	78	76	122	89	68	38	30
$60,000 to $64,999	517	13	127	88	136	86	67	42	25
$65,000 to $69,999	303	5	53	69	71	67	39	31	9
$70,000 to $74,999	301	1	51	72	58	67	52	28	24
$75,000 to $79,999	229	2	54	43	54	48	28	23	6
$80,000 to $84,999	249	4	42	50	70	52	31	19	12
$85,000 to $89,999	176	0	37	37	35	45	22	14	7
$90,000 to $94,999	157	0	22	20	40	42	32	26	6
$95,000 to $99,999	98	0	20	22	27	19	11	11	0
$100,000 to $124,999	480	1	78	107	126	88	80	42	37
$125,000 to $149,999	186	0	32	34	57	34	30	17	12
$150,000 to $174,999	204	0	26	39	41	64	34	19	15
$175,000 to $199,999	57	0	10	7	13	12	13	7	6
$200,000 or more	214	0	18	27	84	54	30	25	6
Median income	**$30,623**	**$17,486**	**$36,019**	**$38,924**	**$35,759**	**$30,507**	**$24,025**	**$26,425**	**$22,216**

PERCENT DISTRIBUTION

	total	15 to 24	25 to 34	35 to 44	45 to 54	55 to 64	65 or older total	65 to 74	75 or older
Total men who live alone	**100.0%**	**100.0%**	**100.0%**	**100.0%**	**100.0%**	**100.0%**	**100.0%**	**100.0%**	**100.0%**
Under $25,000	41.2	67.9	30.9	31.2	36.9	42.2	52.1	47.6	57.0
$25,000 to $49,999	29.9	25.8	35.9	30.1	28.0	29.2	28.9	29.3	28.5
$50,000 to $74,999	15.0	5.4	18.6	20.5	17.1	14.3	10.0	12.0	7.8
$75,000 to $99,999	6.1	0.9	7.5	8.0	7.4	6.4	3.6	5.1	1.9
$100,000 or more	7.7	0.2	7.1	10.0	10.5	7.9	5.4	6.0	4.7

Source: Bureau of the Census, 2012 Current Population Survey, Internet site http://www.census.gov/hhes/www/income/data/ incpovhlth/2011/dtables.html; calculations by New Strategist

Table 4.26 Income Distribution of Women Who Live Alone by Age of Householder, 2011

(number and percent distribution of women who live alone by household income and age of householder, 2011; women who live alone in thousands as of 2012)

	total	15 to 24	25 to 34	35 to 44	45 to 54	55 to 64	65 or older total	65 to 74	75 or older
Total women who live alone	18,354	724	1,758	1,319	2,500	3,697	8,355	3,369	4,987
Under $5,000	1,154	121	123	102	242	284	282	113	168
$5,000 to $9,999	2,038	112	119	87	310	421	989	386	604
$10,000 to $14,999	2,874	90	95	101	237	424	1,926	650	1,276
$15,000 to $19,999	2,289	86	102	70	179	354	1,497	460	1,037
$20,000 to $24,999	1,599	97	117	71	158	232	924	341	584
$25,000 to $29,999	1,300	69	128	57	122	231	692	265	427
$30,000 to $34,999	1,223	51	217	107	190	226	431	206	225
$35,000 to $39,999	1,021	24	147	101	169	265	316	160	156
$40,000 to $44,999	812	24	127	78	130	185	269	137	132
$45,000 to $49,999	613	5	82	94	117	127	189	98	90
$50,000 to $54,999	633	8	104	69	119	152	182	100	82
$55,000 to $59,999	371	13	60	42	71	107	79	58	21
$60,000 to $64,999	453	13	59	65	91	130	96	62	34
$65,000 to $69,999	367	9	48	51	75	110	74	52	21
$70,000 to $74,999	268	2	29	48	71	65	54	38	16
$75,000 to $79,999	219	0	26	32	52	46	63	47	16
$80,000 to $84,999	163	0	27	29	31	45	30	21	9
$85,000 to $89,999	116	0	17	12	15	50	22	17	5
$90,000 to $94,999	115	0	25	9	19	44	18	12	6
$95,000 to $99,999	93	0	10	13	16	15	39	25	15
$100,000 to $124,999	290	0	47	41	52	78	72	54	19
$125,000 to $149,999	115	0	13	7	11	41	39	20	19
$150,000 to $174,999	110	0	15	13	16	23	44	21	23
$175,000 to $199,999	32	0	10	1	0	13	7	7	0
$200,000 or more	86	0	11	17	8	29	21	19	2
Median income	**$22,262**	**$17,546**	**$34,058**	**$38,155**	**$30,048**	**$27,108**	**$18,179**	**$21,006**	**$17,088**
PERCENT DISTRIBUTION									
Total women who live alone	100.0%	100.0%	100.0%	100.0%	100.0%	100.0%	100.0%	100.0%	100.0%
Under $25,000	54.2	69.9	31.6	32.7	45.0	46.4	67.2	57.9	73.6
$25,000 to $49,999	27.1	23.9	39.9	33.1	29.1	28.0	22.7	25.7	20.7
$50,000 to $74,999	11.4	6.2	17.1	20.8	17.1	15.3	5.8	9.2	3.5
$75,000 to $99,999	3.8	0.0	6.0	7.2	5.3	5.4	2.1	3.6	1.0
$100,000 or more	3.4	0.0	5.5	6.0	3.5	5.0	2.2	3.6	1.3

Source: Bureau of the Census, 2012 Current Population Survey, Internet site http://www.census.gov/hhes/www/income/data/incpovhlth/2011/dtables.html; calculations by New Strategist

Most of the Nation's Poor Are Female

The poverty rate of the nation's males is close to a record high.

In 2011, females accounted for the 56 percent majority of people living in poverty. This figure is down slightly from 58 percent in 1990. Overall, 16.3 percent of females are poor, up from 12.6 percent in 2000. The male poverty rate of 13.6 percent in 2011 was close to the record high of 14.0 percent reached in 2010.

Among males and females, blacks are most likely to be poor. In 2011, 29.4 percent of black females and 25.4 percent of black males had incomes below poverty level. Hispanics were not far behind with a poverty rate of 27.7 percent among females and 23.0 percent among males. Non-Hispanic whites have the lowest poverty rates—10.9 percent of females and 8.7 percent of males are poor.

The strong economy of the late 1990s reduced poverty for most Americans—especially for female-headed families. In 1990, 44.5 percent of female-headed families with children under age 18 were poor. The figure fell through the 1990s to a low of 33.0 percent in 2000. Since then, the poverty rate for these families has climbed to 40.9 percent, but still below the 1990 level. Among male-headed families with children, the poverty rate is a smaller 21.9 percent, and only 8.8 percent of married couples with children are poor.

■ Female-headed families with children are vulnerable to poverty because they are likely to have only one or even no earners in the home.

The poverty rate fell then climbed for female-headed families with children

*(percent of female-headed families with children under age 18
living below poverty level, 1990 to 2011)*

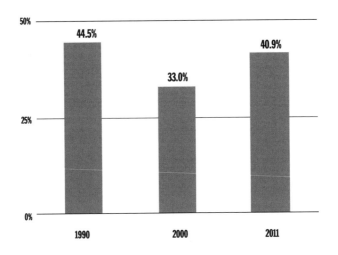

Table 4.27 Females in Poverty, 1990 to 2011

(number and percent of total people below poverty level, number and percent of females below poverty level, and female share of poor, 1990 to 2011; people in thousands as of the following year)

	total poor		females in poverty		
	number	percent	number	percent	share of poor
2011	46,247	15.0%	25,746	16.3%	55.7%
2010	46,343	15.1	25,451	16.3	54.9
2009	43,569	14.3	24,094	15.6	55.3
2008	39,829	13.2	22,131	14.4	55.6
2007	37,276	12.5	20,973	13.8	56.3
2006	36,460	12.3	20,460	13.6	56.1
2005	36,950	12.6	21,000	14.1	56.8
2004	37,040	12.7	20,641	13.9	55.7
2003	35,861	12.5	20,078	13.7	56.0
2002	34,570	12.1	19,408	13.3	56.1
2001	32,907	11.7	18,580	12.9	56.5
2000	31,581	11.3	18,045	12.6	57.1
1999	32,791	11.9	18,712	13.2	57.1
1998	34,476	12.7	19,764	14.3	57.3
1997	35,574	13.3	20,387	14.9	57.3
1996	36,529	13.7	20,918	15.4	57.3
1995	36,425	13.8	20,742	15.4	56.9
1994	38,059	14.5	21,744	16.3	57.1
1993	39,265	15.1	22,365	16.9	57.0
1992	38,014	14.8	21,792	16.6	57.3
1991	35,708	14.2	20,626	16.0	57.8
1990	33,585	13.5	19,373	15.2	57.7

Source: Bureau of the Census, Current Population Surveys, Historical Poverty Tables, Internet site http://www.census.gov/hhes/ www/poverty/data/historical/people.html; calculations by New Strategist

Table 4.28 Males in Poverty, 1990 to 2011

(number and percent of total people below poverty level, number and percent of males below poverty level, and male share of poor, 1990 to 2011; people in thousands as of the following year)

	total poor		males in poverty		
	number	percent	number	percent	share of poor
2011	46,247	15.0%	20,501	13.6%	44.3%
2010	46,343	15.1	20,893	14.0	45.1
2009	43,569	14.3	19,475	13.0	44.7
2008	39,829	13.2	17,698	12.0	44.4
2007	37,276	12.5	16,302	11.1	43.7
2006	36,460	12.3	16,000	11.0	43.9
2005	36,950	12.6	15,950	11.1	43.2
2004	37,040	12.7	16,399	11.5	44.3
2003	35,861	12.5	15,783	11.2	44.0
2002	34,570	12.1	15,162	10.9	43.9
2001	32,907	11.7	14,327	10.4	43.5
2000	31,581	11.3	13,536	9.9	42.9
1999	32,791	11.9	14,079	10.4	42.9
1998	34,476	12.7	14,712	11.1	42.7
1997	35,574	13.3	15,187	11.6	42.7
1996	36,529	13.7	15,611	12.0	42.7
1995	36,425	13.8	15,683	12.2	43.1
1994	38,059	14.5	16,316	12.8	42.9
1993	39,265	15.1	16,900	13.3	43.0
1992	38,014	14.8	16,222	12.9	42.7
1991	35,708	14.2	15,082	12.3	42.2
1990	33,585	13.5	14,211	11.7	42.3

Source: Bureau of the Census, Current Population Surveys, Historical Poverty Tables, Internet site http://www.census.gov/hhes/ www/poverty/data/historical/people.html; calculations by New Strategist

Table 4.29 Females in Poverty by Age, Race, and Hispanic Origin, 2011

(number and percent of females below poverty level by age, race, and Hispanic origin, 2011; females in thousands as of 2012)

NUMBER IN POVERTY	total	Asian	black	Hispanic	non-Hispanic white
Total females	**25,746**	**1,151**	**6,650**	**7,166**	**10,806**
Under age 18	8,002	292	2,413	3,036	2,334
Aged 18 to 24	3,487	222	893	824	1,556
Aged 25 to 34	4,021	177	993	1,203	1,642
Aged 35 to 44	2,827	150	660	873	1,150
Aged 45 to 54	2,656	105	732	494	1,311
Aged 55 to 59	1,221	42	316	197	662
Aged 60 to 64	1,045	42	182	197	599
Aged 65 or older	2,486	121	462	342	1,552
POVERTY RATE					
Total females	**16.3%**	**12.3%**	**29.4%**	**27.7%**	**10.9%**
Under age 18	22.2	12.8	38.1	35.2	12.3
Aged 18 to 24	23.3	24.5	34.2	27.8	18.4
Aged 25 to 34	19.4	11.5	31.7	29.5	13.8
Aged 35 to 44	14.0	10.0	22.6	23.6	9.5
Aged 45 to 54	11.8	8.6	24.0	17.0	8.7
Aged 55 to 59	11.5	7.6	24.2	18.8	8.7
Aged 60 to 64	11.3	10.0	16.8	24.4	8.8
Aged 65 or older	10.7	13.4	20.8	19.7	8.5

Source: Bureau of the Census, 2012 Current Population Survey, Internet site http://www.census.gov/hhes/www/cpstables/ 032012/pov/toc.htm; calculations by New Strategist

Table 4.30 Males in Poverty by Age, Race, and Hispanic Origin, 2011

(number and percent of males below poverty level by age, race, and Hispanic origin, 2011; males in thousands as of 2012)

NUMBER IN POVERTY	total	Asian	black	Hispanic	non-Hispanic white
Total males	**20,501**	**1,038**	**5,079**	**6,078**	**8,366**
Under age 18	8,132	315	2,436	2,972	2,516
Aged 18 to 24	2,722	198	643	683	1,192
Aged 25 to 34	2,516	170	530	758	1,095
Aged 35 to 44	2,046	115	377	707	841
Aged 45 to 54	2,138	112	510	447	1,035
Aged 55 to 59	960	24	260	161	497
Aged 60 to 64	854	41	146	123	532
Aged 65 or older	1,134	64	178	227	658
POVERTY RATE					
Total males	**13.6%**	**12.2%**	**25.4%**	**23.0%**	**8.7%**
Under age 18	21.6	13.8	36.7	33.1	12.6
Aged 18 to 24	18.0	21.2	27.3	20.9	14.0
Aged 25 to 34	12.3	12.1	20.0	17.0	9.1
Aged 35 to 44	10.4	8.8	15.7	18.5	7.0
Aged 45 to 54	10.0	10.1	19.8	15.4	7.0
Aged 55 to 59	9.7	5.7	23.6	16.4	6.8
Aged 60 to 64	10.3	11.2	18.9	17.4	8.4
Aged 65 or older	6.2	9.4	11.9	17.5	4.5

Source: Bureau of the Census, 2012 Current Population Survey, Internet site http://www.census.gov/hhes/www/cpstables/032012/pov/toc.htm; calculations by New Strategist

Table 4.31 Married-Couple Families in Poverty, 1990 to 2011

(total number of married-couple families, and number and percent below poverty level by presence of children under age 18 at home, 1990 to 2011; families in thousands as of the following year)

	total married couples			married couples with children		
		in poverty			in poverty	
	total	number	percent	total	number	percent
2011	58,963	3,652	6.2%	25,081	2,216	8.8%
2010	58,667	3,681	6.3	25,687	2,309	9.0
2009	58,428	3,409	5.8	26,119	2,161	8.3
2008	59,137	3,261	5.5	26,490	1,989	7.5
2007	58,395	2,849	4.9	26,450	1,765	6.7
2006	58,964	2,910	4.9	27,317	1,746	6.4
2005	58,189	2,944	5.1	27,147	1,777	6.5
2004	57,983	3,216	5.5	27,137	1,903	7.0
2003	57,725	3,115	5.4	26,959	1,885	7.0
2002	57,327	3,052	5.3	27,052	1,831	6.8
2001	56,755	2,760	4.9	26,931	1,643	6.1
2000	56,598	2,637	4.7	27,121	1,615	6.0
1999	56,290	2,748	4.9	26,694	1,711	6.4
1998	54,778	2,879	5.3	26,226	1,822	6.9
1997	54,321	2,821	5.2	26,430	1,863	7.1
1996	53,604	3,010	5.6	26,184	1,964	7.5
1995	53,570	2,982	5.6	26,034	1,961	7.5
1994	53,865	3,272	6.1	26,367	2,197	8.3
1993	53,181	3,481	6.5	26,121	2,363	9.0
1992	53,090	3,385	6.4	25,907	2,237	8.6
1991	52,457	3,158	6.0	25,357	2,106	8.3
1990	52,147	2,981	5.7	25,410	1,990	7.8

Source: Bureau of the Census, Current Population Surveys, Historical Poverty Tables, Internet site http://www.census.gov/hhes/ www/poverty/data/historical/people.html; calculations by New Strategist

Table 4.32 Female-Headed Families in Poverty, 1990 to 2011

(total number of female-headed families, and number and percent below poverty level by presence of children under age 18 at home, 1990 to 2011; families in thousands as of the following year)

| | total female-headed families | | | female-headed families with children | | |
| | | in poverty | | | in poverty | |
	total	number	percent	total	number	percent
2011	15,678	4,894	31.2%	10,379	4,243	40.9%
2010	15,243	4,827	31.7	10,178	4,163	40.9
2009	14,857	4,441	29.9	9,872	3,800	38.5
2008	14,482	4,163	28.7	9,796	3,645	37.2
2007	14,411	4,078	28.3	9,718	3,593	37.0
2006	14,424	4,087	28.3	9,894	3,615	36.5
2005	14,095	4,044	28.7	9,638	3,493	36.2
2004	13,981	3,962	28.3	9,676	3,477	35.9
2003	13,791	3,856	28.0	9,614	3,416	35.5
2002	13,626	3,613	26.5	9,414	3,171	33.7
2001	13,146	3,470	26.4	9,171	3,083	33.6
2000	12,903	3,278	25.4	8,813	2,906	33.0
1999	12,818	3,559	27.8	8,793	3,139	35.7
1998	12,796	3,831	29.9	8,934	3,456	38.7
1997	12,652	3,995	31.6	8,822	3,614	41.0
1996	12,790	4,167	32.6	8,957	3,755	41.9
1995	12,514	4,057	32.4	8,751	3,634	41.5
1994	12,220	4,232	34.6	8,665	3,816	44.0
1993	12,411	4,424	35.6	8,758	4,034	46.1
1992	12,061	4,275	35.4	8,375	3,867	46.2
1991	11,693	4,161	35.6	7,991	3,767	47.1
1990	11,268	3,768	33.4	7,707	3,426	44.5

Source: Bureau of the Census, Current Population Surveys, Historical Poverty Tables, Internet site http://www.census.gov/hhes/www/poverty/data/historical/people.html; calculations by New Strategist

Table 4.33 Male-Headed Families in Poverty, 1990 to 2011

(total number of male-headed families, and number and percent below poverty level by presence of children under age 18 at home, 1990 to 2011; families in thousands as of the following year)

	total male-headed families			male-headed families with children		
		in poverty			in poverty	
	total	number	percent	total	number	percent
2011	5,888	950	16.1%	2,976	652	21.9%
2010	5,649	892	15.8	2,789	673	24.1
2009	5,582	942	16.9	2,829	670	23.7
2008	5,255	723	13.8	2,676	471	17.6
2007	5,103	696	13.6	2,700	471	17.5
2006	5,067	671	13.2	2,569	461	17.9
2005	5,134	669	13.0	2,609	459	17.6
2004	4,901	657	13.4	2,562	439	17.1
2003	4,717	636	13.5	2,456	470	19.1
2002	4,663	564	12.1	2,380	395	16.6
2001	4,440	583	13.1	2,325	412	17.7
2000	4,277	485	11.3	2,256	345	15.3
1999	4,099	485	11.8	2,200	360	16.3
1998	3,977	476	12.0	2,107	350	16.6
1997	3,911	507	13.0	2,175	407	18.7
1996	3,847	531	13.8	2,063	412	20.0
1995	3,513	493	14.0	1,934	381	19.7
1994	3,228	549	17.0	1,750	395	22.6
1993	2,914	488	16.8	1,577	354	22.5
1992	3,065	484	15.8	1,569	353	22.5
1991	3,025	392	13.0	1,513	297	19.6
1990	2,907	349	12.0	1,386	260	18.8

Source: Bureau of the Census, Current Population Surveys, Historical Poverty Tables, Internet site http://www.census.gov/hhes/www/poverty/data/historical/people.html; calculations by New Strategist

Labor Force

Labor force participation rate has declined for both men and women.

Participation rate is climbing among men and women aged 55 or older.

More than three out of four Hispanic men are in the labor force.

Hispanic men are more likely to be in the labor force than Asian, black, or white men. Among women, labor force participation rates are similar by race and Hispanic origin.

Dual earners are in the majority.

Fifty-two percent of married couples are dual-earners, while 23 percent have only the husband in the labor force.

Job tenure is rising.

The median number of years men and women have worked for their current employer is rising because of the aging of the labor force.

Many men work in blue-collar occupations.

Thirty-four percent of men are blue-collar workers, and 35 percent are managers or professionals. Among women, 42 percent work in managerial or professional occupations.

The number of older workers in the labor force will rise sharply.

The number of workers aged 65 or older will grow by more than 70 percent between 2010 and 2020 as boomers fill the age group.

Labor Force Participation Has Declined

The largest decline has occurred among teenagers.

The percentage of men and women in the labor force has declined since 2000. The largest drop has been among teenagers. The labor force participation rate of men and women aged 16 to 19 fell 17 to 19 percentage points between 2000 and 2012 as a growing percentage of young adults have gone to college.

In contrast, the labor force participation rate of men and women aged 55 or older has increased. Among men aged 55 to 64, labor force participation climbed from 67 to 70 percent between 2000 and 2012 as early retirement became less common. Among those aged 65 or older, the rate rose from 18 to 24 percent. The labor force participation rate of older women grew even more. Among women aged 55 to 64, the participation rate climbed from 52 to 59 percent. Among women aged 65 or older, the rate climbed from 9 to 14 percent.

■ The labor force participation rate of men and women aged 55 or older will continue to rise as boomers postpone retirement.

The labor force participation rate of older men is rising

(percentage point change in labor force participation rate of men by age, 2000 to 2012)

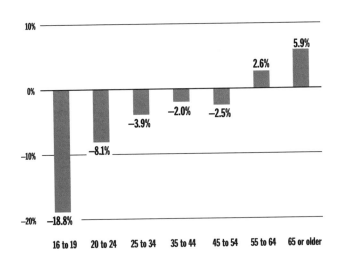

Table 5.1 Labor Force Participation by Sex and Age, 2000 to 2012

(civilian labor force participation rate of people aged 16 or older by sex and age, 2000 to 2012; percentage point change for selected years)

	2012	2010	2007	2000	percentage point change 2007–12	percentage point change 2000–12
Total men	**70.2%**	**71.2%**	**73.2%**	**74.8%**	**–3.0**	**–4.6**
Aged 16 to 19	34.0	34.9	41.1	52.8	–7.1	–18.8
Aged 20 to 24	74.5	74.5	78.7	82.6	–4.2	–8.1
Aged 25 to 34	89.5	89.7	92.2	93.4	–2.7	–3.9
Aged 35 to 44	90.7	91.5	92.3	92.7	–1.6	–2.0
Aged 45 to 54	86.1	86.8	88.2	88.6	–2.1	–2.5
Aged 55 to 64	69.9	70.0	69.6	67.3	0.3	2.6
Aged 65 or older	23.6	22.1	20.5	17.7	3.1	5.9
Total women	**57.7**	**58.6**	**59.3**	**59.9**	**–1.6**	**–2.2**
Aged 16 to 19	34.6	35.0	41.5	51.2	–6.9	–16.6
Aged 20 to 24	67.4	68.3	70.1	73.1	–2.7	–5.7
Aged 25 to 34	74.1	74.7	74.5	76.1	–0.4	–2.0
Aged 35 to 44	74.8	75.2	75.5	77.2	–0.7	–2.4
Aged 45 to 54	74.7	75.7	76.0	76.8	–1.3	–2.1
Aged 55 to 64	59.4	60.2	58.3	51.9	1.1	7.5
Aged 65 or older	14.4	13.8	12.6	9.4	1.8	5.0

Source: Bureau of Labor Statistics, Labor Force Statistics from the Current Population Survey, Internet site http://www.bls.gov/cps/tables.htm#empstat; calculations by New Strategist

Unemployment Is Highest among Young Men

Few middle-aged or older men are unemployed.

In 2012, the unemployment rate among men was 8.2 percent. Among women, it was a slightly lower 7.9 percent. Unemployment is much higher among the young, however. For men and women under age 25, the unemployment rate is in the double digits.

Labor force participation peaks at 91 percent among men in their thirties. At this age, most men are focused on their career as they shoulder the financial responsibilities of marriage and children. Women's labor force participation rate peaks at 76 percent among those in their forties.

Men's labor force participation falls below 80 percent in the 55-to-59 age group and continues to slide with age. Just 61 percent of men aged 60 to 64 are working, a proportion that drops to 37 percent among those aged 65 to 69. Among women, the decline is similar. Sixty-seven percent of women aged 55 to 59 are working, a figure that drops to 50 percent among 60-to-64-year-olds and to 28 percent in the 65-to-69 age group.

■ Unemployment is highest among the young because many are in low-paying, entry-level positions where job turnover is high.

More than 9 out of 10 men aged 35 to 44 are in the labor force

(labor force participation rate of men aged 16 or older, by age, 2012)

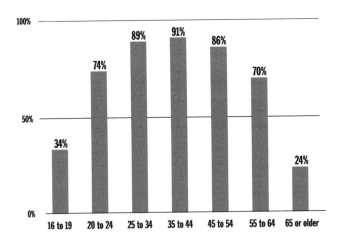

Table 5.2 Employment Status of Men by Age, 2012

(employment status of men aged 16 or older by age, 2012; numbers in thousands)

	civilian noninstitutional population	civilian labor force			unemployed	
		total	percent of population	employed	number	percent
Total men	**117,343**	**82,327**	**70.2%**	**75,555**	**6,771**	**8.2%**
Aged 16 to 19	8,657	2,940	34.0	2,152	787	26.8
Aged 20 to 24	10,889	8,110	74.5	6,948	1,163	14.3
Aged 25 to 34	20,205	18,083	89.5	16,607	1,476	8.2
Aged 35 to 44	19,416	17,607	90.7	16,483	1,124	6.4
Aged 45 to 54	21,339	18,363	86.1	17,221	1,142	6.2
Aged 55 to 64	18,416	12,879	69.9	12,068	811	6.3
Aged 65 or older	18,422	4,345	23.6	4,077	268	6.2
Total men	**117,343**	**82,327**	**70.2**	**75,555**	**6,771**	**8.2**
Aged 16 to 17	4,550	950	20.9	659	291	30.6
Aged 18 to 19	4,107	1,990	48.5	1,493	497	25.0
Aged 20 to 24	10,889	8,110	74.5	6,948	1,163	14.3
Aged 25 to 29	10,216	9,027	88.4	8,219	808	9.0
Aged 30 to 34	9,989	9,055	90.7	8,387	668	7.4
Aged 35 to 39	9,309	8,502	91.3	7,930	572	6.7
Aged 40 to 44	10,107	9,106	90.1	8,553	552	6.1
Aged 45 to 49	10,449	9,205	88.1	8,633	572	6.2
Aged 50 to 54	10,890	9,157	84.1	8,588	570	6.2
Aged 55 to 59	9,922	7,737	78.0	7,243	494	6.4
Aged 60 to 64	8,495	5,142	60.5	4,826	317	6.2
Aged 65 or older	18,422	4,345	23.6	4,077	268	6.2
Aged 65 to 69	6,499	2,412	37.1	2,252	159	6.6
Aged 70 to 74	4,537	1,096	24.2	1,025	71	6.5
Aged 75 or older	7,386	837	11.3	800	37	4.4

Note: The civilian labor force equals the number of the employed plus the number of the unemployed. The civilian population equals the number in the labor force plus the number not in the labor force.
Source: Bureau of Labor Statistics, Labor Force Statistics from the Current Population Survey, Internet site http://www.bls .gov/cps/tables.htm#empstat

Table 5.3 Employment Status of Women by Age, 2012

(employment status of women aged 16 or older by age, 2012; numbers in thousands)

	civilian noninstitutional population	civilian labor force				
		total	percent of population	employed	unemployed	
					number	percent
Total women	**125,941**	**72,648**	**57.7%**	**66,914**	**5,734**	**7.9%**
Aged 16 to 19	8,327	2,883	34.6	2,274	609	21.1
Aged 20 to 24	10,910	7,352	67.4	6,460	891	12.1
Aged 25 to 34	20,770	15,382	74.1	14,094	1,288	8.4
Aged 35 to 44	20,226	15,127	74.8	14,093	1,034	6.8
Aged 45 to 54	22,358	16,692	74.7	15,653	1,039	6.2
Aged 55 to 64	19,902	11,830	59.4	11,171	659	5.6
Aged 65 or older	23,447	3,383	14.4	3,168	214	6.3
Total women	**125,941**	**72,648**	**57.7**	**66,914**	**5,734**	**7.9**
Aged 16 to 17	4,341	1,003	23.1	760	242	24.2
Aged 18 to 19	3,986	1,880	47.2	1,514	367	19.5
Aged 20 to 24	10,910	7,352	67.4	6,460	891	12.1
Aged 25 to 29	10,437	7,765	74.4	7,073	692	8.9
Aged 30 to 34	10,333	7,617	73.7	7,021	597	7.8
Aged 35 to 39	9,716	7,156	73.7	6,630	526	7.3
Aged 40 to 44	10,510	7,970	75.8	7,462	508	6.4
Aged 45 to 49	10,909	8,251	75.6	7,738	513	6.2
Aged 50 to 54	11,449	8,440	73.7	7,915	525	6.2
Aged 55 to 59	10,653	7,171	67.3	6,773	398	5.6
Aged 60 to 64	9,249	4,660	50.4	4,399	261	5.6
Aged 65 or older	23,447	3,383	14.4	3,168	214	6.3
Aged 65 to 69	7,301	2,015	27.6	1,880	135	6.7
Aged 70 to 74	5,316	821	15.4	769	52	6.4
Aged 75 or older	10,830	546	5.0	519	27	4.9

Note: The civilian labor force equals the number of the employed plus the number of the unemployed. The civilian population equals the number in the labor force plus the number not in the labor force.
Source: Bureau of Labor Statistics, Labor Force Statistics from the Current Population Survey, Internet site http://www.bls.gov/cps/tables.htm#empstat

Hispanic Men Are Most Likely to Work

Among women, labor force participation rates are similar by race and Hispanic origin.

Seventy-six percent of Hispanic men are in the labor force—the highest labor force participation rate among racial and ethnic groups. The participation rate of Hispanic men exceeds that of Asians (72 percent), whites (71 percent), or blacks (64 percent). Among women, labor force participation rates are more similar, with 57 percent of Asians, Hispanics, and whites in the labor force and 60 percent of blacks.

Among Asian men, labor force participation is well below average for those under age 25 and above average for those aged 35 or older. Behind this pattern is the fact that most Asian men earn a bachelor's degree, keeping them out of the labor force until they graduate from college. Once in the labor force, these well-educated workers remain at work longer than average.

■ The labor force participation rate of black men is lower than that of Hispanics or whites in part because many black men are discouraged workers.

More than three of four Hispanic men are in the labor force

(labor force participation rate of men aged 16 or older, by race and Hispanic origin, 2012)

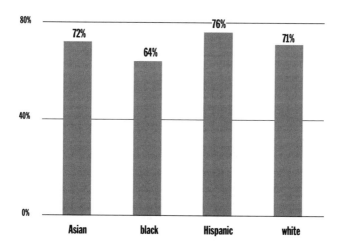

Table 5.4 Men's Labor Force Participation by Age, Race, and Hispanic Origin, 2012

(labor force participation rate of men aged 16 or older by age, race, and Hispanic origin, 2012)

	total	Asian	black	Hispanic	white
Total men	**70.2%**	**72.2%**	**63.6%**	**76.1%**	**71.0%**
Aged 16 to 19	34.0	18.7	25.6	33.0	36.7
Aged 20 to 24	74.5	57.0	66.4	78.5	77.2
Aged 25 to 34	89.5	87.3	82.5	91.6	90.9
Aged 35 to 44	90.7	92.4	83.5	91.1	91.8
Aged 45 to 54	86.1	90.6	75.9	87.3	87.5
Aged 55 to 64	69.9	75.2	57.1	70.3	71.6
Aged 65 or older	23.6	23.9	19.4	21.1	24.0

Note: The labor force includes both the employed and the unemployed.
Source: Bureau of Labor Statistics, Labor Force Statistics from the Current Population Survey, Internet site http://www.bls .gov/cps/tables.htm#empstat

Table 5.5 Women's Labor Force Participation by Age, Race, and Hispanic Origin, 2012

(labor force participation rate of women aged 16 or older by age, race, and Hispanic origin, 2012)

	total	Asian	black	Hispanic	white
Total women	**57.7%**	**56.5%**	**59.8%**	**56.6%**	**57.4%**
Aged 16 to 19	34.6	21.7	28.2	28.8	37.1
Aged 20 to 24	67.4	48.7	66.5	63.3	69.0
Aged 25 to 34	74.1	67.0	76.9	65.6	74.3
Aged 35 to 44	74.8	70.8	78.4	69.0	74.5
Aged 45 to 54	74.7	73.0	73.3	69.4	75.2
Aged 55 to 64	59.4	59.5	53.9	51.4	60.5
Aged 65 or older	14.4	13.9	14.4	13.2	14.4

Note: The labor force includes both the employed and the unemployed.
Source: Bureau of Labor Statistics, Labor Force Statistics from the Current Population Survey, Internet site http://www.bls .gov/cps/tables.htm#empstata

Most Working Men Have Full-Time Jobs

Many men who work part-time are looking for full-time work.

Eighty-one percent of working men have full-time jobs. The proportion of working men with full-time jobs rises from a low of 28 percent among men aged 16 to 19 to a high of 87 percent among those aged 25 to 54. Among working women, more than two out of three (68 percent) work full-time, including 74 percent of those aged 25 to 54.

Many men and women with part-time jobs would prefer full-time employment. Among men who work part-time, 29 percent are doing so only because of their difficulty in getting a full-time position. Among men aged 25 to 54 who work part-time, more than one-third (37 percent) would rather have a full-time job. About one in five women who work part-time would rather have a full-time job, a proportion that does not vary much by age.

■ Part-time work is more common among young and old because it provides a more flexible schedule for students and retirees.

More than one-third of men aged 25 to 54 who work part-time would prefer full-time employment

(among men who work part-time, percent who work part-time for economic reasons, by age, 2012)

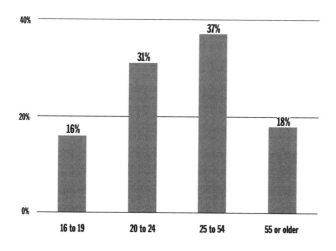

Table 5.6 Men Working Full- or Part-Time by Age, 2012

(number and percent distribution of employed men aged 16 or older by age and full- or part-time employment status, 2012; numbers in thousands)

	total	full-time		part-time	
		number	percent	number	percent
Total employed men	**71,765**	**58,149**	**81.0%**	**13,616**	**19.0%**
Aged 16 to 19	2,004	567	28.3	1,437	71.7
Aged 20 to 24	6,660	4,213	63.3	2,447	36.7
Aged 25 or older	63,100	53,369	84.6	9,731	15.4
Aged 25 to 54	48,174	41,828	86.8	6,346	13.2
Aged 55 or older	14,926	11,541	77.3	3,385	22.7

Note: "Full-time" is defined as 35 hours or more per week. "Part-time" is defined as less than 35 hours per week.
Source: Bureau of Labor Statistics, Labor Force Statistics from the Current Population Survey, Internet site http://www.bls
.gov/cps/tables.htm#empstat

Table 5.7 Women Working Full- or Part-Time by Age, 2012

(number and percent distribution of employed women aged 16 or older by age and full- or part-time employment status, 2012; numbers in thousands)

	total	full-time		part-time	
		number	percent	number	percent
Total employed women	**63,470**	**43,233**	**68.1%**	**20,236**	**31.9%**
Aged 16 to 19	2,155	408	18.9	1,747	81.1
Aged 20 to 24	6,220	3,233	52.0	2,987	48.0
Aged 25 or older	55,094	39,592	71.9	15,503	28.1
Aged 25 to 54	41,727	30,843	73.9	10,884	26.1
Aged 55 or older	13,367	8,749	65.5	4,618	34.5

Note: "Full-time" is defined as 35 hours or more per week. "Part-time" is defined as less than 35 hours per week.
Source: Bureau of Labor Statistics, Labor Force Statistics from the Current Population Survey, Internet site http://www.bls
.gov/cps/tables.htm#empstat

Table 5.8 Part-Time Workers for Economic Reasons, 2012

(number of people aged 16 or older who work part-time, and number and percent who work part-time for economic reasons, by sex and age, 2012; numbers in thousands)

		for economic reasons	
	total	number	share of total
Men who work part-time	**13,616**	**3,981**	**29.2%**
Aged 16 to 19	1,437	225	15.7
Aged 20 to 24	2,447	758	31.0
Aged 25 or older	9,731	2,997	30.8
Aged 25 to 54	6,346	2,372	37.4
Aged 55 or older	3,385	626	18.5
Women who work part-time	**20,236**	**4,022**	**19.9**
Aged 16 to 19	1,747	194	11.1
Aged 20 to 24	2,987	730	24.4
Aged 25 or older	15,503	3,098	20.0
Aged 25 to 54	10,884	2,418	22.2
Aged 55 or older	4,618	680	14.7

Note: "Part-time" is defined as less than 35 hours per week. Part-timers for economic reasons are people who work part-time because of slack work or poor business conditions, people who cannot find full-time jobs, and people who have seasonal jobs.
Source: Bureau of Labor Statistics, Labor Force Statistics from the Current Population Survey, Internet site http://www.bls.gov/cps/tables.htm#empstat

Working Parents Are the Norm

Few families can afford a stay-at-home mother.

In 2012, fully 58 percent of married couples with children under age 18 were dual-earners. The proportion reaches 63 percent among couples with school-aged children and is a smaller 53 percent among those with preschoolers.

Couples in which the husband works while the wife stays at home are in the minority but are still substantial in number. The husband is the only spouse employed in 7 million couples with children under age 18 (or 30 percent). Among couples with preschoolers, the father is the only one employed in an even larger 37 percent. Among female-headed families with children under age 18, 66 percent of mothers are in the labor force.

The majority of mothers are in the labor force regardless of the age of their children. Among women with children under age 1, the 56 percent majority is in the labor force—although only 34 percent work full-time. Fifty-three percent of women with school-aged children work full-time.

■ With working parents now the norm, family schedules, eating habits, and even vacation plans have changed.

Most married couples with children are dual-earners

(percent distribution of married couples with children under age 18 by parents' employment status, 2011)

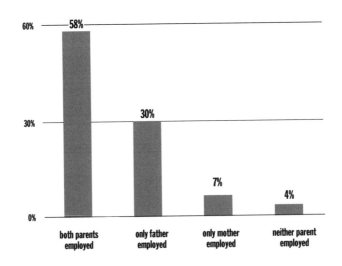

Table 5.9 Labor Force Status of Parents with Children under Age 18, 2011

(number and percent distribution of families with children under age 18 by family type and employment status of parent, 2011; numbers in thousands)

	with children under age 18	
	number	percent distribution
Married couples	**23,334**	**100.0%**
One or both parents employed	22,360	95.8
Mother employed	15,267	65.4
Both parents employed	13,649	58.5
Mother employed, not father	1,618	6.9
Father employed, not mother	7,093	30.4
Neither parent employed	974	4.2
Female-headed families	**8,538**	**100.0**
Mother employed	5,622	65.8
Mother not employed	2,916	34.2
Male-headed families	**2,397**	**100.0**
Father employed	1,908	79.6
Father not employed	489	20.4

Source: Bureau of Labor Statistics, Employment Characteristics of Families, Internet site http://www.bls.gov/news.release/famee.toc.htm

Table 5.10 Labor Force Status of Families with Children Aged 6 to 17, 2011

(number and percent distribution of families with children aged 6 to 17 and none younger by family type and employment status of parent, 2011; numbers in thousands)

	with children aged 6 to 17, none younger	
	number	percent distribution
Married couples	**12,927**	**100.0%**
One or both parents employed	12,388	95.8
Mother employed	9,118	70.5
Both parents employed	8,136	62.9
Mother employed, not father	982	7.6
Father employed, not mother	3,270	25.3
Neither parent employed	539	4.2
Female-headed families	**5,043**	**100.0**
Mother employed	3,575	70.9
Mother not employed	1,468	29.1
Male-headed families	**1,330**	**100.0**
Father employed	1,063	79.9
Father not employed	267	20.1

Source: Bureau of Labor Statistics, Employment Characteristics of Families, Internet site http://www.bls.gov/news.release/ famee.toc.htm

Table 5.11 Labor Force Status of Families with Children under Age 6, 2011

(number and percent distribution of families with children under age 6 by family type and employment status of parent, 2011; numbers in thousands)

	with children under age 6 only	
	number	percent distribution
Married couples	**10,407**	**100.0%**
One or both parents employed	9,972	95.8
Mother employed	6,149	59.1
Both parents employed	5,512	53.0
Mother employed, not father	636	6.1
Father employed, not mother	3,824	36.7
Neither parent employed	435	4.2
Female-headed families	**3,495**	**100.0**
Mother employed	2,047	58.6
Mother not employed	1,448	41.4
Male-headed families	**1,067**	**100.0**
Father employed	845	79.2
Father not employed	222	20.8

Source: Bureau of Labor Statistics, Employment Characteristics of Families, Internet site http://www.bls.gov/news.release/famee.toc.htm

Table 5.12 Labor Force Status of Men by Presence of Children under Age 18 at Home, 2011

(number and percent distribution of men aged 16 or older by labor force status and presence and age of children under age 18 at home, 2011; numbers in thousands)

	civilian population	civilian labor force total	employed total	full-time	part-time
Total men	**116,318**	**81,975**	**74,290**	**64,332**	**9,958**
No children under age 18	88,175	55,673	49,671	41,087	8,584
With children under age 18	28,143	26,302	24,619	23,245	1,374
Children aged 6 to 17, none younger	15,431	14,289	13,422	12,735	686
Children under age 6	12,712	12,013	11,197	10,510	687
Total men	**100.0%**	**70.5%**	**63.9%**	**55.3%**	**8.6%**
No children under age 18	100.0	63.1	56.3	46.6	9.7
With children under age 18	100.0	93.5	87.5	82.6	4.9
Children aged 6 to 17, none younger	100.0	92.6	87.0	82.5	4.4
Children under age 6	100.0	94.5	88.1	82.7	5.4

Source: Bureau of Labor Statistics, Employment Characteristics of Families, Internet site http://www.bls.gov/news.release/famee.toc.htm

Table 5.13 Labor Force Status of Women by Presence of Children under Age 18 at Home, 2011

(number and percent distribution of women aged 16 or older by labor force status and presence and age of own children under age 18 at home, 2011; numbers in thousands)

| | | civilian labor force | | | |
| | | | employed | | |
	civilian population	total	total	full-time	part-time
Total women	**123,301**	**71,642**	**65,579**	**48,223**	**17,356**
No children under age 18	87,558	46,423	42,620	31,194	11,426
With children under age 18	35,743	25,219	22,959	17,029	5,930
Children aged 6 to 17, none younger	19,596	14,904	13,756	10,450	3,306
Children under age 6	16,146	10,315	9,203	6,579	2,624
Children under age 3	9,259	5,613	4,977	3,486	1,492
Children under age 1	3,013	1,682	1,488	1,021	467
Total women	**100.0%**	**58.1%**	**53.2%**	**39.1%**	**14.1%**
No children under age 18	100.0	53.0	48.7	35.6	13.0
With children under age 18	100.0	70.6	64.2	47.6	16.6
Children aged 6 to 17, none younger	100.0	76.1	70.2	53.3	16.9
Children under age 6	100.0	63.9	57.0	40.7	16.3
Children under age 3	100.0	60.6	53.8	37.6	16.1
Children under age 1	100.0	55.8	49.4	33.9	15.5

Source: Bureau of Labor Statistics, Employment Characteristics of Families, Internet site http://www.bls.gov/news.release/famee.toc.htm

Dual-Earners Account for the Majority of Couples

In 52 percent of the nation's married couples, both husband and wife are in the labor force.

In nearly every age group, the majority of couples are dual-earners. The dual-earner share reaches 69 percent among couples aged 40 to 44. Only among couples aged 55 or older are dual-earners in the minority.

Twenty-three percent of the nation's married couples have only the husband in the labor force. This arrangement is most common among the youngest couples because many are new parents.

In 18 percent of couples, neither husband nor wife is in the labor force—most of them retirees. Neither spouse works in 54 percent of couples aged 65 to 74 and 82 percent of couples aged 75 or older.

■ As boomers age, a growing share of couples will have neither spouse in the labor force.

Fewer than one in four couples has only the husband in the labor force

(percent distribution of married couples by labor force status of husband and wife, 2012)

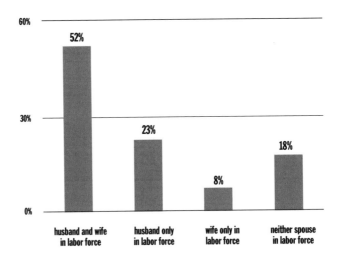

Table 5.14 Labor Force Status of Married-Couple Family Groups, 2012

(number and percent distribution of married-couple family groups aged 20 or older by age of householder and labor force status of husband and wife, 2012; numbers in thousands)

| | total | husband and/or wife in labor force | | | neither husband nor wife in labor force |
		husband and wife	husband only	wife only	
Married couples	**61,047**	**31,803**	**13,820**	**4,595**	**10,830**
Under age 25	1,247	653	491	52	51
Aged 25 to 29	3,576	2,217	1,118	149	91
Aged 30 to 34	5,482	3,618	1,564	195	105
Aged 35 to 39	5,727	3,803	1,616	203	104
Aged 40 to 44	6,622	4,593	1,583	257	189
Aged 45 to 54	13,822	9,335	3,071	834	582
Aged 55 to 64	12,431	6,188	2,726	1,625	1,891
Aged 65 to 74	7,751	1,208	1,288	1,059	4,197
Aged 75 or older	4,391	188	364	220	3,619
Married couples	**100.0%**	**52.1%**	**22.6%**	**7.5%**	**17.7%**
Under age 25	100.0	52.4	39.4	4.2	4.1
Aged 25 to 29	100.0	62.0	31.3	4.2	2.5
Aged 30 to 34	100.0	66.0	28.5	3.6	1.9
Aged 35 to 39	100.0	66.4	28.2	3.5	1.8
Aged 40 to 44	100.0	69.4	23.9	3.9	2.9
Aged 45 to 54	100.0	67.5	22.2	6.0	4.2
Aged 55 to 64	100.0	49.8	21.9	13.1	15.2
Aged 65 to 74	100.0	15.6	16.6	13.7	54.1
Aged 75 or older	100.0	4.3	8.3	5.0	82.4

Source: Bureau of the Census, America's Families and Living Arrangements: 2012, detailed tables, Internet site http://www.census.gov/hhes/families/data/cps2012.html; calculations by New Strategist

Job Tenure Has Increased

Among older workers, a growing share has been with their current employer for 10 or more years.

The median number of years male and female workers have been with their current employer has increased. Overall, male workers aged 25 or older had been with their current employer for a median of 5.5 years in 2012, up from 4.9 years in 2000. Female workers had been with their current employer a median of 5.4 years, up from 4.4 years in 2000. Behind the rise are two factors: the aging of the labor force and the postponement of retirement. Median job tenure for men aged 65 or older climbed from 9.0 to 10.2 years between 2000 and 2012. For their female counterparts, the median grew from 9.7 to 10.5 years.

Long-term employment has dropped among middle-aged men and women, but has climbed in the older age groups as workers postpone retirement. Among men ranging in age from 35 to 49, the percentage with long-term jobs fell by 3 to 4 percentage points between 2000 and 2012. But among men aged 55 or older, the percentage with long-term jobs increased. Among men aged 65 or older, the figure climbed from 49 percent to more than 55 percent. Long-term employment also climbed among older women.

■ The rise in long-term employment among older Americans is evidence of an end to early retirement.

Long-term employment has increased among men aged 65 or older

(percentage of men aged 65 or older who have been with their current employer for 10 or more years, 2000 and 2012)

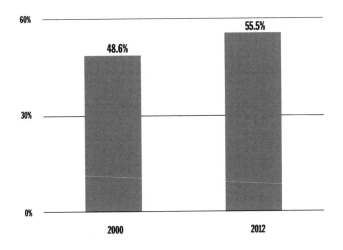

Table 5.15 Job Tenure of Men by Age, 2000 to 2012

(median number of years men aged 25 or older have been with their current employer by age, 2000 to 2012; change in years, 2000–12)

	2012	2010	2000	change in years 2000–12
Men, aged 25 or older	**5.5 yrs.**	**5.3 yrs.**	**4.9 yrs.**	**0.6 yrs.**
Aged 25 to 34	3.2	3.2	2.7	0.5
Aged 35 to 44	5.4	5.3	5.3	0.1
Aged 45 to 54	8.5	8.5	9.5	–1.0
Aged 55 to 64	10.7	10.4	10.2	0.5
Aged 65 or older	10.2	9.7	9.0	1.2

Source: Bureau of Labor Statistics, Employee Tenure, Internet site http://www.bls.gov/news.release/tenure.nr0.htm; calculations by New Strategist

Table 5.16 Job Tenure of Women by Age, 2000 to 2012

(median number of years women aged 25 or older have been with their current employer by age, 2000 to 2012; change in years, 2000–12)

	2012	2010	2000	change in years 2000–12
Women, aged 25 or older	**5.4 yrs.**	**5.1 yrs.**	**4.4 yrs.**	**1.0 yrs.**
Aged 25 to 34	3.1	3.0	2.5	0.6
Aged 35 to 44	5.2	4.9	4.3	0.9
Aged 45 to 54	7.3	7.1	7.3	0.0
Aged 55 to 64	10.0	9.7	9.9	0.1
Aged 65 or older	10.5	10.1	9.7	0.8

Source: Bureau of Labor Statistics, Employee Tenure, Internet site http://www.bls.gov/news.release/tenure.nr0.htm; calculations by New Strategist

Table 5.17 Long-Term Employment among Men by Age, 2000 to 2012

(percent of men aged 25 or older who have worked for their current employer for 10 years or more by age, 2000 and 2012; percentage point change, 2000–12)

	2012	2010	2000	percentage point change 2000–12
Men, aged 25 or older	**34.6%**	**34.3%**	**33.4%**	**1.2**
Aged 25 to 29	2.6	3.1	3.0	–0.4
Aged 30 to 34	13.2	14.3	15.1	–1.9
Aged 35 to 39	25.7	27.2	29.4	–3.7
Aged 40 to 44	36.9	37.5	40.2	–3.3
Aged 45 to 49	44.8	43.7	49.0	–4.2
Aged 50 to 54	51.4	51.3	51.6	–0.2
Aged 55 to 59	55.7	53.6	53.7	2.0
Aged 60 to 64	56.2	56.8	52.4	3.8
Aged 65 or older	55.5	51.9	48.6	6.9

Source: Bureau of Labor Statistics, Employee Tenure, Internet site http://www.bls.gov/news.release/tenure.nr0.htm; calculations by New Strategist

Table 5.18 Long-Term Employment among Women by Age, 2000 to 2012

(percent of women aged 25 or older who have worked for their current employer for 10 years or more by age, 2000 and 2012; percentage point change, 2000–12)

	2012	2010	2000	percentage point change 2000–12
Women, aged 25 or older	**32.8%**	**31.9%**	**29.5%**	**3.3**
Aged 25 to 29	2.3	1.6	1.9	0.4
Aged 30 to 34	11.8	11.1	12.5	–0.7
Aged 35 to 39	24.7	24.0	22.3	2.4
Aged 40 to 44	33.2	32.9	31.2	2.0
Aged 45 to 49	38.3	38.0	41.4	–3.1
Aged 50 to 54	45.5	46.5	45.8	–0.3
Aged 55 to 59	52.6	51.2	52.5	0.1
Aged 60 to 64	54.0	52.2	53.6	0.4
Aged 65 or older	55.6	54.3	51.0	4.6

Source: Bureau of Labor Statistics, Employee Tenure, Internet site http://www.bls.gov/news.release/tenure.nr0.htm; calculations by New Strategist

Men Dominate Most Occupations

Blue-collar jobs are overwhelmingly filled by men.

Although white-collar employment has been growing much faster than blue-collar for decades, many men continue to work in blue-collar occupations. In 2012, more than one-third (34 percent) of men worked in natural resources, construction, maintenance, production, or transportation occupations. This figure is nearly equal to the 35 percent of men who are managers or professionals. Another 31 percent of men are sales or service workers. Men account for 98 percent of electricians, 96 percent of aircraft pilots, and 95 percent of wastewater treatment plant operators.

Women are more likely than men to work in white-collar occupations. Forty-two percent of working women are managers or professionals, 31 percent are in sales or office occupations, and 21 percent are in service jobs. Only 6 percent work in blue-collar jobs. Women dominate some occupations. They account for 73 percent of human resource managers and psychologists, 98 percent of preschool teachers, and 99 percent of dental hygienists. In a few occupations, men and women are more evenly split, such as veterinarians (55 percent female), editors (51 percent), and postsecondary teachers (48 percent).

■ The earnings gap between the sexes is partly due to the different occupational choices of men and women.

Women choose different jobs from men

(female share of workers by selected occupation, 2012)

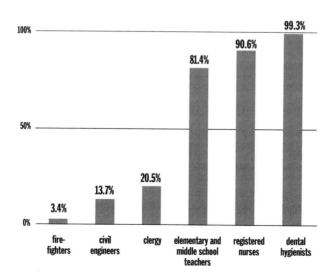

Table 5.19 Male Workers by Occupation, 2012

(total number of employed workers aged 16 or older in the civilian labor force, number and percent distribution of employed men, and male share of total, by occupation, 2012; numbers in thousands)

	total	men number	men percent distribution	men share of total
TOTAL EMPLOYED	**142,469**	**75,555**	**100.0%**	**53.0%**
Management, professional and related occupations	**54,043**	**26,208**	**34.7**	**48.5**
Management, business, and financial operations	22,678	12,779	16.9	56.3
Management	16,042	9,849	13.0	61.4
Business and financial operations	6,636	2,931	3.9	44.2
Professional and related occupations	31,365	13,429	17.8	42.8
Computer and mathematical	3,816	2,841	3.8	74.4
Architecture and engineering	2,846	2,457	3.3	86.3
Life, physical, and social science	1,316	720	1.0	54.7
Community and social services	2,265	819	1.1	36.2
Legal	1,786	885	1.2	49.6
Education, training, and library	8,543	2,253	3.0	26.4
Art, design, entertainment, sports, and media	2,814	1,456	1.9	51.7
Health care practitioner and technical occupations	7,977	1,998	2.6	25.0
Service occupations	**25,459**	**11,135**	**14.7**	**43.7**
Health care support	3,496	434	0.6	12.4
Protective service	3,096	2,449	3.2	79.1
Food preparation and serving related	8,018	3,648	4.8	45.5
Building and grounds cleaning and maintenance	5,591	3,430	4.5	61.3
Personal care and service	5,258	1,173	1.6	22.3
Sales and office occupations	**33,152**	**12,653**	**16.7**	**38.2**
Sales and related	15,457	7,922	10.5	51.3
Office and administrative support	17,695	4,730	6.3	26.7
Natural resources, construction, and maintenance occupations	**12,821**	**12,266**	**16.2**	**95.7**
Farming, fishing, and forestry	994	768	1.0	77.3
Construction and extraction	7,005	6,832	9.0	97.5
Installation, maintenance, and repair	4,821	4,666	6.2	96.8
Production, transportation, and material-moving occupations	**16,994**	**13,294**	**17.6**	**78.2**
Production	8,455	6,109	8.1	72.3
Transportation and material moving	8,540	7,185	9.5	84.1

Source: Bureau of Labor Statistics, Labor Force Statistics from the Current Population Survey, Internet site http://www.bls.gov/cps/tables.htm#empstat

Table 5.20 Female Workers by Occupation, 2012

(total number of employed workers aged 16 or older in the civilian labor force, number and percent distribution of employed women, and female share of total, by occupation, 2012; numbers in thousands)

	total	women number	women percent distribution	women share of total
TOTAL EMPLOYED	**142,469**	**66,914**	**100.0%**	**47.0%**
Management, professional and related occupations	**54,043**	**27,834**	**41.6**	**51.5**
Management, business, and financial operations	22,678	9,899	14.8	43.7
Management	16,042	6,194	9.3	38.6
Business and financial operations	6,636	3,705	5.5	55.8
Professional and related occupations	31,365	17,936	26.8	57.2
Computer and mathematical	3,816	976	1.5	25.6
Architecture and engineering	2,846	390	0.6	13.7
Life, physical, and social science	1,316	596	0.9	45.3
Community and social services	2,265	1,446	2.2	63.8
Legal	1,786	901	1.3	50.4
Education, training, and library	8,543	6,290	9.4	73.6
Art, design, entertainment, sports, and media	2,814	1,358	2.0	48.3
Health care practitioner and technical occupations	7,977	5,979	8.9	75.0
Service occupations	**25,459**	**14,324**	**21.4**	**56.3**
Health care support	3,496	3,062	4.6	87.6
Protective service	3,096	647	1.0	20.9
Food preparation and serving related	8,018	4,370	6.5	54.5
Building and grounds cleaning and maintenance	5,591	2,160	3.2	38.6
Personal care and service	5,258	4,085	6.1	77.7
Sales and office occupations	**33,152**	**20,500**	**30.6**	**61.8**
Sales and related	15,457	7,535	11.3	48.7
Office and administrative support	17,695	12,965	19.4	73.3
Natural resources, construction, and maintenance occupations	**12,821**	**554**	**0.8**	**4.3**
Farming, fishing, and forestry	994	226	0.3	22.7
Construction and extraction	7,005	173	0.3	2.5
Installation, maintenance, and repair	4,821	156	0.2	3.2
Production, transportation, and material-moving occupations	**16,994**	**3,701**	**5.5**	**21.8**
Production	8,455	2,346	3.5	27.7
Transportation and material moving	8,540	1,355	2.0	15.9

Source: Bureau of Labor Statistics, Labor Force Statistics from the Current Population Survey, Internet site http://www.bls.gov/cps/tables.htm#empstat

Table 5.21 Employment by Detailed Occupation and Sex, 2012

(total number of employed workers aged 16 or older in the civilian labor force and female and male share of total, by occupation, 2012; numbers in thousands)

	total	female share of total	male share of total
TOTAL EMPLOYED	**142,469**	**47.0%**	**53.0%**
Management, professional and related occupations	**54,043**	**51.5**	**48.5**
Management, business, and financial operations occupations	22,678	43.6	56.4
Management occupations	16,042	38.6	61.4
Chief executives	1,513	27.4	72.6
General and operations managers	1,064	29.1	70.9
Legislators	11	–	–
Advertising and promotions managers	77	49.4	50.6
Marketing and sales managers	967	45.2	54.8
Public relations and fundraising managers	58	69.3	30.7
Administrative services managers	144	44.1	55.9
Computer and information systems managers	605	26.8	73.2
Financial managers	1,228	53.5	46.5
Compensation and benefits managers	15	–	–
Human resources managers	224	72.7	27.3
Training and development managers	36	–	–
Industrial production managers	261	17.6	82.4
Purchasing managers	218	50.9	49.1
Transportation, storage, and distribution managers	287	15.6	84.4
Farmers, ranchers, and other agricultural managers	944	24.5	75.5
Construction managers	983	6.4	93.6
Education administrators	811	64.4	35.6
Architectural and engineering managers	120	10.9	89.1
Food service managers	1,085	47.2	52.8
Funeral service managers	13	–	–
Gaming managers	26	–	–
Lodging managers	154	45.0	55.0
Medical and health services managers	585	69.7	30.3
Natural sciences managers	18	–	–
Postmasters and mail superintendents	39	–	–
Property, real estate, and community association managers	644	50.7	49.3
Social and community service managers	315	70.5	29.5
Emergency management directors	6	–	–
Managers, all other	3,594	35.0	65.0
Business and financial operations occupations	6,636	55.8	44.2
Agents and business managers of artists, performers, and athletes	47	–	–
Buyers and purchasing agents, farm products	13	–	–
Wholesale and retail buyers, except farm products	198	55.2	44.8
Purchasing agents, except wholesale, retail, and farm products	261	55.1	44.9
Claims adjusters, appraisers, examiners, and investigators	323	63.4	36.6

	total	female share of total	male share of total
Compliance officers	199	50.6%	49.4%
Cost estimators	114	11.7	88.3
Human resources workers	603	71.8	28.2
Compensation, benefits, and job analysis specialists	71	81.1	18.9
Training and development specialists	126	56.4	43.6
Logisticians	94	36.8	63.2
Management analysts	773	39.8	60.2
Meeting, convention, and event planners	127	73.3	26.7
Fundraisers	86	75.3	24.7
Market research analysts and marketing specialists	219	54.2	45.8
Business operations specialists, all other	251	67.3	32.7
Accountants and auditors	1,765	60.9	39.1
Appraisers and assessors of real estate	93	40.6	59.4
Budget analysts	55	52.5	47.5
Credit analysts	30	–	–
Financial analysts	89	36.8	63.2
Personal financial advisors	378	31.2	68.8
Insurance underwriters	103	70.4	29.6
Financial examiners	14	–	–
Credit counselors and loan officers	333	59.2	40.8
Tax examiners and collectors, and revenue agents	82	62.4	37.6
Tax preparers	107	59.6	40.4
Financial specialists, all other	82	66.5	33.5
Professional and related occupations	31,365	57.2	42.8
Computer and mathematical occupations	3,816	25.6	74.4
Computer and information research scientists	29	–	–
Computer systems analysts	499	30.9	69.1
Information security analysts	52	15.1	84.9
Computer programmers	480	22.5	77.5
Software developers, applications and systems software	1,084	19.7	80.3
Web developers	190	33.7	66.3
Computer support specialists	476	27.1	72.9
Database administrators	101	36.6	63.4
Network and computer systems administrators	226	25.0	75.0
Computer network architects	127	8.1	91.9
Computer occupations, all other	341	24.4	75.6
Actuaries	26	–	–
Mathematicians	4	–	–
Operations research analysts	130	54.9	45.1
Statisticians	47	–	–
Miscellaneous mathematical science occupations	3	–	–
Architecture and engineering occupations	2,846	13.7	86.3
Architects, except naval	195	23.5	76.5
Surveyors, cartographers, and photogrammetrists	51	27.8	72.2

	total	female share of total	male share of total
Aerospace engineers	119	9.0%	91.0%
Agricultural engineers	4	–	–
Biomedical engineers	10	–	–
Chemical engineers	71	17.7	82.3
Civil engineers	358	13.7	86.3
Computer hardware engineers	91	15.1	84.9
Electrical and electronics engineers	335	9.0	91.0
Environmental engineers	43	–	–
Industrial engineers, including health and safety	197	18.8	81.2
Marine engineers and naval architects	8	–	–
Materials engineers	40	–	–
Mechanical engineers	288	4.5	95.5
Mining and geological engineers, including mining safety engineers	9	–	–
Nuclear engineers	11	–	–
Petroleum engineers	38	–	–
Engineers, all other	359	13.2	86.8
Drafters	149	16.6	83.4
Engineering technicians, except drafters	395	16.3	83.7
Surveying and mapping technicians	77	4.3	95.7
Life, physical, and social science occupations	1,316	45.3	54.7
Agricultural and food scientists	42	–	–
Biological scientists	101	50.1	49.9
Conservation scientists and foresters	25	–	–
Medical scientists	136	52.8	47.2
Astronomers and physicists	25	–	–
Atmospheric and space scientists	15	–	–
Chemists and materials scientists	105	44.2	55.8
Environmental scientists and geoscientists	105	25.7	74.3
Physical scientists, all other	154	35.1	64.9
Economists	26	–	–
Survey researchers	2	–	–
Psychologists	178	72.7	27.3
Sociologists	7	–	–
Urban and regional planners	28	–	–
Miscellaneous social scientists and related workers	57	54.3	45.7
Agricultural and food science technicians	32	–	–
Biological technicians	19	–	–
Chemical technicians	70	29.9	70.1
Geological and petroleum technicians	21	–	–
Nuclear technicians	3	–	–
Social science research assistants	3	–	–
Miscellaneous life, physical, and social science technicians	160	52.8	47.2
Community and social service occupations	2,265	63.8	36.2
Counselors	661	69.3	30.7

	total	female share of total	male share of total
Social workers	734	80.6%	19.4%
Probation officers and correctional treatment specialists	88	47.5	52.5
Social and human service assistants	151	77.1	22.9
Miscellaneous community and social service specialists, including health educators and community health workers	94	75.7	24.3
Clergy	408	20.5	79.5
Directors, religious activities and education	61	66.3	33.7
Religious workers, all other	69	62.4	37.6
Legal occupations	1,786	50.4	49.6
Lawyers	1,061	31.1	68.9
Judicial law clerks	17	–	–
Judges, magistrates, and other judicial workers	67	39.0	61.0
Paralegals and legal assistants	418	85.9	14.1
Miscellaneous legal support workers	223	79.0	21.0
Education, training, and library occupations	8,543	73.6	26.4
Postsecondary teachers	1,350	48.2	51.8
Preschool and kindergarten teachers	678	98.1	1.9
Elementary and middle school teachers	2,838	81.4	18.6
Secondary school teachers	1,127	57.3	42.7
Special education teachers	366	86.2	13.8
Other teachers and instructors	860	65.6	34.4
Archivists, curators, and museum technicians	46	–	–
Librarians	181	86.8	13.2
Library technicians	45	–	–
Teacher assistants	898	91.1	8.9
Other education, training, and library workers	153	67.3	32.7
Arts, design, entertainment, sports, and media occupations	2,814	48.3	51.7
Artists and related workers	212	51.6	48.4
Designers	756	55.3	44.7
Actors	37	–	–
Producers and directors	121	40.8	59.2
Athletes, coaches, umpires, and related workers	267	36.5	63.5
Dancers and choreographers	21	–	–
Musicians, singers, and related workers	203	35.5	64.5
Entertainers and performers, sports and related workers, all other	41	–	–
Announcers	50	23.6	76.4
News analysts, reporters, and correspondents	82	45.7	54.3
Public relations specialists	155	58.2	41.8
Editors	159	50.7	49.3
Technical writers	58	55.5	44.5
Writers and authors	208	55.6	44.4
Miscellaneous media and communication workers	98	79.2	20.8
Broadcast and sound engineering technicians and radio operators	108	8.4	91.6
Photographers	178	52.2	47.8

	total	female share of total	male share of total
Television, video, and motion picture camera operators and editors	57	21.4%	78.6%
Media and communication equipment workers, all other	2	–	–
Health care practitioners and technical occupations	7,977	75.0	25.0
Chiropractors	58	22.3	77.7
Dentists	167	24.2	75.8
Dietitians and nutritionists	116	93.3	6.7
Optometrists	33	–	–
Pharmacists	286	53.7	46.3
Physicians and surgeons	911	34.3	65.7
Physician assistants	108	69.4	30.6
Podiatrists	9	–	–
Audiologists	14	–	–
Occupational therapists	118	94.0	6.0
Physical therapists	211	70.7	29.3
Radiation therapists	14	–	–
Recreational therapists	13	–	–
Respiratory therapists	111	60.4	39.6
Speech–language pathologists	146	95.2	4.8
Exercise physiologists	2	–	–
Therapists, all other	148	83.6	16.4
Veterinarians	85	54.7	45.3
Registered nurses	2,875	90.6	9.4
Nurse anesthetists	27	–	–
Nurse midwives	3	–	–
Nurse practitioners	103	86.1	13.9
Health diagnosing and treating practitioners, all other	23	–	–
Clinical laboratory technologists and technicians	319	72.8	27.2
Dental hygienists	163	99.3	0.7
Diagnostic related technologists and technicians	308	74.5	25.5
Emergency medical technicians and paramedics	172	31.2	68.8
Health practitioner support technologists and technicians	544	83.6	16.4
Licensed practical and licensed vocational nurses	531	94.2	5.8
Medical records and health information technicians	90	89.3	10.7
Opticians, dispensing	54	59.6	40.4
Miscellaneous health technologists and technicians	140	60.2	39.8
Other health care practitioners and technical occupations	75	50.3	49.7
Service occupations	**25,459**	**56.3**	**43.7**
Health care support occupations	3,496	87.6	12.4
Nursing, psychiatric, and home health aides	2,119	87.9	12.1
Occupational therapy assistants and aides	18	–	–
Physical therapist assistants and aides	66	66.4	33.6
Massage therapists	158	81.5	18.5
Dental assistants	274	97.9	2.1

	total	female share of total	male share of total
Medical assistants	429	93.8%	6.2%
Medical transcriptionists	55	98.2	1.8
Pharmacy aides	45	–	–
Veterinary assistants and laboratory animal caretakers	47	–	–
Phlebotomists	119	80.2	19.8
Miscellaneous health care support occupations, including medical equipment preparers	166	69.0	31.0
Protective service occupations	3,096	20.9	79.1
First-line supervisors of correctional officers	46	–	–
First-line supervisors of police and detectives	112	15.2	84.8
First-line supervisors of firefighting and prevention workers	64	0.5	99.5
First-line supervisors of protective service workers, all other	93	29.9	70.1
Firefighters	295	3.4	96.6
Fire inspectors	18	–	–
Bailiffs, correctional officers, and jailers	371	28.0	72.0
Detectives and criminal investigators	160	24.8	75.2
Fish and game wardens	7	–	–
Parking enforcement workers	4	–	–
Police and sheriff's patrol officers	657	12.6	87.4
Transit and railroad police	3	–	–
Animal control workers	11	–	–
Private detectives and investigators	103	44.0	56.0
Security guards and gaming surveillance officers	903	18.5	81.5
Crossing guards	61	55.3	44.7
Transportation security screeners	25	–	–
Lifeguards and other recreational, and all other protective service workers	162	52.6	47.4
Food preparation and serving related occupations	8,018	54.5	45.5
Chefs and head cooks	403	21.5	78.5
First-line supervisors of food preparation and serving workers	552	59.3	40.7
Cooks	1,970	37.7	62.3
Food preparation workers	868	58.0	42.0
Bartenders	412	59.9	40.1
Combined food preparation and serving workers, including fast food	343	64.9	35.1
Counter attendants, cafeteria, food concession, and coffee shop	233	70.8	29.2
Waiters and waitresses	2,124	71.2	28.8
Food servers, nonrestaurant	217	64.9	35.1
Dining room and cafeteria attendants and bartender helpers	359	43.4	56.6
Dishwashers	271	18.7	81.3
Hosts and hostesses, restaurant, lounge, and coffee shop	260	81.5	18.5
Food preparation and serving related workers, all other	6	–	–
Building and grounds cleaning and maintenance occupations	5,591	38.6	61.4
First-line supervisors of housekeeping and janitorial workers	277	47.1	52.9
First-line supervisors of landscaping, lawn service, and groundskeeping workers	281	7.6	92.4

	total	female share of total	male share of total
Janitors and building cleaners	2,205	29.7%	70.3%
Maids and housekeeping cleaners	1,457	88.1	11.9
Pest control workers	73	4.7	95.3
Grounds maintenance workers	1,298	5.1	94.9
Personal care and service occupations	5,258	77.7	22.3
First-line supervisors of gaming workers	146	43.0	57.0
First-line supervisors of personal service workers	246	70.3	29.7
Animal trainers	44	–	–
Nonfarm animal caretakers	179	74.2	25.8
Gaming services workers	106	51.0	49.0
Motion picture projectionists	2	–	–
Ushers, lobby attendants, and ticket takers	43	–	–
Miscellaneous entertainment attendants and related workers	180	45.4	54.6
Embalmers and funeral attendants	16	–	–
Morticians, undertakers, and funeral directors	38	–	–
Barbers	109	21.9	78.1
Hairdressers, hairstylists, and cosmetologists	785	92.8	7.2
Miscellaneous personal appearance workers	300	81.5	18.5
Baggage porters, bellhops, and concierges	68	25.0	75.0
Tour and travel guides	51	36.9	63.1
Childcare workers	1,314	94.1	5.9
Personal care aides	1,071	84.7	15.3
Recreation and fitness workers	406	66.5	33.5
Residential advisors	58	61.4	38.6
Personal care and service workers, all other	95	45.7	54.3
Sales and office occupations	**33,152**	**61.8**	**38.2**
Sales and related occupations	15,457	48.7	51.3
First-line supervisors of retail sales workers	3,237	43.4	56.6
First-line supervisors of non–retail sales workers	1,151	24.7	75.3
Cashiers	3,275	71.8	28.2
Counter and rental clerks	139	53.4	46.6
Parts salespersons	106	13.3	86.7
Retail salespersons	3,341	50.2	49.8
Advertising sales agents	230	47.4	52.6
Insurance sales agents	540	44.1	55.9
Securities, commodities, and financial services sales agents	280	27.9	72.1
Travel agents	73	79.0	21.0
Sales representatives, services, all other	457	31.0	69.0
Sales representatives, wholesale and manufacturing	1,277	27.0	73.0
Models, demonstrators, and product promoters	65	83.4	16.6
Real estate brokers and sales agents	761	57.1	42.9
Sales engineers	27	–	–
Telemarketers	97	50.3	49.7

	total	female share of total	male share of total
Door-to-door sales workers, news and street vendors, and related workers	198	62.2%	37.8%
Sales and related workers, all other	204	47.9	52.1
Office and administrative support occupations	17,695	73.3	26.7
First-line supervisors of office and administrative support workers	1,416	68.5	31.5
Switchboard operators, including answering service	35	–	–
Telephone operators	42	–	–
Communications equipment operators, all other	9	–	–
Bill and account collectors	206	69.1	30.9
Billing and posting clerks	475	90.1	9.9
Bookkeeping, accounting, and auditing clerks	1,268	89.1	10.9
Gaming cage workers	8	–	–
Payroll and timekeeping clerks	155	92.6	7.4
Procurement clerks	27	–	–
Tellers	380	87.3	12.7
Financial clerks, all other	52	68.4	31.6
Brokerage clerks	5	–	–
Correspondence clerks	6	–	–
Court, municipal, and license clerks	85	77.2	22.8
Credit authorizers, checkers, and clerks	43	–	–
Customer service representatives	1,956	67.8	32.2
Eligibility interviewers, government programs	92	81.4	18.6
File clerks	292	81.3	18.7
Hotel, motel, and resort desk clerks	110	64.6	35.4
Interviewers, except eligibility and loan	135	83.7	16.3
Library assistants, clerical	97	84.0	16.0
Loan interviewers and clerks	144	81.2	18.8
New accounts clerks	26	–	–
Order clerks	104	58.2	41.8
Human resources assistants, except payroll and timekeeping	132	82.7	17.3
Receptionists and information clerks	1,237	91.5	8.5
Reservation and transportation ticket agents and travel clerks	117	58.6	41.4
Information and record clerks, all other	104	80.2	19.8
Cargo and freight agents	25	–	–
Couriers and messengers	213	15.5	84.5
Dispatchers	277	61.5	38.5
Meter readers, utilities	29	–	–
Postal service clerks	148	50.0	50.0
Postal service mail carriers	318	37.7	62.3
Postal service mail sorters, processors, and processing machine operators	66	47.6	52.4
Production, planning, and expediting clerks	272	55.0	45.0
Shipping, receiving, and traffic clerks	527	27.8	72.2
Stock clerks and order fillers	1,453	35.5	64.5
Weighers, measurers, checkers, and samplers, recordkeeping	74	49.1	50.9

	total	female share of total	male share of total
Secretaries and administrative assistants	2,904	95.3%	4.7%
Computer operators	102	50.7	49.3
Data entry keyers	337	77.0	23.0
Word processors and typists	119	88.7	11.3
Desktop publishers	3	–	–
Insurance claims and policy processing clerks	230	81.9	18.1
Mail clerks and mail machine operators, except postal service	81	41.2	58.8
Office clerks, general	1,103	83.4	16.6
Office machine operators, except computer	46	–	–
Proofreaders and copy markers	10	–	–
Statistical assistants	32	–	–
Office and administrative support workers, all other	570	77.3	22.7
Natural resources, construction, and maintenance occupations	**12,821**	**4.3**	**95.7**
Farming, fishing, and forestry occupations	994	22.7	77.3
First-line supervisors of farming, fishing, and forestry workers	50	14.1	85.9
Agricultural inspectors	16	–	–
Animal breeders	6	–	–
Graders and sorters, agricultural products	118	59.8	40.2
Miscellaneous agricultural workers	711	18.9	81.1
Fishers and related fishing workers	33	–	–
Hunters and trappers	2	–	–
Forest and conservation workers	9	–	–
Logging workers	49	–	–
Construction and extraction occupations	7,005	2.5	97.5
First-line supervisors of construction trades and extraction workers	634	2.8	97.2
Boilermakers	23	–	–
Brickmasons, blockmasons, and stonemasons	122	0.1	99.9
Carpenters	1,223	1.6	98.4
Carpet, floor, and tile installers and finishers	150	2.2	97.8
Cement masons, concrete finishers, and terrazzo workers	68	2.7	97.3
Construction laborers	1,387	2.9	97.1
Paving, surfacing, and tamping equipment operators	23	–	–
Pile-driver operators	4	–	–
Operating engineers and other construction equipment operators	348	1.3	98.7
Drywall installers, ceiling tile installers, and tapers	129	0.3	99.7
Electricians	692	1.8	98.2
Glaziers	46	–	–
Insulation workers	44	–	–
Painters, construction and maintenance	485	5.5	94.5
Paperhangers	7	–	–
Pipelayers, plumbers, pipefitters, and steamfitters	534	1.3	98.7
Plasterers and stucco masons	18	–	–
Reinforcing iron and rebar workers	8	–	–

	total	female share of total	male share of total
Roofers	196	1.5%	98.5%
Sheet metal workers	123	4.6	95.4
Structural iron and steel workers	65	2.8	97.2
Solar photovoltaic installers	7	–	–
Helpers, construction trades	53	4.5	95.5
Construction and building inspectors	118	7.8	92.2
Elevator installers and repairers	29	–	–
Fence erectors	33	–	–
Hazardous materials removal workers	38	–	–
Highway maintenance workers	108	1.5	98.5
Rail-track laying and maintenance equipment operators	10	–	–
Septic tank servicers and sewer pipe cleaners	8	–	–
Miscellaneous construction and related workers	32	–	–
Derrick, rotary drill, and service unit operators, oil, gas, and mining	37	–	–
Earth drillers, except oil and gas	35	–	–
Explosives workers, ordnance handling experts, and blasters	8	–	–
Mining machine operators	65	0.3	99.7
Roof bolters, mining	3	–	–
Roustabouts, oil and gas	14	–	–
Helpers—extraction workers	5	–	–
Other extraction workers	75	4.5	95.5
Installation, maintenance, and repair occupations	4,821	3.2	96.8
First-line supervisors of mechanics, installers, and repairers	292	5.9	94.1
Computer, automated teller, and office machine repairers	296	10.7	89.3
Radio and telecommunications equipment installers and repairers	158	5.8	94.2
Avionics technicians	14	–	–
Electric motor, power tool, and related repairers	37	–	–
Electrical and electronics installers and repairers, transportation equipment	5	–	–
Electrical and electronics repairers, industrial and utility	12	–	–
Electronic equipment installers and repairers, motor vehicles	18	–	–
Electronic home entertainment equipment installers and repairers	50	0.5	99.5
Security and fire alarm systems installers	41	–	–
Aircraft mechanics and service technicians	153	1.6	98.4
Automotive body and related repairers	140	1.8	98.2
Automotive glass installers and repairers	22	–	–
Automotive service technicians and mechanics	867	1.2	98.8
Bus and truck mechanics and diesel engine specialists	316	0.5	99.5
Heavy vehicle and mobile equipment service technicians and mechanics	194	1.0	99.0
Small engine mechanics	56	1.4	98.6
Miscellaneous vehicle and mobile equipment mechanics, installers, and repairers	87	1.8	98.2
Control and valve installers and repairers	27	–	–
Heating, air conditioning, and refrigeration mechanics and installers	340	1.6	98.4
Home appliance repairers	47	–	–

	total	female share of total	male share of total
Industrial and refractory machinery mechanics	454	1.9%	98.1%
Maintenance and repair workers, general	442	2.2	97.8
Maintenance workers, machinery	28	–	–
Millwrights	53	6.4	93.6
Electrical power line installers and repairers	110	2.4	97.6
Telecommunications line installers and repairers	177	4.8	95.2
Precision instrument and equipment repairers	60	16.0	84.0
Wind turbine service technicians	3	–	–
Coin, vending, and amusement machine servicers and repairers	33	–	–
Commercial divers	3	–	–
Locksmiths and safe repairers	31	–	–
Manufactured building and mobile home installers	5	–	–
Riggers	13	–	–
Signal and track switch repairers	5	–	–
Helpers—installation, maintenance, and repair workers	30	–	–
Other installation, maintenance, and repair workers	205	3.6	96.4
Production, transportation, and material-moving occupations	**16,994**	**21.8**	**78.2**
Production occupations	8,455	27.7	72.3
First-line supervisors of production and operating workers	808	19.5	80.5
Aircraft structure, surfaces, rigging, and systems assemblers	23	–	–
Electrical, electronics, and electromechanical assemblers	166	52.8	47.2
Engine and other machine assemblers	32	–	–
Structural metal fabricators and fitters	25	–	–
Miscellaneous assemblers and fabricators	919	38.4	61.6
Bakers	199	53.9	46.1
Butchers and other meat, poultry, and fish processing workers	311	23.0	77.0
Food and tobacco roasting, baking, and drying machine operators and tenders	11	–	–
Food batchmakers	84	59.6	40.4
Food cooking machine operators and tenders	14	–	–
Food processing workers, all other	117	29.5	70.5
Computer control programmers and operators	67	8.4	91.6
Extruding and drawing machine setters, operators, and tenders, metal and plastic	10	–	–
Forging machine setters, operators, and tenders, metal and plastic	10	–	–
Rolling machine setters, operators, and tenders, metal and plastic	8	–	–
Cutting, punching, and press machine setters, operators, and tenders, metal and plastic	87	18.9	81.1
Drilling and boring machine tool setters, operators, and tenders, metal and plastic	3	–	–
Grinding, lapping, polishing, and buffing machine tool setters, operators, and tenders, metal and plastic	54	6.6	93.4
Lathe and turning machine tool setters, operators, and tenders, metal and plastic	17	–	–

	total	female share of total	male share of total
Milling and planing machine setters, operators, and tenders, metal and plastic	3	–	–
Machinists	397	3.8%	96.2%
Metal furnace operators, tenders, pourers, and casters	17	–	–
Model makers and patternmakers, metal and plastic	11	–	–
Molders and molding machine setters, operators, and tenders, metal and plastic	37	–	–
Multiple machine tool setters, operators, and tenders, metal and plastic	5	–	–
Tool and die makers	56	0.8	99.2
Welding, soldering, and brazing workers	593	4.8	95.2
Heat treating equipment setters, operators, and tenders, metal and plastic	4	–	–
Layout workers, metal and plastic	4	–	–
Plating and coating machine setters, operators, and tenders, metal and plastic	18	–	–
Tool grinders, filers, and sharpeners	3	–	–
Metal workers and plastic workers, all other	375	19.5	80.5
Prepress technicians and workers	33	–	–
Printing press operators	201	17.2	82.8
Print binding and finishing workers	22	–	–
Laundry and dry-cleaning workers	185	53.3	46.7
Pressers, textile, garment, and related materials	54	70.6	29.4
Sewing machine operators	166	74.2	25.8
Shoe and leather workers and repairers	11	–	–
Shoe machine operators and tenders	11	–	–
Tailors, dressmakers, and sewers	86	77.1	22.9
Textile bleaching and dyeing machine operators and tenders	5	–	–
Textile cutting machine setters, operators, and tenders	12	–	–
Textile knitting and weaving machine setters, operators, and tenders	7	–	–
Textile winding, twisting, and drawing out machine setters, operators, and tenders	14	–	–
Extruding and forming machine setters, operators, and tenders, synthetic and glass fibers	1	–	–
Fabric and apparel patternmakers	3	–	–
Upholsterers	34	–	–
Textile, apparel, and furnishings workers, all other	14	–	–
Cabinetmakers and bench carpenters	45	–	–
Furniture finishers	7	–	–
Sawing machine setters, operators, and tenders, wood	30	–	–
Woodworking machine setters, operators, and tenders, except sawing	21	–	–
Woodworkers, all other	21	–	–
Power plant operators, distributors, and dispatchers	44	–	–
Stationary engineers and boiler operators	121	5.5	94.5
Water and wastewater treatment plant and system operators	72	4.5	95.5
Miscellaneous plant and system operators	39	–	–
Chemical processing machine setters, operators, and tenders	68	16.2	83.8

	total	female share of total	male share of total
Crushing, grinding, polishing, mixing, and blending workers	100	15.0%	85.0%
Cutting workers	67	19.2	80.8
Extruding, forming, pressing, and compacting machine setters, operators, and tenders	45	–	–
Furnace, kiln, oven, drier, and kettle operators and tenders	16	–	–
Inspectors, testers, sorters, samplers, and weighers	689	33.4	66.6
Jewelers and precious stone and metal workers	46	–	–
Medical, dental, and ophthalmic laboratory technicians	95	50.7	49.3
Packaging and filling machine operators and tenders .	261	52.3	47.7
Painting workers	150	15.1	84.9
Photographic process workers and processing machine operators	55	45.6	54.4
Semiconductor processors	4	–	–
Adhesive bonding machine operators and tenders	9	–	–
Cleaning, washing, and metal pickling equipment operators and tenders	7	–	–
Cooling and freezing equipment operators and tenders	2	–	–
Etchers and engravers	6	–	–
Molders, shapers, and casters, except metal and plastic	41	–	–
Paper goods machine setters, operators, and tenders	35	–	–
Tire builders	19	–	–
Helpers—production workers	59	34.8	65.2
Production workers, all other	933	26.3	73.7
Transportation and material-moving occupations	8,540	15.9	84.1
Supervisors of transportation and material-moving workers	200	23.0	77.0
Aircraft pilots and flight engineers	129	4.1	95.9
Air traffic controllers and airfield operations specialists	44	–	–
Flight attendants	88	77.6	22.4
Ambulance drivers and attendants, except emergency medical technicians	20	–	–
Bus drivers	558	45.5	54.5
Driver/sales workers and truck drivers	3,201	5.4	94.6
Taxi drivers and chauffeurs	336	13.2	86.8
Motor vehicle operators, all other	63	13.3	86.7
Locomotive engineers and operators	41	–	–
Railroad brake, signal, and switch operators	10	–	–
Railroad conductors and yardmasters	52	5.6	94.4
Subway, streetcar, and other rail transportation workers	11	–	–
Sailors and marine oilers	16	–	–
Ship and boat captains and operators	37	–	–
Ship engineers	7	–	–
Bridge and lock tenders	7	–	–
Parking lot attendants	81	11.6	88.4
Automotive and watercraft service attendants	94	9.2	90.8
Transportation inspectors	36	–	–
Transportation attendants, except flight attendants	38	–	–
Other transportation workers	17	–	–

	total	female share of total	male share of total
Conveyor operators and tenders	4	–	–
Crane and tower operators	62	4.0%	96.0%
Dredge, excavating, and loading machine operators	42	–	–
Hoist and winch operators	5	–	–
Industrial truck and tractor operators	537	7.4	92.6
Cleaners of vehicles and equipment	315	15.2	84.8
Laborers and freight, stock, and material movers, hand	1,849	18.7	81.3
Machine feeders and offbearers	27	–	–
Packers and packagers, hand	431	53.1	46.9
Pumping station operators	25	–	–
Refuse and recyclable material collectors	106	6.6	93.4
Mine shuttle car operators	1	–	–
Tank car, truck, and ship loaders	4	–	–
Material-moving workers, all other	45	–	–

Note: "–" means sample is too small to make a reliable estimate.
Source: Bureau of Labor Statistics, Labor Force Statistics from the Current Population Survey, Internet site http://www.bls .gov/cps/tables.htm#empstat; calculations by New Strategist

One in Four Men Works in Manufacturing or Construction

More than one-third of women work in the education and health service industry.

While women account for nearly half of all workers, the share varies greatly by industry. In some industries, workers are overwhelmingly female, while in others women account for few of the employed. Women account for just 9 percent of workers in the construction industry and 29 percent of workers in the manufacturing industry, for example. But they are 74 percent of workers in the education and health care service industry, which includes teachers and nurses.

Men dominate a number of industries. They account for 91 percent of construction workers, 87 percent of those employed in the mining industry, and 71 percent of workers in the manufacturing industry.

■ The rapid growth of the education and health service industry over the past few decades has drawn millions of women into the workforce.

Women dominate education and health services, men manufacturing and construction

(percent distribution of workers in selected industries, by sex, 2012)

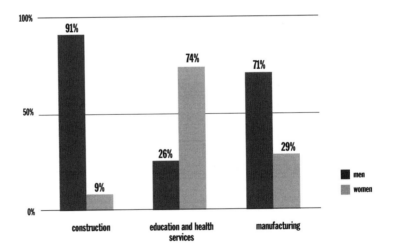

Table 5.22 Male Workers by Industry, 2012

(total number of employed people aged 16 or older, number and percent distribution of employed men and male share of total, by industry, 2012; numbers in thousands)

	total	men number	men percent distribution	men share of total
Total employed	**142,469**	**75,555**	**100.0%**	**53.0%**
Agriculture, forestry, fishing, and hunting	2,186	1,626	2.2	74.4
Mining	957	831	1.1	86.8
Construction	8,964	8,162	10.8	91.1
Manufacturing	14,686	10,432	13.8	71.0
Durable goods	9,244	6,932	9.2	75.0
Nondurable goods	5,443	3,499	4.6	64.3
Wholesale/retail trade	19,876	11,004	14.6	55.4
Wholesale trade	3,694	2,638	3.5	71.4
Retail trade	16,182	8,367	11.1	51.7
Transportation and utilities	7,271	5,581	7.4	76.8
Information	2,971	1,838	2.4	61.9
Financial activities	9,590	4,482	5.9	46.7
Professional and business services	16,539	9,741	12.9	58.9
Educational and health services	32,350	8,263	10.9	25.5
Leisure and hospitality	13,193	6,487	8.6	49.2
Other services	7,168	3,439	4.6	48.0
Other services except private households	6,430	3,357	4.4	52.2
Private households	738	82	0.1	11.1
Public administration	6,717	3,669	4.9	54.6

Source: Bureau of Labor Statistics, Labor Force Statistics from the Current Population Survey, Internet site http://www.bls.gov/cps/tables.htm#empstat

Table 5.23 Female Workers by Industry, 2012

(total number of employed people aged 16 or older, number and percent distribution of employed women and female share of total, by industry, 2012; numbers in thousands)

	total	women number	women percent distribution	women share of total
Total employed	**142,469**	**66,914**	**100.0%**	**47.0%**
Agriculture, forestry, fishing, and hunting	2,186	560	0.8	25.6
Mining	957	126	0.2	13.2
Construction	8,964	802	1.2	8.9
Manufacturing	14,686	4,255	6.4	29.0
Durable goods	9,244	2,311	3.5	25.0
Nondurable goods	5,443	1,943	2.9	35.7
Wholesale/retail trade	19,876	8,871	13.3	44.6
Wholesale trade	3,694	1,056	1.6	28.6
Retail trade	16,182	7,815	11.7	48.3
Transportation and utilities	7,271	1,691	2.5	23.3
Information	2,971	1,134	1.7	38.2
Financial activities	9,590	5,108	7.6	53.3
Professional and business services	16,539	6,798	10.2	41.1
Educational and health services	32,350	24,087	36.0	74.5
Leisure and hospitality	13,193	6,706	10.0	50.8
Other services	7,168	3,728	5.6	52.0
Other services except private households	6,430	3,072	4.6	47.8
Private households	738	656	1.0	88.9
Public administration	6,717	3,048	4.6	45.4

Source: Bureau of Labor Statistics, Labor Force Statistics from the Current Population Survey, Internet site http://www.bls.gov/cps/ tables.htm#empstat

Many Older Men Are Self-Employed

Few young adults work for themselves.

Among workers, only 8 percent of men and 6 percent of women were self-employed in 2012, according to the Bureau of Labor Statistics. The bureau counts as self-employed only those whose longest job in the previous 12 months was self-employment. It does not include people who run their own business on the side.

The proportion of male and female workers who are self-employed rises with age. Among men under age 55 and women under age 65, fewer than 10 percent of workers are self-employed. The share rises to 14 percent among women aged 65 or older and peaks at 20 percent among men aged 65 or older. Self-employment rises sharply in the 65-or-older age group because the federal government's Medicare program provides their health insurance, allowing workers the security to experiment with entrepreneurship.

■ As boomer men and women become eligible for Medicare, the number of self-employed should grow substantially.

Self-employment is much more common among older Americans

(percent of total workers and workers aged 65 or older who are self-employed, by sex, 2012)

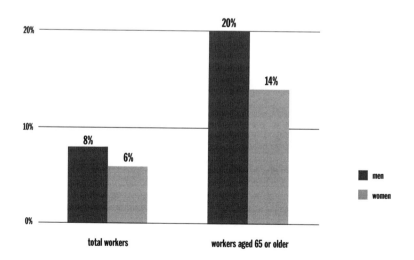

Table 5.24 Self-Employed Men by Age, 2012

(number of men aged 16 or older in the civilian labor force, number and percent who are self-employed, and percent distribution of self-employed men by age, 2012; numbers in thousands)

	total employed	self-employed number	self-employed percent of total	self-employed percent distribution
Total men	**75,556**	**5,828**	**7.7%**	**100.0%**
Aged 16 to 19	2,152	55	2.6	0.9
Aged 20 to 24	6,948	150	2.2	2.6
Aged 25 to 34	16,606	758	4.6	13.0
Aged 35 to 44	16,483	1,171	7.1	20.1
Aged 45 to 54	17,220	1,508	8.8	25.9
Aged 55 to 64	12,068	1,376	11.4	23.6
Aged 65 or older	4,077	812	19.9	13.9

Source: Bureau of Labor Statistics, Current Population Survey, Internet site http://www.bls.gov/cps/tables.htm#empstat

Table 5.25 Self-Employed Women by Age, 2012

(number of women aged 16 or older in the labor force, number and percent who are self-employed, and percent distribution of self-employed women by age, 2012; numbers in thousands)

	total employed	self-employed number	self-employed percent of total	self-employed percent distribution
Total women	**66,913**	**3,701**	**5.5%**	**100.0%**
Aged 16 to 19	2,274	22	1.0	0.6
Aged 20 to 24	6,460	105	1.6	2.8
Aged 25 to 34	14,094	535	3.8	14.5
Aged 35 to 44	14,093	765	5.4	20.7
Aged 45 to 54	15,653	1,003	6.4	27.1
Aged 55 to 64	11,171	840	7.5	22.7
Aged 65 or older	3,168	431	13.6	11.6

Source: Bureau of Labor Statistics, Current Population Survey, Internet site http://www.bls.gov/cps/tables.htm#empstat

Middle-Aged Men Are Most Likely to Be Union Members

Union representation is highest among men aged 55 to 64.

Union membership has been slipping for decades as employment in service industries—where unions have been slow to organize—outpaces employment in manufacturing. Only 13 percent of the nation's 66 million male wage and salary workers are represented by unions. Among the 62 million female wage and salary workers, the figure is 12 percent.

Union representation rises with age and peaks in the 55-to-64 age group. Sixteen percent of women and 17 percent of men aged 55 to 64 are represented by a union.

■ Without union representation, workers lack the power to demand better pay or benefits.

Seventeen percent of men aged 55 to 64 are represented by unions

(percent of male wage and salary workers represented by unions, by age, 2012)

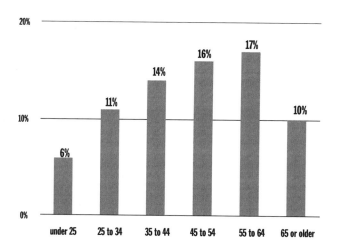

Table 5.26 Union Representation of Men by Age, 2012

(number of employed male wage and salary workers aged 16 or older, and number and percent represented by unions, by age, 2012; numbers in thousands)

	total employed	represented by unions	
		number	percent
Total men	**65,898**	**8,611**	**13.1%**
Aged 16 to 24	8,830	521	5.9
Aged 25 to 34	15,465	1,688	10.9
Aged 35 to 44	14,481	2,085	14.4
Aged 45 to 54	14,601	2,385	16.3
Aged 55 to 64	9,728	1,655	17.0
Aged 65 or older	2,792	277	9.9

Note: Workers represented by unions are either members of a labor union or similar employee association or workers who report no union affiliation but whose jobs are covered by a union or an employee association contract.
Source: Bureau of Labor Statistics, Current Population Survey, Internet site http://www.bls.gov/cps/tables.htm#empstat

Table 5.27 Union Representation of Women by Age, 2012

(number of employed female wage and salary workers aged 16 or older, and number and percent represented by unions, by age, 2012; numbers in thousands)

	total employed	represented by unions	
		number	percent
Total women	**61,679**	**7,311**	**11.9%**
Aged 16 to 24	8,586	347	4.0
Aged 25 to 34	13,410	1,396	10.4
Aged 35 to 44	12,961	1,661	12.8
Aged 45 to 54	14,164	2,052	14.5
Aged 55 to 64	9,966	1,579	15.8
Aged 65 or older	2,593	277	10.7

Note: Workers represented by unions are either members of a labor union or similar employee association or workers who report no union affiliation but whose jobs are covered by a union or an employee association contract.
Source: Bureau of Labor Statistics, Current Population Survey, Internet site http://www.bls.gov/cps/tables.htm#empstat

Women Account for the Majority of Minimum Wage Workers

Few women earn minimum wage or less, however.

Among the nation's 3.8 million workers who earn minimum wage or less, women account for the 63 percent majority. Overall, 6 percent of women who are paid by the hour earn minimum wage or less. Among men, the proportion is 4 percent.

Young workers are most likely to earn minimum wage or less. Among workers aged 16 to 19 who are paid by the hour, 25 percent of women and 20 percent of men earn minimum wage or less. The proportion who earn minimum wage or less bottoms out for both men and women in the 55-to-64 age group at just 2 to 3 percent. Among women workers aged 65 or older who are paid by the hour, a larger 6 percent earn minimum wage or less.

■ The number of workers who earn minimum wage or less increased over the past few years along with the rise in the minimum wage threshold.

Teens and young adults are most likely to be minimum-wage workers

(percent of female workers making minimum wage or less, by age, 2012)

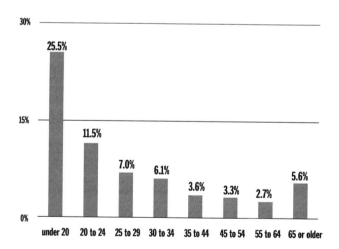

Table 5.28 Men Earning Minimum Wage by Age, Race, and Hispanic Origin, 2011

(total number of male workers paid hourly rates, and number and percent paid at or below prevailing federal minimum wage, by age, race, and Hispanic origin, 2011; numbers in thousands)

	total men paid hourly rates	at or below minimum wage	
		number	percent
Total men aged 16 or older	**36,457**	**1,433**	**3.9%**
Aged 16 to 19	1,872	373	19.9
Aged 20 to 24	5,418	413	7.6
Aged 25 to 29	4,893	157	3.2
Aged 30 to 34	4,238	122	2.9
Aged 35 to 44	7,036	142	2.0
Aged 45 to 54	7,167	113	1.6
Aged 55 to 64	4,491	72	1.6
Aged 65 or older	1,341	42	3.1
Aged 65 to 69	754	21	2.8
Aged 70 or older	587	22	3.7
Total men aged 16 or older	**36,457**	**1,433**	**3.9**
Asian	1,425	41	2.9
Black	4,252	222	5.2
Hispanic	7,703	326	4.2
White	29,743	1,108	3.7

Source: Bureau of Labor Statistics, Characteristics of Minimum Wage Workers: 2011, Internet site http://www.bls.gov/cps/minwage2011tbls.htm; calculations by New Strategist

Table 5.29 Women Earning Minimum Wage by Age, Race, and Hispanic Origin, 2011

(total number of female workers paid hourly rates, and number and percent paid at or below prevailing federal minimum wage, by age, race, and Hispanic origin, 2011; numbers in thousands)

	total women paid hourly rates	at or below minimum wage	
		number	percent
Total women aged 16 or older	**37,469**	**2,395**	**6.4%**
Aged 16 to 19	2,064	526	25.5
Aged 20 to 24	5,083	583	11.5
Aged 25 to 29	4,336	303	7.0
Aged 30 to 34	3,688	225	6.1
Aged 35 to 44	7,132	257	3.6
Aged 45 to 54	8,164	270	3.3
Aged 55 to 64	5,555	150	2.7
Aged 65 or older	1,448	81	5.6
Aged 65 to 69	815	46	5.6
Aged 70 or older	633	33	5.2
Total women aged 16 or older	**37,469**	**2,395**	**6.4**
Asian	1,612	58	3.6
Black	5,271	356	6.8
Hispanic	5,561	394	7.1
White	29,571	1,898	6.4

Source: Bureau of Labor Statistics, Characteristics of Minimum Wage Workers: 2011, Internet site http://www.bls.gov/cps/ minwage2011tbls.htm; calculations by New Strategist

Table 5.30 Female Share of Minimum Wage Workers by Age, Race, and Hispanic Origin, 2011

(total number of workers paid hourly rates at or below the prevailing federal minimum wage, females paid at or below minimum wage, and female share of total, by age, race, and Hispanic origin, 2011; numbers in thousands)

	total minimum wage workers	women paid at or below minimum wage	
		number	share of total
Total aged 16 or older	**3,828**	**2,395**	**62.6%**
Aged 16 to 19	899	526	58.5
Aged 20 to 24	996	583	58.5
Aged 25 to 29	460	303	65.9
Aged 30 to 34	347	225	64.8
Aged 35 to 44	399	257	64.4
Aged 45 to 54	383	270	70.5
Aged 55 to 64	222	150	67.6
Aged 65 or older	123	81	65.9
Aged 65 to 69	67	46	68.7
Aged 70 or older	55	33	60.0
Total aged 16 or older	**3,828**	**2,395**	**62.6**
Asian	99	58	58.6
Black	578	356	61.6
Hispanic	720	394	54.7
White	3,006	1,898	63.1

Source: Bureau of Labor Statistics, Characteristics of Minimum Wage Workers: 2011, Internet site http://www.bls.gov/cps/minwage2011tbls.htm; calculations by New Strategist

More Older Workers Will Be in the Labor Force

Participation rate is projected to climb in the older age groups.

Early retirement has come to an end. Labor force participation rates among older men and women are projected to climb, according to the Bureau of Labor Statistics. Men's overall labor force participation rate should fall by 3.0 percentage point between 2010 and 2020, but only because of a decline in participation among younger men and the aging of the population. Labor force participation among men aged 65 or older is projected to increase by 4.6 percentage points between 2010 and 2020, to 26.7 percent. Women's labor force participation rate also will rise in the older age groups.

As boomers enter their late sixties, the number of older workers will soar. The number of workers aged 65 or older is projected to increase by more than 70 percent between 2010 and 2020.

■ Many baby boomers will have to remain in the labor force well into their sixties as they try to save for retirement.

Number of male workers aged 65 or older will grow rapidly

(percent change in number of male workers by age, 2010 to 2020)

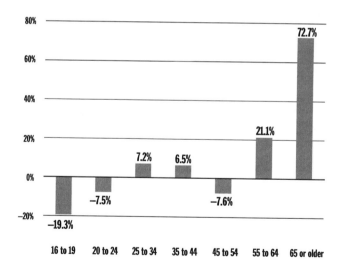

Table 5.31 Men in the Labor Force by Age, 2010 to 2020

(number and percent of men aged 16 or older in the civilian labor force by age, 2010 and 2020; percent change in number and percentage point change in rate, 2010–20; numbers in thousands)

NUMBER	2010	2020	percent change
Men in labor force	81,985	87,128	6.3%
Aged 16 to 19	2,991	2,413	–19.3
Aged 20 to 24	7,864	7,276	–7.5
Aged 25 to 34	18,352	19,667	7.2
Aged 35 to 44	18,119	19,303	6.5
Aged 45 to 54	18,856	17,415	–7.6
Aged 55 to 64	12,103	14,662	21.1
Aged 65 or older	3,700	6,391	72.7
Aged 65 to 74	2,971	5,236	76.2
Aged 75 or older	729	1,155	58.4

PARTICIPATION RATE	2010	2020	percentage point change
Men in labor force	71.2%	68.2%	–3.0
Aged 16 to 19	34.9	27.9	–7.0
Aged 20 to 24	74.5	69.4	–5.1
Aged 25 to 34	90.3	86.9	–3.4
Aged 35 to 44	91.5	91.3	–0.2
Aged 45 to 54	86.8	86.0	–0.8
Aged 55 to 64	70.0	71.1	1.1
Aged 65 or older	22.1	26.7	4.6
Aged 65 to 74	30.4	35.1	4.7
Aged 75 or older	10.4	12.8	2.4

Source: Bureau of Labor Statistics, Labor Force Projections to 2020: A More Slowly Growing Workforce, Monthly Labor Review, January 2012, Internet site http://www.bls.gov/opub/mlr/2012/01/home.htm

Table 5.32 Women in the Labor Force by Age, 2010 to 2020

(number and percent of women aged 16 or older in the civilian labor force by age, 2010 and 2020; percent change in number and percentage point change in rate, 2010–20; numbers in thousands)

NUMBER	2010	2020	percent change
Women in labor force	**71,904**	**77,232**	**7.4%**
Aged 16 to 19	2,914	2,134	−26.8
Aged 20 to 24	7,164	6,506	−9.2
Aged 25 to 34	15,263	16,754	9.8
Aged 35 to 44	15,247	15,844	3.9
Aged 45 to 54	17,104	15,635	−8.6
Aged 55 to 64	11,194	14,637	30.8
Aged 65 or older	3,017	5,174	71.5
Aged 65 to 74	2,453	4,709	92.0
Aged 75 or older	564	1,012	79.4

PARTICIPATION RATE	2010	2020	percentage point change
Women in labor force	**58.6%**	**57.1%**	**−1.5**
Aged 16 to 19	35.0	25.2	−9.8
Aged 20 to 24	68.3	62.3	−6.0
Aged 25 to 34	74.7	74.2	−0.5
Aged 35 to 44	75.2	74.0	−1.2
Aged 45 to 54	75.7	75.7	0.0
Aged 55 to 64	60.2	66.6	6.4
Aged 65 or older	13.8	19.2	5.4
Aged 65 to 74	21.6	27.5	5.9
Aged 75 or older	5.3	8.0	2.7

Source: Bureau of Labor Statistics, Labor Force Projections to 2020: A More Slowly Growing Workforce, Monthly Labor Review, January 2012, Internet site http://www.bls.gov/opub/mlr/2012/01/home.htm

Living Arrangements

Median age at first marriage is at a record high.

Both men and women are marrying later than ever.

Most men and women are married.

Fifty-four percent of men and just over 50 percent of women aged 18 or older are currently married.

Living arrangements of men and women diverge with age.

Most men aged 35 or older are husbands. Most women from age 30 to 74 are wives, but widows outnumber wives among those aged 75 or older.

Married couples head a smaller share of households.

The married-couple share of households fell from 53 to 49 percent between 2000 and 2012. The number of married couples with children under age 18 declined during those years.

Few households include children under age 18.

Only 29 percent of households include children under age 18.

Husbands and wives are alike in many ways.

Most are close in age, of the same race/Hispanic origin, and of equal educational attainment.

Divorce is common among baby boomers.

Thirty-seven percent of women in their fifties have experienced divorce.

The Census Bureau is now profiling same-sex couples.

The nation's same-sex couples are more educated and affluent than opposite-sex married couples.

Men and Women Are Postponing Marriage

Among young adults, the growing majority has never married.

Men and women are postponing marriage as going to college and looking for a stable job prevents them from making commitments. The median age at first marriage climbed to 28.6 years for men and 26.6 years for women in 2012—a record high for both. Since 1950, the median age at which men and women marry for the first time has increased by six years.

The percentage of young men and women who have never married has surged over the past few decades. Among men aged 20 to 24, the share that has never married climbed from 55 percent in 1970 to 89 percent in 2012. Among their female counterparts, the figure has grown from 36 to 81 percent. Since 1970, the percentage of men and women who have never married has increased in all but one age group. Only people aged 65 or older are less likely to be single.

■ Young men and women had been postponing marriage well before the Great Recession, largely because of rising college enrollment rates.

Median age at first marriage is at a record high

(median age at first marriage for men and women, 2012)

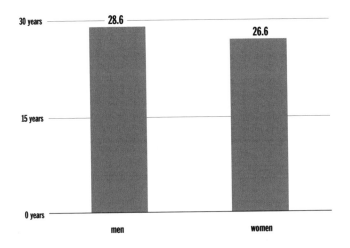

Table 6.1 Median Age at First Marriage by Sex, 1890 to 2012

(median age at first marriage by sex, 1890 to 2012; change in years for selected years)

	men	women
2012	28.6 yrs.	26.6 yrs.
2011	28.4	26.4
2010	28.2	26.1
2009	28.1	25.9
2008	27.6	25.9
2007	27.5	25.6
2006	27.5	25.5
2005	27.1	25.3
2004	27.4	25.3
2003	27.1	25.3
2002	26.9	25.3
2001	26.9	25.1
2000	26.8	25.1
1990	26.1	23.9
1980	24.7	22.0
1970	23.2	20.8
1960	22.8	20.3
1950	22.8	20.3
1940	24.3	21.5
1930	24.3	21.3
1920	24.6	21.2
1910	25.1	21.6
1900	25.9	21.9
1890	26.1	22.0

Change in years

2000 to 2012	1.8 yrs.	1.5 yrs.
1950 to 2012	5.8	6.3
1890 to 1950	–3.3	–1.7

Source: Bureau of the Census, Families and Living Arrangements, Historical Time Series, Internet site http://www.census .gov/hhes/families/data/historical.html; calculations by New Strategist

Table 6.2 Never-Married People by Sex and Age, 1970 to 2012

(percent of people who have never been married, by sex and age, 1970 to 2012; percentage point change 1970–2012)

	2012	2010	2000	1990	1980	1970	percentage point change 1970–2012
MEN							
Aged 20 to 24	89.2%	88.7%	83.7%	79.3%	68.8%	54.7%	34.5
Aged 25 to 29	63.5	62.2	51.7	45.2	33.1	19.1	44.4
Aged 30 to 34	39.1	36.5	30.1	27.0	15.9	9.4	29.7
Aged 35 to 39	24.4	23.5	20.3	14.7	7.8	7.2	17.2
Aged 40 to 44	20.1	20.4	15.7	10.5	7.1	6.3	13.8
Aged 45 to 54	14.9	14.9	9.5	6.3	6.1	7.5	7.4
Aged 55 to 64	9.4	9.1	5.5	5.8	5.3	7.8	1.6
Aged 65 or older	4.5	4.1	4.2	4.2	4.9	7.5	–3.0
WOMEN							
Aged 20 to 24	81.3	79.3	72.8	62.8	50.2	35.8	45.5
Aged 25 to 29	51.0	47.8	38.9	31.1	20.9	10.5	40.5
Aged 30 to 34	29.7	27.2	21.9	16.4	9.5	6.2	23.5
Aged 35 to 39	20.1	17.7	14.3	10.4	6.2	5.4	14.7
Aged 40 to 44	15.0	13.8	11.8	8.0	4.8	4.9	10.1
Aged 45 to 54	11.7	11.0	8.6	5.0	4.7	4.9	6.8
Aged 55 to 64	8.7	7.1	4.9	3.9	4.5	6.8	1.9
Aged 65 or older	4.3	4.5	3.6	4.9	5.9	7.7	–3.4

Source: Bureau of the Census, America's Families and Living Arrangements, Internet site http://www.census.gov/hhes/families/ data/cps.html; calculations by New Strategist

Most Men and Women Are Married

Among the oldest women, most are widows.

Among Americans aged 18 or older, 54 percent of men and 50 percent of women are currently married and living with their spouse. The proportion of men who are married crosses the 50 percent threshold in the 30-to-34 age group and stays there regardless of advancing age. Among women, the percentage currently married reaches the majority in the 30-to-34 age group but falls below 50 percent in the 75-to-84 age group. Nearly half (46 percent) of women aged 75 to 84 are currently widowed as are 73 percent of those aged 85 or older.

The marital status of men and women varies greatly by race and Hispanic origin. Among men and women aged 18 or older, the majority of non-Hispanic whites and Asians are currently married. The figures are only 45 and 47 percent among Hispanic men and women, respectively. Only 36 percent of black men and 28 percent of black women are currently married.

■ Male life expectancy has been rising slightly faster than female, reducing the percentage of older women who are widows.

Most Asian and non-Hispanic white women are currently married

(percentage of women who are currently married and living with their spouse, by race and Hispanic origin, 2012)

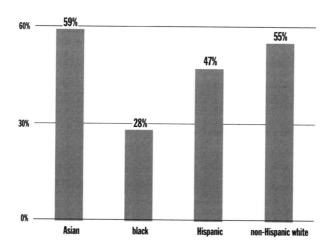

Table 6.3 Marital Status of Women by Age, 2012

(number and percent distribution of women aged 18 or older by age and marital status, 2012; numbers in thousands)

	total	never married	married, spouse present	married, spouse absent	separated	divorced	widowed
Total women	**121,385**	**30,061**	**61,021**	**1,764**	**3,141**	**14,208**	**11,190**
Aged 18 to 19	4,083	3,938	65	30	26	14	11
Aged 20 to 24	10,888	8,850	1,527	149	214	124	23
Aged 25 to 29	10,459	5,338	4,226	141	258	463	33
Aged 30 to 34	10,284	3,055	5,807	171	387	836	28
Aged 35 to 39	9,714	1,953	5,939	179	442	1,122	80
Aged 40 to 44	10,530	1,580	6,792	171	379	1,464	144
Aged 45 to 49	10,999	1,426	6,960	185	400	1,786	243
Aged 50 to 54	11,460	1,202	7,247	183	338	2,024	466
Aged 55 to 64	19,808	1,716	12,123	300	458	3,588	1,622
Aged 65 to 74	12,393	588	6,875	117	168	1,929	2,717
Aged 75 to 84	7,574	290	2,940	95	50	708	3,491
Aged 85 or older	3,193	125	521	43	21	152	2,332
Total women	**100.0%**	**24.8%**	**50.3%**	**1.5%**	**2.6%**	**11.7%**	**9.2%**
Aged 18 to 19	100.0	96.4	1.6	0.7	0.6	0.3	0.3
Aged 20 to 24	100.0	81.3	14.0	1.4	2.0	1.1	0.2
Aged 25 to 29	100.0	51.0	40.4	1.3	2.5	4.4	0.3
Aged 30 to 34	100.0	29.7	56.5	1.7	3.8	8.1	0.3
Aged 35 to 39	100.0	20.1	61.1	1.8	4.6	11.6	0.8
Aged 40 to 44	100.0	15.0	64.5	1.6	3.6	13.9	1.4
Aged 45 to 49	100.0	13.0	63.3	1.7	3.6	16.2	2.2
Aged 50 to 54	100.0	10.5	63.2	1.6	2.9	17.7	4.1
Aged 55 to 64	100.0	8.7	61.2	1.5	2.3	18.1	8.2
Aged 65 to 74	100.0	4.7	55.5	0.9	1.4	15.6	21.9
Aged 75 to 84	100.0	3.8	38.8	1.3	0.7	9.3	46.1
Aged 85 or older	100.0	3.9	16.3	1.3	0.7	4.8	73.0

Source: Bureau of the Census, America's Families and Living Arrangements: 2012, Internet site http://www.census.gov/hhes/families/data/cps2012.html; calculations by New Strategist

Table 6.4 Marital Status of Men by Age, 2012

(number and percent distribution of men aged 18 or older by age and marital status, 2012; numbers in thousands)

	total	never married	married, spouse present	married, spouse absent	separated	divorced	widowed
Total men	**113,213**	**34,471**	**61,039**	**1,730**	**2,421**	**10,688**	**2,864**
Aged 18 to 19	4,172	4,051	46	20	40	12	4
Aged 20 to 24	10,982	9,800	879	88	135	70	9
Aged 25 to 29	10,430	6,620	3,151	154	189	305	10
Aged 30 to 34	10,028	3,924	5,087	176	230	602	8
Aged 35 to 39	9,418	2,294	5,842	159	239	847	38
Aged 40 to 44	10,252	2,057	6,414	241	302	1,212	27
Aged 45 to 49	10,569	1,846	6,618	175	388	1,462	81
Aged 50 to 54	10,894	1,356	7,296	188	296	1,631	127
Aged 55 to 64	18,137	1,707	12,491	271	395	2,826	446
Aged 65 to 74	10,980	541	8,199	126	146	1,278	690
Aged 75 to 84	5,543	196	4,056	89	51	383	769
Aged 85 or older	1,809	79	961	43	10	61	656
Total men	**100.0%**	**30.4%**	**53.9%**	**1.5%**	**2.1%**	**9.4 %**	**2.5%**
Aged 18 to 19	100.0	97.1	1.1	0.5	1.0	0.3	0.1
Aged 20 to 24	100.0	89.2	8.0	0.8	1.2	0.6	0.1
Aged 25 to 29	100.0	63.5	30.2	1.5	1.8	2.9	0.1
Aged 30 to 34	100.0	39.1	50.7	1.8	2.3	6.0	0.1
Aged 35 to 39	100.0	24.4	62.0	1.7	2.5	9.0	0.4
Aged 40 to 44	100.0	20.1	62.6	2.4	2.9	11.8	0.3
Aged 45 to 49	100.0	17.5	62.6	1.7	3.7	13.8	0.8
Aged 50 to 54	100.0	12.4	67.0	1.7	2.7	15.0	1.2
Aged 55 to 64	100.0	9.4	68.9	1.5	2.2	15.6	2.5
Aged 65 to 74	100.0	4.9	74.7	1.1	1.3	11.6	6.3
Aged 75 to 84	100.0	3.5	73.2	1.6	0.9	6.9	13.9
Aged 85 or older	100.0	4.4	53.1	2.4	0.6	3.4	36.3

Source: Bureau of the Census, America's Families and Living Arrangements: 2012, Internet site http://www.census.gov/hhes/families/data/cps2012.html; calculations by New Strategist

Table 6.5 Marital Status of Women by Race and Hispanic Origin, 2012

(number and percent distribution of women aged 18 or older by marital status, race, and Hispanic origin, 2012; numbers in thousands)

	total	Asian	black	Hispanic	non-Hispanic white
Total women	**121,385**	**7,028**	**16,319**	**17,240**	**80,232**
Never married	30,061	1,733	7,058	5,246	15,977
Married, spouse present	61,021	4,135	4,533	8,104	43,920
Married, spouse absent	1,764	241	357	390	780
Separated	3,141	94	804	820	1,426
Divorced	14,208	395	2,116	1,708	9,889
Widowed	11,190	430	1,452	972	8,241

PERCENT DISTRIBUTION BY MARITAL STATUS

Total women	**100.0%**	**100.%**	**100.0%**	**100.0%**	**100.0%**
Never married	24.8	24.7	43.3	30.4	19.9
Married, spouse present	50.3	58.8	27.8	47.0	54.7
Married, spouse absent	1.5	3.4	2.2	2.3	1.0
Separated	2.6	1.3	4.9	4.8	1.8
Divorced	11.7	5.6	13.0	9.9	12.3
Widowed	9.2	6.1	8.9	5.6	10.3

PERCENT DISTRIBUTION BY RACE AND HISPANIC ORIGIN

Total women	**100.0**	**5.8**	**13.4**	**14.2**	**66.1**
Never married	100.0	5.8	23.5	17.5	53.1
Married, spouse present	100.0	6.8	7.4	13.3	72.0
Married, spouse absent	100.0	13.7	20.2	22.1	44.2
Separated	100.0	3.0	25.6	26.1	45.4
Divorced	100.0	2.8	14.9	12.0	69.6
Widowed	100.0	3.8	13.0	8.7	73.6

Note: Numbers do not sum to total because Asians and blacks are those who identify themselves as being of the race alone and those who identify themselves as being of the race in combination with other races, not all races are shown, and Hispanics may be of any race. Non-Hispanic whites are those who identify themselves as being white alone and not Hispanic.
Source: Bureau of the Census, America's Families and Living Arrangements: 2012, Current Population Survey Annual Social and Economic Supplement, Internet site http://www.census.gov/hhes/families/data/cps2012.html; calculations by New Strategist

Table 6.6 Marital Status of Men by Race and Hispanic Origin, 2012

(number and percent distribution of men aged 18 or older by marital status, race, and Hispanic origin, 2012; numbers in thousands)

	total	Asian	black	Hispanic	non-Hispanic white
Total men	**113,213**	**6,200**	**13,340**	**17,425**	**75,700**
Never married	34,471	2,043	5,973	6,958	19,459
Married, spouse present	61,039	3,648	4,824	7,870	44,320
Married, spouse absent	1,730	182	235	660	671
Separated	2,421	49	598	536	1,233
Divorced	10,688	214	1,400	1,147	7,823
Widowed	2,864	64	310	253	2,194

PERCENT DISTRIBUTION BY MARITAL STATUS

	total	Asian	black	Hispanic	non-Hispanic white
Total men	**100.0%**	**100.%**	**100.0%**	**100.0%**	**100.0%**
Never married	30.4	33.0	44.8	39.9	25.7
Married, spouse present	53.9	58.8	36.2	45.2	58.5
Married, spouse absent	1.5	2.9	1.8	3.8	0.9
Separated	2.1	0.8	4.5	3.1	1.6
Divorced	9.4	3.5	10.5	6.6	10.3
Widowed	2.5	1.0	2.3	1.5	2.9

PERCENT DISTRIBUTION BY RACE AND HISPANIC ORIGIN

	total	Asian	black	Hispanic	non-Hispanic white
Total men	**100.0%**	**5.5%**	**11.8%**	**15.4%**	**66.9%**
Never married	100.0	5.9	17.3	20.2	56.5
Married, spouse present	100.0	6.0	7.9	12.9	72.6
Married, spouse absent	100.0	10.5	13.6	38.2	38.8
Separated	100.0	2.0	24.7	22.1	50.9
Divorced	100.0	2.0	13.1	10.7	73.2
Widowed	100.0	2.2	10.8	8.8	76.6

Note: Numbers do not sum to total because Asians and blacks are those who identify themselves as being of the race alone and those who identify themselves as being of the race in combination with other races, not all races are shown, and Hispanics may be of any race. Non-Hispanic whites are those who identify themselves as being white alone and not Hispanic.
Source: Bureau of the Census, America's Families and Living Arrangements: 2012, Current Population Survey Annual Social and Economic Supplement, Internet site http://www.census.gov/hhes/families/data/cps2012.html; calculations by New Strategist

Most Men Are Householders

Many young men live with their parents.

Among the nation's 120 million men aged 15 or older, 70 percent head households as a married-couple householder or spouse, a male family head, a single-person householder, or a householder living with nonrelatives. Among women aged 15 or older, an even larger 75 percent are householders or the spouse of a married-couple householder.

Being a married-couple householder or spouse is the most common living arrangement for both men and women. The second most common arrangement for women is living alone, with 14 percent of women aged 15 or older heading single-person households. Ranking third among women is being the child of the householder (13 percent). Among men, the second most common living arrangement is child of householder (18 percent) and a smaller 12 percent live alone.

■ Among young adults, men are more likely than women to live with their parents because men marry at an older age.

Nearly half of men are a married-couple householder or spouse

(percent distribution of men aged 15 or older by householder status, 2012)

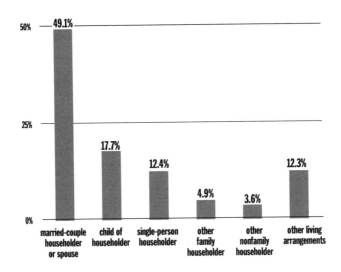

Table 6.7 Living Arrangements of Women by Age, 2012

(number and percent distribution of women aged 15 or older by living arrangement and age, 2012; numbers in thousands)

	total	under 20	20–24	25–29	30–34	35–44	45–54	55–64	65–74	75–84	85+
TOTAL WOMEN	127,695	10,393	10,888	10,459	10,284	20,244	22,459	19,808	12,393	7,574	3,193
Householder	96,000	397	3,910	7,126	8,492	17,669	19,814	17,919	11,293	6,730	2,652
Married couple householder or spouse	58,949	69	1,355	4,030	5,619	12,344	13,701	11,765	6,716	2,854	498
Other family householder	15,668	231	1,224	1,610	1,809	3,672	3,136	2,013	1,011	680	282
Living alone	18,354	51	673	947	811	1,319	2,501	3,697	3,369	3,130	1,857
Living with nonrelatives	3,029	46	658	539	253	334	476	444	197	66	15
Not a householder	31,695	9,996	6,979	3,333	1,792	2,575	2,644	1,888	1,100	844	541
Child of householder	17,120	8,682	4,595	1,494	661	859	550	228	47	0	0
Other relative of householder	7,730	910	825	513	330	775	1,156	1,093	866	763	501
In nonfamily household	6,845	404	1,559	1,326	801	941	938	567	187	81	40

PERCENT DISTRIBUTION BY LIVING ARRANGEMENT

	total	under 20	20–24	25–29	30–34	35–44	45–54	55–64	65–74	75–84	85+
TOTAL WOMEN	100.0%	100.0%	100.0%	100.0%	100.0%	100.0%	100.0%	100.0%	100.0%	100.0%	100.0%
Householder	75.2	3.8	35.9	68.1	82.6	51.3	50.9	90.5	91.1	88.9	83.1
Married couple householder or spouse	46.2	0.7	12.4	38.5	54.6	25.0	23.7	59.4	54.2	37.7	15.6
Other family householder	12.3	2.2	11.2	15.4	17.6	18.1	14.0	10.2	8.2	9.0	8.8
Living alone	14.4	0.5	6.2	9.1	7.9	6.5	11.1	18.7	27.2	41.3	58.2
Living with nonrelatives	2.4	0.4	6.0	5.2	2.5	1.6	2.1	2.2	1.6	0.9	0.5
Not a householder	24.8	96.2	64.1	31.9	17.4	48.7	49.1	9.5	8.9	11.1	16.9
Child of householder	13.4	83.5	42.2	14.3	6.4	4.2	2.4	1.2	0.4	0.0	0.0
Other relative of householder	6.1	8.8	7.6	4.9	3.2	3.8	5.1	5.5	7.0	10.1	15.7
In nonfamily household	5.4	3.9	14.3	12.7	7.8	4.6	4.2	2.9	1.5	1.1	1.3

Source: Bureau of the Census, America's Families and Living Arrangements: 2012, Detailed Tables, Internet site http://www.census .gov/hhes/families/data/cps2012.html; calculations by New Strategist

Table 6.8 Living Arrangements of Men by Age, 2012

(number and percent distribution of men aged 15 or older by living arrangement and age, 2012; numbers in thousands)

	total	under 20	20–24	25–29	30–34	35–44	45–54	55–64	65–74	75–84	85+
TOTAL MEN	**119,877**	**10,836**	**10,982**	**10,430**	**10,028**	**19,670**	**21,463**	**18,137**	**10,980**	**5,543**	**1,809**
Householder	**84,032**	**425**	**2,611**	**5,704**	**7,385**	**15,850**	**18,207**	**16,654**	**10,338**	**5,203**	**1,656**
Married couple householder or spouse	58,949	33	763	2,960	4,912	11,888	13,425	12,123	7,994	3,933	919
Other family householder	5,888	273	546	767	665	1,157	1,111	795	317	153	103
Living alone	14,835	58	596	1,147	1,176	2,137	3,052	3,206	1,829	1,018	615
Living with nonrelatives	4,360	61	706	830	632	668	619	530	198	99	19
Not a householder	**35,844**	**10,412**	**8,370**	**4,725**	**2,643**	**3,820**	**3,255**	**1,483**	**641**	**340**	**154**
Child of householder	21,195	9,194	5,896	2,321	1,138	1,407	997	206	33	0	0
Other relative of householder	6,720	905	1,022	804	455	936	1,099	699	409	262	131
In nonfamily household	7,929	313	1,452	1,600	1,050	1,477	1,159	578	199	78	23

PERCENT DISTRIBUTION BY LIVING ARRANGEMENT

TOTAL MEN	**100.0%**	**100.0%**	**100.0%**	**100.0%**	**100.0%**	**100.0%**	**100.0%**	**100.0%**	**100.0%**	**100.0%**	**100.0%**
Householder	**70.1**	**3.8**	**23.8**	**54.7**	**73.6**	**55.2**	**59.4**	**91.8**	**94.2**	**93.9**	**91.5**
Married couple householder or spouse	49.2	0.2	6.9	28.4	49.0	35.0	37.2	66.8	72.8	71.0	50.8
Other family householder	4.9	2.5	5.0	7.4	6.6	5.9	5.2	4.4	2.9	2.8	5.7
Living alone	12.4	0.5	5.4	11.0	11.7	10.9	14.2	17.7	16.7	18.4	34.0
Living with nonrelatives	3.6	0.6	6.4	8.0	6.3	3.4	2.9	2.9	1.8	1.8	1.1
Not a householder	**29.9**	**96.2**	**76.2**	**45.3**	**26.4**	**44.8**	**40.6**	**8.2**	**5.8**	**6.1**	**8.5**
Child of householder	17.7	84.8	53.7	22.3	11.3	7.2	4.6	1.1	0.3	0.0	0.0
Other relative of householder	5.6	8.4	9.3	7.7	4.5	4.8	5.1	3.9	3.7	4.7	7.2
In nonfamily household	6.6	2.9	13.2	15.3	10.5	7.5	5.4	3.2	1.8	1.4	1.3

Source: Bureau of the Census, America's Families and Living Arrangements: 2012, Detailed Tables, Internet site http://www.census.gov/hhes/families/data/cps2012.html; calculations by New Strategist

Many Children Live with Their Mother Only

Only 58 percent live with both biological parents who are married to one another.

In 2012, 68 percent of children under age 18 lived with two parents, 64 percent lived with two married parents, and 58 percent lived with two married parents who were the child's biological mother and father. The percentage of children who live with their married, biological parents ranges from a high of 76 percent among Asians to a low of 29 percent among blacks.

Nearly one in four children lives with his or her mother only. Among Asians, just 12 percent of children live with their mother only. The figure is 49 percent among blacks. Few children live with their father only, the proportion being 3 to 4 percent regardless of race or Hispanic origin.

■ Only 6 percent of children live with a stepparent and just 2 percent live with an adoptive parent.

Most children still live with two parents

(percent distribution of children by living arrangement, 2012)

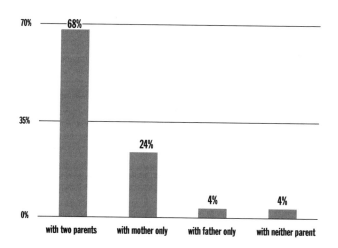

Table 6.9 Living Arrangements of Children by Race and Hispanic Origin, 2012

(number and percent distribution of children under age 18 by living arrangement, race, and Hispanic origin, 2012; numbers in thousands)

	total	Asian	black	Hispanic	non-Hispanic white
TOTAL CHILDREN	73,817	4,542	13,012	17,570	39,062
Living with two parents	50,267	3,785	5,200	11,542	29,881
Married parents	47,330	3,657	4,537	10,364	28,806
Unmarried parents	2,937	129	663	1,178	1,075
Biological mother and father	45,221	3,554	4,364	10,589	26,888
Married parents	42,691	3,431	3,816	9,528	25,997
Biological mother and stepfather	3,016	73	518	680	1,742
Biological father and stepmother	919	29	160	125	587
Biological mother and adoptive father	185	10	22	29	118
Biological father and adoptive mother	34	2	3	1	28
Adoptive mother and father	661	109	101	86	364
Other	231	8	32	31	154
Living with one parent	20,916	662	6,958	5,465	8,090
Mother only	17,991	548	6,414	4,926	6,423
Father only	2,924	114	545	539	1,667
Living with no parents	2,634	95	853	563	1,091
Grandparents	1,454	29	494	265	627
Other	1,180	66	360	298	463
Living with at least one biological parent	69,941	4,290	11,907	16,822	37,339
Living with at least one stepparent	4,287	121	750	864	2,519
Living with at least one adoptive parent	1,126	150	205	160	600

	total	Asian	black	Hispanic	non-Hispanic white
PERCENT DISTRIBUTION BY LIVING ARRANGEMENT					
TOTAL CHILDREN	**100.0%**	**100.0%**	**100.0%**	**100.0%**	**100.0%**
Living with two parents	**68.1**	**83.3**	**40.0**	**65.7**	**76.5**
Married parents	64.1	80.5	34.9	59.0	73.7
Unmarried parents	4.0	2.8	5.1	6.7	2.8
Biological mother and father	61.3	78.2	33.5	60.3	68.8
Married parents	57.8	75.5	29.3	54.2	66.6
Biological mother and stepfather	4.1	1.6	4.0	3.9	4.5
Biological father and stepmother	1.2	0.6	1.2	0.7	1.5
Biological mother and adoptive father	0.3	0.2	0.2	0.2	0.3
Biological father and adoptive mother	0.0	0.0	0.0	0.0	0.1
Adoptive mother and father	0.9	2.4	0.8	0.5	0.9
Other	0.3	0.2	0.2	0.2	0.4
Living with one parent	**28.3**	**14.6**	**53.5**	**31.1**	**20.7**
Mother only	24.4	12.1	49.3	28.0	16.4
Father only	4.0	2.5	4.2	3.1	4.3
Living with no parents	**3.6**	**2.1**	**6.6**	**3.2**	**2.8**
Grandparents	2.0	0.6	3.8	1.5	1.6
Other	1.6	1.5	2.8	1.7	1.2
Living with at least one biological parent	**94.7**	**94.5**	**91.5**	**95.7**	**95.6**
Living with at least one stepparent	**5.8**	**2.7**	**5.8**	**4.9**	**6.4**
Living with at least one adoptive parent	**1.5**	**3.3**	**1.6**	**0.9**	**1.5**

Note: Numbers do not sum to total because Asians and blacks are those who identify themselves as being of the race alone and those who identify themselves as being of the race in combination with other races, not all races are shown, and Hispanics may be of any race.

Source: Bureau of the Census, America's Families and Living Arrangements: 2012, Detailed Tables, Internet site http://www .census.gov/hhes/families/data/cps2012.html; calculations by New Strategist

Married Couples Are a Shrinking Share of Households

They accounted for only 49 percent of households in 2012.

The proportion of households headed by married couples fell from 53 to 49 percent between 2000 and 2012. The number of married couples has not grown at all since 2007 as young adults postpone marriage. The number of nuclear families—married couples with children under age 18 at home—fell 8 percent between 2007 and 2012.

Households headed by the youngest and oldest adults are the most diverse as men and women transition into and out of marriage over the life course. By race and Hispanic origin, black and Hispanic households are most diverse. Married couples head only 28 percent of black households, while female-headed families head another 28 percent. Among Hispanics, 48 percent of households are headed by married couples and 21 percent are female-headed families. Living alone is more common among blacks and non-Hispanic whites than among Asians or Hispanics.

■ Unrelated people who live together—such as friends or cohabiting partners—account for nearly one in four households headed by people under age 25.

Women who live alone is the second most common household type

(percent distribution of households by type ranked by share, 2012)

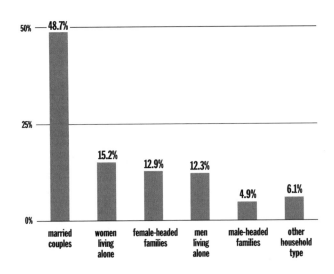

Table 6.10 Households by Type, 2000 to 2012

(number and percent distribution of households by household type, 2000 to 2012; percent change in number for selected years; numbers in thousands)

NUMBER	2012	2010	2007	2000	percent change 2007–2012	percent change 2000–2012
TOTAL HOUSEHOLDS	**121,084**	**117,538**	**116,011**	**104,705**	**4.4%**	**15.6%**
Family households	**80,506**	**78,833**	**78,425**	**72,025**	**2.7**	**11.8**
Married couples	58,949	58,410	58,945	55,311	0.0	6.6
With children under age 18	25,114	26,171	27,350	26,359	–8.2	–4.7
Female householders, no spouse present	15,669	14,843	14,416	12,687	8.7	23.5
With children under age 18	10,380	9,867	9,883	8,727	5.0	18.9
Male householders, no spouse present	5,888	5,580	5,063	4,028	16.3	46.2
With children under age 18	2,982	2,851	2,587	2,164	15.3	37.8
Nonfamily households	**40,578**	**38,705**	**37,587**	**32,680**	**8.0**	**24.2**
Female householders	21,383	20,442	20,249	18,039	5.6	18.5
Living alone	18,354	17,428	17,604	15,543	4.3	18.1
Male householders	19,195	18,263	17,338	14,641	10.7	31.1
Living alone	14,835	13,971	13,528	11,181	9.7	32.7

PERCENT DISTRIBUTION					percentage point change 2007–2012	percentage point change 2000–2012
TOTAL HOUSEHOLDS	**100.0%**	**100.0%**	**100.0%**	**100.0%**	–	–
Family households	**66.5**	**67.1**	**67.6**	**68.8**	**–1.1**	**–2.3**
Married couples	48.7	49.7	50.8	52.8	–2.1	–4.1
With children under age 18	20.7	22.3	23.6	25.2	–2.8	–4.4
Female householders, no spouse present	12.9	12.6	12.4	12.1	0.5	0.8
With children under age 18	8.6	8.4	8.5	8.3	0.1	0.2
Male householders, no spouse present	4.9	4.7	4.4	3.8	0.5	1.0
With children under age 18	2.5	2.4	2.2	2.1	0.2	0.4
Nonfamily households	**33.5**	**32.9**	**32.4**	**31.2**	**1.1**	**2.3**
Female householders	17.7	17.4	17.5	17.2	0.2	0.4
Living alone	15.2	14.8	15.2	14.8	0.0	0.3
Male householders	15.9	15.5	14.9	14.0	0.9	1.9
Living alone	12.3	11.9	11.7	10.7	0.6	1.6

Note: "–" means not applicable.
Source: Bureau of the Census, Current Population Survey Annual Social and Economic Supplement, Internet site http://www .census.gov/hhes/www/income/data/incpovhlth/2011/index.html; calculations by New Strategist

Table 6.11 Households by Household Type and Age of Householder, 2012

(number and percent distribution of households by household type and age of householder, 2012; numbers in thousands)

	total	under 25	25 to 34	35 to 44	45 to 54	55 to 64	65 or older
TOTAL HOUSEHOLDS	121,084	6,180	19,846	21,241	24,195	22,779	26,843
Family households	80,506	3,333	13,511	16,782	17,547	14,902	14,431
Married couples	58,949	1,058	8,658	11,954	13,299	12,093	11,886
With own children under age 18	23,704	597	6,153	9,643	6,048	1,079	183
Female householders, no spouse present	15,669	1,455	3,420	3,672	3,137	2,013	1,972
With own children under age 18	8,869	970	3,077	3,010	1,531	224	57
Male householders, no spouse present	5,888	819	1,432	1,157	1,112	795	573
With own children under age 18	2,415	171	765	804	514	124	37
Nonfamily households	40,578	2,848	6,335	4,458	6,648	7,877	12,412
Female householders	21,383	1,427	2,551	1,653	2,977	4,141	8,634
Living alone	18,354	724	1,758	1,319	2,500	3,697	8,355
Male householders	19,195	1,421	3,784	2,805	3,671	3,736	3,778
Living alone	14,835	654	2,323	2,137	3,052	3,206	3,462

PERCENT DISTRIBUTION BY HOUSEHOLD TYPE

	total	under 25	25 to 34	35 to 44	45 to 54	55 to 64	65 or older
TOTAL HOUSEHOLDS	100.0%	100.0%	100.0%	100.0%	100.0%	100.0%	100.0%
Family households	66.5	53.9	68.1	79.0	72.5	65.4	53.8
Married couples	48.7	17.1	43.6	56.3	55.0	53.1	44.3
With own children under age 18	19.6	9.7	31.0	45.4	25.0	4.7	0.7
Female householders, no spouse present	12.9	23.5	17.2	17.3	13.0	8.8	7.3
With own children under age 18	7.3	15.7	15.5	14.2	6.3	1.0	0.2
Male householders, no spouse present	4.9	13.3	7.2	5.4	4.6	3.5	2.1
With own children under age 18	2.0	2.8	3.9	3.8	2.1	0.5	0.1
Nonfamily households	33.5	46.1	31.9	21.0	27.5	34.6	46.2
Female householders	17.7	23.1	12.9	7.8	12.3	18.2	32.2
Living alone	15.2	11.7	8.9	6.2	10.3	16.2	31.1
Male householders	15.9	23.0	19.1	13.2	15.2	16.4	14.1
Living alone	12.3	10.6	11.7	10.1	12.6	14.1	12.9

PERCENT DISTRIBUTION BY AGE OF HOUSEHOLDER

	total	under 25	25 to 34	35 to 44	45 to 54	55 to 64	65 or older
TOTAL HOUSEHOLDS	**100.0%**	**5.1%**	**16.4%**	**17.5%**	**20.0%**	**18.8%**	**22.2%**
Family households	**100.0**	**4.1**	**16.8**	**20.8**	**21.8**	**18.5**	**17.9**
Married couples	100.0	1.8	14.7	20.3	22.6	20.5	20.2
With own children under age 18	100.0	2.5	26.0	40.7	25.5	4.6	0.8
Female householders, no spouse present	100.0	9.3	21.8	23.4	20.0	12.8	12.6
With own children under age 18	100.0	10.9	34.7	33.9	17.3	2.5	0.6
Male householders, no spouse present	100.0	13.9	24.3	19.6	18.9	13.5	9.7
With own children under age 18	100.0	7.1	31.7	33.3	21.3	5.1	1.5
Nonfamily households	**100.0**	**7.0**	**15.6**	**11.0**	**16.4**	**19.4**	**30.6**
Female householders	100.0	6.7	11.9	7.7	13.9	19.4	40.4
Living alone	100.0	3.9	9.6	7.2	13.6	20.1	45.5
Male householders	100.0	7.4	19.7	14.6	19.1	19.5	19.7
Living alone	100.0	4.4	15.7	14.4	20.6	21.6	23.3

Note: "Own children" are sons and daughters of the householder, including stepchildren and adopted children.
Source: Bureau of the Census, 2012 Current Population Survey Annual Social and Economic Supplement, Internet site http://www.census.gov/hhes/www/cpstables/032012/hhinc/toc.htm; calculations by New Strategist

Table 6.12 Households by Household Type, Race, and Hispanic Origin of Householder, 2012

(number and percent distribution of households by household type, race, and Hispanic origin of householder, 2012; numbers in thousands)

	total	Asian	black	Hispanic	non-Hispanic white
TOTAL HOUSEHOLDS	121,084	5,705	16,165	14,939	83,573
Family households	80,506	4,342	10,025	11,585	54,146
Married couples	58,949	3,435	4,546	7,222	43,376
With children under age 18	25,114	1,842	2,333	4,672	16,258
Female householders, no spouse present	15,669	573	4,477	3,086	7,539
With children under age 18	10,380	306	3,208	2,358	4,549
Male householders, no spouse present	5,888	334	1,002	1,277	3,231
With children under age 18	2,982	120	514	725	1,599
Nonfamily households	40,578	1,362	6,141	3,353	29,426
Female householders	21,383	685	3,374	1,535	15,635
Living alone	18,354	534	3,039	1,251	13,395
Male householders	19,195	677	2,767	1,818	13,792
Living alone	14,835	480	2,367	1,264	10,629

PERCENT DISTRIBUTION BY HOUSEHOLD TYPE

	total	Asian	black	Hispanic	non-Hispanic white
TOTAL HOUSEHOLDS	100.0%	100.0%	100.0%	100.0%	100.0%
Family households	66.5	76.1	62.0	77.6	64.8
Married couples	48.7	60.2	28.1	48.3	51.9
With children under age 18	20.7	32.3	14.4	31.3	19.5
Female householders, no spouse present	12.9	10.0	27.7	20.7	9.0
With children under age 18	8.6	5.4	19.8	15.8	5.4
Male householders, no spouse present	4.9	5.9	6.2	8.5	3.9
With children under age 18	2.5	2.1	3.2	4.9	1.9
Nonfamily households	33.5	23.9	38.0	22.4	35.2
Female householders	17.7	12.0	20.9	10.3	18.7
Living alone	15.2	9.4	18.8	8.4	16.0
Male householders	15.9	11.9	17.1	12.2	16.5
Living alone	12.3	8.4	14.6	8.5	12.7

PERCENT DISTRIBUTION BY RACE AND HISPANIC ORIGIN	total	Asian	black	Hispanic	non-Hispanic white
TOTAL HOUSEHOLDS	**100.0%**	**4.7%**	**13.4%**	**12.3%**	**69.0%**
Family households	**100.0**	**5.4**	**12.5**	**14.4**	**67.3**
Married couples	100.0	5.8	7.7	12.3	73.6
With children under age 18	100.0	7.3	9.3	18.6	64.7
Female householders, no spouse present	100.0	3.7	28.6	19.7	48.1
With children under age 18	100.0	2.9	30.9	22.7	43.8
Male householders, no spouse present	100.0	5.7	17.0	21.7	54.9
With children under age 18	100.0	4.0	17.2	24.3	53.6
Nonfamily households	**100.0**	**3.4**	**15.1**	**8.3**	**72.5**
Female householders	100.0	3.2	15.8	7.2	73.1
Living alone	100.0	2.9	16.6	6.8	73.0
Male householders	100.0	3.5	14.4	9.5	71.9
Living alone	100.0	3.2	16.0	8.5	71.7

Note: Numbers do not add to total because Hispanics may be of any race, not all races are shown, and some householders may be of more than one race. Asians and blacks are those who identify themselves as being of the race alone and those who identify themselves as being of the race in combination with other races. Non-Hispanic whites are those who identify themselves as being white alone and not Hispanic.
Source: Bureau of the Census, 2012 Current Population Survey Annual Social and Economic Supplement, Internet site http:// www.census.gov/hhes/www/cpstables/032012/hhinc/toc.htm; calculations by New Strategist

Women Outnumber Men among People Who Live Alone

Men account for the majority in most age groups, however.

Thirty-three million Americans lived alone in 2012, the 55 percent majority of them women. In most age groups, however, men who live alone outnumber women. Women who live alone outnumber their male counterparts only among those under age 25 and aged 60 or older.

Overall, 12 percent of men live by themselves. The proportion of men who live alone varies little by age, ranging from 10 to 18 percent from ages 25 through 74. The figure is a somewhat higher 22 percent among men aged 75 or older. Among women, 14 percent live alone, and the figure varies widely by age. Fewer than 10 percent of women under age 50 live alone. Among women aged 75 or older, fully 46 percent live by themselves.

■ The lifestyles of people who live alone vary greatly depending on their age.

Men are the majority of people who live alone in the 25-to-59 age group

(male share of people who live alone by age, 2012)

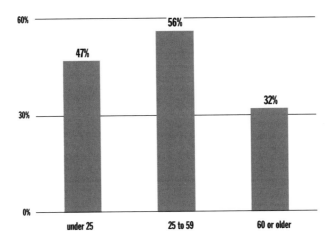

Table 6.13 People Living Alone by Sex and Age, 2012

(total number of people aged 15 or older, number and percent living alone, and percent distribution of people who live alone, by sex and age, 2012; numbers in thousands)

	total	number	percent	percent distribution
Total people	**247,696**	**33,189**	**13.4%**	**100.0%**
Aged 15 to 24	43,117	1,378	3.2	4.2
Aged 25 to 29	20,893	2,094	10.0	6.3
Aged 30 to 34	20,326	1,987	9.8	6.0
Aged 35 to 39	19,140	1,627	8.5	4.9
Aged 40 to 44	20,787	1,829	8.8	5.5
Aged 45 to 49	21,583	2,455	11.4	7.4
Aged 50 to 54	22,372	3,098	13.8	9.3
Aged 55 to 59	20,470	3,432	16.8	10.3
Aged 60 to 64	17,501	3,471	19.8	10.5
Aged 65 to 69	13,599	2,865	21.1	8.6
Aged 70 to 74	9,784	2,332	23.8	7.0
Aged 75 or older	18,123	6,620	36.5	19.9
Total men	**119,946**	**14,835**	**12.4**	**100.0**
Aged 15 to 24	21,826	654	3.0	4.4
Aged 25 to 29	10,430	1,147	11.0	7.7
Aged 30 to 34	10,034	1,176	11.7	7.9
Aged 35 to 39	9,421	985	10.5	6.6
Aged 40 to 44	10,255	1,152	11.2	7.8
Aged 45 to 49	10,584	1,427	13.5	9.6
Aged 50 to 54	10,906	1,625	14.9	11.0
Aged 55 to 59	9,879	1,730	17.5	11.7
Aged 60 to 64	8,278	1,476	17.8	9.9
Aged 65 to 69	6,461	1,084	16.8	7.3
Aged 70 to 74	4,519	745	16.5	5.0
Aged 75 or older	7,353	1,633	22.2	11.0
Total women	**127,751**	**18,354**	**14.4**	**100.0**
Aged 15 to 24	21,291	724	3.4	3.9
Aged 25 to 29	10,464	947	9.1	5.2
Aged 30 to 34	10,292	811	7.9	4.4
Aged 35 to 39	9,719	642	6.6	3.5
Aged 40 to 44	10,532	677	6.4	3.7
Aged 45 to 49	11,000	1,028	9.3	5.6
Aged 50 to 54	11,466	1,473	12.8	8.0
Aged 55 to 59	10,592	1,702	16.1	9.3
Aged 60 to 64	9,223	1,995	21.6	10.9
Aged 65 to 69	7,139	1,781	24.9	9.7
Aged 70 to 74	5,265	1,587	30.1	8.6
Aged 75 or older	10,771	4,987	46.3	27.2

Source: Bureau of the Census, 2012 Current Population Survey Annual Social and Economic Supplement, Internet site http://www.census.gov/hhes/www/cpstables/032012/hhinc/toc.htm; calculations by New Strategist

Few Households Include Children under Age 18

Children under age 18 are present in most female-headed families, however.

Among the nation's 121 million households, only 29 percent include children under age 18. Forty percent of married-couple households have children under age 18, as do 41 percent of male-headed families. Among female-headed families, the 57 percent majority include children under age 18. By age, most households headed by people ranging in age from 30 to 44 have children under age 18 in their home.

Only 18 percent of all married couples have preschoolers in their home, but more than half of married couples with a householder under age 35 are raising preschoolers. Twenty-three percent of female-headed families have preschoolers, including most of those under age 30. The percentage of male-headed families with preschoolers peaks at 38 percent among householders in their thirties.

■ Only 32 percent of married couples with preschoolers have a stay-at-home mom.

Male-headed families are unlikely to include children under age 18

(percent of households with children under age 18, by household type, 2012)

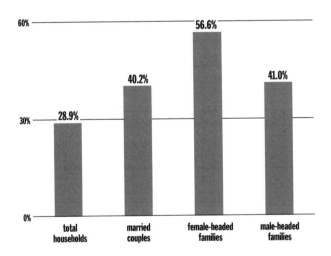

Table 6.14 Total Households by Age of Householder, Type of Household, and Presence of Children under Age 18, 2012

(number and percent distribution of households by age of householder, type of household, and presence of own children under age 18, 2012; numbers in thousands)

	all households		married couples		female-headed families		male-headed families	
	total	with children under 18	total	with children under 18	total	with children under 18	total	with children under 18
Total households	**121,084**	**34,989**	**58,949**	**23,704**	**15,669**	**8,869**	**5,888**	**2,415**
Under age 25	6,180	1,737	1,059	597	1,456	970	819	171
Aged 25 to 29	9,208	3,820	3,366	2,063	1,611	1,401	768	356
Aged 30 to 34	10,638	6,176	5,292	4,090	1,809	1,676	665	409
Aged 35 to 39	10,111	6,772	5,557	4,690	1,871	1,666	560	415
Aged 40 to 44	11,129	6,686	6,397	4,953	1,801	1,344	596	389
Aged 45 to 49	11,763	5,213	6,438	3,872	1,722	998	605	343
Aged 50 to 54	12,433	2,880	6,861	2,176	1,414	533	506	171
Aged 55 to 64	22,779	1,428	12,093	1,079	2,013	224	795	124
Aged 65 or older	26,843	277	11,886	183	1,972	57	573	37

PERCENT OF HOUSEHOLDS WITH CHILDREN BY TYPE

	all households		married couples		female-headed families		male-headed families	
Total households	**100.0%**	**28.9%**	**100.0%**	**40.2%**	**100.0%**	**56.6%**	**100.0%**	**41.0%**
Under age 25	100.0	28.1	100.0	56.4	100.0	66.6	100.0	20.9
Aged 25 to 29	100.0	41.5	100.0	61.3	100.0	87.0	100.0	46.4
Aged 30 to 34	100.0	58.1	100.0	77.3	100.0	92.6	100.0	61.5
Aged 35 to 39	100.0	67.0	100.0	84.4	100.0	89.0	100.0	74.1
Aged 40 to 44	100.0	60.1	100.0	77.4	100.0	74.6	100.0	65.3
Aged 45 to 49	100.0	44.3	100.0	60.1	100.0	58.0	100.0	56.7
Aged 50 to 54	100.0	23.2	100.0	31.7	100.0	37.7	100.0	33.8
Aged 55 to 64	100.0	6.3	100.0	8.9	100.0	11.1	100.0	15.6
Aged 65 or older	100.0	1.0	100.0	1.5	100.0	2.9	100.0	6.5

Source: Bureau of the Census, America's Families and Living Arrangements: 2012, Detailed Tables, Internet site http://www .census.gov/hhes/families/data/cps2012.html; calculations by New Strategist

Table 6.15 Married Couples by Age of Householder and Age of Children, 2012

(number and percent distribution of married-couple households by presence of own children at home, by age of householder and age of children, 2012; numbers in thousands)

	total	of any age	under age 18	aged 12 to 17	aged 6 to 11	under age 6	under age 1
		with children at home					
Total married couples	**58,949**	**30,882**	**23,704**	**11,152**	**11,204**	**10,676**	**2,015**
Under age 25	1,059	598	597	28	83	552	199
Aged 25 to 29	3,366	2,072	2,063	102	754	1,835	538
Aged 30 to 34	5,292	4,127	4,090	814	1,947	3,164	693
Aged 35 to 39	5,557	4,765	4,690	1,760	2,807	2,644	413
Aged 40 to 44	6,397	5,327	4,953	2,871	2,888	1,601	113
Aged 45 to 49	6,438	4,871	3,872	2,847	1,740	570	35
Aged 50 to 54	6,861	3,914	2,176	1,739	663	180	17
Aged 55 to 64	12,093	3,754	1,079	871	260	90	4
Aged 65 or older	11,886	1,454	183	118	61	40	4
Total married couples	**100.0%**	**52.4%**	**40.2%**	**18.9%**	**19.0%**	**18.1%**	**3.4%**
Under age 25	100.0	56.5	56.4	2.6	7.8	52.1	18.8
Aged 25 to 29	100.0	61.6	61.3	3.0	22.4	54.5	16.0
Aged 30 to 34	100.0	78.0	77.3	15.4	36.8	59.8	13.1
Aged 35 to 39	100.0	85.7	84.4	31.7	50.5	47.6	7.4
Aged 40 to 44	100.0	83.3	77.4	44.9	45.1	25.0	1.8
Aged 45 to 49	100.0	75.7	60.1	44.2	27.0	8.9	0.5
Aged 50 to 54	100.0	57.0	31.7	25.3	9.7	2.6	0.2
Aged 55 to 64	100.0	31.0	8.9	7.2	2.2	0.7	0.0
Aged 65 or older	100.0	12.2	1.5	1.0	0.5	0.3	0.0

Note: Numbers do not add to total because households may contain children in more than one age group.
Source: Bureau of the Census, America's Families and Living Arrangements: 2012, Detailed Tables, Internet site http://www.census.gov/hhes/families/data/cps2012.html; calculations by New Strategist

Table 6.16 Female-Headed Families by Age of Householder and Age of Children, 2012

(number and percent distribution of female-headed families by presence of own children at home, by age of householder and age of children, 2012; numbers in thousands)

	total	with children at home					
		of any age	under age 18	aged 12 to 17	aged 6 to 11	under age 6	under age 1
Total female-headed families	**15,669**	**13,397**	**8,869**	**4,262**	**4,102**	**3,636**	**559**
Under age 25	1,456	980	970	9	131	920	232
Aged 25 to 29	1,611	1,411	1,401	99	812	1,066	160
Aged 30 to 34	1,809	1,689	1,676	722	1,135	818	102
Aged 35 to 39	1,871	1,763	1,666	1,080	897	495	54
Aged 40 to 44	1,801	1,691	1,344	926	631	214	10
Aged 45 to 49	1,722	1,571	998	742	338	73	0
Aged 50 to 54	1,414	1,251	533	464	94	19	0
Aged 55 to 64	2,013	1,536	224	190	37	18	2
Aged 65 or older	1,972	1,506	57	30	25	12	0
Total female-headed families	**100.0%**	**85.5%**	**56.6%**	**27.2%**	**26.2%**	**23.2%**	**3.6%**
Under age 25	100.0	67.3	66.6	0.6	9.0	63.2	15.9
Aged 25 to 29	100.0	87.6	87.0	6.1	50.4	66.2	9.9
Aged 30 to 34	100.0	93.4	92.6	39.9	62.7	45.2	5.6
Aged 35 to 39	100.0	94.2	89.0	57.7	47.9	26.5	2.9
Aged 40 to 44	100.0	93.9	74.6	51.4	35.0	11.9	0.6
Aged 45 to 49	100.0	91.2	58.0	43.1	19.6	4.2	0.0
Aged 50 to 54	100.0	88.5	37.7	32.8	6.6	1.3	0.0
Aged 55 to 64	100.0	76.3	11.1	9.4	1.8	0.9	0.1
Aged 65 or older	100.0	76.4	2.9	1.5	1.3	0.6	0.0

Note: Numbers do not add to total because households may contain children in more than one age group.
Source: Bureau of the Census, America's Families and Living Arrangements: 2012, Detailed Tables, Internet site http://www.census.gov/hhes/families/data/cps2012.html; calculations by New Strategist

Table 6.17 Male-Headed Families by Age of Householder and Age of Children, 2012

(number and percent distribution of male-headed families by presence of own children at home, by age of householder and age of children, 2012; numbers in thousands)

| | total | with children at home | | | | | |
		of any age	under age 18	aged 12 to 17	aged 6 to 11	under age 6	under age 1
Total male-headed families	**5,888**	**3,633**	**2,415**	**1,034**	**957**	**1,031**	**228**
Under age 25	819	171	171	4	17	155	55
Aged 25 to 29	768	371	356	20	119	292	75
Aged 30 to 34	665	411	409	74	233	256	60
Aged 35 to 39	560	431	415	216	207	150	16
Aged 40 to 44	596	445	389	227	170	98	13
Aged 45 to 49	605	473	343	240	115	45	7
Aged 50 to 54	506	378	171	129	54	19	3
Aged 55 to 64	795	504	124	97	32	10	0
Aged 65 or older	573	451	37	28	10	4	0
Total male-headed families	**100.0%**	**61.7%**	**41.0%**	**17.6**	**16.3**	**17.5%**	**3.9%**
Under age 25	100.0	20.9	20.9	0.5	2.1	18.9	6.7
Aged 25 to 29	100.0	48.3	46.4	2.6	15.5	38.0	9.8
Aged 30 to 34	100.0	61.8	61.5	11.1	35.0	38.5	9.0
Aged 35 to 39	100.0	77.0	74.1	38.6	37	26.8	2.9
Aged 40 to 44	100.0	74.7	65.3	38.1	28.5	16.4	2.2
Aged 45 to 49	100.0	78.2	56.7	39.7	19.0	7.4	1.2
Aged 50 to 54	100.0	74.7	33.8	25.5	10.7	3.8	0.6
Aged 55 to 64	100.0	63.4	15.6	12.2	4.0	1.3	0.0
Aged 65 or older	100.0	78.7	6.5	4.9	1.7	0.7	0.0

Note: Numbers do not add to total because households may contain children in more than one age group.
Source: Bureau of the Census, America's Families and Living Arrangements: 2012, Detailed Tables, Internet site http://www
.census.gov/hhes/families/data/cps2012.html; calculations by New Strategist

Table 6.18 Stay-at-Home Parents among Married Couples, 2012

(number and percent distribution of married-couple family groups with children under age 15 by stay-at-home status of mother and father and age of child, 2012; numbers in thousands)

	with children under age 15		with children under age 6	
	number	percent distribution	number	percent distribution
Total married-couple family groups	**21,334**	**100.0%**	**11,055**	**100.0%**
Mother's labor force status in past year				
In labor force one or more weeks	14,564	68.3	7,096	64.2
Not in labor force, caring for family	5,737	26.9	3,494	31.6
Not in labor force, other reason	1,033	4.8	466	4.2
Father's labor force status in past year				
In labor force one or more weeks	19,943	93.5	10,400	94.1
Not in labor force, caring for family	276	1.3	170	1.5
Not in labor force, other reason	1,115	5.2	485	4.4

Note: Married-couple family groups include married-couple householders and married couples living in households headed by others.
Source: Bureau of the Census, Current Population Survey Annual Social and Economic Supplement, America's Families and Living Arrangements: 2012, Detailed Tables, Internet site http://www.census.gov/hhes/families/data/cps2012.html; calculations by New Strategist

Husbands and Wives Are Alike in Many Ways

Most couples are close in age, of the same race and ethnicity, and share the same educational level.

Men usually marry slightly younger women, but most husbands and wives are close in age. Thirty-three percent are within one year of each other in age, and in another 34 percent the husband is only two to five years older than the wife.

Both husband and wife are non-Hispanic white in 69 percent of the nation's married couples. In 11 percent both are Hispanic, in 6 percent both are non-Hispanic black, and in another 6 percent both are non-Hispanic other (primarily Asian). No single mixed race/Hispanic origin combination accounts for more than about 2 percent of couples, the most common being a non-Hispanic white husband and a Hispanic wife.

In the 54 percent majority of married couples, neither husband nor wife has a bachelor's degree. In another 22 percent, one has a bachelor's degree and the other does not, and both husband and wife have a bachelor's degree in 24 percent.

■ The similarities between husbands and wives mean that high earners tend to marry one another, boosting incomes.

Most husbands and wives are close in age

(percent distribution of married couples by age difference between husband and wife, 2012)

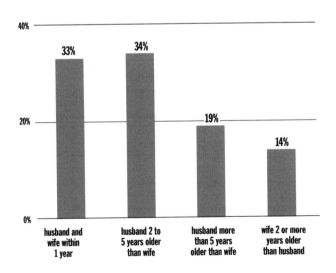

Table 6.19 Age Difference between Husbands and Wives, 2012

(number and percent distribution of married-couple family groups by age difference between husband and wife, 2012; numbers in thousands)

AGE DIFFERENCE	number	percent distribution
Total married couples	**61,047**	**100.0%**
Husband 20 or more years older than wife	590	1.0
Husband 15 to 19 years older than wife	962	1.6
Husband 10 to 14 years older than wife	3,024	5.0
Husband 6 to 9 years older than wife	6,935	11.4
Husband 4 to 5 years older than wife	8,083	13.2
Husband 2 to 3 years older than wife	12,433	20.4
Husband and wife within 1 year	20,344	33.3
Wife 2 to 3 years older than husband	3,983	6.5
Wife 4 to 5 years older than husband	1,998	3.3
Wife 6 to 9 years older than husband	1,682	2.8
Wife 10 to 14 years older than husband	631	1.0
Wife 15 to 19 years older than husband	182	0.3
Wife 20 or more years older than husband	200	0.3

Note: Married-couple family groups include married-couple householders and married couples living in households headed by others.
Source: Bureau of the Census, America's Families and Living Arrangements: 2012, Current Population Survey Annual Social and Economic Supplement, Internet site http://www.census.gov/hhes/families/data/cps2012.html; calculations by New Strategist

Table 6.20 Race and Hispanic Origin Difference between Husbands and Wives, 2012

(number and percent distribution of married-couple family groups by race and Hispanic origin differences between husband and wife, 2012; numbers in thousands)

RACE AND HISPANIC ORIGIN DIFFERENCE	number	percent distribution
Total married-couple family groups	**61,047**	**100.0%**
Both white	41,996	68.8
Both Hispanic	6,730	11.0
Both black	3,860	6.3
Both other	3,616	5.9
Mixed race/Hispanic origin couples	4,507	7.4
Husband white, wife black	144	0.2
Husband white, wife Hispanic	1,098	1.8
Husband white, wife other	1,084	1.8
Husband black, wife white	315	0.5
Husband black, wife Hispanic	166	0.3
Husband black, wife other	85	0.1
Husband Hispanic, wife white	977	1.6
Husband Hispanic, wife black	36	0.1
Husband Hispanic, wife other	132	0.2
Husband other, wife white	644	1.1
Husband other, wife black	43	0.1
Husband other, wife Hispanic	121	0.2

Note: Whites, blacks, and "others" are non-Hispanic. "Others" include Asians and American Indians. Hispanics may be of any race. Married-couple family groups include married-couple householders and married couples living in households headed by others.
Source: Bureau of the Census, America's Families and Living Arrangements: 2012, Current Population Survey Annual Social and Economic Supplement, Internet site http://www.census.gov/hhes/families/data/cps2012.html; calculations by New Strategist

Table 6.21 Educational Attainment Difference between Husbands and Wives, 2012

(number and percent distribution of married-couple family groups by educational difference between husband and wife, 2012; numbers in thousands)

EDUCATIONAL DIFFERENCE	number	percent distribution
Total married couples	**61,047**	**100.0%**
Neither has bachelor's degree	33,034	54.1
One has bachelor's degree, other has less	13,665	22.4
Both have bachelor's degree	14,348	23.5

Note: Married-couple family groups include married-couple householders and married couples living in households headed by others.
Source: Bureau of the Census, America's Families and Living Arrangements: 2012, Current Population Survey Annual Social and Economic Supplement, Internet site http://www.census.gov/hhes/families/data/cps2012.html; calculations by New Strategist

Divorce Is Highest among Fifty-Something Women

One in four women aged 50 to 59 has married at least twice.

Fully 37 percent of women aged 50 to 59 have experienced divorce, according to a Census Bureau study of marriage and divorce through 2009. Among men, the percentage that has ever divorced exceeds 35 percent among those ranging in age from 50 to 69. Despite the high level of divorce, most men aged 30 or older have married only once and are still married to their first wife.

Among women and men ever married, aged 15 to 44, the 52 to 56 percent majority of marriages have lasted 20 years. Those most likely to have a lasting marriage are the more educated, those who had not been married before, and those who did not have children before marrying.

■ One reason for the high divorce rate among boomer men and women may be the revolutionary changes in women's roles, which occurred as boomers were becoming adults.

Divorce is less common among the oldest women

(percent of women aged 25 or older who have ever divorced, by age, 2009)

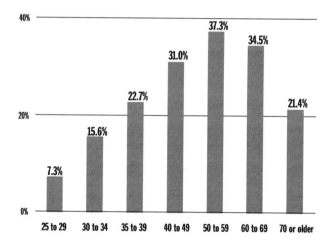

Table 6.22 Marital History of Women by Age, 2009

(number of women aged 15 or older and percent distribution by marital history and age, 2009; numbers in thousands)

	total	15–19	20–24	25–29	30–34	35–39	40–49	50–59	60–69	70+
Total women, number	123,272	10,478	10,158	10,408	9,645	10,267	22,119	20,702	14,288	15,207
Total women, percent	100.0%	100.0%	100.0%	100.0%	100.0%	100.0%	100.0%	100.0%	100.0%	100.0%
Never married	27.2	97.5	77.3	46.8	26.7	17.3	13.0	9.1	6.0	4.3
Ever married	72.8	2.5	22.7	53.2	73.3	82.7	87.0	90.9	94.0	95.7
Married once	57.5	2.5	22.4	50.8	64.5	69.3	67.4	65.5	67.7	76.1
Still married	40.6	1.9	19.7	43.2	54.5	55.8	51.6	47.5	45.7	30.1
Married twice	12.1	0.1	0.3	2.3	8.0	11.6	15.8	19.5	20.1	15.2
Still married	7.9	0.6	0.2	2.0	6.9	9.1	11.3	13.4	13.2	5.2
Married three or more times	3.2	0.0	0.0	0.0	0.8	1.9	3.8	5.9	6.2	4.4
Still married	1.9	0.0	0.0	0.0	0.7	1.4	2.5	4.1	3.6	1.4
Ever divorced	22.4	0.2	1.8	7.3	15.6	22.7	31.0	37.3	34.5	21.4
Currently divorced	11.3	0.1	1.5	5.3	8.1	11.8	16.4	18.6	16.0	9.9
Ever widowed	10.0	0.3	0.1	0.2	0.6	1.4	2.6	6.5	17.0	51.2
Currently widowed	8.9	0.3	0.1	0.1	0.4	0.8	1.8	4.9	13.9	48.3

Source: Bureau of the Census, Number, Timing, and Duration of Marriages and Divorces: 2009, Current Population Reports P70-125, 2011, Internet site http://www.census.gov/hhes/socdemo/marriage/data/sipp/index.html; calculations by New Strategist

Table 6.23 Marital History of Men by Age, 2009

(number of men aged 15 or older and percent distribution by marital history and age, 2009; numbers in thousands)

	total	15–19	20–24	25–29	30–34	35–39	40–49	50–59	60–69	70+
Total men, number	115,797	10,870	10,152	10,567	9,518	9,995	21,504	19,568	12,774	10,849
Total men, percent	100.0%	100.0%	100.0%	100.0%	100.0%	100.0%	100.0%	100.0%	100.0%	100.0%
Never married	33.0	98.0	87.5	59.7	35.6	23.5	16.4	10.8	4.6	3.4
Ever married	67.0	2.0	12.5	40.3	64.4	76.5	83.6	89.2	95.4	96.6
Married once	52.3	1.9	12.5	38.8	59.4	66.9	65.8	63.4	64.8	72.3
Still married	42.5	1.3	11.2	34.2	52.2	56.1	52.2	50.4	53.5	54.0
Married twice	11.6	0.1	0.0	1.5	4.8	8.7	14.8	20.0	22.1	18.9
Still married	9.0	0.1	0.0	1.3	4.0	7.4	11.3	15.5	17.5	13.2
Married three or more times	3.1	0.0	0.0	0.1	0.2	1.0	3.0	5.8	8.5	5.4
Still married	2.3	0.0	0.0	0.1	0.2	0.8	2.2	4.3	6.5	3.8
Ever divorced	20.5	0.3	0.8	5.0	10.5	17.9	28.5	35.7	36.5	23.4
Currently divorced	9.1	0.2	0.7	3.7	6.2	9.5	14.2	15.5	12.4	7.2
Ever widowed	3.6	0.4	0.1	0.3	0.2	0.5	1.3	2.5	6.4	22.6
Currently widowed	2.6	0.3	0.1	0.3	0.1	0.3	0.9	1.6	3.9	17.4

Source: Bureau of the Census, Number, Timing, and Duration of Marriages and Divorces: 2009, Current Population Reports P70-125, 2011, Internet site http://www.census.gov/hhes/socdemo/marriage/data/sipp/index.html; calculations by New Strategist

Table 6.24 Women's Probability of Reaching Marriage Anniversary, 2006–10

(number of women ever married, aged 15 to 44, and percentage whose first marriage survived for specified years, by selected characteristics, 2006–10; numbers in thousands)

	total first marriages		percent of first marriages surviving			
	number	percent distribution	5 years	10 years	15 years	20 years
Total women ever married aged 15 to 44	**32,904**	**100.0%**	**80%**	**68%**	**60%**	**52%**
Age at first marriage						
Under age 20	6,874	20.9	70	54	46	37
Aged 20 to 24	14,166	43.1	81	69	60	55
Aged 25 or older	11,863	36.1	86	78	73	–
Race and Hispanic origin						
Asian, non-Hispanic	1,438	4.4	91	83	78	69
Black, non-Hispanic	3,134	9.5	72	56	45	37
Hispanic	5,412	16.4	84	73	64	53
White, non-Hispanic	21,703	66.0	80	68	61	54
Education						
Not a high school graduate	4,524	14.1	76	60	53	39
High school graduate or GED	8,078	25.1	75	60	51	41
Some college, no degree	9,007	28.0	76	63	54	49
Bachelor's degree	7,511	23.3	90	85	79	78
Master's degree or more	3,066	9.5	88	82	78	–
Family structure at age 14						
Living with both parents	22,707	69.0	83	73	66	58
Other	10,197	31.0	73	57	47	38
Religion raised						
None	2,495	7.6	73	61	58	43
Protestant	15,738	47.8	77	65	56	50
Catholic	11,215	34.1	84	73	63	53
Other religions	3,390	10.3	86	75	68	65

	total first marriages		percent of first marriages surviving			
	number	percent distribution	5 years	10 years	15 years	20 years
Births at time of first marriage						
No births	25,234	76.7%	82%	71%	64%	56%
One or more births	7,670	23.3	74	56	44	33
First birth timing relative to first marriage						
No first birth	6,164	18.7	72	56	50	–
Birth before marriage	7,670	23.3	74	56	44	33
Birth 0 to 7 months after marriage	3,188	9.7	76	55	48	41
Birth 8 or more months after marriage	14,320	43.5	93	85	77	68
Cohabitation with first husband before marriage						
Yes, cohabited and engaged	9,855	30.0	81	67	58	46
Yes, cohabited but not engaged	8,062	24.5	78	61	53	45
No, did not cohabit with first husband	14,954	45.4	80	71	63	57
First husband ever married before this marriage						
Yes	4,498	13.7	75	62	53	38
No	28,379	86.2	81	69	61	54
First husband had children from previous relationship						
Yes	5,425	16.5	72	57	48	37
No	27,428	83.4	82	70	62	54

Note: Education categories include only people aged 22 to 44. "–" means sample is too small to make a reliable estimate.
Source: National Center for Health Statistics, First Marriages in the United States: Data from the 2006–2010 National Survey of Family Growth, National Health Statistics Reports, No. 49, 2012, Internet site http://www.cdc.gov/nchs/nsfg/new_nsfg.htm

Table 6.25 Men's Probability of Reaching Marriage Anniversary, 2006–10

(number of men ever married, aged 15 to 44, and percentage whose first marriage survived for specified years, by selected characteristics, 2006–10; numbers in thousands)

	total first marriages		percent of first marriages surviving			
	number	percent distribution	5 years	10 years	15 years	20 years
Total men ever married aged 15 to 44	**28,094**	**100.0%**	**81%**	**70%**	**62%**	**56%**
Age at first marriage						
Under age 20	2,438	8.7	66	48	46	41
Aged 20 to 24	11,709	41.7	81	70	60	54
Aged 25 or older	13,947	49.6	84	76	68	–
Race and Hispanic origin						
Black, non-Hispanic	2,567	9.1	75	64	55	53
Hispanic	5,073	18.1	82	73	67	62
White, non-Hispanic	17,813	63.4	82	70	61	54
Education						
Not a high school graduate	5,024	18.0	79	66	56	54
High school graduate or GED	7,446	26.7	80	66	54	47
Some college, no degree	7,209	25.9	76	64	57	54
Bachelor's degree	5,255	18.9	87	80	75	65
Master's degree or more	2,912	10.5	90	88	83	–
Family structure at age 14						
Living with both parents	20,423	72.7	84	74	66	60
Other	7,671	27.3	75	60	49	44
Religion raised						
None	2,420	8.6	79	68	54	–
Protestant	13,375	47.6	80	67	58	53
Catholic	9,392	33.4	83	74	67	59
Other religions	2,850	10.1	83	73	72	–

	total first marriages		percent of first marriages surviving			
	number	percent distribution	5 years	10 years	15 years	20 years
Biological children at time of first marriage						
No children	22,250	79.2%	83%	74%	65%	59%
One or more children	5,843	20.8	74	55	48	43
Timing of first child's birth relative to first marriage						
No first birth	5,948	21.2	73	63	52	–
Birth before marriage	5,843	20.8	74	55	48	43
Birth 0 to 7 months after marriage	2,645	9.4	78	68	55	42
Birth 8 or more months after marriage	12,262	43.6	95	86	78	74
Cohabitation with first wife before marriage						
Yes, cohabited and engaged	8,386	29.8	81	71	63	57
Yes, cohabited but not engaged	7,062	25.1	79	66	55	49
No, did not cohabit with first wife	12,492	44.5	82	73	65	60
First wife ever married before this marriage						
Yes	3,342	11.9	76	59	50	–
No	24,459	87.1	82	72	64	58
First wife had children from previous relationship						
Yes	4,487	16.0	72	55	39	–
No	23,311	83.0	84	74	67	61

Note: Education categories include only people aged 22 to 44. "–" means sample is too small to make a reliable estimate.
Source: National Center for Health Statistics, First Marriages in the United States: Data from the 2006–2010 National Survey of Family Growth, National Health Statistics Reports, No. 49, 2012; Internet site http://www.cdc.gov/nchs/nsfg/new_nsfg.htm

Males Outnumber Females among Same-Sex Couples

Females outnumber males among those who are married.

According to the 2011 American Community Survey, there were 605,472 same-sex couples in the United States—284,295 male couples and 321,177 female couples. Among same-sex couples, most identify themselves as unmarried partners. But 98,570 females and 69,522 males say they are spouses of a same-sex partner.

On average, same-sex couples are younger than married couples, but older than unmarried opposite-sex couples. They are far more educated and just as or even more affluent than opposite-sex married couples. The average household income of male same-sex couples was a substantial $120,786 in 2011, and female same-sex couples had an average income of $94,333. This compares with an average income of $95,506 for opposite-sex married couples and $64,562 for opposite-sex unmarried couples.

■ Same-sex couples who identify themselves as spouses are older than same-sex unmarried partners. They are more likely to have children in the household and more likely to be homeowners.

Same-sex couples are affluent

(average income of couples by type, 2011)

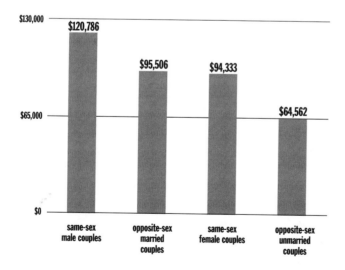

Table 6.26 Characteristics of Opposite-Sex and Same-Sex Couple Households, 2011

(number of households with opposite and same-sex spouses or partners and percent distribution by selected characteristics, 2011)

	opposite-sex couples		same-sex couples		
	married	unmarried	total	male	female
Total couples (number)	**55,519,648**	**6,109,902**	**605,472**	**284,295**	**321,177**
Age of householder					
Under age 25	1.4%	13.2%	3.9%	3.0%	4.7%
Aged 25 to 34	13.6	35.3	16.5	15.0	17.8
Aged 35 to 44	20.6	21.3	20.8	21.4	20.2
Aged 45 to 54	23.4	16.3	29.1	30.5	27.9
Aged 55 to 64	21.0	9.3	17.2	18.5	16.0
Aged 65 or older	20.0	4.6	12.6	11.6	13.5
Average age of householder (years)	**51.3**	**38.3**	**47.7**	**48.0**	**47.5**
Average age of spouse/partner (years)	**50.3**	**37.5**	**45.8**	**45.8**	**45.8**
Race and Hispanic origin of householder					
Asian	5.0%	2.2%	2.4%	2.6%	2.1%
Black	6.9	11.6	7.0	5.9	8.1
Hispanic	11.8	18.3	9.8	10.2	9.4
Non-Hispanic white	74.7	65.2	78.6	79.5	77.9
Educational attainment of householder					
Householder has a bachelor's degree	35.8	21.7	48.8	52.3	45.7
Both partners have a bachelor's degree	22.3	11.2	31.0	32.4	29.8
Employment status					
Householder employed	67.5	75.0	73.2	74.4	72.2
Both partners employed	47.2	54.7	58.0	58.4	57.6
Children in the household	**40.7**	**41.8**	**17.5**	**11.0**	**23.2**
Household income					
Under $35,000	17.2	32.5	16.4	13.1	19.3
$35,000 to $49,999	12.5	16.6	10.7	9.4	11.9
$50,000 to $74,999	20.5	21.3	17.3	16.1	18.4
$75,000 to $99,999	16.3	12.8	15.8	15.9	15.7
$100,000 or more	33.5	16.7	39.8	45.5	34.7
Average household income	**$95,506**	**$64,562**	**$106,753**	**$120,786**	**$94,333**
Housing tenure					
Owner	80.7%	42.3%	70.1%	71.5%	68.9%
Renter	19.3	57.7	29.9	28.5	31.1

Source: Bureau of the Census, 2011 American Community Survey, Internet site http://www.census.gov/hhes/samesex/

Table 6.27 Characteristics of Same-Sex Couple Households by Marital Status, 2011

(number of same-sex couple households by marital status and percent distribution by selected characteristics, 2011)

	couples reported as spouses		unmarried partners	
	male-male	female-female	male-male	female-female
Total couples (number)	**69,522**	**98,570**	**214,773**	**222,607**
Age of householder				
Under age 25	2.2%	1.2%	3.2%	6.2%
Aged 25 to 34	11.4	11.9	16.2	20.3
Aged 35 to 44	17.9	17.6	22.5	21.4
Aged 45 to 54	27.7	23.4	31.4	29.9
Aged 55 to 64	21.2	15.9	17.6	16.0
Aged 65 or older	19.6	30.0	9.0	6.1
Average age of householder (years)	**51.8**	**54.7**	**46.8**	**44.3**
Average age of spouse/partner (years)	**50.4**	**52.9**	**44.4**	**42.7**
Race and Hispanic origin of householder				
Asian	4.6%	3.6%	2.0%	1.5%
Black	7.4	9.5	5.4	7.4
Hispanic	14.2	8.1	8.9	9.9
Non-Hispanic white	71.9	76.8	82.0	78.3
Children in the household	**26.1**	**26.2**	**6.1**	**21.9**
Household income				
Under $35,000	16.5%	23.2%	12.0%	17.6%
$35,000 to $49,999	10.7	10.8	9.0	12.4
$50,000 to $74,999	15.6	20.2	16.3	17.6
$75,000 to $99,999	14.1	14.4	16.5	16.3
$100,000 or more	43.2	31.4	46.3	36.1
Average household income	**$118,259**	**$92,362**	**$121,603**	**$95,205**
Housing tenure				
Owner	79.1%	76.9%	69.0%	65.3%
Renter	20.9	23.1	31.0	34.7

Source: Bureau of the Census, 2011 American Community Survey, Internet site http://www.census.gov/hhes/samesex/

Population

Females outnumber males by 5 million in the United States.

Women account for 57 percent of the 65-or-older population. An even larger 67 percent of people aged 85 or older are women.

Fewer than two-thirds of the nation's males and females are non-Hispanic white.

Between 2012 and 2050, the number of non-Hispanic white males and females will decline, becoming a minority by 2050.

The South has the fastest-growing male and female populations.

By state, the number of males and females grew fastest in Nevada between 2000 and 2011, while the male and female population declined in Michigan.

Twelve percent of males and females moved between 2011 and 2012.

Women aged 20 to 24 and men aged 25 to 29 are most likely to move.

Females account for 51 percent of the nation's foreign-born.

They are the 55 percent majority of legal immigrants.

Women Outnumber Men

Among both men and women, the 60-to-64 age group grew the fastest between 2000 and 2011.

The number of females in the United States grew 10 percent between 2000 and 2011, climbing from 144 million to 158 million. The number of males grew by a slightly faster 11 percent during those years, from 138 million to 153 million. Females outnumber males in the United States and will continue to do so for the foreseeable future. Although more boys than girls are born each year, higher male mortality rates eventually result in the female numerical advantage.

The aging of the baby-boom generation is behind the increase in the number of men and women in their late fifties and early sixties. The oldest boomers, born in 1946, turned 65 in 2011. Between 2012 and 2050, the Census Bureau projects a 26 to 29 percent increase in the number of females and males, respectively. The number of males and females aged 65 or older will nearly double during those years.

■ Because women are the majority of older Americans, they are by far the primary consumers of the health care industry.

Females outnumber males in the United States by more than 5 million

(total population by sex, 2011)

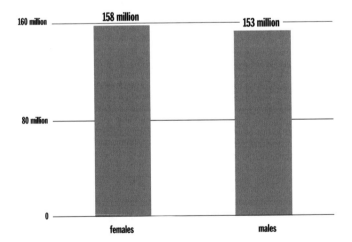

Table 7.1 Females by Age, 2000 to 2011

(number of females by age, 2000 to 2011, percent change, 2000–11; numbers in thousands)

	2011	2010	2000	percent change 2000–11
Total females	**158,301**	**157,242**	**143,719**	**10.1%**
Under age 5	9,863	9,883	9,368	5.3
Aged 5 to 9	9,950	9,975	9,984	–0.3
Aged 10 to 14	10,118	10,107	10,063	0.5
Aged 15 to 19	10,525	10,696	9,855	6.8
Aged 20 to 24	10,841	10,612	9,350	16.0
Aged 25 to 29	10,518	10,477	9,532	10.3
Aged 30 to 34	10,228	10,030	10,195	0.3
Aged 35 to 39	9,833	10,086	11,358	–13.4
Aged 40 to 44	10,571	10,500	11,352	–6.9
Aged 45 to 49	11,205	11,465	10,266	9.1
Aged 50 to 54	11,494	11,399	9,076	26.6
Aged 55 to 59	10,439	10,199	7,009	49.0
Aged 60 to 64	9,264	8,829	5,696	62.6
Aged 65 to 69	6,802	6,623	5,125	32.7
Aged 70 to 74	5,204	5,057	4,950	5.1
Aged 75 to 79	4,156	4,130	4,382	–5.2
Aged 80 to 84	3,446	3,448	3,132	10.1
Aged 85 or older	3,843	3,726	3,027	27.0
Aged 18 to 24	15,167	15,028	13,343	13.7
Aged 18 or older	122,172	120,998	108,442	12.7
Aged 65 or older	23,451	22,984	20,615	13.8

Source: Bureau of the Census, Population Estimates, Internet site http://www.census.gov/popest/; calculations by New Strategist

Table 7.2 Males by Age, 2000 to 2011

(number of males by age, 2000 to 2011, percent change, 2000–11; numbers in thousands)

	2011	2010	2000	percent change 2000–11
Total males	**153,291**	**152,108**	**138,443**	**10.7%**
Under age 5	10,300	10,318	9,811	5.0
Aged 5 to 9	10,384	10,407	10,479	–0.9
Aged 10 to 14	10,587	10,587	10,575	0.1
Aged 15 to 19	11,119	11,263	10,440	6.5
Aged 20 to 24	11,313	11,056	9,767	15.8
Aged 25 to 29	10,762	10,676	9,748	10.4
Aged 30 to 34	10,283	10,063	10,329	–0.4
Aged 35 to 39	9,761	9,997	11,293	–13.6
Aged 40 to 44	10,462	10,399	11,166	–6.3
Aged 45 to 49	10,953	11,183	9,953	10.0
Aged 50 to 54	11,067	10,966	8,703	27.2
Aged 55 to 59	9,816	9,580	6,557	49.7
Aged 60 to 64	8,542	8,159	5,167	65.3
Aged 65 to 69	6,072	5,892	4,398	38.0
Aged 70 to 74	4,404	4,269	3,910	12.6
Aged 75 to 79	3,233	3,184	3,057	5.8
Aged 80 to 84	2,340	2,302	1,853	26.3
Aged 85 or older	1,894	1,284	885	114.1
Aged 18 to 24	15,897	15,680	13,972	13.8
Aged 18 or older	115,486	114,156	101,344	14.0
Aged 65 or older	17,943	17,454	14,454	24.1

Source: Bureau of the Census, Population Estimates, Internet site http://www.census.gov/popest/; calculations by New Strategist

Table 7.3 Female Share of the Population by Age, 2011

(total number of people by sex and female share of total, by age, 2011; numbers in thousands)

	total	females number	share of total
Total people	**311,592**	**158,301**	**50.8%**
Under age 5	20,162	9,863	48.9
Aged 5 to 9	20,334	9,950	48.9
Aged 10 to 14	20,705	10,118	48.9
Aged 15 to 19	21,644	10,525	48.6
Aged 20 to 24	22,154	10,841	48.9
Aged 25 to 29	21,280	10,518	49.4
Aged 30 to 34	20,511	10,228	49.9
Aged 35 to 39	19,594	9,833	50.2
Aged 40 to 44	21,034	10,571	50.3
Aged 45 to 49	22,158	11,205	50.6
Aged 50 to 54	22,560	11,494	50.9
Aged 55 to 59	20,256	10,439	51.5
Aged 60 to 64	17,807	9,264	52.0
Aged 65 to 69	12,874	6,802	52.8
Aged 70 to 74	9,608	5,204	54.2
Aged 75 to 79	7,389	4,156	56.2
Aged 80 to 84	5,787	3,446	59.6
Aged 85 or older	5,737	3,843	67.0
Aged 18 to 24	31,065	15,167	48.8
Aged 18 or older	237,658	122,172	51.4
Aged 65 or older	41,394	23,451	56.7

Source: Bureau of the Census, Population Estimates, Internet site http://www.census.gov/popest/; calculations by New Strategist

Table 7.4 Male Share of the Population by Age, 2011

(total number of people by sex and male share of total, by age, 2011; numbers in thousands)

	total	males number	males share of total
Total people	**311,592**	**153,291**	**49.2%**
Under age 5	20,162	10,300	51.1
Aged 5 to 9	20,334	10,384	51.1
Aged 10 to 14	20,705	10,587	51.1
Aged 15 to 19	21,644	11,119	51.4
Aged 20 to 24	22,154	11,313	51.1
Aged 25 to 29	21,280	10,762	50.6
Aged 30 to 34	20,511	10,283	50.1
Aged 35 to 39	19,594	9,761	49.8
Aged 40 to 44	21,034	10,462	49.7
Aged 45 to 49	22,158	10,953	49.4
Aged 50 to 54	22,560	11,067	49.1
Aged 55 to 59	20,256	9,816	48.5
Aged 60 to 64	17,807	8,542	48.0
Aged 65 to 69	12,874	6,072	47.2
Aged 70 to 74	9,608	4,404	45.8
Aged 75 to 79	7,389	3,233	43.8
Aged 80 to 84	5,787	2,340	40.4
Aged 85 or older	5,737	1,894	33.0
Aged 18 to 24	31,065	15,897	51.2
Aged 18 or older	237,658	115,486	48.6
Aged 65 or older	41,394	17,943	43.3

Source: Bureau of the Census, Population Estimates, Internet site http://www.census.gov/popest/; calculations by New Strategist

Table 7.5 Projections of the Female Population by Age, 2012 to 2050

(projected number of females by age, 2012 to 2050, percent change, 2012–50; numbers in thousands)

	2012	2020	2030	2040	2050	percent change 2012–50
Total females	**159,458**	**169,084**	**181,148**	**191,681**	**201,034**	**26.1%**
Under age 5	9,917	10,658	10,875	11,243	11,786	18.9
Aged 5 to 9	10,006	10,411	10,968	11,181	11,717	17.1
Aged 10 to 14	10,088	10,078	10,921	11,178	11,563	14.6
Aged 15 to 19	10,379	10,166	10,699	11,295	11,522	11.0
Aged 20 to 24	11,020	10,541	10,666	11,585	11,873	7.7
Aged 25 to 29	10,538	11,372	11,063	11,728	12,377	17.5
Aged 30 to 34	10,412	11,253	11,389	11,654	12,627	21.3
Aged 35 to 39	9,771	10,877	11,931	11,736	12,444	27.4
Aged 40 to 44	10,564	10,203	11,546	11,763	12,069	14.2
Aged 45 to 49	10,956	10,101	10,965	12,078	11,925	8.8
Aged 50 to 54	11,495	10,363	10,133	11,511	11,772	2.4
Aged 55 to 59	10,700	11,148	9,903	10,801	11,949	11.7
Aged 60 to 64	9,275	10,914	10,023	9,866	11,267	21.5
Aged 65 to 69	7,368	9,538	10,528	9,437	10,378	40.8
Aged 70 to 74	5,412	7,905	9,898	9,200	9,157	69.2
Aged 75 to 79	4,197	5,523	8,092	9,063	8,244	96.4
Aged 80 to 84	3,425	3,722	5,968	7,626	7,240	111.4
Aged 85 or older	3,935	4,311	5,580	8,736	11,124	182.7
Aged 18 to 24	15,273	14,632	14,886	16,130	16,499	8.0
Aged 18 or older	123,322	131,862	141,904	151,329	159,071	29.0
Aged 65 or older	24,337	30,999	40,066	44,062	46,144	89.6

Source: Bureau of the Census, Population Estimates, Internet site http://www.census.gov/popest/; calculations by New Strategist

Table 7.6 Projections of the Male Population by Age, 2012 to 2050

(projected number of males by age, 2012 to 2050, percent change, 2012–50; numbers in thousands)

	2012	2020	2030	2040	2050	percent change 2012–50
Total males	**154,546**	**164,812**	**177,323**	**188,335**	**198,770**	**28.6%**
Under age 5	10,357	11,150	11,377	11,761	12,329	19.0
Aged 5 to 9	10,451	10,896	11,482	11,705	12,266	17.4
Aged 10 to 14	10,551	10,538	11,443	11,715	12,119	14.9
Aged 15 to 19	10,947	10,640	11,247	11,879	12,120	10.7
Aged 20 to 24	11,534	11,109	11,274	12,278	12,590	9.2
Aged 25 to 29	10,837	11,994	11,650	12,423	13,115	21.0
Aged 30 to 34	10,489	11,653	11,951	12,270	13,322	27.0
Aged 35 to 39	9,708	10,991	12,491	12,267	13,069	34.6
Aged 40 to 44	10,453	10,158	11,858	12,237	12,586	20.4
Aged 45 to 49	10,722	9,907	10,970	12,517	12,337	15.1
Aged 50 to 54	11,077	10,103	9,950	11,665	12,095	9.2
Aged 55 to 59	10,069	10,599	9,490	10,583	12,145	20.6
Aged 60 to 64	8,533	10,103	9,431	9,377	11,081	29.9
Aged 65 to 69	6,605	8,515	9,549	8,654	9,767	47.9
Aged 70 to 74	4,597	6,839	8,618	8,174	8,253	79.5
Aged 75 to 79	3,290	4,487	6,630	7,576	6,998	112.7
Aged 80 to 84	2,356	2,748	4,545	5,875	5,723	142.9
Aged 85 or older	1,970	2,382	3,366	5,378	6,854	248.0
Aged 18 to 24	16,045	15,396	15,720	17,069	17,468	8.9
Aged 18 or older	116,752	125,875	136,219	146,066	154,814	32.6
Aged 65 or older	18,818	24,970	32,709	35,657	37,595	99.8

Source: Bureau of the Census, Population Estimates, Internet site http://www.census.gov/popest/; calculations by New Strategist

Non-Hispanic Whites Are the Majority of Females and Males

Hispanics are the largest minority, followed by blacks.

Non-Hispanic whites are the majority of the nation's females and males, but the minority share is expanding rapidly as the Asian, black, and Hispanic populations grow faster than the non-Hispanic white. In 2011, only 63 percent of the female and male populations were non-Hispanic white. Hispanics are the largest minority, accounting for 16 percent of the female and 17 percent of the male population. Blacks are 14 percent of each group and Asians 6 percent.

Children are far more diverse than adults. Among boys and girls under age 5, only half are non-Hispanic white and Hispanics are a substantial 26 percent. Among men and women aged 65 or older, fully 79 to 80 percent are non-Hispanic white and only 7 percent are Hispanic. By 2050, according to Census Bureau projections, minorities will be the majority of both the male and female populations. The number of non-Hispanic whites is projected to decline by 6 percent between 2012 and 2050, while the Asian and Hispanic populations will more than double in size.

■ Females account for the majority of the Asian, black, and non-Hispanic white populations, but males are the majority of Hispanics in the United States.

Children are much more diverse than adults

*(percent distribution of females under age 5 and aged 65 or older,
by race and Hispanic origin, 2011)*

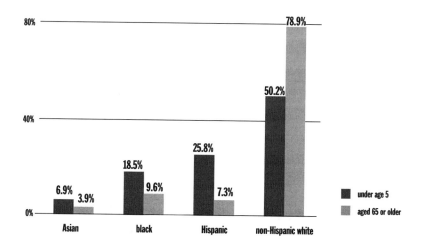

Table 7.7 Females by Race and Hispanic Origin, 2011

(total number of people, number of females, female share of total, and percent distribution of females by race and Hispanic origin, 2011)

| | | females | | |
	total	number	share of total	percent distribution by race and Hispanic origin
Total people	**311,592**	**158,301**	**50.8%**	**100.0%**
Asian	18,206	9,480	52.1	6.0
Black	43,884	22,906	52.2	14.5
Hispanic	52,045	25,602	49.2	16.2
Non-Hispanic white	197,511	100,352	50.8	63.4

Note: Numbers do not add to total because Asians and blacks are those who identify themselves as being of the race alone and those who identify themselves as being of the race in combination with other races and because Hispanics may be of any race. Non-Hispanic whites are those who identify themselves as being white alone and non-Hispanic.
Source: Bureau of the Census, Population Estimates, Internet site http://www.census.gov/popest/; calculations by New Strategist

Table 7.8 Males by Race and Hispanic Origin, 2011

(total number of people, number of males, male share of total, and percent distribution of males by race and Hispanic origin, 2011; numbers in thousands)

| | | males | | |
	total	number	share of total	percent distribution by race and Hispanic origin
Total people	**311,592**	**153,291**	**49.2%**	**100.0%**
Asian	18,206	8,726	47.9	5.7
Black	43,884	20,978	47.8	13.7
Hispanic	52,045	26,443	50.8	17.3
Non-Hispanic white	197,511	97,158	49.2	63.4

Note: Numbers do not add to total because Asians and blacks are those who identify themselves as being of the race alone and those who identify themselves as being of the race in combination with other races and because Hispanics may be of any race. Non-Hispanic whites are those who identify themselves as being white alone and non-Hispanic.
Source: Bureau of the Census, Population Estimates, Internet site http://www.census.gov/popest/; calculations by New Strategist

Table 7.9 Females by Age, Race, and Hispanic Origin, 2011

(total number of females and percent distribution by age, race, and Hispanic origin, 2011; numbers in thousands)

	total		Asian	black	Hispanic	non-Hispanic white
	number	percent				
Total females	**158,301**	**100.0%**	**6.0%**	**14.5%**	**16.2%**	**63.4%**
Under age 5	9,863	100.0	6.9	18.5	25.8	50.2
Aged 5 to 9	9,950	100.0	6.7	17.4	24.2	52.5
Aged 10 to 14	10,118	100.0	6.1	17.4	22.4	54.5
Aged 15 to 19	10,525	100.0	5.8	17.8	21.0	55.7
Aged 20 to 24	10,841	100.0	6.4	17.1	19.4	57.4
Aged 25 to 29	10,518	100.0	7.4	15.4	19.5	58.0
Aged 30 to 34	10,228	100.0	7.7	15.4	19.8	57.4
Aged 35 to 39	9,833	100.0	8.0	14.9	19.5	57.7
Aged 40 to 44	10,571	100.0	6.9	14.3	16.5	62.2
Aged 45 to 49	11,205	100.0	5.8	14.0	13.8	66.0
Aged 50 to 54	11,494	100.0	5.2	13.3	11.3	69.7
Aged 55 to 59	10,439	100.0	5.1	12.5	9.7	72.1
Aged 60 to 64	9,264	100.0	4.8	11.3	8.4	74.9
Aged 65 to 69	6,802	100.0	4.4	10.4	8.2	76.4
Aged 70 to 74	5,204	100.0	4.3	10.3	8.0	77.0
Aged 75 to 79	4,156	100.0	4.0	9.8	7.5	78.3
Aged 80 to 84	3,446	100.0	3.4	8.5	6.5	81.2
Aged 85 or older	3,843	100.0	2.7	7.7	5.1	84.2
Aged 18 to 24	15,167	100.0	6.2	17.4	19.7	56.9
Aged 18 or older	122,172	100.0	5.9	13.5	14.0	66.5
Aged 65 or older	23,451	100.0	3.9	9.6	7.3	78.9

Note: Numbers do not add to total because Asians and blacks are those who identify themselves as being of the race alone and those who identify themselves as being of the race in combination with other races and because Hispanics may be of any race. Non-Hispanic whites are those who identify themselves as being white alone and non-Hispanic.
Source: Bureau of the Census, Population Estimates, Internet site http://www.census.gov/popest/; calculations by New Strategist

Table 7.10 Males by Age, Race, and Hispanic Origin, 2011

(total number of males and percent distribution by age, race, and Hispanic origin, 2011; numbers in thousands)

	total		Asian	black	Hispanic	non-Hispanic white
	number	percent				
Total males	**153,291**	**100.0%**	**5.7%**	**13.7%**	**17.3%**	**63.4%**
Under age 5	10,300	100.0	6.8	18.2	25.7	50.4
Aged 5 to 9	10,384	100.0	6.5	17.1	24.1	53.0
Aged 10 to 14	10,587	100.0	6.0	17.2	22.3	55.0
Aged 15 to 19	11,119	100.0	5.7	17.4	21.3	55.8
Aged 20 to 24	11,313	100.0	6.3	16.1	21.0	56.8
Aged 25 to 29	10,762	100.0	6.7	14.1	21.6	57.8
Aged 30 to 34	10,283	100.0	6.8	13.8	21.5	58.1
Aged 35 to 39	9,761	100.0	7.2	13.3	20.7	58.9
Aged 40 to 44	10,462	100.0	6.2	12.9	17.5	63.3
Aged 45 to 49	10,953	100.0	5.3	12.7	14.5	67.0
Aged 50 to 54	11,067	100.0	4.7	12.2	11.6	71.0
Aged 55 to 59	9,816	100.0	4.5	11.2	9.8	73.9
Aged 60 to 64	8,542	100.0	4.2	10.0	8.2	76.9
Aged 65 to 69	6,072	100.0	4.1	9.0	7.6	78.7
Aged 70 to 74	4,404	100.0	4.2	8.7	7.3	79.2
Aged 75 to 79	3,233	100.0	3.8	8.0	6.9	80.7
Aged 80 to 84	2,340	100.0	3.3	6.7	6.4	83.3
Aged 85 or older	1,894	100.0	3.3	6.1	5.6	84.8
Aged 18 to 24	15,897	100.0	6.1	16.6	21.0	56.5
Aged 18 or older	115,486	100.0	5.5	12.4	15.2	66.7
Aged 65 or older	17,943	100.0	3.9	8.1	7.1	80.4

Note: Numbers do not add to total because Asians and blacks are those who identify themselves as being of the race alone and those who identify themselves as being of the race in combination with other races and because Hispanics may be of any race. Non-Hispanic whites are those who identify themselves as being white alone and non-Hispanic.
Source: Bureau of the Census, Population Estimates, Internet site http://www.census.gov/popest/; calculations by New Strategist

Table 7.11 Female Share of the Asian Population by Age, 2011

(total number of Asians, number of Asian females, and female share of total, by age, 2011; numbers in thousands)

	total	females	
		number	share of total
Total Asians	**18,206**	**9,480**	**52.1%**
Under age 5	1,383	678	49.0
Aged 5 to 9	1,346	668	49.7
Aged 10 to 14	1,250	619	49.5
Aged 15 to 19	1,244	609	49.0
Aged 20 to 24	1,407	697	49.5
Aged 25 to 29	1,497	775	51.8
Aged 30 to 34	1,484	789	53.2
Aged 35 to 39	1,485	784	52.8
Aged 40 to 44	1,370	726	53.0
Aged 45 to 49	1,235	653	52.8
Aged 50 to 54	1,117	597	53.4
Aged 55 to 59	976	531	54.4
Aged 60 to 64	806	444	55.1
Aged 65 to 69	550	301	54.7
Aged 70 to 74	407	222	54.6
Aged 75 to 79	288	164	57.1
Aged 80 to 84	195	118	60.4
Aged 85 or older	166	105	63.0
Aged 18 to 24	1,915	945	49.4
Aged 18 or older	13,492	7,154	53.0
Aged 65 or older	1,605	909	56.6

Note: Asians are those who identify themselves as being of the race alone and those who identify themselves as being of the race in combination with other races.
Source: Bureau of the Census, Population Estimates, Internet site http://www.census.gov/popest/; calculations by New Strategist

Table 7.12 Male Share of the Asian Population by Age, 2011

(total number of Asians, number of Asian males, and male share of total, by age, 2011; numbers in thousands)

		males	
	total	number	share of total
Total Asians	**18,206**	**8,726**	**47.9%**
Under age 5	1,383	705	51.0
Aged 5 to 9	1,346	677	50.3
Aged 10 to 14	1,250	631	50.5
Aged 15 to 19	1,244	635	51.0
Aged 20 to 24	1,407	710	50.5
Aged 25 to 29	1,497	722	48.2
Aged 30 to 34	1,484	695	46.8
Aged 35 to 39	1,485	701	47.2
Aged 40 to 44	1,370	645	47.0
Aged 45 to 49	1,235	582	47.2
Aged 50 to 54	1,117	520	46.6
Aged 55 to 59	976	445	45.6
Aged 60 to 64	806	362	44.9
Aged 65 to 69	550	249	45.3
Aged 70 to 74	407	185	45.4
Aged 75 to 79	288	123	42.9
Aged 80 to 84	195	77	39.6
Aged 85 or older	166	62	37.0
Aged 18 to 24	1,915	970	50.6
Aged 18 or older	13,492	6,338	47.0
Aged 65 or older	1,605	696	43.4

Note: Asians are those who identify themselves as being of the race alone and those who identify themselves as being of the race in combination with other races.
Source: Bureau of the Census, Population Estimates, Internet site http://www.census.gov/popest/; calculations by New Strategist

Table 7.13 Female Share of the Black Population by Age, 2011

(total number of blacks, number of black females, and female share of total, by age, 2011; numbers in thousands)

		females	
	total	number	share of total
Total blacks	**43,884**	**22,906**	**52.2%**
Under age 5	3,701	1,821	49.2
Aged 5 to 9	3,507	1,730	49.3
Aged 10 to 14	3,585	1,765	49.2
Aged 15 to 19	3,804	1,871	49.2
Aged 20 to 24	3,679	1,853	50.4
Aged 25 to 29	3,141	1,625	51.7
Aged 30 to 34	2,990	1,573	52.6
Aged 35 to 39	2,765	1,466	53.0
Aged 40 to 44	2,864	1,515	52.9
Aged 45 to 49	2,961	1,567	52.9
Aged 50 to 54	2,877	1,531	53.2
Aged 55 to 59	2,404	1,300	54.1
Aged 60 to 64	1,904	1,049	55.1
Aged 65 to 69	1,255	709	56.5
Aged 70 to 74	920	536	58.3
Aged 75 to 79	668	408	61.1
Aged 80 to 84	449	292	65.1
Aged 85 or older	410	295	71.8
Aged 18 to 24	5,266	2,632	50.0
Aged 18 or older	30,874	16,499	53.4
Aged 65 or older	3,702	2,241	60.5

Note: Blacks are those who identify themselves as being of the race alone and those who identify themselves as being of the race in combination with other races.
Source: Bureau of the Census, Population Estimates, Internet site http://www.census.gov/popest/; calculations by New Strategist

Table 7.14 Male Share of the Black Population by Age, 2011

(total number of blacks, number of black males, and male share of total, by age, 2011; numbers in thousands)

		males	
	total	number	share of total
Total blacks	**43,884**	**20,978**	**47.8%**
Under age 5	3,701	1,879	50.8
Aged 5 to 9	3,507	1,778	50.7
Aged 10 to 14	3,585	1,820	50.8
Aged 15 to 19	3,804	1,933	50.8
Aged 20 to 24	3,679	1,827	49.6
Aged 25 to 29	3,141	1,516	48.3
Aged 30 to 34	2,990	1,418	47.4
Aged 35 to 39	2,765	1,299	47.0
Aged 40 to 44	2,864	1,348	47.1
Aged 45 to 49	2,961	1,394	47.1
Aged 50 to 54	2,877	1,346	46.8
Aged 55 to 59	2,404	1,104	45.9
Aged 60 to 64	1,904	855	44.9
Aged 65 to 69	1,255	546	43.5
Aged 70 to 74	920	383	41.7
Aged 75 to 79	668	260	38.9
Aged 80 to 84	449	156	34.9
Aged 85 or older	410	116	28.2
Aged 18 to 24	5,266	2,634	50.0
Aged 18 or older	30,874	14,375	46.6
Aged 65 or older	3,702	1,461	39.5

Note: Blacks are those who identify themselves as being of the race alone and those who identify themselves as being of the race in combination with other races.
Source: Bureau of the Census, Population Estimates, Internet site http://www.census.gov/popest/; calculations by New Strategist

Table 7.15 Female Share of the Hispanic Population by Age, 2011

(total number of Hispanics, number of Hispanic females, and female share of total, by age, 2011; numbers in thousands)

	total	females number	females share of total
Total Hispanics	**52,045**	**25,602**	**49.2%**
Under age 5	5,192	2,541	48.9
Aged 5 to 9	4,910	2,406	49.0
Aged 10 to 14	4,628	2,264	48.9
Aged 15 to 19	4,582	2,213	48.3
Aged 20 to 24	4,478	2,102	46.9
Aged 25 to 29	4,368	2,047	46.9
Aged 30 to 34	4,237	2,023	47.8
Aged 35 to 39	3,933	1,916	48.7
Aged 40 to 44	3,575	1,746	48.8
Aged 45 to 49	3,137	1,546	49.3
Aged 50 to 54	2,579	1,296	50.2
Aged 55 to 59	1,975	1,018	51.5
Aged 60 to 64	1,483	782	52.8
Aged 65 to 69	1,019	556	54.5
Aged 70 to 74	736	414	56.2
Aged 75 to 79	535	311	58.1
Aged 80 to 84	375	225	60.1
Aged 85 or older	304	197	64.8
Aged 18 to 24	6,340	2,993	47.2
Aged 18 or older	34,595	17,069	49.3
Aged 65 or older	2,969	1,702	57.3

Source: Bureau of the Census, Population Estimates, Internet site http://www.census.gov/popest/; calculations by New Strategist

Table 7.16 Male Share of the Hispanic Population by Age, 2011

(total number of Hispanics, number of Hispanic males, and male share of total, by age, 2011; numbers in thousands)

		males	
	total	number	share of total
Total Hispanics	**52,045**	**26,443**	**50.8%**
Under age 5	5,192	2,651	51.1
Aged 5 to 9	4,910	2,504	51.0
Aged 10 to 14	4,628	2,364	51.1
Aged 15 to 19	4,582	2,369	51.7
Aged 20 to 24	4,478	2,376	53.1
Aged 25 to 29	4,368	2,321	53.1
Aged 30 to 34	4,237	2,214	52.2
Aged 35 to 39	3,933	2,016	51.3
Aged 40 to 44	3,575	1,829	51.2
Aged 45 to 49	3,137	1,591	50.7
Aged 50 to 54	2,579	1,283	49.8
Aged 55 to 59	1,975	957	48.5
Aged 60 to 64	1,483	700	47.2
Aged 65 to 69	1,019	463	45.5
Aged 70 to 74	736	323	43.8
Aged 75 to 79	535	224	41.9
Aged 80 to 84	375	149	39.9
Aged 85 or older	304	107	35.2
Aged 18 to 24	6,340	3,346	52.8
Aged 18 or older	34,595	17,526	50.7
Aged 65 or older	2,969	1,267	42.7

Source: Bureau of the Census, Population Estimates, Internet site http://www.census.gov/popest/; calculations by New Strategist

Table 7.17 Female Share of the Non-Hispanic White Population by Age, 2011

(total number of non-Hispanic whites, number of non-Hispanic white females, and female share of total, by age, 2011; numbers in thousands)

	total	females number	share of total
Total non-Hispanic whites	**197,511**	**100,352**	**50.8%**
Under age 5	10,141	4,947	48.8
Aged 5 to 9	10,734	5,226	48.7
Aged 10 to 14	11,339	5,518	48.7
Aged 15 to 19	12,065	5,858	48.6
Aged 20 to 24	12,640	6,218	49.2
Aged 25 to 29	12,321	6,097	49.5
Aged 30 to 34	11,844	5,870	49.6
Aged 35 to 39	11,423	5,677	49.7
Aged 40 to 44	13,189	6,570	49.8
Aged 45 to 49	14,739	7,398	50.2
Aged 50 to 54	15,866	8,010	50.5
Aged 55 to 59	14,781	7,530	50.9
Aged 60 to 64	13,505	6,935	51.4
Aged 65 to 69	9,975	5,199	52.1
Aged 70 to 74	7,494	4,006	53.5
Aged 75 to 79	5,865	3,256	55.5
Aged 80 to 84	4,748	2,800	59.0
Aged 85 or older	4,843	3,237	66.9
Aged 18 to 24	17,609	8,633	49.0
Aged 18 or older	158,202	81,218	51.3
Aged 65 or older	32,926	18,498	56.2

Note: Non-Hispanic whites are those who identify themselves as white alone and not Hispanic.
Source: Bureau of the Census, Population Estimates, Internet site http://www.census.gov/popest/; calculations by New Strategist

Table 7.18 Male Share of the Non-Hispanic White Population by Age, 2011

(total number of non-Hispanic whites, number of non-Hispanic white males, and male share of total, by age, 2011; numbers in thousands)

	total	males number	share of total
Total non-Hispanic whites	**197,511**	**97,158**	**49.2%**
Under age 5	10,141	5,194	51.2
Aged 5 to 9	10,734	5,508	51.3
Aged 10 to 14	11,339	5,821	51.3
Aged 15 to 19	12,065	6,206	51.4
Aged 20 to 24	12,640	6,422	50.8
Aged 25 to 29	12,321	6,224	50.5
Aged 30 to 34	11,844	5,974	50.4
Aged 35 to 39	11,423	5,746	50.3
Aged 40 to 44	13,189	6,619	50.2
Aged 45 to 49	14,739	7,341	49.8
Aged 50 to 54	15,866	7,856	49.5
Aged 55 to 59	14,781	7,251	49.1
Aged 60 to 64	13,505	6,570	48.6
Aged 65 to 69	9,975	4,776	47.9
Aged 70 to 74	7,494	3,488	46.5
Aged 75 to 79	5,865	2,610	44.5
Aged 80 to 84	4,748	1,949	41.0
Aged 85 or older	4,843	1,605	33.1
Aged 18 to 24	17,609	8,976	51.0
Aged 18 or older	158,202	76,984	48.7
Aged 65 or older	32,926	14,428	43.8

Note: Non-Hispanic whites are those who identify themselves as white alone and not Hispanic.
Source: Bureau of the Census, Population Estimates, Internet site http://www.census.gov/popest/; calculations by New Strategist

Table 7.19 Projections of the Female Population by Race and Hispanic Origin, 2012 to 2050

(projected number of females by race and Hispanic origin, 2012 to 2050, percent change, 2012–50; numbers in thousands)

NUMBER	2012	2020	2030	2040	2050	percent change 2012–50
Total females	**159,458**	**169,084**	**181,148**	**191,681**	**201,034**	**26.1%**
Asian	9,709	11,653	14,311	17,112	19,950	105.5
Black	23,193	25,619	28,795	32,057	35,541	53.2
Hispanic	26,191	31,214	38,280	46,014	54,113	106.6
Non-Hispanic white	100,445	101,055	100,841	98,436	94,460	–6.0

PERCENT DISTRIBUTION						percentage point change, 2012–50
Total females	**100.0%**	**100.0%**	**100.0%**	**100.0%**	**100.0%**	–
Asian	6.1	6.9	7.9	8.9	9.9	3.8
Black	14.5	15.2	15.9	16.7	17.7	3.1
Hispanic	16.4	18.5	21.1	24.0	26.9	10.5
Non-Hispanic white	63.0	59.8	55.7	51.4	47.0	–16.0

Note: Numbers by race and Hispanic origin do not sum to total because Asians and blacks are those who identify themselves as being of the race alone and those who identify themselves as being of the race in combination with other races, Hispanics may be of any race, and not all races are shown. Non-Hispanic whites are those who identify themselves as being white alone and not Hispanic. "–" means not applicable.
Source: Bureau of the Census, Population Projections, Internet site http://www.census.gov/population/projections/; calculations by New Strategist

Table 7.20 Projections of the Male Population by Race and Hispanic Origin, 2012 to 2050

(projected number and percent distribution of males by race and Hispanic origin, 2012 to 2050, percent and percentage point change, 2012–50; numbers in thousands)

NUMBER	2012	2020	2030	2040	2050	percent change 2012–50
Total males	**154,546**	**164,812**	**177,323**	**188,335**	**198,770**	**28.6%**
Asian	8,937	10,731	13,171	15,764	18,457	106.5
Black	21,269	23,719	26,932	30,293	33,984	59.8
Hispanic	27,082	32,570	40,375	48,862	57,619	112.8
Non-Hispanic white	97,317	98,258	97,976	95,451	91,874	–5.6

PERCENT DISTRIBUTION						percentage point change, 2012–50
Total males	**100.0%**	**100.0%**	**100.0%**	**100.0%**	**100.0%**	–
Asian	5.8	6.5	7.4	8.4	9.3	3.5
Black	13.8	14.4	15.2	16.1	17.1	3.3
Hispanic	17.5	19.8	22.8	25.9	29.0	11.5
Non-Hispanic white	63.0	59.6	55.3	50.7	46.2	–16.7

Note: Numbers by race and Hispanic origin do not sum to total because Asians and blacks are those who identify themselves as being of the race alone and those who identify themselves as being of the race in combination with other races, Hispanics may be of any race, and not all races are shown. Non-Hispanic whites are those who identify themselves as being white alone and not Hispanic. "–" means not applicable.
Source: Bureau of the Census, Population Projections, Internet site http://www.census.gov/population/projections/; calculations by New Strategist

Both Female and Male Populations Are Growing Fastest in the South

Nevada saw the biggest gain, while several states saw declines.

The number of males and females grew 10 to 11 percent nationally between 2000 and 2011, but in the South their numbers rose by a larger 16 percent. By state, the male and female population grew the fastest in Nevada between 2000 and 2011 (up 35 and 38 percent, respectively). The female population declined in Michigan and Rhode Island during those years, while the male population fell only in Michigan.

Females outnumber males in most states, although the margin is small. The District of Columbia has the largest share of females (52.7 percent). Males outnumber females in nine states: Alaska, Colorado, Hawaii, Idaho, Montana, Nevada, North Dakota, Utah, and Wyoming.

■ States with older populations, such as Pennsylvania, tend to have more females than males. States with youthful populations, such as Utah, tend to have more males than females.

The South is home to the largest share of females

(percent distribution of females by region, 2011)

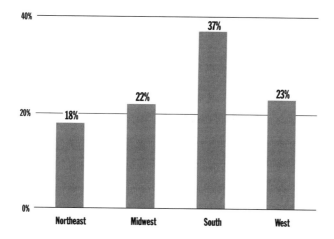

Table 7.21 Females by Region, 2000 to 2011

(number and percent distribution of females by region, 2000 to 2011, percent change in number, 2000–11; numbers in thousands)

	2011	2010	2000	percent change 2000–11
Total females	**158,301**	**156,964**	**143,368**	**10.4%**
Northeast	28,523	28,448	27,697	3.0
Midwest	34,099	33,999	32,837	3.8
South	59,150	58,421	51,180	15.6
West	36,529	36,096	31,654	15.4

Source: Bureau of the Census, Gender: 2000, Census 2000 Brief; and Population Estimates, Internet site http://www.census .gov/popest/; calculations by New Strategist

Table 7.22 Males by Region, 2000 to 2011

(number and percent distribution of males by region, 2000 to 2011, percent change in number, 2000–11; numbers in thousands)

	2011	2010	2000	percent change 2000–11
Total males	**153,291**	**151,781**	**138,054**	**11.0%**
Northeast	26,999	26,869	25,897	4.3
Midwest	33,060	32,928	31,555	4.8
South	56,897	56,135	49,057	16.0
West	36,335	35,850	31,543	15.2

Source: Bureau of the Census, Gender: 2000, Census 2000 Brief; and Population Estimates, Internet site http://www.census .gov/popest/; calculations by New Strategist

Table 7.23 Female Share of the Population by Region, 2011

(total number of people, number of females, female share of total, and percent distribution of females by region, 2011)

		females		
	total	number	share of total	percent distribution by region
Total people	**311,592**	**158,301**	**50.8%**	**100.0%**
Northeast	55,522	28,523	51.4	18.0
Midwest	67,159	34,099	50.8	21.5
South	116,047	59,150	51.0	37.4
West	72,865	36,529	50.1	23.1

Source: Bureau of the Census, Population Estimates, Internet site http://www.census.gov/popest/; calculations by New Strategist

Table 7.24 Male Share of the Population by Region, 2011

(total number of people, number of males, male share of total, and percent distribution of males by region, 2011)

		males		
	total	number	share of total	percent distribution by region
Total people	**311,592**	**153,291**	**49.2%**	**100.0%**
Northeast	55,522	26,999	48.6	17.6
Midwest	67,159	33,060	49.2	21.6
South	116,047	56,897	49.0	37.1
West	72,865	36,335	49.9	23.7

Source: Bureau of the Census, Population Estimates, Internet site http://www.census.gov/popest/; calculations by New Strategist

Table 7.25 Females by State, 2000 to 2011

(number of females by state, 2000 to 2011, percent change, 2000–11; numbers in thousands)

	2011	2010	2000	percent change 2000–11
Total females	**158,301**	**156,964**	**143,368**	**10.4%**
Alabama	2,473	2,460	2,301	7.5
Alaska	348	341	303	14.8
Arizona	3,259	3,216	2,570	26.8
Arkansas	1,495	1,484	1,369	9.2
California	18,944	18,736	16,997	11.5
Colorado	2,550	2,509	2,135	19.4
Connecticut	1,836	1,834	1,756	4.5
Delaware	467	463	403	15.9
District of Columbia	326	318	303	7.6
Florida	9,736	9,612	8,185	19.0
Georgia	5,012	4,958	4,159	20.5
Hawaii	685	679	603	13.6
Idaho	791	782	645	22.6
Illinois	6,555	6,538	6,339	3.4
Indiana	3,310	3,294	3,098	6.8
Iowa	1,545	1,538	1,491	3.6
Kansas	1,445	1,438	1,360	6.3
Kentucky	2,219	2,204	2,066	7.4
Louisiana	2,336	2,314	2,306	1.3
Maine	678	678	655	3.6
Maryland	3,008	2,982	2,739	9.8
Massachusetts	3,398	3,381	3,290	3.3
Michigan	5,030	5,036	5,065	–0.7
Minnesota	2,690	2,672	2,484	8.3
Mississippi	1,532	1,526	1,471	4.1
Missouri	3,066	3,055	2,875	6.7
Montana	497	493	453	9.8
Nebraska	927	920	868	6.9
Nevada	1,349	1,337	980	37.6
New Hampshire	667	667	628	6.2
New Jersey	4,521	4,512	4,332	4.4
New Mexico	1,052	1,042	925	13.8
New York	10,033	10,001	9,830	2.1
North Carolina	4,953	4,890	4,107	20.6
North Dakota	338	333	322	5.0
Ohio	5,906	5,904	5,841	1.1
Oklahoma	1,914	1,894	1,755	9.1
Oregon	1,955	1,935	1,725	13.4
Pennsylvania	6,528	6,512	6,351	2.8

	2011	2010	2000	percent change 2000–11
Rhode Island	543	544	545	–0.3%
South Carolina	2,403	2,375	2,063	16.5
South Dakota	411	407	380	8.1
Tennessee	3,282	3,253	2,919	12.4
Texas	12,932	12,673	10,499	23.2
Utah	1,402	1,376	1,114	25.8
Vermont	318	318	310	2.3
Virginia	4,120	4,075	3,607	14.2
Washington	3,420	3,375	2,960	15.6
West Virginia	940	939	929	1.2
Wisconsin	2,876	2,865	2,715	5.9
Wyoming	278	276	245	13.4

Source: Bureau of the Census, Gender: 2000, Census 2000 Brief; Age and Sex Composition: 2010, 2010 Census Brief; and Population Estimates, Internet site http://www.census.gov/popest/; calculations by New Strategist

Table 7.26 Males by State, 2000 to 2011

(number of males by state, 2000 and 2011, percent change, 2000–11; numbers in thousands)

	2011	2010	2000	percent change 2000–11
Total males	**153,291**	**151,781**	**138,054**	**11.0%**
Alabama	2,329	2,320	2,147	8.5
Alaska	375	370	324	15.8
Arizona	3,224	3,176	2,561	25.9
Arkansas	1,443	1,432	1,305	10.6
California	18,748	18,518	16,875	11.1
Colorado	2,567	2,521	2,166	18.5
Connecticut	1,745	1,740	1,649	5.8
Delaware	440	435	381	15.6
District of Columbia	292	284	269	8.5
Florida	9,321	9,189	7,798	19.5
Georgia	4,803	4,729	4,027	19.3
Hawaii	690	681	609	13.3
Idaho	794	785	649	22.3
Illinois	6,314	6,292	6,080	3.8
Indiana	3,207	3,190	2,982	7.5
Iowa	1,517	1,508	1,436	5.7
Kansas	1,426	1,415	1,328	7.3
Kentucky	2,150	2,135	1,975	8.8
Louisiana	2,238	2,219	2,163	3.5
Maine	650	650	620	4.8
Maryland	2,821	2,792	2,558	10.3
Massachusetts	3,190	3,167	3,059	4.3
Michigan	4,846	4,848	4,873	–0.6
Minnesota	2,655	2,632	2,436	9.0
Mississippi	1,447	1,441	1,374	5.3
Missouri	2,944	2,933	2,720	8.2
Montana	501	497	449	11.5
Nebraska	915	906	843	8.5
Nevada	1,375	1,364	1,018	35.0
New Hampshire	651	649	608	7.1
New Jersey	4,300	4,280	4,083	5.3
New Mexico	1,030	1,017	894	15.2
New York	9,432	9,377	9,147	3.1
North Carolina	4,704	4,645	3,943	19.3
North Dakota	346	340	321	8.0
Ohio	5,639	5,632	5,512	2.3
Oklahoma	1,878	1,857	1,696	10.7
Oregon	1,917	1,896	1,697	13.0
Pennsylvania	6,215	6,190	5,930	4.8
Rhode Island	508	508	504	0.9

	2011	2010	2000	percent change 2000–11
South Carolina	2,277	2,250	1,949	16.8%
South Dakota	413	407	375	10.3
Tennessee	3,121	3,094	2,770	12.7
Texas	12,742	12,472	10,353	23.1
Utah	1,416	1,388	1,119	26.5
Vermont	309	308	298	3.5
Virginia	3,976	3,926	3,472	14.5
Washington	3,410	3,350	2,934	16.2
West Virginia	915	914	879	4.1
Wisconsin	2,836	2,822	2,649	7.1
Wyoming	290	287	248	16.7

Source: Bureau of the Census, Gender: 2000, Census 2000 Brief; Age and Sex Composition: 2010, 2010 Census Brief; and Population Estimates, Internet site http://www.census.gov/popest/; calculations by New Strategist

Table 7.27 Female Share of the Population by State, 2011

(total number of people, number of females, and female share of total, by state, 2011; numbers in thousands)

	total	females number	females share of total
Total people	**311,592**	**158,324**	**50.8%**
Alabama	4,803	2,478	51.6
Alaska	723	350	48.4
Arizona	6,483	3,254	50.2
Arkansas	2,938	1,490	50.7
California	37,692	18,941	50.3
Colorado	5,117	2,548	49.8
Connecticut	3,581	1,837	51.3
Delaware	907	467	51.5
District of Columbia	618	326	52.7
Florida	19,058	9,736	51.1
Georgia	9,815	5,006	51.0
Hawaii	1,375	686	49.9
Idaho	1,585	790	49.8
Illinois	12,869	6,560	51.0
Indiana	6,517	3,310	50.8
Iowa	3,062	1,550	50.6
Kansas	2,871	1,448	50.4
Kentucky	4,369	2,226	50.9
Louisiana	4,575	2,339	51.1
Maine	1,328	677	51.0
Maryland	5,828	3,008	51.6
Massachusetts	6,588	3,400	51.6
Michigan	9,876	5,028	50.9
Minnesota	5,345	2,688	50.3
Mississippi	2,979	1,532	51.4
Missouri	6,011	3,065	51.0
Montana	998	498	49.9
Nebraska	1,843	930	50.5
Nevada	2,723	1,351	49.6
New Hampshire	1,318	667	50.6
New Jersey	8,821	4,523	51.3
New Mexico	2,082	1,046	50.2
New York	19,465	10,027	51.5
North Carolina	9,656	4,969	51.5
North Dakota	684	340	49.7
Ohio	11,545	5,903	51.1
Oklahoma	3,792	1,914	50.5
Oregon	3,872	1,958	50.6
Pennsylvania	12,743	6,526	51.2
Rhode Island	1,051	543	51.6
South Carolina	4,679	2,405	51.4

	total	females	
		number	share of total
South Dakota	824	414	50.2%
Tennessee	6,403	3,284	51.3
Texas	25,675	12,934	50.4
Utah	2,817	1,400	49.7
Vermont	626	318	50.8
Virginia	8,097	4,118	50.9
Washington	6,830	3,422	50.1
West Virginia	1,855	941	50.7
Wisconsin	5,712	2,877	50.4
Wyoming	568	279	49.1

Source: Bureau of the Census, 2011 American Community Survey, Internet site http://factfinder2.census.gov/faces/nav/jsf/pages/ index.xhtml; calculations by New Strategist

Table 7.28 Male Share of the Population by State, 2011

(total number of people, number of males, and male share of total, by state, 2011; numbers in thousands)

		males	
	total	**number**	**share of total**
Total people	**311,592**	**153,268**	**49.2%**
Alabama	4,803	2,324	48.4
Alaska	723	373	51.6
Arizona	6,483	3,229	49.8
Arkansas	2,938	1,448	49.3
California	37,692	18,751	49.7
Colorado	5,117	2,569	50.2
Connecticut	3,581	1,744	48.7
Delaware	907	440	48.5
District of Columbia	618	292	47.3
Florida	19,058	9,321	48.9
Georgia	9,815	4,809	49.0
Hawaii	1,375	689	50.1
Idaho	1,585	795	50.2
Illinois	12,869	6,309	49.0
Indiana	6,517	3,206	49.2
Iowa	3,062	1,512	49.4
Kansas	2,871	1,423	49.6
Kentucky	4,369	2,144	49.1
Louisiana	4,575	2,236	48.9
Maine	1,328	651	49.0
Maryland	5,828	2,820	48.4
Massachusetts	6,588	3,188	48.4
Michigan	9,876	4,849	49.1
Minnesota	5,345	2,656	49.7
Mississippi	2,979	1,447	48.6
Missouri	6,011	2,946	49.0
Montana	998	500	50.1
Nebraska	1,843	912	49.5
Nevada	2,723	1,373	50.4
New Hampshire	1,318	651	49.4
New Jersey	8,821	4,299	48.7
New Mexico	2,082	1,037	49.8
New York	19,465	9,438	48.5
North Carolina	9,656	4,688	48.5
North Dakota	684	344	50.3
Ohio	11,545	5,642	48.9
Oklahoma	3,792	1,878	49.5
Oregon	3,872	1,914	49.4
Pennsylvania	12,743	6,217	48.8
Rhode Island	1,051	508	48.4
South Carolina	4,679	2,274	48.6

	total	males	
		number	share of total
South Dakota	824	411	49.8%
Tennessee	6,403	3,119	48.7
Texas	25,675	12,741	49.6
Utah	2,817	1,418	50.3
Vermont	626	308	49.2
Virginia	8,097	3,979	49.1
Washington	6,830	3,408	49.9
West Virginia	1,855	914	49.3
Wisconsin	5,712	2,835	49.6
Wyoming	568	289	50.9

Source: Bureau of the Census, 2011 American Community Survey, Internet site http://factfinder2.census.gov/faces/nav/jsf/pages/index.xhtml; calculations by New Strategist

Only 12 Percent of Males and Females Move Each Year

Most move within the same county.

The mobility rate is highest among men and women in their twenties, with women's peak mobility rate slightly exceeding men's. Twenty-seven percent of women aged 20 to 24 moved between March 2011 and March 2012. Among men, mobility peaks at 25 percent among those aged 25 to 29. Some young adults are moving out of their parents' home into their own apartment. Some are going to college, while others are leaving college for jobs elsewhere. The mobility rate falls with age as people buy homes and establish roots in a community. The lowest mobility rate is found among men and women aged 65 or older, with only 3 to 4 percent moving during a year's time.

Most moves are local. Nearly two-thirds of male and female movers remain within the same county. Only 14 percent moved to a different state between 2011 and 2012. The most common reason for moving is for better housing, with 16 percent of both male and female movers saying they moved because they wanted a new or better home or apartment.

■ Americans are far less likely to move today than in decades past, in part because of the increase in two-income couples.

Few moves are out-of-state

(percent distribution of male movers by type of move, 2011–12)

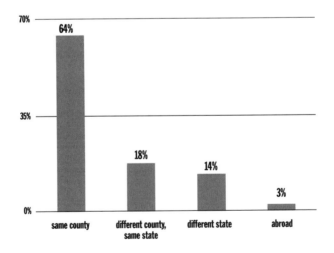

Table 7.29 Geographical Mobility of Females by Relationship to Householder and Age, 2011–12

(total number of females aged 1 or older, and number and percent who moved between March 2011 and March 2012; by relationship to householder and age; numbers in thousands)

		movers	
	total	number	share of total
Total females	**155,739**	**18,587**	**11.9%**
Householder, spouse present	22,950	1,757	7.7
Other family householder	15,678	2,745	17.5
Spouse of householder	36,014	2,707	7.5
Child of householder	42,060	5,120	12.2
Other relative of householder	10,283	1,400	13.6
Nonrelative of householder	7,340	2,118	28.9
Nonfamily householder	21,383	2,729	12.8
Total females	**155,739**	**18,587**	**11.9%**
Under age 15	27,988	4,111	14.7
Aged 15 to 17	6,311	686	10.9
Aged 18 to 19	4,089	564	13.8
Aged 20 to 24	10,891	2,966	27.2
Aged 25 to 29	10,464	2,545	24.3
Aged 30 to 34	10,292	1,790	17.4
Aged 35 to 44	20,251	2,287	11.3
Aged 45 to 64	42,280	2,812	6.7
Aged 65 or older	23,174	828	3.6

Source: Bureau of the Census, Geographic Mobility: 2011 to 2012, Internet site http://www.census.gov/hhes/migration/; calculations by New Strategist

Table 7.30 Geographical Mobility of Males by Relationship to Householder and Age, 2011–12

(total number of males aged 1 or older, and number and percent who moved between March 2011 and March 2012; by relationship to householder and age; numbers in thousands)

		movers	
	total	number	share of total
Total males	**149,185**	**17,901**	**12.0%**
Householder, spouse present	36,014	2,636	7.3
Other family householder	5,888	861	14.6
Spouse of householder	22,950	1,806	7.9
Child of householder	47,372	5,453	11.5
Other relative of householder	9,269	1,331	14.4
Nonrelative of householder	8,451	2,480	29.3
Nonfamily householder	19,195	3,321	17.3
Total males	**149,185**	**17,901**	**12.0%**
Under age 15	29,239	4,246	14.5
Aged 15 to 17	6,666	625	9.4
Aged 18 to 19	4,173	589	14.1
Aged 20 to 24	10,987	2,421	22.0
Aged 25 to 29	10,430	2,593	24.9
Aged 30 to 34	10,034	1,873	18.7
Aged 35 to 44	19,677	2,265	11.5
Aged 45 to 64	39,646	2,690	6.8
Aged 65 or older	18,332	598	3.3

Source: Bureau of the Census, Geographic Mobility: 2011 to 2012, Internet site http://www.census.gov/hhes/migration/; calculations by New Strategist

Table 7.31 Geographical Mobility of Females by Age and Type of Move, 2011–12

(number and percent distribution of females aged 1 or older who moved between March 2011 and March 2012, by age and type of move; numbers in thousands)

	total	same county	different county, same state	different state total	different state same region	different state different region	movers from abroad
Total female movers	**18,587**	**12,021**	**3,489**	**2,542**	**1,178**	**1,364**	**535**
Under age 15	4,111	2,811	693	504	226	278	103
Aged 15 to 17	686	456	118	91	43	48	20
Aged 18 to 19	564	367	119	64	10	54	14
Aged 20 to 24	2,966	1,925	528	417	199	218	97
Aged 25 to 29	2,545	1,613	452	371	201	170	108
Aged 30 to 34	1,790	1,153	341	234	107	127	61
Aged 35 to 44	2,287	1,467	429	328	137	191	62
Aged 45 to 64	2,812	1,752	601	405	195	210	54
Aged 65 or older	828	478	208	126	58	68	15

PERCENT DISTRIBUTION BY TYPE OF MOVE

	total	same county	different county, same state	different state total	different state same region	different state different region	movers from abroad
Total female movers	**100.0%**	**64.7%**	**18.8%**	**13.7%**	**6.3%**	**7.3%**	**2.9%**
Under age 15	100.0	68.4	16.9	12.3	5.5	6.8	2.5
Aged 15 to 17	100.0	66.5	17.2	13.3	6.3	7.0	2.9
Aged 18 to 19	100.0	65.1	21.1	11.3	1.8	9.6	2.5
Aged 20 to 24	100.0	64.9	17.8	14.1	6.7	7.3	3.3
Aged 25 to 29	100.0	63.4	17.8	14.6	7.9	6.7	4.2
Aged 30 to 34	100.0	64.4	19.1	13.1	6.0	7.1	3.4
Aged 35 to 44	100.0	64.1	18.8	14.3	6.0	8.4	2.7
Aged 45 to 64	100.0	62.3	21.4	14.4	6.9	7.5	1.9
Aged 65 or older	100.0	57.7	25.1	15.2	7.0	8.2	1.8

Source: Bureau of the Census, Geographic Mobility: 2011 to 2012, Internet site http://www.census.gov/hhes/migration/; calculations by New Strategist

Table 7.32 Geographical Mobility of Males by Age and Type of Move, 2011–12

(number and percent distribution of males aged 1 or older who moved between March 2011 and March 2012, by age and type of move; numbers in thousands)

	total	same county	different county, same state	different state total	different state same region	different state different region	movers from abroad
Total male movers	17,901	11,472	3,293	2,518	1,142	1,376	619
Under age 15	4,246	2,881	727	536	237	299	102
Aged 15 to 17	625	424	107	80	46	34	14
Aged 18 to 19	589	377	129	54	38	16	29
Aged 20 to 24	2,421	1,561	429	315	135	180	116
Aged 25 to 29	2,593	1,591	460	425	210	215	117
Aged 30 to 34	1,873	1,188	333	287	129	158	65
Aged 35 to 44	2,265	1,427	426	319	117	202	94
Aged 45 to 64	2,690	1,678	547	394	170	224	71
Aged 65 or older	598	344	136	108	60	48	11

PERCENT DISTRIBUTION BY TYPE OF MOVE

	total	same county	different county, same state	different state total	different state same region	different state different region	movers from abroad
Total male movers	100.0%	64.1%	18.4%	14.1%	6.4%	7.7%	3.5%
Under age 15	100.0	67.9	17.1	12.6	5.6	7.0	2.4
Aged 15 to 17	100.0	67.8	17.1	12.8	7.4	5.4	2.2
Aged 18 to 19	100.0	64.0	21.9	9.2	6.5	2.7	4.9
Aged 20 to 24	100.0	64.5	17.7	13.0	5.6	7.4	4.8
Aged 25 to 29	100.0	61.4	17.7	16.4	8.1	8.3	4.5
Aged 30 to 34	100.0	63.4	17.8	15.3	6.9	8.4	3.5
Aged 35 to 44	100.0	63.0	18.8	14.1	5.2	8.9	4.2
Aged 45 to 64	100.0	62.4	20.3	14.6	6.3	8.3	2.6
Aged 65 or older	100.0	57.5	22.7	18.1	10.0	8.0	1.8

Source: Bureau of the Census, Geographic Mobility: 2011 to 2012, Internet site http://www.census.gov/hhes/migration/; calculations by New Strategist

Table 7.33 Geographical Mobility of Females by Reason for Move, 2011–12

(number and percent distribution of females aged 1 or older who moved between March 2011 and March 2012, by main reason for move and type of move; numbers in thousands)

	total moves		move within county		move to different county	
	total	percent distribution	total	percent distribution	total	percent distribution
Total female movers	**18,587**	**100.0%**	**12,021**	**100.0%**	**6,031**	**100.0%**
Family reasons, total	**5,691**	**30.6**	**3,708**	**30.8**	**1,813**	**30.1**
Change in marital status	1,239	6.7	807	6.7	410	6.8
To establish own household	2,109	11.3	1,627	13.5	419	6.9
Other family reason	2,343	12.6	1,274	10.6	984	16.3
Employment reasons, total	**3,368**	**18.1**	**1,051**	**8.7**	**2,130**	**35.3**
New job or job transfer	1,685	9.1	233	1.9	1,328	22.0
To look for work or lost job	291	1.6	90	0.7	164	2.7
To be closer to work/easier commute	953	5.1	588	4.9	353	5.9
Retired	96	0.5	30	0.2	63	1.0
Other job-related reason	343	1.8	110	0.9	222	3.7
Housing reasons, total	**9,197**	**49.5**	**7,081**	**58.9**	**1,954**	**32.4**
Wanted own home/not rent	855	4.6	711	5.9	141	2.3
Wanted new or better home/apartment	2,980	16.0	2,521	21.0	449	7.4
Wanted better neighborhood/less crime	634	3.4	451	3.8	181	3.0
Wanted cheaper housing	1,698	9.1	1,422	11.8	272	4.5
Foreclosure or eviction	389	2.1	299	2.5	87	1.4
Other housing reasons	2,641	14.2	1,677	14.0	824	13.7
Other reasons, total	**331**	**1.8**	**177**	**1.5**	**136**	**2.3**
To attend or leave college	73	0.4	25	0.2	37	0.6
Change of climate	8	0.0	6	0.0	2	0.0
Health reasons	42	0.2	27	0.2	16	0.3
Natural disaster	25	0.1	15	0.1	10	0.2
Other reasons	183	1.0	104	0.9	71	1.2

Note: Numbers by type of move do not sum to total because movers from abroad are not shown.
Source: Bureau of the Census, Geographic Mobility: 2011 to 2012, Internet site http://www.census.gov/hhes/migration/; calculations by New Strategist

Table 7.34 Geographical Mobility of Males by Reason for Move, 2011–12

(number and percent distribution of males aged 1 or older who moved between March 2011 and March 2012, by main reason for move and type of move; numbers in thousands)

	total moves		move within county		move to different county	
	total	percent distribution	total	percent distribution	total	percent distribution
Total male movers	**17,901**	**100.0%**	**11,472**	**100.0%**	**5,810**	**100.0%**
Family reasons, total	**5,002**	**27.9**	**3,398**	**29.6**	**1,437**	**24.7**
Change in marital status	1,061	5.9	737	6.4	309	5.3
To establish own household	1,797	10.0	1,431	12.5	308	5.3
Other family reason	2,144	12.0	1,230	10.7	820	14.1
Employment reasons, total	**3,689**	**20.6**	**1,170**	**10.2**	**2,260**	**38.9**
New job or job transfer	1,784	10.0	281	2.4	1,334	23.0
To look for work or lost job	368	2.1	117	1.0	207	3.6
To be closer to work/easier commute	1,044	5.8	628	5.5	401	6.9
Retired	86	0.5	27	0.2	53	0.9
Other job-related reason	407	2.3	117	1.0	265	4.6
Housing reasons, total	**8,842**	**49.4**	**6,736**	**58.7**	**1,945**	**33.5**
Wanted own home/not rent	855	4.8	712	6.2	137	2.4
Wanted new or better home/apartment	2,829	15.8	2,408	21.0	416	7.2
Wanted better neighborhood/less crime	596	3.3	440	3.8	152	2.6
Wanted cheaper housing	1,562	8.7	1,253	10.9	303	5.2
Foreclosure or eviction	403	2.3	300	2.6	93	1.6
Other housing reasons	2,597	14.5	1,623	14.1	844	14.5
Other reasons, total	**368**	**2.1**	**169**	**1.5**	**170**	**2.9**
To attend or leave college	125	0.7	52	0.5	55	0.9
Change of climate	8	0.0	3	0.0	5	0.1
Health reasons	59	0.3	22	0.2	36	0.6
Natural disaster	30	0.2	17	0.1	13	0.2
Other reasons	146	0.8	75	0.7	61	1.0

Note: Numbers by type of move do not sum to total because movers from abroad are not shown.
Source: Bureau of the Census, Geographic Mobility: 2011 to 2012, Internet site http://www.census.gov/hhes/migration/; calculations by New Strategist

More than Half the Nation's Foreign-Born Are Female

More than one in three foreign-born males and females came to the United States since 2000.

The nation's foreign-born females number more than 20 million and accounted for 13 percent of the total female population in 2011. The male foreign-born population numbers nearly 20 million and accounts for 13 percent of the male population. The 51 percent majority of foreign-born females are from Latin America. Among foreign-born males, Latin America accounts for an even larger 55 percent of the total.

The U.S. population gains more than 1 million legal immigrants a year, 55 percent of them female. Males outnumber females only among immigrants aged 1 to 19. In all other age groups, females outnumber males, sometimes by a wide margin.

■ Many immigrants to the United States are the relatives of America's foreign-born population, including wives, mothers, and sisters.

More than 500,000 females immigrated to the United States in 2011

(number of legal immigrants by sex, 2011)

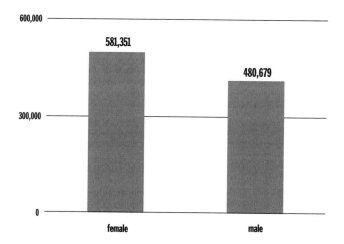

Table 7.35 Foreign-Born Females by Selected Characteristics, 2011

(number and percent distribution of females by foreign-born status, and foreign-born females by selected characteristics, 2011; numbers in thousands)

	number	percent distribution
Total females	**158,324**	**100.0%**
Foreign-born females	20,617	13.0
Total foreign-born	**40,378**	**100.0**
Foreign-born females	20,617	51.1
CITIZENSHIP STATUS		
Total foreign-born females	**20,617**	**100.0**
Naturalized citizen	9,832	47.7
Not a citizen	10,785	52.3
REGION OF BIRTH		
Total foreign-born females	**20,617**	**100.0**
Asia	6,180	30.0
Europe	2,672	13.0
Latin America	10,434	50.6
Caribbean	2,065	10.0
Central America	6,912	33.5
Mexico	5,446	26.4
Other Central America	1,467	7.1
South America	1,456	7.1
Other areas	1,331	6.5
YEAR OF ENTRY		
Total foreign-born females	**20,617**	**100.0**
2000 or later	7,241	35.1
Before 2000	13,376	64.9

Source: Bureau of the Census, 2011 American Community Survey, Internet site http://factfinder2.census.gov/faces/nav/jsf/pages/index.xhtml; calculations by New Strategist

Table 7.36 Foreign-Born Males by Selected Characteristics, 2011

(number and percent distribution of males by foreign-born status, and foreign-born males by selected characteristics, 2011; numbers in thousands)

	number	percent distribution
Total males	**153,268**	**100.0%**
Foreign-born males	19,761	12.9
Total foreign-born	**40,378**	**100.0**
Foreign-born males	19,761	48.9
CITIZENSHIP STATUS		
Total foreign-born males	**19,761**	**100.0**
Naturalized citizen	8,308	42.0
Not a citizen	11,452	58.0
REGION OF BIRTH		
Total foreign-born males	**19,761**	**100.0**
Asia	5,382	27.2
Europe	2,218	11.2
Latin America	10,811	54.7
Caribbean	1,711	8.7
Central America	7,846	39.7
Mexico	6,227	31.5
Other Central America	1,619	8.2
South America	1,254	6.3
Other areas	1,350	6.8
YEAR OF ENTRY		
Total foreign-born males	**19,761**	**100.0**
2000 or later	7,170	36.3
Before 2000	12,591	63.7

Source: Bureau of the Census, 2011 American Community Survey, Internet site http://factfinder2.census.gov/faces/nav/jsf/pages/index.xhtml; calculations by New Strategist

Table 7.37 Female Share of Legal Immigrants by Age, 2011

(total number of immigrants admitted for legal permanent residence, number and percent distribution of female immigrants, and female share of total, by age, fiscal year 2011)

	total	females		
		number	percent distribution	share of total
Total legal immigrants	**1,062,040**	**581,351**	**100.0%**	**54.7%**
Under age 1	4,361	2,247	0.4	51.5
Aged 1 to 4	34,017	16,910	2.9	49.7
Aged 5 to 9	52,828	25,725	4.4	48.7
Aged 10 to 14	70,295	34,073	5.9	48.5
Aged 15 to 19	88,970	43,852	7.5	49.3
Aged 20 to 24	110,144	61,015	10.5	55.4
Aged 25 to 29	122,128	71,170	12.2	58.3
Aged 30 to 34	130,789	71,132	12.2	54.4
Aged 35 to 39	112,983	59,737	10.3	52.9
Aged 40 to 44	84,394	47,130	8.1	55.8
Aged 45 to 49	68,174	39,241	6.7	57.6
Aged 50 to 54	52,623	30,898	5.3	58.7
Aged 55 to 59	42,941	26,156	4.5	60.9
Aged 60 to 64	34,257	20,670	3.6	60.3
Aged 65 to 74	39,386	23,244	4.0	59.0
Aged 75 or older	13,740	8,147	1.4	59.3

Note: Numbers do not add to total because immigrants of unknown age are not shown.
Source: Department of Homeland Security, 2011 Yearbook of Immigration Statistics, Internet site http://www.dhs.gov/yearbook-immigration-statistics

Table 7.38 Male Share of Legal Immigrants by Age, 2011

(total number of immigrants admitted for legal permanent residence, number and percent distribution of male immigrants, and male share of total, by age, fiscal year 2011)

		males		
	total	number	percent distribution	share of total
Total legal immigrants	**1,062,040**	**480,679**	**100.0%**	**45.3%**
Under age 1	4,361	2,114	0.4	48.5
Aged 1 to 4	34,017	17,107	3.6	50.3
Aged 5 to 9	52,828	27,103	5.6	51.3
Aged 10 to 14	70,295	36,222	7.5	51.5
Aged 15 to 19	88,970	45,115	9.4	50.7
Aged 20 to 24	110,144	49,127	10.2	44.6
Aged 25 to 29	122,128	50,957	10.6	41.7
Aged 30 to 34	130,789	59,655	12.4	45.6
Aged 35 to 39	112,983	53,245	11.1	47.1
Aged 40 to 44	84,394	37,264	7.8	44.2
Aged 45 to 49	68,174	28,933	6.0	42.4
Aged 50 to 54	52,623	21,725	4.5	41.3
Aged 55 to 59	42,941	16,785	3.5	39.1
Aged 60 to 64	34,257	13,586	2.8	39.7
Aged 65 to 74	39,386	16,142	3.4	41.0
Aged 75 or older	13,740	5,593	1.2	40.7

Note: Numbers do not add to total because immigrants of unknown age are not shown.
Source: Department of Homeland Security, 2011 Yearbook of Immigration Statistics, Internet site http://www.dhs.gov/yearbook-immigration-statistics

8

Spending

Married couples with children spend the most.

They spent $69,724 in 2011—or 40 percent more than the average household. Those with school-aged children spend more than twice the average on household personal services, largely daycare.

Married couples without children at home spend more on some items.

Many are empty-nesters and big spenders on public transportation, which includes cruises and airline fares. They also spend more on alcoholic beverages, health care, reading material, cash contributions, and gifts.

Single parents spend less than married couples.

The $37,553 spent by single parents, most of whom are women, was only 76 percent as much as the average household spent.

Men aged 25 to 34 who live alone are big spenders on alcoholic beverages.

They spend 80 percent more than the average household on alcoholic beverages, 94 percent more than average on rent, and twice the average on men's clothes.

Women aged 25 to 34 who live alone are big spenders on women's clothes.

They spend 65 percent more than the average household on women's clothes. They are also above-average spenders on personal care products and services.

Married Couples Spend More than Average

Those with children at home spend the most.

Because the majority of men and women are married, examining the spending patterns of married couples reveals much of what men and women do with their money. Married couples spent an average of $63,972 in 2011, a substantial 29 percent more than the $49,705 spent by the average household. Married couples with children spent a larger $69,724—or 40 percent more than the average household. Many married couples have two earners in the home, boosting incomes and spending.

Spending by households headed by single parents (79 percent of whom are women) was only 76 percent of the average ($37,553) in 2011. Behind the lower spending of single parents is the fact that most have only one earner in the home.

The Bureau of Labor Statistics collects spending data from households rather than individuals. The average spending table shows how much married couples and single parents spent in 2011. The indexed spending table compares the spending of each type of household to the spending of the average household. An index of 100 means the household type spends an average amount on an item. An index above 100 means the household type spends more than average on an item, while an index below 100 signifies below-average spending.

Married couples without children at home spend less than those with children

(average annual spending of households by type, 2011)

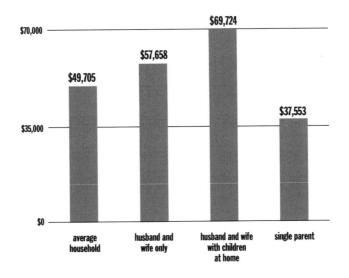

Married couples with children at home spend more than average on most items because of their larger-than-average household size. They spend 51 percent more than average on food at home and 44 percent more on food away from home. They are big spenders on household personal services (mostly daycare), with an index of 251. They spend well above average on children's clothes, household furnishings, vehicles, entertainment, and education. They spend only an average amount on alcoholic beverages, with an index of 101.

Married couples without children at home (many of them empty-nesters) spend only 16 percent more than the average household. But they spend 34 percent more than average on alcoholic beverages. They spend 36 percent more on public transportation, which includes cruises and airline fares. They spend well above average on cash contributions, health care, household furnishings, and gifts for people living in other households.

Single parents spend well below average on most items, although they spend close to the average on some foods such as milk and more than average on fish and seafood as well as poultry. Single-parent households spend 72 percent more than average on household personal services, most of which is daycare. They spend more than twice the average on boys' and girls' clothes, and 18 percent more than average on footwear.

■ With boomers becoming empty-nesters and postponing retirement, the spending of married couples without children at home is likely to rise.

Table 8.1 Average Spending of Married-Couple and Single-Parent Households, 2011

(average annual spending of households by type of household, 2011)

	total households	total married couples	married couples, no children at home	married couples with children at home				single parent, at least one child under 18 at home
				total	oldest child under 6	oldest child 6 to 17	oldest child 18 or older	
Number of households (in 000s)	122,287	60,144	25,270	29,097	5,825	14,661	8,612	6,956
Average number of persons per household	2.5	3.2	2.0	4.0	3.5	4.2	3.9	2.9
Average annual spending	$49,705	$63,972	$57,658	$69,724	$65,948	$70,709	$70,412	$37,553
FOOD	$6,458	$8,315	$6,895	$9,557	$8,028	$9,813	$10,042	$5,676
Food at home	3,838	4,944	3,935	5,785	5,010	5,877	6,080	3,526
Cereals and bakery products	531	687	535	820	673	864	832	519
Cereals and cereal products	175	225	168	275	232	295	266	194
Bakery products	356	462	367	545	441	569	566	325
Meats, poultry, fish, and eggs	832	1,084	820	1,275	921	1,276	1,480	790
Beef	223	298	225	337	219	344	393	207
Pork	162	209	162	242	175	245	276	144
Other meats	123	166	116	210	145	223	224	102
Poultry	154	197	137	243	190	226	301	167
Fish and seafood	121	153	132	171	131	166	205	126
Eggs	50	62	48	73	61	72	81	45
Dairy products	407	533	420	636	597	650	635	355
Fresh milk and cream	150	194	140	238	239	239	238	139
Other dairy products	257	339	279	398	358	411	397	216
Fruits and vegetables	715	926	761	1,067	996	1,059	1,122	600
Fresh fruits	247	325	272	374	353	369	395	208
Fresh vegetables	224	294	255	325	298	321	349	159
Processed fruits	116	144	108	175	168	177	176	113
Processed vegetables	128	164	126	192	177	191	203	121
Other food at home	1,353	1,714	1,400	1,987	1,824	2,030	2,011	1,262
Sugar and other sweets	144	188	152	219	183	229	223	124
Fats and oils	110	142	119	158	121	155	184	91
Miscellaneous foods	690	866	687	1,033	1,078	1,037	998	684
Nonalcoholic beverages	361	445	361	510	383	533	546	343
Food prepared by consumer unit on trips	48	72	81	68	58	76	60	19
Food away from home	2,620	3,370	2,960	3,772	3,018	3,936	3,962	2,150
ALCOHOLIC BEVERAGES	456	515	610	459	424	459	479	246
HOUSING	16,803	20,664	18,329	22,788	25,009	23,158	20,648	14,563
Shelter	9,825	11,780	10,404	13,122	14,571	13,609	11,311	8,426
Owned dwellings	6,148	8,620	7,622	9,646	10,295	9,974	8,649	3,405
Mortgage interest and charges	3,184	4,591	3,341	5,694	6,808	5,944	4,515	1,967
Property taxes	1,845	2,565	2,558	2,658	2,412	2,748	2,673	930
Maintenance, repair, insurance, other expenses	1,120	1,464	1,724	1,294	1,074	1,282	1,461	508
Rented dwellings	3,029	2,145	1,471	2,649	3,608	2,792	1,758	4,851
Other lodging	648	1,015	1,312	826	668	843	905	170
Utilities, fuels, and public services	3,727	4,540	4,073	4,797	3,989	4,856	5,244	3,445
Natural gas	420	505	452	542	444	558	579	371
Electricity	1,423	1,713	1,563	1,783	1,484	1,809	1,942	1,428

	total households	total married couples	married couples, no children at home	married couples with children at home				single parent, at least one child under 18 at home
				total	oldest child under 6	oldest child 6 to 17	oldest child 18 or older	
Fuel oil and other fuels	$157	$198	$212	$185	$142	$185	$213	$63
Telephone services	1,226	1,498	1,275	1,640	1,377	1,636	1,825	1,165
Water and other public services	501	626	571	647	543	667	685	419
Household services	**1,122**	**1,451**	**1,021**	**1,891**	**3,679**	**1,660**	**1,074**	**1,185**
Personal services	398	549	69	997	2,817	768	157	683
Other household services	724	902	952	893	862	892	917	502
Housekeeping supplies	**615**	**826**	**800**	**860**	**834**	**851**	**890**	**392**
Laundry and cleaning supplies	145	188	172	200	169	210	203	138
Other household products	340	460	439	495	500	468	537	196
Postage and stationery	130	178	189	165	165	174	150	58
Household furnishings and equipment	**1,514**	**2,067**	**2,029**	**2,118**	**1,935**	**2,182**	**2,129**	**1,115**
Household textiles	109	141	144	138	159	124	151	140
Furniture	358	472	437	512	484	537	487	347
Floor coverings	20	29	37	23	14	21	31	12
Major appliances	194	271	275	275	267	293	249	163
Small appliances and miscellaneous housewares	89	121	138	110	109	106	118	51
Miscellaneous household equipment	744	1,031	999	1,060	902	1,101	1,092	402
APPAREL AND RELATED SERVICES	**1,740**	**2,184**	**1,715**	**2,541**	**2,157**	**2,587**	**2,687**	**1,835**
Men and boys	**404**	**515**	**363**	**612**	**405**	**649**	**673**	**336**
Men, aged 16 or older	324	405	338	433	278	393	592	138
Boys, aged 2 to 15	80	110	25	179	126	256	80	198
Women and girls	**721**	**889**	**737**	**1,004**	**636**	**1,045**	**1,154**	**851**
Women, aged 16 or older	604	726	691	733	528	634	1,018	577
Girls, aged 2 to 15	117	163	47	272	108	411	136	274
Children under age 2	**68**	**93**	**30**	**151**	**512**	**99**	**26**	**104**
Footwear	**321**	**407**	**297**	**490**	**337**	**522**	**525**	**380**
Other apparel products and services	**226**	**280**	**288**	**283**	**268**	**273**	**309**	**163**
TRANSPORTATION	**8,293**	**10,972**	**9,474**	**12,182**	**10,698**	**12,218**	**13,120**	**5,471**
Vehicle purchases	**2,669**	**3,609**	**2,793**	**4,302**	**3,562**	**4,382**	**4,666**	**1,394**
Cars and trucks, new	1,265	1,848	1,557	2,134	1,830	2,085	2,421	334
Cars and trucks, used	1,339	1,683	1,158	2,074	1,725	2,136	2,206	1,028
Other vehicles	64	78	77	94	8	160	40	33
Gasoline and motor oil	**2,655**	**3,472**	**2,923**	**3,852**	**3,205**	**3,921**	**4,173**	**2,119**
Other vehicle expenses	**2,454**	**3,204**	**3,056**	**3,319**	**3,297**	**3,168**	**3,588**	**1,636**
Vehicle finance charges	233	330	248	391	452	383	364	144
Maintenance and repairs	805	1,041	981	1,105	933	1,159	1,124	520
Vehicle insurance	983	1,243	1,244	1,203	1,248	1,084	1,377	699
Vehicle rentals, leases, licenses, other charges	433	590	583	620	663	542	723	273
Public transportation	**516**	**687**	**702**	**709**	**633**	**747**	**693**	**323**
HEALTH CARE	**3,313**	**4,479**	**5,127**	**3,910**	**3,486**	**3,753**	**4,465**	**1,892**
Health insurance	1,922	2,619	3,004	2,268	2,161	2,157	2,530	797
Medical services	768	1,026	1,089	990	883	960	1,111	821
Drugs	489	661	829	505	328	485	658	211
Medical supplies	134	173	205	148	113	151	166	63
ENTERTAINMENT	**2,572**	**3,418**	**3,286**	**3,591**	**2,956**	**4,086**	**3,161**	**1,821**
Fees and admissions	594	872	719	1,044	698	1,367	724	424

	total households	total married couples	married couples, no children at home	married couples with children at home				single parent, at least one child under 18 at home
				total	oldest child under 6	oldest child 6 to 17	oldest child 18 or older	
Audio and visual equipment and services	$977	$1,180	$1,071	$1,278	$1,073	$1,355	$1,282	$827
Pets, toys, and playground equipment	631	794	809	774	681	801	788	405
Other entertainment products and services	370	572	687	495	504	563	367	164
PERSONAL CARE PRODUCTS AND SERVICES	634	819	761	884	707	915	938	548
READING	115	148	177	132	107	136	141	52
EDUCATION	1,051	1,340	716	1,904	729	1,739	2,978	553
TOBACCO PRODUCTS AND SMOKING SUPPLIES	351	342	293	320	204	312	411	322
MISCELLANEOUS	775	897	902	865	973	811	883	668
CASH CONTRIBUTIONS	1,721	2,227	2,824	1,833	1,589	1,877	1,924	665
PERSONAL INSURANCE AND PENSIONS	5,424	7,652	6,549	8,759	8,882	8,843	8,533	3,241
Life and other personal insurance	317	463	473	473	509	443	501	135
Pensions and Social Security	5,106	7,189	6,077	8,286	8,373	8,400	8,032	3,107
PERSONAL TAXES	2,012	2,940	3,216	2,976	3,141	2,233	4,128	−11
Federal income taxes	1,370	2,024	2,362	1,957	2,076	1,424	2,786	−279
State and local income taxes	505	719	637	832	817	662	1,130	226
Other taxes	136	197	216	187	248	147	212	42
GIFTS FOR PEOPLE IN OTHER HOUSEHOLDS	1,037	1,332	1,635	1,171	744	1,052	1,660	450

Note: Number of married couples by type does not add to total married couples because not all types of married-couple households are shown. Seventy-nine percent of single-parent families are headed by women and 21 percent are headed by men. Gift spending is also included in the preceding product and service categories.
Source: Bureau of Labor Statistics, 2011 Consumer Expenditure Survey, Internet site http://www.bls.gov/cex/; calculations by New Strategist

Table 8.2 Indexed Spending of Married-Couple and Single-Parent Households, 2011

(indexed average annual spending of households by type of household, 2011)

| | total households | total married couples | married couples, no children at home | married couples with children at home | | | | single parent, at least one child under 18 at home |
				total	oldest child under 6	oldest child 6 to 17	oldest child 18 or older	
Average annual spending	$49,705	$63,972	$57,658	$69,724	$65,948	$70,709	$70,412	$37,553
Average annual spending, index	100	129	116	140	133	142	142	76
FOOD	100	129	107	148	124	152	155	88
Food at home	100	129	103	151	131	153	158	92
Cereals and bakery products	100	129	101	154	127	163	157	98
Cereals and cereal products	100	129	96	157	133	169	152	111
Bakery products	100	130	103	153	124	160	159	91
Meats, poultry, fish, and eggs	100	130	99	153	111	153	178	95
Beef	100	134	101	151	98	154	176	93
Pork	100	129	100	149	108	151	170	89
Other meats	100	135	94	171	118	181	182	83
Poultry	100	128	89	158	123	147	195	108
Fish and seafood	100	126	109	141	108	137	169	104
Eggs	100	124	96	146	122	144	162	90
Dairy products	100	131	103	156	147	160	156	87
Fresh milk and cream	100	129	93	159	159	159	159	93
Other dairy products	100	132	109	155	139	160	154	84
Fruits and vegetables	100	130	106	149	139	148	157	84
Fresh fruits	100	132	110	151	143	149	160	84
Fresh vegetables	100	131	114	145	133	143	156	71
Processed fruits	100	124	93	151	145	153	152	97
Processed vegetables	100	128	98	150	138	149	159	95
Other food at home	100	127	103	147	135	150	149	93
Sugar and other sweets	100	131	106	152	127	159	155	86
Fats and oils	100	129	108	144	110	141	167	83
Miscellaneous foods	100	126	100	150	156	150	145	99
Nonalcoholic beverages	100	123	100	141	106	148	151	95
Food prepared by consumer unit on trips	100	150	169	142	121	158	125	40
Food away from home	100	129	113	144	115	150	151	82
ALCOHOLIC BEVERAGES	100	113	134	101	93	101	105	54
HOUSING	100	123	109	136	149	138	123	87
Shelter	100	120	106	134	148	139	115	86
Owned dwellings	100	140	124	157	167	162	141	55
Mortgage interest and charges	100	144	105	179	214	187	142	62
Property taxes	100	139	139	144	131	149	145	50
Maintenance, repair, insurance, other expenses	100	131	154	116	96	114	130	45
Rented dwellings	100	71	49	87	119	92	58	160
Other lodging	100	157	202	127	103	130	140	26
Utilities, fuels, and public services	100	122	109	129	107	130	141	92
Natural gas	100	120	108	129	106	133	138	88
Electricity	100	120	110	125	104	127	136	100

	total households	total married couples	married couples, no children at home	married couples with children at home				single parent, at least one child under 18 at home
				total	oldest child under 6	oldest child 6 to 17	oldest child 18 or older	
Fuel oil and other fuels	100	126	135	118	90	118	136	40
Telephone services	100	122	104	134	112	133	149	95
Water and other public services	100	125	114	129	108	133	137	84
Household services	**100**	**129**	**91**	**169**	**328**	**148**	**96**	**106**
Personal services	100	138	17	251	708	193	39	172
Other household services	100	125	131	123	119	123	127	69
Housekeeping supplies	**100**	**134**	**130**	**140**	**136**	**138**	**145**	**64**
Laundry and cleaning supplies	100	130	119	138	117	145	140	95
Other household products	100	135	129	146	147	138	158	58
Postage and stationery	100	137	145	127	127	134	115	45
Household furnishings and equipment	**100**	**137**	**134**	**140**	**128**	**144**	**141**	**74**
Household textiles	100	129	132	127	146	114	139	128
Furniture	100	132	122	143	135	150	136	97
Floor coverings	100	145	185	115	70	105	155	60
Major appliances	100	140	142	142	138	151	128	84
Small appliances and miscellaneous housewares	100	136	155	124	122	119	133	57
Miscellaneous household equipment	100	139	134	142	121	148	147	54
APPAREL AND RELATED SERVICES	**100**	**126**	**99**	**146**	**124**	**149**	**154**	**105**
Men and boys	**100**	**127**	**90**	**151**	**100**	**161**	**167**	**83**
Men, aged 16 or older	100	125	104	134	86	121	183	43
Boys, aged 2 to 15	100	138	31	224	158	320	100	248
Women and girls	**100**	**123**	**102**	**139**	**88**	**145**	**160**	**118**
Women, aged 16 or older	100	120	114	121	87	105	169	96
Girls, aged 2 to 15	100	139	40	232	92	351	116	234
Children under age 2	**100**	**137**	**44**	**222**	**753**	**146**	**38**	**153**
Footwear	**100**	**127**	**93**	**153**	**105**	**163**	**164**	**118**
Other apparel products and services	**100**	**124**	**127**	**125**	**119**	**121**	**137**	**72**
TRANSPORTATION	**100**	**132**	**114**	**147**	**129**	**147**	**158**	**66**
Vehicle purchases	**100**	**135**	**105**	**161**	**133**	**164**	**175**	**52**
Cars and trucks, new	100	146	123	169	145	165	191	26
Cars and trucks, used	100	126	86	155	129	160	165	77
Other vehicles	100	122	120	147	13	250	63	52
Gasoline and motor oil	**100**	**131**	**110**	**145**	**121**	**148**	**157**	**80**
Other vehicle expenses	**100**	**131**	**125**	**135**	**134**	**129**	**146**	**67**
Vehicle finance charges	100	142	106	168	194	164	156	62
Maintenance and repairs	100	129	122	137	116	144	140	65
Vehicle insurance	100	126	127	122	127	110	140	71
Vehicle rentals, leases, licenses, other charges	100	136	135	143	153	125	167	63
Public transportation	**100**	**133**	**136**	**137**	**123**	**145**	**134**	**63**
HEALTH CARE	**100**	**135**	**155**	**118**	**105**	**113**	**135**	**57**
Health insurance	100	136	156	118	112	112	132	41
Medical services	100	134	142	129	115	125	145	107
Drugs	100	135	170	103	67	99	135	43
Medical supplies	100	129	153	110	84	113	124	47
ENTERTAINMENT	**100**	**133**	**128**	**140**	**115**	**159**	**123**	**71**
Fees and admissions	100	147	121	176	118	230	122	71

| | total households | total married couples | married couples, no children at home | married couples with children at home | | | | single parent, at least one child under 18 at home |
				total	oldest child under 6	oldest child 6 to 17	oldest child 18 or older	
Audio and visual equipment and services	100	121	110	131	110	139	131	85
Pets, toys, and playground equipment	100	126	128	123	108	127	125	64
Other entertainment products and services	100	155	186	134	136	152	99	44
PERSONAL CARE PRODUCTS AND SERVICES	**100**	**129**	**120**	**139**	**112**	**144**	**148**	**86**
READING	**100**	**129**	**154**	**115**	**93**	**118**	**123**	**45**
EDUCATION	**100**	**127**	**68**	**181**	**69**	**165**	**283**	**53**
TOBACCO PRODUCTS AND SMOKING SUPPLIES	**100**	**97**	**83**	**91**	**58**	**89**	**117**	**92**
MISCELLANEOUS	**100**	**116**	**116**	**112**	**126**	**105**	**114**	**86**
CASH CONTRIBUTIONS	**100**	**129**	**164**	**107**	**92**	**109**	**112**	**39**
PERSONAL INSURANCE AND PENSIONS	**100**	**141**	**121**	**161**	**164**	**163**	**157**	**60**
Life and other personal insurance	100	146	149	149	161	140	158	43
Pensions and Social Security	100	141	119	162	164	165	157	61
PERSONAL TAXES	**100**	**146**	**160**	**148**	**156**	**111**	**205**	**–1**
Federal income taxes	100	148	172	143	152	104	203	–20
State and local income taxes	100	142	126	165	162	131	224	45
Other taxes	100	145	159	138	182	108	156	31
GIFTS FOR PEOPLE IN OTHER HOUSEHOLDS	**100**	**128**	**158**	**113**	**72**	**101**	**160**	**43**

Note: An index of 100 is the average for all households. An index of 125 means households of that type spend 25 percent more than the average household. An index of 75 means households of that type spend 25 percent less than the average household. Seventy-nine percent of single-parent families are headed by women and 21 percent are headed by men.
Source: Calculations by New Strategist based on the Bureau of Labor Statistics 2011 Consumer Expenditure Survey, Internet site http://www.bls.gov/cex/home.htm

Table 8.3 Market Shares of Married-Couple and Single-Parent Households, 2011

(share of total annual spending accounted for by type of household, 2011)

| | total households | total married couples | married couples, no children at home | married couples with children at home | | | | single parent, at least one child under 18 at home |
				total	oldest child under 6	oldest child 6 to 17	oldest child 18 or older	
Share of total households	100.0%	49.2%	20.7%	23.8%	4.8%	12.0%	7.0%	5.7%
Share of total annual spending	100.0	63.3	24.0	33.4	6.3	17.1	10.0	4.3
FOOD	100.0%	63.3%	22.1%	35.2%	5.9%	18.2%	11.0%	5.0%
Food at home	100.0	63.4	21.2	35.9	6.2	18.4	11.2	5.2
Cereals and bakery products	100.0	63.6	20.8	36.7	6.0	19.5	11.0	5.6
Cereals and cereal products	100.0	63.2	19.8	37.4	6.3	20.2	10.7	6.3
Bakery products	100.0	63.8	21.3	36.4	5.9	19.2	11.2	5.2
Meats, poultry, fish, and eggs	100.0	64.1	20.4	36.5	5.3	18.4	12.5	5.4
Beef	100.0	65.7	20.8	36.0	4.7	18.5	12.4	5.3
Pork	100.0	63.5	20.7	35.5	5.1	18.1	12.0	5.1
Other meats	100.0	66.4	19.5	40.6	5.6	21.7	12.8	4.7
Poultry	100.0	62.9	18.4	37.5	5.9	17.6	13.8	6.2
Fish and seafood	100.0	62.2	22.5	33.6	5.2	16.4	11.9	5.9
Eggs	100.0	61.0	19.8	34.7	5.8	17.3	11.4	5.1
Dairy products	100.0	64.4	21.3	37.2	7.0	19.1	11.0	5.0
Fresh milk and cream	100.0	63.6	19.3	37.8	7.6	19.1	11.2	5.3
Other dairy products	100.0	64.9	22.4	36.8	6.6	19.2	10.9	4.8
Fruits and vegetables	100.0	63.7	22.0	35.5	6.6	17.8	11.1	4.8
Fresh fruits	100.0	64.7	22.8	36.0	6.8	17.9	11.3	4.8
Fresh vegetables	100.0	64.6	23.5	34.5	6.3	17.2	11.0	4.0
Processed fruits	100.0	61.1	19.2	35.9	6.9	18.3	10.7	5.5
Processed vegetables	100.0	63.0	20.3	35.7	6.6	17.9	11.2	5.4
Other food at home	100.0	62.3	21.4	34.9	6.4	18.0	10.5	5.3
Sugar and other sweets	100.0	64.2	21.8	36.2	6.1	19.1	10.9	4.9
Fats and oils	100.0	63.5	22.4	34.2	5.2	16.9	11.8	4.7
Miscellaneous foods	100.0	61.7	20.6	35.6	7.4	18.0	10.2	5.6
Nonalcoholic beverages	100.0	60.6	20.7	33.6	5.1	17.7	10.7	5.4
Food prepared by consumer unit on trips	100.0	73.8	34.9	33.7	5.8	19.0	8.8	2.3
Food away from home	100.0	63.3	23.3	34.3	5.5	18.0	10.6	4.7
ALCOHOLIC BEVERAGES	100.0	55.5	27.6	24.0	4.4	12.1	7.4	3.1
HOUSING	100.0	60.5	22.5	32.3	7.1	16.5	8.7	4.9
Shelter	100.0	59.0	21.9	31.8	7.1	16.6	8.1	4.9
Owned dwellings	100.0	69.0	25.6	37.3	8.0	19.4	9.9	3.2
Mortgage interest and charges	100.0	70.9	21.7	42.6	10.2	22.4	10.0	3.5
Property taxes	100.0	68.4	28.7	34.3	6.2	17.9	10.2	2.9
Maintenance, repair, insurance, other expenses	100.0	64.3	31.8	27.5	4.6	13.7	9.2	2.6
Rented dwellings	100.0	34.8	10.0	20.8	5.7	11.1	4.1	9.1
Other lodging	100.0	77.0	41.8	30.3	4.9	15.6	9.8	1.5
Utilities, fuels, and public services	100.0	59.9	22.6	30.6	5.1	15.6	9.9	5.3
Natural gas	100.0	59.1	22.2	30.7	5.0	15.9	9.7	5.0
Electricity	100.0	59.2	22.7	29.8	5.0	15.2	9.6	5.7

	total households	total married couples	married couples, no children at home	married couples with children at home				single parent, at least one child under 18 at home
				total	oldest child under 6	oldest child 6 to 17	oldest child 18 or older	
Fuel oil and other fuels	100.0%	62.0%	27.9%	28.0%	4.3%	14.1%	9.6%	2.3%
Telephone services	100.0	60.1	21.5	31.8	5.4	16.0	10.5	5.4
Water and other public services	100.0	61.5	23.6	30.7	5.2	16.0	9.6	4.8
Household services	**100.0**	**63.6**	**18.8**	**40.1**	**15.6**	**17.7**	**6.7**	**6.0**
Personal services	100.0	67.8	3.6	59.6	33.7	23.1	2.8	9.8
Other household services	100.0	61.3	27.2	29.3	5.7	14.8	8.9	3.9
Housekeeping supplies	**100.0**	**66.1**	**26.9**	**33.3**	**6.5**	**16.6**	**10.2**	**3.6**
Laundry and cleaning supplies	100.0	63.8	24.5	32.8	5.6	17.4	9.9	5.4
Other household products	100.0	66.5	26.7	34.6	7.0	16.5	11.1	3.3
Postage and stationery	100.0	67.3	30.0	30.2	6.0	16.0	8.1	2.5
Household furnishings and equipment	**100.0**	**67.1**	**27.7**	**33.3**	**6.1**	**17.3**	**9.9**	**4.2**
Household textiles	100.0	63.6	27.3	30.1	6.9	13.6	9.8	7.3
Furniture	100.0	64.8	25.2	34.0	6.4	18.0	9.6	5.5
Floor coverings	100.0	71.3	38.2	27.4	3.3	12.6	10.9	3.4
Major appliances	100.0	68.7	29.3	33.7	6.6	18.1	9.0	4.8
Small appliances and miscellaneous housewares	100.0	66.9	32.0	29.4	5.8	14.3	9.3	3.3
Miscellaneous household equipment	100.0	68.2	27.7	33.9	5.8	17.7	10.3	3.1
APPAREL AND RELATED SERVICES	**100.0**	**61.7**	**20.4**	**34.7**	**5.9**	**17.8**	**10.9**	**6.0**
Men and boys	**100.0**	**62.7**	**18.6**	**36.0**	**4.8**	**19.3**	**11.7**	**4.7**
Men, aged 16 or older	100.0	61.5	21.6	31.8	4.1	14.5	12.9	2.4
Boys, aged 2 to 15	100.0	67.6	6.5	53.2	7.5	38.4	7.0	14.1
Women and girls	**100.0**	**60.6**	**21.1**	**33.1**	**4.2**	**17.4**	**11.3**	**6.7**
Women, aged 16 or older	100.0	59.1	23.6	28.9	4.2	12.6	11.9	5.4
Girls, aged 2 to 15	100.0	68.5	8.3	55.3	4.4	42.1	8.2	13.3
Children under age 2	**100.0**	**67.3**	**9.1**	**52.8**	**35.9**	**17.5**	**2.7**	**8.7**
Footwear	**100.0**	**62.4**	**19.1**	**36.3**	**5.0**	**19.5**	**11.5**	**6.7**
Other apparel products and services	**100.0**	**60.9**	**26.3**	**29.8**	**5.6**	**14.5**	**9.6**	**4.1**
TRANSPORTATION	**100.0**	**65.1**	**23.6**	**35.0**	**6.1**	**17.7**	**11.1**	**3.8**
Vehicle purchases	**100.0**	**66.5**	**21.6**	**38.4**	**6.4**	**19.7**	**12.3**	**3.0**
Cars and trucks, new	100.0	71.8	25.4	40.1	6.9	19.8	13.5	1.5
Cars and trucks, used	100.0	61.8	17.9	36.9	6.1	19.1	11.6	4.4
Other vehicles	100.0	59.9	24.9	34.9	0.6	30.0	4.4	2.9
Gasoline and motor oil	**100.0**	**64.3**	**22.8**	**34.5**	**5.8**	**17.7**	**11.1**	**4.5**
Other vehicle expenses	**100.0**	**64.2**	**25.7**	**32.2**	**6.4**	**15.5**	**10.3**	**3.8**
Vehicle finance charges	100.0	69.7	22.0	39.9	9.2	19.7	11.0	3.5
Maintenance and repairs	100.0	63.6	25.2	32.7	5.5	17.3	9.8	3.7
Vehicle insurance	100.0	62.2	26.2	29.1	6.0	13.2	9.9	4.0
Vehicle rentals, leases, licenses, other charges	100.0	67.0	27.8	34.1	7.3	15.0	11.8	3.6
Public transportation	**100.0**	**65.5**	**28.1**	**32.7**	**5.8**	**17.4**	**9.5**	**3.6**
HEALTH CARE	**100.0**	**66.5**	**32.0**	**28.1**	**5.0**	**13.6**	**9.5**	**3.2**
Health insurance	100.0	67.0	32.3	28.1	5.4	13.5	9.3	2.4
Medical services	100.0	65.7	29.3	30.7	5.5	15.0	10.2	6.1
Drugs	100.0	66.5	35.0	24.6	3.2	11.9	9.5	2.5
Medical supplies	100.0	63.5	31.6	26.3	4.0	13.5	8.7	2.7
ENTERTAINMENT	**100.0**	**65.4**	**26.4**	**33.2**	**5.5**	**19.0**	**8.7**	**4.0**
Fees and admissions	100.0	72.2	25.0	41.8	5.6	27.6	8.6	4.1

	total households	total married couples	married couples, no children at home	married couples with children at home				single parent, at least one child under 18 at home
				total	oldest child under 6	oldest child 6 to 17	oldest child 18 or older	
Audio and visual equipment and services	100.0%	59.4%	22.7%	31.1%	5.2%	16.6%	9.2%	4.8%
Pets, toys, and playground equipment	100.0	61.9	26.5	29.2	5.1	15.2	8.8	3.7
Other entertainment products and services	100.0	76.0	38.4	31.8	6.5	18.2	7.0	2.5
PERSONAL CARE PRODUCTS AND SERVICES	**100.0**	**63.5**	**24.8**	**33.2**	**5.3**	**17.3**	**10.4**	**4.9**
READING	**100.0**	**63.3**	**31.8**	**27.3**	**4.4**	**14.2**	**8.6**	**2.6**
EDUCATION	**100.0**	**62.7**	**14.1**	**43.1**	**3.3**	**19.8**	**20.0**	**3.0**
TOBACCO PRODUCTS AND SMOKING SUPPLIES	**100.0**	**47.9**	**17.2**	**21.7**	**2.8**	**10.7**	**8.2**	**5.2**
MISCELLANEOUS	**100.0**	**56.9**	**24.1**	**26.6**	**6.0**	**12.5**	**8.0**	**4.9**
CASH CONTRIBUTIONS	**100.0**	**63.6**	**33.9**	**25.3**	**4.4**	**13.1**	**7.9**	**2.2**
PERSONAL INSURANCE AND PENSIONS	**100.0**	**69.4**	**25.0**	**38.4**	**7.8**	**19.5**	**11.1**	**3.4**
Life and other personal insurance	100.0	71.8	30.8	35.5	7.6	16.8	11.1	2.4
Pensions and Social Security	100.0	69.2	24.6	38.6	7.8	19.7	11.1	3.5
PERSONAL TAXES	**100.0**	**71.9**	**33.0**	**35.2**	**7.4**	**13.3**	**14.4**	**0.0**
Federal income taxes	100.0	72.7	35.6	34.0	7.2	12.5	14.3	−1.2
State and local income taxes	100.0	70.0	26.1	39.2	7.7	15.7	15.8	2.5
Other taxes	100.0	71.2	32.8	32.7	8.7	13.0	11.0	1.8
GIFTS FOR PEOPLE IN OTHER HOUSEHOLDS	**100.0**	**63.2**	**32.6**	**26.9**	**3.4**	**12.2**	**11.3**	**2.5**

Note: Percentages do not add to total married couples because not all types of married couples are shown. Seventy-nine percent of single-parent families are headed by women and 21 percent are headed by men.
Source: Calculations by New Strategist based on the Bureau of Labor Statistics 2011 Consumer Expenditure Survey, Internet site http://www.bls.gov/cex/home.htm

Men Who Live Alone Spend Less than Average

They spend more than the average household on alcoholic beverages, however.

On average, men who live alone spent an annual average of $31,288 in 2010–11, only 64 percent of the $48,926 spent by the average household during that time period.

The Bureau of Labor Statistics collects spending data from households rather than individuals. The data in this chapter, showing the spending of married couples, single parents, and people who live alone, include most of the nation's men and women. The average spending table shows how much men who live alone spent in 2010–11 by age group. The indexed spending table compares the spending of men who live alone to the spending of the average consumer unit. An index of 100 means men in the age group spend an average amount on an item. An index above 100 means men in the age group spend more than average on an item, while an index below 100 signifies below-average spending.

Among men who live alone, those under age 25 spend much more than the average household on education, with an index of 233. Many are students paying college tuition.

Men aged 25 to 64 who live alone have higher incomes and spend more than younger men. Men under age 55 who live alone spend more than the average household on alcoholic beverages, despite their small household size. Men aged 25 to 34 who live alone spent $782 on alcoholic beverages in 2010–11—more than any other household type. Men aged 25 to 34 who live alone spend twice the average on men's clothes, devoting more to men's clothing than far more affluent married couples.

Men aged 65 or older who live alone spend less than their middle-aged counterparts, an average of $28,725 in 2010–11. They spend more than the average household on cash contributions.

■ As single-person households become a larger share of all households, their spending will become increasingly important to the economy.

Among men living alone, those aged 35 to 54 spend the most

(average annual spending of men who live alone by age, 2010–11)

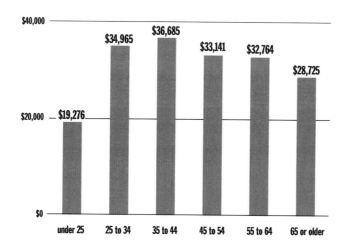

Table 8.4 Average Spending of Single-Person Households Headed by Men by Age, 2010–11

(average annual spending of total households and single-person households headed by men by age, 2010–11)

	total households	single-person households headed by men						
		total	under 25	25 to 34	35 to 44	45 to 54	55 to 64	65 or older
Number of households (in 000s)	121,697	16,630	2,055	2,913	2,322	3,009	2,873	3,459
Average annual spending	$48,926	$31,288	$19,276	$34,965	$36,685	$33,141	$32,764	$28,725
FOOD	$6,294	$3,916	$2,771	$4,589	$4,408	$4,014	$4,021	$3,464
Food at home	3,731	1,871	1,060	1,702	1,979	2,022	2,120	1,998
Cereals and bakery products	516	255	166	198	251	266	299	298
Cereals and cereal products	170	83	55	70	84	86	89	97
Bakery products	346	172	112	128	166	180	210	201
Meats, poultry, fish, and eggs	808	397	185	437	433	439	451	367
Beef	220	95	42	128	99	119	94	75
Pork	155	77	31	64	79	79	104	85
Other meats	120	68	45	55	71	89	76	62
Poultry	146	70	34	100	78	72	74	54
Fish and seafood	119	62	15	65	77	56	75	68
Eggs	48	25	18	25	29	25	27	24
Dairy products	394	187	111	161	179	207	221	202
Fresh milk and cream	145	74	47	61	78	81	82	79
Other dairy products	248	113	63	100	101	126	139	122
Fruits and vegetables	697	338	164	278	353	363	374	413
Fresh fruits	240	116	55	88	122	123	132	145
Fresh vegetables	217	100	49	89	101	109	116	113
Processed fruits	114	62	33	45	70	64	61	86
Processed vegetables	126	60	26	55	61	67	65	70
Other food at home	1,316	694	434	627	763	746	774	719
Sugar and other sweets	138	61	30	50	67	62	61	79
Fats and oils	106	49	26	41	57	57	54	53
Miscellaneous foods	679	366	221	333	398	371	401	411
Nonalcoholic beverages	347	193	141	180	219	230	230	148
Food prepared by consumer unit on trips	45	25	16	24	23	26	28	29
Food away from home	2,562	2,046	1,712	2,887	2,429	1,992	1,902	1,465
ALCOHOLIC BEVERAGES	434	507	611	782	628	454	409	287
HOUSING	16,687	11,203	6,495	12,546	13,315	11,949	11,132	10,842
Shelter	9,819	7,411	4,545	8,731	9,300	8,040	7,008	6,521
Owned dwellings	6,212	3,231	389	2,540	4,112	4,068	3,783	3,725
Mortgage interest and charges	3,267	1,590	227	1,721	2,593	2,209	1,612	1,059
Property taxes	1,829	1,006	97	565	953	1,223	1,296	1,524
Maintenance, repair, insurance, other expenses	1,116	635	65	254	566	637	874	1,141
Rented dwellings	2,965	3,806	3,845	5,765	4,806	3,703	2,816	2,373
Other lodging	642	374	311	425	382	270	409	423
Utilities, fuels, and public services	3,693	2,232	907	2,005	2,459	2,461	2,462	2,666
Natural gas	430	260	81	227	287	267	284	349
Electricity	1,418	880	364	743	950	976	1,018	1,057
Fuel oil and other fuels	149	101	3	43	66	128	84	220
Telephone services	1,202	713	382	776	855	787	732	679
Water and other public services	495	279	77	216	301	302	344	362

	total households	single-person households headed by men						
		total	under 25	25 to 34	35 to 44	45 to 54	55 to 64	65 or older
Household services	$1,074	$497	$220	$416	$574	$454	$594	$635
Personal services	369	58	9	33	150	52	86	28
Other household services	705	439	211	384	424	401	508	607
Housekeeping supplies	613	252	91	199	207	294	296	333
Laundry and cleaning supplies	148	67	33	59	59	59	76	92
Other household products	334	134	38	97	107	167	164	176
Postage and stationery	131	52	21	43	40	68	56	65
Household furnishings and equipment	1,487	811	732	1,194	775	700	771	687
Household textiles	106	48	16	29	45	34	52	88
Furniture	351	244	203	445	276	106	305	148
Floor coverings	28	27	4	87	17	5	12	30
Major appliances	202	81	56	112	68	71	55	109
Small appliances, miscellaneous housewares	98	48	63	51	30	56	40	49
Miscellaneous household equipment	703	363	390	470	339	428	308	264
APPAREL AND RELATED SERVICES	1,720	746	623	1,103	1,006	622	765	443
Men and boys	393	393	365	642	499	286	444	189
Men, aged 16 or older	314	383	364	627	476	273	438	186
Boys, aged 2 to 15	79	10	1	16	23	13	6	2
Women and girls	693	64	9	54	115	81	38	73
Women, aged 16 or older	583	48	8	46	86	55	30	53
Girls, aged 2 to 15	110	16	1	9	29	26	8	20
Children under age 2	79	11	2	23	5	19	9	5
Footwear	312	128	113	191	181	86	138	78
Other apparel products and services	243	150	135	192	206	150	137	99
TRANSPORTATION	7,987	4,769	3,246	5,892	5,290	5,011	4,938	3,982
Vehicle purchases	2,629	1,364	1,025	2,191	1,511	1,228	1,430	833
Cars and trucks, new	1,242	515	128	848	652	441	698	285
Cars and trucks, used	1,329	794	870	1,269	827	721	610	543
Other vehicles	58	55	27	74	32	67	123	5
Gasoline and motor oil	2,395	1,516	1,211	1,660	1,771	1,712	1,526	1,226
Other vehicle expenses	2,459	1,571	781	1,569	1,614	1,788	1,681	1,684
Vehicle finance charges	238	111	66	152	170	120	116	53
Maintenance and repairs	796	576	404	573	651	662	576	556
Vehicle insurance	997	628	179	530	462	767	764	808
Vehicle rentals, leases, licenses, other charges	428	256	132	314	332	240	225	268
Public transportation	504	318	229	473	393	283	302	239
HEALTH CARE	3,235	1,654	262	887	1,372	1,434	1,881	3,311
Health insurance	1,877	980	139	578	890	852	1,015	1,962
Medical services	745	367	57	172	282	317	457	741
Drugs	487	239	43	96	140	181	345	498
Medical supplies	127	67	23	41	60	83	62	110
ENTERTAINMENT	2,547	1,545	991	1,801	1,848	1,503	1,522	1,511
Fees and admissions	588	310	259	369	455	348	218	236
Audio and visual equipment and services	972	718	515	802	861	669	743	703
Pets, toys, and playground equipment	618	270	96	291	285	322	332	241
Other entertainment products and services	369	247	121	338	247	166	229	330
PERSONAL CARE PRODUCTS AND SERVICES	608	194	133	231	253	180	170	191
READING	$108	$76	$43	$59	$78	$72	$84	$107

	total households	single-person households headed by men						
		total	under 25	25 to 34	35 to 44	45 to 54	55 to 64	65 or older
EDUCATION	$1,063	$908	$2,482	$1,733	$365	$452	$552	$336
TOBACCO PRODUCTS AND SMOKING SUPPLIES	356	364	223	329	343	556	473	235
MISCELLANEOUS	812	690	126	493	651	958	1,211	515
CASH CONTRIBUTIONS	1,677	1,629	164	903	2,429	1,732	1,651	2,466
PERSONAL INSURANCE AND PENSIONS	5,398	3,086	1,103	3,616	4,701	4,204	3,957	1,037
Life and other personal insurance	318	131	15	45	118	176	178	201
Pensions and Social Security	5,081	2,955	1,089	3,572	4,583	4,028	3,779	835
PERSONAL TAXES	1,891	1,566	435	1,654	2,617	2,217	2,033	504
Federal income taxes	1,254	1,130	311	1,118	1,955	1,611	1,487	357
State and local income taxes	494	373	121	478	616	508	457	85
Other taxes	143	63	3	58	46	98	89	63
GIFTS FOR PEOPLE IN OTHER HOUSEHOLDS	1,037	818	168	588	848	1,117	998	959

Note: Spending by category does not add to total spending because gift spending is also included in the preceding product and service categories.
Source: Bureau of Labor Statistics, 2010 and 2011 Consumer Expenditure Surveys, Internet site http://www.bls.gov/cex/

Table 8.5 Indexed Spending of Single-Person Households Headed by Men by Age, 2010–11

(indexed average annual spending of total households and single-person households headed by men by age, 2010–11)

	total households	single-person households headed by men						
		total	under 25	25 to 34	35 to 44	45 to 54	55 to 64	65 or older
Average annual spending	$48,926	$31,288	$19,276	$34,965	$36,685	$33,141	$32,764	$28,725
Average annual spending, index	100	64	39	71	75	68	67	59
FOOD	100	62	44	73	70	64	64	55
Food at home	100	50	28	46	53	54	57	54
Cereals and bakery products	100	49	32	38	49	52	58	58
Cereals and cereal products	100	49	32	41	49	51	52	57
Bakery products	100	50	32	37	48	52	61	58
Meats, poultry, fish, and eggs	100	49	23	54	54	54	56	45
Beef	100	43	19	58	45	54	43	34
Pork	100	50	20	41	51	51	67	55
Other meats	100	57	38	46	59	74	63	52
Poultry	100	48	23	68	53	49	51	37
Fish and seafood	100	52	13	55	65	47	63	57
Eggs	100	52	38	52	60	52	56	50
Dairy products	100	47	28	41	45	53	56	51
Fresh milk and cream	100	51	32	42	54	56	57	54
Other dairy products	100	46	25	40	41	51	56	49
Fruits and vegetables	100	48	24	40	51	52	54	59
Fresh fruits	100	48	23	37	51	51	55	60
Fresh vegetables	100	46	23	41	47	50	53	52
Processed fruits	100	54	29	39	61	56	54	75
Processed vegetables	100	48	21	44	48	53	52	56
Other food at home	100	53	33	48	58	57	59	55
Sugar and other sweets	100	44	22	36	49	45	44	57
Fats and oils	100	46	25	39	54	54	51	50
Miscellaneous foods	100	54	33	49	59	55	59	61
Nonalcoholic beverages	100	56	41	52	63	66	66	43
Food prepared by consumer unit on trips	100	56	36	53	51	58	62	64
Food away from home	100	80	67	113	95	78	74	57
ALCOHOLIC BEVERAGES	100	117	141	180	145	105	94	66
HOUSING	100	67	39	75	80	72	67	65
Shelter	100	75	46	89	95	82	71	66
Owned dwellings	100	52	6	41	66	65	61	60
Mortgage interest and charges	100	49	7	53	79	68	49	32
Property taxes	100	55	5	31	52	67	71	83
Maintenance, repair, insurance, other expenses	100	57	6	23	51	57	78	102
Rented dwellings	100	128	130	194	162	125	95	80
Other lodging	100	58	48	66	60	42	64	66
Utilities, fuels, and public services	100	60	25	54	67	67	67	72
Natural gas	100	60	19	53	67	62	66	81
Electricity	100	62	26	52	67	69	72	75
Fuel oil and other fuels	100	68	2	29	44	86	56	148
Telephone services	100	59	32	65	71	65	61	56
Water and other public services	100	56	16	44	61	61	69	73

	total households	single-person households headed by men						
		total	under 25	25 to 34	35 to 44	45 to 54	55 to 64	65 or older
Household services	100	46	20	39	53	42	55	59
Personal services	100	16	2	9	41	14	23	8
Other household services	100	62	30	54	60	57	72	86
Housekeeping supplies	100	41	15	32	34	48	48	54
Laundry and cleaning supplies	100	45	22	40	40	40	51	62
Other household products	100	40	11	29	32	50	49	53
Postage and stationery	100	40	16	33	31	52	43	50
Household furnishings and equipment	100	55	49	80	52	47	52	46
Household textiles	100	45	15	27	42	32	49	83
Furniture	100	70	58	127	79	30	87	42
Floor coverings	100	96	14	311	61	18	43	107
Major appliances	100	40	28	55	34	35	27	54
Small appliances, miscellaneous housewares	100	49	64	52	31	57	41	50
Miscellaneous household equipment	100	52	55	67	48	61	44	38
APPAREL AND RELATED SERVICES	100	43	36	64	58	36	44	26
Men and boys	100	100	93	163	127	73	113	48
Men, aged 16 or older	100	122	116	200	152	87	139	59
Boys, aged 2 to 15	100	13	1	20	29	16	8	3
Women and girls	100	9	1	8	17	12	5	11
Women, aged 16 or older	100	8	1	8	15	9	5	9
Girls, aged 2 to 15	100	15	1	8	26	24	7	18
Children under age 2	100	14	3	29	6	24	11	6
Footwear	100	41	36	61	58	28	44	25
Other apparel products and services	100	62	56	79	85	62	56	41
TRANSPORTATION	100	60	41	74	66	63	62	50
Vehicle purchases	100	52	39	83	57	47	54	32
Cars and trucks, new	100	41	10	68	52	36	56	23
Cars and trucks, used	100	60	65	95	62	54	46	41
Other vehicles	100	95	47	128	55	116	212	9
Gasoline and motor oil	100	63	51	69	74	71	64	51
Other vehicle expenses	100	64	32	64	66	73	68	68
Vehicle finance charges	100	47	28	64	71	50	49	22
Maintenance and repairs	100	72	51	72	82	83	72	70
Vehicle insurance	100	63	18	53	46	77	77	81
Vehicle rentals, leases, licenses, other charges	100	60	31	73	78	56	53	63
Public transportation	100	63	45	94	78	56	60	47
HEALTH CARE	100	51	8	27	42	44	58	102
Health insurance	100	52	7	31	47	45	54	105
Medical services	100	49	8	23	38	43	61	99
Drugs	100	49	9	20	29	37	71	102
Medical supplies	100	53	18	32	47	65	49	87
ENTERTAINMENT	100	61	39	71	73	59	60	59
Fees and admissions	100	53	44	63	77	59	37	40
Audio and visual equipment and services	100	74	53	83	89	69	76	72
Pets, toys, and playground equipment	100	44	16	47	46	52	54	39
Other entertainment products and services	100	67	33	92	67	45	62	89
PERSONAL CARE PRODUCTS AND SERVICES	100	32	22	38	42	30	28	31
READING	100	70	40	55	72	67	78	99

	total households	single-person households headed by men						
		total	under 25	25 to 34	35 to 44	45 to 54	55 to 64	65 or older
EDUCATION	100	85	233	163	34	43	52	32
TOBACCO PRODUCTS AND SMOKING SUPPLIES	100	102	63	92	96	156	133	66
MISCELLANEOUS	100	85	16	61	80	118	149	63
CASH CONTRIBUTIONS	100	97	10	54	145	103	98	147
PERSONAL INSURANCE AND PENSIONS	100	57	20	67	87	78	73	19
Life and other personal insurance	100	41	5	14	37	55	56	63
Pensions and Social Security	100	58	21	70	90	79	74	16
PERSONAL TAXES	100	83	23	87	138	117	108	27
Federal income taxes	100	90	25	89	156	128	119	28
State and local income taxes	100	76	24	97	125	103	93	17
Other taxes	100	44	2	41	32	69	62	44
GIFTS FOR PEOPLE IN OTHER HOUSEHOLDS	100	79	16	57	82	108	96	92

Note: An index of 100 is the average for all households. An index of 125 means men who live alone spend 25 percent more than the average household. An index of 75 means men who live alone spend 25 percent less than the average household.
Source: Calculations by New Strategist based on the Bureau of Labor Statistics' 2010 and 2011 Consumer Expenditure Surveys

Women Who Live Alone Spend Less than Average

Many are older and depend on Social Security.

On average, women who live alone spent an annual average of $28,688 in 2010–11, only 59 percent of the $48,926 spent by the average household during that time period. Forty-one percent of women who live alone are aged 65 or older, many of them elderly widows with low incomes.

The Bureau of Labor Statistics collects spending data from households rather than individuals. The data in this chapter, showing the spending of married couples, single parents, and people who live alone, include most of the nation's men and women. The average spending table shows how much women who live alone spent in 2010–11 by age group. The indexed spending table compares the spending of women who live alone to the spending of the average consumer unit. An index of 100 means women in the age group who live alone spend an average amount on an item. An index above 100 means women in the age group who live alone spend more than average on an item, while an index below 100 signifies below-average spending.

Among women who live alone, spending peaks in the 35-to-44 age group, at $36,379 in 2010–11. Women under age 25 who live alone spend much more than the average household on education, with an index of 257. Many are students paying college tuition. Women under age 65 who live alone spend more than the average household on women's clothes, spending peaking at 65 percent more than average among women aged 25 to 34. Women aged 65 or older spend less than their middle-aged counterparts, an average of $25,341. But they spend more than the average household on reading material, postage and stationary, and health care.

■ As single-person households become a larger share of all households, their spending will become increasingly important to the economy.

Among women who live alone, those aged 35 to 44 spend the most

(average annual spending of women living alone by age, 2010–11)

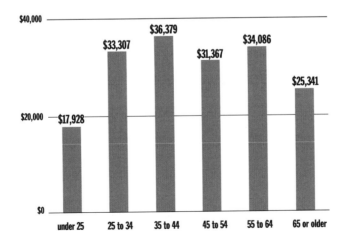

Table 8.6 Average Spending of Single-Person Households Headed by Women by Age, 2010–11

(average annual spending of total households and single-person households headed by women by age, 2010–11)

	total households	single-person households headed by women						
		total	under 25	25 to 34	35 to 44	45 to 54	55 to 64	65 or older
Number of households (in 000s)	121,697	19,164	1,835	1,780	1,469	2,536	3,598	7,947
Average annual spending	$48,926	$28,688	$17,928	$33,307	$36,379	$31,367	$34,086	$25,341
FOOD	$6,294	$3,241	$2,570	$3,670	$3,801	$3,375	$3,641	$2,924
Food at home	3,731	2,057	1,202	1,803	2,175	2,179	2,329	2,093
Cereals and bakery products	516	284	188	241	259	307	294	304
Cereals and cereal products	170	89	70	99	91	98	87	88
Bakery products	346	195	118	142	168	209	207	216
Meats, poultry, fish, and eggs	808	383	221	303	391	420	462	382
Beef	220	88	59	57	92	104	112	84
Pork	155	73	35	52	80	86	79	77
Other meats	120	54	30	49	52	58	60	56
Poultry	146	69	45	60	65	74	82	67
Fish and seafood	119	69	34	58	74	71	93	65
Eggs	48	29	18	26	28	27	34	31
Dairy products	394	223	129	205	231	228	255	228
Fresh milk and cream	145	76	47	69	73	80	81	80
Other dairy products	248	147	82	136	158	149	174	148
Fruits and vegetables	697	419	254	396	400	431	452	441
Fresh fruits	240	153	93	142	145	148	175	160
Fresh vegetables	217	136	76	140	134	138	146	140
Processed fruits	114	63	38	56	63	63	65	69
Processed vegetables	126	68	47	59	57	81	66	72
Other food at home	1,316	748	410	657	895	792	866	738
Sugar and other sweets	138	85	35	62	94	86	102	90
Fats and oils	106	64	29	59	57	71	67	68
Miscellaneous foods	679	387	232	355	476	388	435	385
Nonalcoholic beverages	347	191	105	160	235	224	231	176
Food prepared by consumer unit on trips	45	22	7	21	33	23	31	18
Food away from home	2,562	1,184	1,369	1,867	1,625	1,196	1,312	831
ALCOHOLIC BEVERAGES	434	215	352	366	372	197	236	120
HOUSING	16,687	11,459	6,217	13,455	14,141	12,330	12,817	10,824
Shelter	9,819	7,037	4,632	9,638	9,331	7,790	7,806	5,998
Owned dwellings	6,212	3,654	189	2,956	4,680	4,339	5,075	3,558
Mortgage interest and charges	3,267	1,450	122	1,820	3,066	2,336	2,343	687
Property taxes	1,829	1,173	47	632	1,068	1,105	1,471	1,461
Maintenance, repair, insurance, other expenses	1,116	1,031	19	503	546	898	1,261	1,410
Rented dwellings	2,965	3,093	4,086	6,295	4,418	3,179	2,353	2,209
Other lodging	642	291	358	387	233	271	379	232
Utilities, fuels, and public services	3,693	2,464	759	2,117	2,659	2,786	2,806	2,640
Natural gas	430	312	69	209	323	297	337	383
Electricity	1,418	948	315	819	1,037	1,145	1,050	998
Fuel oil and other fuels	149	117	2	26	38	54	117	198
Telephone services	1,202	750	319	855	933	959	917	650
Water and other public services	495	336	54	208	327	331	385	411

	total households	single-person households headed by women						
		total	under 25	25 to 34	35 to 44	45 to 54	55 to 64	65 or older
Household services	$1,074	$713	$160	$451	$691	$542	$771	$931
Personal services	369	162	2	30	117	7	22	349
Other household services	705	551	158	421	574	535	750	582
Housekeeping supplies	613	426	164	244	442	362	483	518
Laundry and cleaning supplies	148	91	59	65	96	96	102	97
Other household products	334	228	80	118	254	171	269	282
Postage and stationery	131	107	25	62	92	94	112	139
Household furnishings and equipment	1,487	820	502	1,004	1,018	851	951	736
Household textiles	106	72	26	68	49	54	73	93
Furniture	351	184	146	333	278	162	191	147
Floor coverings	28	17	4	19	16	45	16	12
Major appliances	202	110	22	75	144	116	159	108
Small appliances, miscellaneous housewares	98	59	55	81	71	62	65	49
Miscellaneous household equipment	703	376	249	429	459	413	447	327
APPAREL AND RELATED SERVICES	1,720	1,046	1,107	1,494	1,357	1,043	1,197	798
Men and boys	393	75	49	75	94	57	98	72
Men, aged 16 or older	314	60	45	69	76	43	77	55
Boys, aged 2 to 15	79	15	3	6	18	13	22	17
Women and girls	693	638	709	979	689	620	721	493
Women, aged 16 or older	583	608	705	964	650	591	660	472
Girls, aged 2 to 15	110	30	4	15	38	29	61	21
Children under age 2	79	20	11	14	9	52	18	14
Footwear	312	178	241	192	410	157	217	112
Other apparel products and services	243	135	97	234	156	157	141	107
TRANSPORTATION	7,987	3,690	2,255	4,946	4,616	4,535	5,027	2,681
Vehicle purchases	2,629	938	441	1,342	1,129	1,213	1,667	511
Cars and trucks, new	1,242	547	188	744	485	751	1,015	320
Cars and trucks, used	1,329	381	240	597	643	392	652	191
Other vehicles	58	10	13	–	–	70	–	–
Gasoline and motor oil	2,395	1,080	894	1,455	1,520	1,450	1,287	746
Other vehicle expenses	2,459	1,357	638	1,598	1,609	1,588	1,695	1,183
Vehicle finance charges	238	88	48	185	142	133	123	36
Maintenance and repairs	796	418	234	488	486	532	556	334
Vehicle insurance	997	616	246	477	699	629	775	627
Vehicle rentals, leases, licenses, other charges	428	235	110	447	283	294	241	186
Public transportation	504	315	281	552	358	285	377	241
HEALTH CARE	3,235	2,429	384	1,296	1,803	1,919	2,675	3,320
Health insurance	1,877	1,399	174	696	906	1,001	1,339	2,083
Medical services	745	524	121	384	547	505	743	550
Drugs	487	402	68	160	267	328	499	534
Medical supplies	127	106	22	57	83	85	94	152
ENTERTAINMENT	2,547	1,432	814	1,450	1,962	1,737	1,702	1,244
Fees and admissions	588	250	202	374	408	274	288	178
Audio and visual equipment and services	972	632	368	613	800	688	727	607
Pets, toys, and playground equipment	618	472	193	385	647	643	606	400
Other entertainment products and services	369	78	50	78	107	132	82	60
PERSONAL CARE PRODUCTS AND SERVICES	608	524	321	688	756	528	540	478
READING	108	93	38	73	87	83	93	116

	total households	single-person households headed by women						
		total	under 25	25 to 34	35 to 44	45 to 54	55 to 64	65 or older
EDUCATION	$1,063	$503	$2,732	$913	$594	$254	$245	$78
TOBACCO PRODUCTS AND SMOKING SUPPLIES	356	172	90	162	307	290	274	85
MISCELLANEOUS	812	645	121	411	1,713	624	809	570
CASH CONTRIBUTIONS	1,677	1,098	125	649	892	864	1,225	1,478
PERSONAL INSURANCE AND PENSIONS	5,398	2,139	802	3,734	3,977	3,588	3,606	625
Life and other personal insurance	318	188	1	85	95	166	445	162
Pensions and Social Security	5,081	1,951	801	3,649	3,882	3,422	3,161	463
PERSONAL TAXES	1,891	973	−148	1,709	1,987	1,885	1,277	452
Federal income taxes	1,254	635	−186	1,182	1,422	1,452	821	212
State and local income taxes	494	221	34	495	524	360	329	55
Other taxes	143	117	5	33	41	73	126	185
GIFTS FOR PEOPLE IN OTHER HOUSEHOLDS	1,037	816	314	623	818	941	1,182	762

Note: Spending by category does not add to total spending because gift spending is also included in the preceding product and service categories. "−" means sample is too small to make a reliable estimate.
Source: Bureau of Labor Statistics, 2010 and 2011 Consumer Expenditure Surveys, Internet site http://www.bls.gov/cex/

Table 8.7 Indexed Spending of Single-Person Households Headed by Women by Age, 2010–11

(indexed average annual spending of total households and single-person households headed by women by age, 2010–11)

	total households	single-person households headed by women						
		total	under 25	25 to 34	35 to 44	45 to 54	55 to 64	65 or older
Average annual spending	$48,926	$28,688	$17,928	$33,307	$36,379	$31,367	$34,086	$25,341
Average annual spending, index	100	59	37	68	74	64	70	52
FOOD	100	51	41	58	60	54	58	46
Food at home	100	55	32	48	58	58	62	56
Cereals and bakery products	100	55	36	47	50	59	57	59
Cereals and cereal products	100	52	41	58	54	58	51	52
Bakery products	100	56	34	41	49	60	60	62
Meats, poultry, fish, and eggs	100	47	27	38	48	52	57	47
Beef	100	40	27	26	42	47	51	38
Pork	100	47	23	34	52	55	51	50
Other meats	100	45	25	41	43	48	50	47
Poultry	100	47	31	41	45	51	56	46
Fish and seafood	100	58	29	49	62	60	78	55
Eggs	100	60	38	54	58	56	71	65
Dairy products	100	57	33	52	59	58	65	58
Fresh milk and cream	100	52	32	48	50	55	56	55
Other dairy products	100	59	33	55	64	60	70	60
Fruits and vegetables	100	60	36	57	57	62	65	63
Fresh fruits	100	64	39	59	60	62	73	67
Fresh vegetables	100	63	35	65	62	64	67	65
Processed fruits	100	55	33	49	55	55	57	61
Processed vegetables	100	54	37	47	45	64	52	57
Other food at home	100	57	31	50	68	60	66	56
Sugar and other sweets	100	62	25	45	68	62	74	65
Fats and oils	100	60	27	56	54	67	63	64
Miscellaneous foods	100	57	34	52	70	57	64	57
Nonalcoholic beverages	100	55	30	46	68	65	67	51
Food prepared by consumer unit on trips	100	49	16	47	73	51	69	40
Food away from home	100	46	53	73	63	47	51	32
ALCOHOLIC BEVERAGES	100	50	81	84	86	45	54	28
HOUSING	100	69	37	81	85	74	77	65
Shelter	100	72	47	98	95	79	79	61
Owned dwellings	100	59	3	48	75	70	82	57
Mortgage interest and charges	100	44	4	56	94	72	72	21
Property taxes	100	64	3	35	58	60	80	80
Maintenance, repair, insurance, other expenses	100	92	2	45	49	80	113	126
Rented dwellings	100	104	138	212	149	107	79	75
Other lodging	100	45	56	60	36	42	59	36
Utilities, fuels, and public services	100	67	21	57	72	75	76	71
Natural gas	100	73	16	49	75	69	78	89
Electricity	100	67	22	58	73	81	74	70
Fuel oil and other fuels	100	79	1	17	26	36	79	133
Telephone services	100	62	27	71	78	80	76	54
Water and other public services	100	68	11	42	66	67	78	83

	total households	single-person households headed by women						
		total	under 25	25 to 34	35 to 44	45 to 54	55 to 64	65 or older
Household services	100	**66**	**15**	**42**	**64**	**50**	**72**	**87**
Personal services	100	44	1	8	32	2	6	95
Other household services	100	78	22	60	81	76	106	83
Housekeeping supplies	100	**69**	**27**	**40**	**72**	**59**	**79**	**85**
Laundry and cleaning supplies	100	61	40	44	65	65	69	66
Other household products	100	68	24	35	76	51	81	84
Postage and stationery	100	82	19	47	70	72	85	106
Household furnishings and equipment	100	**55**	**34**	**68**	**68**	**57**	**64**	**49**
Household textiles	100	68	25	64	46	51	69	88
Furniture	100	52	42	95	79	46	54	42
Floor coverings	100	61	14	68	57	161	57	43
Major appliances	100	54	11	37	71	57	79	53
Small appliances, miscellaneous housewares	100	60	56	83	72	63	66	50
Miscellaneous household equipment	100	53	35	61	65	59	64	47
APPAREL AND RELATED SERVICES	100	**61**	**64**	**87**	**79**	**61**	**70**	**46**
Men and boys	100	**19**	**12**	**19**	**24**	**15**	**25**	**18**
Men, aged 16 or older	100	19	14	22	24	14	25	18
Boys, aged 2 to 15	100	19	4	8	23	16	28	22
Women and girls	100	**92**	**102**	**141**	**99**	**89**	**104**	**71**
Women, aged 16 or older	100	104	121	165	111	101	113	81
Girls, aged 2 to 15	100	27	4	14	35	26	55	19
Children under age 2	100	**25**	**14**	**18**	**11**	**66**	**23**	**18**
Footwear	100	**57**	**77**	**62**	**131**	**50**	**70**	**36**
Other apparel products and services	100	**56**	**40**	**96**	**64**	**65**	**58**	**44**
TRANSPORTATION	100	**46**	**28**	**62**	**58**	**57**	**63**	**34**
Vehicle purchases	100	**36**	**17**	**51**	**43**	**46**	**63**	**19**
Cars and trucks, new	100	44	15	60	39	60	82	26
Cars and trucks, used	100	29	18	45	48	29	49	14
Other vehicles	100	17	22	–	–	121	–	–
Gasoline and motor oil	100	**45**	**37**	**61**	**63**	**61**	**54**	**31**
Other vehicle expenses	100	**55**	**26**	**65**	**65**	**65**	**69**	**48**
Vehicle finance charges	100	37	20	78	60	56	52	15
Maintenance and repairs	100	53	29	61	61	67	70	42
Vehicle insurance	100	62	25	48	70	63	78	63
Vehicle rentals, leases, licenses, other charges	100	55	26	104	66	69	56	43
Public transportation	100	**63**	**56**	**110**	**71**	**57**	**75**	**48**
HEALTH CARE	100	**75**	**12**	**40**	**56**	**59**	**83**	**103**
Health insurance	100	75	9	37	48	53	71	111
Medical services	100	70	16	52	73	68	100	74
Drugs	100	83	14	33	55	67	102	110
Medical supplies	100	83	17	45	65	67	74	120
ENTERTAINMENT	100	**56**	**32**	**57**	**77**	**68**	**67**	**49**
Fees and admissions	100	43	34	64	69	47	49	30
Audio and visual equipment and services	100	65	38	63	82	71	75	62
Pets, toys, and playground equipment	100	76	31	62	105	104	98	65
Other entertainment products and services	100	21	14	21	29	36	22	16
PERSONAL CARE PRODUCTS AND SERVICES	100	**86**	**53**	**113**	**124**	**87**	**89**	**79**
READING	100	**86**	**35**	**68**	**81**	**77**	**86**	**107**

	total households	single-person households headed by women						
		total	under 25	25 to 34	35 to 44	45 to 54	55 to 64	65 or older
EDUCATION	100	47	257	86	56	24	23	7
TOBACCO PRODUCTS AND SMOKING SUPPLIES	100	48	25	46	86	81	77	24
MISCELLANEOUS	100	79	15	51	211	77	100	70
CASH CONTRIBUTIONS	100	65	7	39	53	52	73	88
PERSONAL INSURANCE AND PENSIONS	100	40	15	69	74	66	67	12
Life and other personal insurance	100	59	0	27	30	52	140	51
Pensions and Social Security	100	38	16	72	76	67	62	9
PERSONAL TAXES	100	51	–8	90	105	100	68	24
Federal income taxes	100	51	–15	94	113	116	65	17
State and local income taxes	100	45	7	100	106	73	67	11
Other taxes	100	82	3	23	29	51	88	129
GIFTS FOR PEOPLE IN OTHER HOUSEHOLDS	100	79	30	60	79	91	114	73

Note: Spending by category does not add to total spending because gift spending is also included in the preceding product and service categories. "–" means sample is too small to make a reliable estimate.
Source: Bureau of Labor Statistics, 2010 and 2011 Consumer Expenditure Surveys, Internet site http://www.bls.gov/cex/

People Who Live Alone Control One-Third of the Rental Market

Men and women who live alone account for 18 percent of household spending.

Women who live alone control a slightly larger share of total household spending than their male counterparts—9.2 percent versus 8.7 percent in 2010–11. But men who live alone control twice as large a share of spending on alcoholic beverages as their female counterparts—16 percent versus 8 percent. Men who live alone account for a larger share of spending than women who live alone on food away from home, other vehicles (mostly motorcycles), and tobacco. Women who live alone account for a larger share of spending than their male counterparts on pets, toys, and playground equipment (12 versus 6 percent). They also control a larger share of the market for drugs (13 versus 7 percent) and for postage and stationary (13 versus 5 percent).

Together, men and women who live alone control a substantial share of some markets. They account for 34 percent of household spending on rent, 24 percent of spending on alcoholic beverages, 23 percent of spending on reading material, and 23 percent of spending on gifts for people in other households.

■ The share of spending controlled by single-person households will climb as the large baby-boom generation ages and more people live alone.

People who live alone account for a large share of some markets

(percent of total household spending accounted for by men and women who live alone, 2010–11)

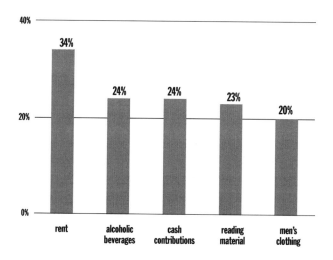

Table 8.8 Market Share of Spending Accounted for by Men and Women Who Live Alone, 2010–11

(share of total annual household spending accounted for by people who live alone, by sex, 2010–11)

	total households	total who live alone	men who live alone	women who live alone
Share of total households	100.0%	29.4%	13.7%	15.7%
Share of total annual spending	100.0	18.0	8.7	9.2
FOOD	100.0	16.6	8.5	8.1
Food at home	100.0	15.5	6.9	8.7
Cereals and bakery products	100.0	15.4	6.8	8.7
Cereals and cereal products	100.0	14.9	6.7	8.2
Bakery products	100.0	15.7	6.8	8.9
Meats, poultry, fish, and eggs	100.0	14.2	6.7	7.5
Beef	100.0	12.2	5.9	6.3
Pork	100.0	14.2	6.8	7.4
Other meats	100.0	14.8	7.7	7.1
Poultry	100.0	14.0	6.6	7.4
Fish and seafood	100.0	16.3	7.1	9.1
Eggs	100.0	16.6	7.1	9.5
Dairy products	100.0	15.4	6.5	8.9
Fresh milk and cream	100.0	15.2	7.0	8.3
Other dairy products	100.0	15.6	6.2	9.3
Fruits and vegetables	100.0	16.1	6.6	9.5
Fresh fruits	100.0	16.6	6.6	10.0
Fresh vegetables	100.0	16.2	6.3	9.9
Processed fruits	100.0	16.1	7.4	8.7
Processed vegetables	100.0	15.0	6.5	8.5
Other food at home	100.0	16.2	7.2	9.0
Sugar and other sweets	100.0	15.7	6.0	9.7
Fats and oils	100.0	15.8	6.3	9.5
Miscellaneous foods	100.0	16.3	7.4	9.0
Nonalcoholic beverages	100.0	16.3	7.6	8.7
Food prepared by household on trips	100.0	15.3	7.6	7.7
Food away from home	100.0	18.2	10.9	7.3
ALCOHOLIC BEVERAGES	100.0	23.8	16.0	7.8
HOUSING	100.0	20.0	9.2	10.8
Shelter	100.0	21.6	10.3	11.3
Owned dwellings	100.0	16.4	7.1	9.3
Mortgage interest and charges	100.0	13.6	6.7	7.0
Property taxes	100.0	17.6	7.5	10.1
Maintenance, repairs, insurance, other expenses	100.0	22.3	7.8	14.5
Rented dwellings	100.0	34.0	17.5	16.4
Other lodging	100.0	15.1	8.0	7.1
Utilities, fuels, and public services	100.0	18.8	8.3	10.5
Natural gas	100.0	19.7	8.3	11.4

	total households	total who live alone	men who live alone	women who live alone
Electricity	100.0%	19.0%	8.5%	10.5%
Fuel oil and other fuels	100.0	21.6	9.3	12.4
Telephone services	100.0	17.9	8.1	9.8
Water and other public services	100.0	18.4	7.7	10.7
Household services	**100.0**	**16.8**	**6.3**	**10.5**
Personal services	100.0	9.1	2.1	6.9
Other household services	100.0	20.8	8.5	12.3
Housekeeping supplies	**100.0**	**16.6**	**5.6**	**10.9**
Laundry and cleaning supplies	100.0	15.9	6.2	9.7
Other household products	100.0	16.2	5.5	10.7
Postage and stationery	100.0	18.3	5.4	12.9
Household furnishings and equipment	**100.0**	**16.1**	**7.5**	**8.7**
Household textiles	100.0	16.9	6.2	10.7
Furniture	100.0	17.8	9.5	8.3
Floor coverings	100.0	22.7	13.2	9.6
Major appliances	100.0	14.1	5.5	8.6
Small appliances, miscellaneous housewares	100.0	16.2	6.7	9.5
Miscellaneous household equipment	100.0	15.5	7.1	8.4
APPAREL AND SERVICES	**100.0**	**15.5**	**5.9**	**9.6**
Men and boys	**100.0**	**16.7**	**13.7**	**3.0**
Men, aged 16 or older	100.0	19.7	16.7	3.0
Boys, aged 2 to 15	100.0	4.7	1.7	3.0
Women and girls	**100.0**	**15.8**	**1.3**	**14.5**
Women, aged 16 or older	100.0	17.5	1.1	16.4
Girls, aged 2 to 15	100.0	6.3	2.0	4.3
Children under age 2	**100.0**	**5.9**	**1.9**	**4.0**
Footwear	**100.0**	**14.6**	**5.6**	**9.0**
Other apparel products and services	**100.0**	**17.2**	**8.4**	**8.7**
TRANSPORTATION	**100.0**	**15.4**	**8.2**	**7.3**
Vehicle purchases	**100.0**	**12.7**	**7.1**	**5.6**
Cars and trucks, new	100.0	12.6	5.7	6.9
Cars and trucks, used	100.0	12.7	8.2	4.5
Other vehicles	100.0	15.7	13.0	2.7
Gasoline and motor oil	**100.0**	**15.8**	**8.6**	**7.1**
Other vehicle expenses	**100.0**	**17.4**	**8.7**	**8.7**
Vehicle finance charges	100.0	12.2	6.4	5.8
Maintenance and repairs	100.0	18.2	9.9	8.3
Vehicle insurance	100.0	18.3	8.6	9.7
Vehicle rental, leases, licenses, other charges	100.0	16.8	8.2	8.6
Public transportation	**100.0**	**18.5**	**8.6**	**9.8**
HEALTH CARE	**100.0**	**18.8**	**7.0**	**11.8**
Health insurance	100.0	18.9	7.1	11.7
Medical services	100.0	17.8	6.7	11.1
Drugs	100.0	19.7	6.7	13.0
Medical supplies	100.0	20.4	7.2	13.1

	total households	total who live alone	men who live alone	women who live alone
ENTERTAINMENT	**100.0%**	**17.1%**	**8.3%**	**8.9%**
Fees and admissions	100.0	13.9	7.2	6.7
Television, radio, sound equipment	100.0	20.3	10.1	10.2
Pets, toys, and playground equipment	100.0	18.0	6.0	12.0
Other entertainment supplies, services	100.0	12.5	9.1	3.3
PERSONAL CARE PRODUCTS AND SERVICES	**100.0**	**17.9**	**4.4**	**13.6**
READING	**100.0**	**23.2**	**9.6**	**13.6**
EDUCATION	**100.0**	**19.1**	**11.7**	**7.5**
TOBACCO PRODUCTS AND SMOKING SUPPLIES	**100.0**	**21.6**	**14.0**	**7.6**
MISCELLANEOUS	**100.0**	**24.1**	**11.6**	**12.5**
CASH CONTRIBUTIONS	**100.0**	**23.6**	**13.3**	**10.3**
PERSONAL INSURANCE AND PENSIONS	**100.0**	**14.1**	**7.8**	**6.2**
Life and other personal insurance	100.0	14.9	5.6	9.3
Pensions and Social Security	100.0	14.0	7.9	6.0
PERSONAL TAXES	**100.0**	**19.4**	**11.3**	**8.1**
Federal income taxes	100.0	20.3	12.3	8.0
State and local income taxes	100.0	17.4	10.3	7.0
Other taxes	100.0	18.9	6.0	12.9
GIFTS FOR PEOPLE IN OTHER HOUSEHOLDS	**100.0**	**23.2**	**10.8**	**12.4**

Source: Calculations by New Strategist based on the Bureau of Labor Statistics' 2010 and 2011 Consumer Expenditure Surveys, Internet site http://www.bls.gov/cex/home.htm

Time Use

Leisure activities rank second in time use.

Men spend 4.88 hours per day in leisure pursuits, and women spend 4.43 hours.

Work is the third most time-consuming activity.

Men work an average of 3.89 hours per day, and women work 2.73 hours.

Among dual-income couples, husbands spend more time at work.

Wives spend more time in the kitchen and caring for kids.

More than half of leisure time is spent watching television.

Men watch television an average of 2.99 hours per day, and women watch 2.52 hours.

Men spend more time than women caring for their lawns.

Women spend more time than men cooking, cleaning, and doing laundry.

Teenage girls spend the most time on the telephone.

Women aged 65 or older spend the most time participating in religious activities.

Women are more likely than men to vote.

In the 2012 presidential election, women were the 54 percent majority of voters.

Leisure Ranks Second in Time Use among Men and Women

Work ranks third, well behind leisure.

The American Time Use Survey collects data on time use by asking a representative sample of Americans aged 15 or older about their activities during the past 24 hours. These "diary" data are combined and analyzed by type of activity and demographic characteristic, revealing how much time people devote to eating, shopping, working, and playing.

Men and women spend the largest amount of time in personal care activities—including sleeping and grooming. In 2011, the average man devoted 9.23 hours and the average woman 9.71 hours to personal care activities. Leisure pursuits took up an average of 4.88 hours for men and 4.43 hours for women—most of this time spent in front of a television. Work ranks third for both men and women, with men spending 3.89 hours at work and in work-related activities and women 2.73 hours. This figure seems relatively low because it includes people in the labor force, students, and retirees, and because it includes weekdays and weekends.

Men spend 1.36 hours involved in household activities (housework) on an average day, including cooking, housecleaning, laundry, and lawn care. They spend 0.27 hours caring for other household members (such as children). Women spend a larger 2.18 hours a day doing household activities and 0.58 hours caring for other household members.

■ Researchers and public policymakers use the results of the time use survey to determine how people balance work and family issues.

On an average day, men spend more time at work

(average number of hours per day people aged 15 or older spend working and in work-related activities, by sex, 2011)

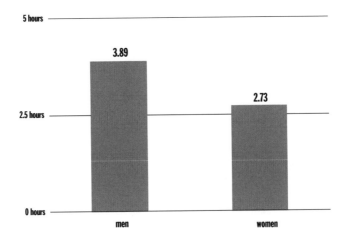

Table 9.1 Time Use by Primary Activity and Sex, 2011

(average number of hours per day people aged 15 or older spent in primary activities, and index of time use by sex to average, 2011)

	total	men	women
Total, all activities	**24.00 hrs.**	**24.00 hrs.**	**24.00 hrs.**
Personal care	9.47	9.23	9.71
Household activities	1.78	1.36	2.18
Caring for and helping household members	0.43	0.27	0.58
Caring for and helping people in other households	0.15	0.13	0.16
Work and work-related activities	3.29	3.89	2.73
Education	0.44	0.46	0.42
Consumer purchases (store, telephone, Internet)	0.37	0.31	0.43
Professional and personal care services	0.07	0.05	0.10
Household services	0.01	0.01	0.01
Government services and civic obligations	0.01	0.01	0.00
Eating and drinking	1.12	1.16	1.09
Socializing, relaxing, and leisure	4.65	4.88	4.43
Sports, exercise, and recreation	0.34	0.43	0.25
Religious and spiritual activities	0.15	0.12	0.19
Volunteer activities	0.15	0.13	0.16
Telephone calls	0.10	0.06	0.13
Traveling	1.21	1.25	1.16

INDEX OF TIME USE BY SEX TO AVERAGE

Total, all activities	**100**	**100**	**100**
Personal care	100	97	103
Household activities	100	76	122
Caring for and helping household members	100	63	135
Caring for and helping people in other households	100	87	107
Work and work-related activities	100	118	83
Education	100	105	95
Consumer purchases (store, telephone, Internet)	100	84	116
Professional and personal care services	100	71	143
Eating and drinking	100	104	97
Socializing, relaxing, and leisure	100	105	95
Sports, exercise, and recreation	100	126	74
Religious and spiritual activities	100	80	127
Volunteer activities	100	87	107
Telephone calls	100	60	130
Traveling	100	103	96

Note: Primary activities are those respondents identified as their main activity. Other activities done simultaneously, such as eating while watching TV, are not included. Numbers do not add to 24.00 because not all activities could be coded due to insufficient detail, respondent could not remember, etc. The index is calculated by dividing time use of each age/sex group by time use of the average person and multiplying by 100.
Source: Bureau of Labor Statistics, unpublished tables from the 2011 American Time Use Survey, Internet site http://www.bls .gov/tus/home.htm; calculations by New Strategist

Older Men Spend the Most Time Eating and Drinking

Older women spend the most time in religious activities.

Time use varies greatly by age. The youngest and oldest adults spend more time than the middle-aged in personal care activities and leisure pursuits, in large part because they have more free time. Middle-aged Americans work the most.

The average man works 3.89 hours per day. This figure seems low because it includes workers as well as retirees, weekdays and weekends. Men aged 25 to 44 spend 33 to 42 percent more time working than the average man. Middle-aged men devote more time to work than to leisure. Men and women aged 25 to 44 spend more time than average caring for other household members, mostly children. Women aged 35 or older spend more than two hours a day involved in household activities (cooking, cleaning, laundry, and so on). For men, average time spent in household activities rises above two hours per day only among those aged 65 or older.

Not surprisingly, the youngest men and women spend the most time in educational activities, an average of more than three hours per day. Women aged 75 or older spend 84 percent more time than the average woman in religious activities.

■ It is no coincidence that men and women aged 25 to 44, who spend the most time working and caring for other household members, have the least amount of leisure time.

Men and women aged 25 to 44 have the least amount of time for socializing and leisure

(average number of hours per day total people aged 15 or older and people aged 25 to 44 spend in leisure as a primary activity, by sex, 2011)

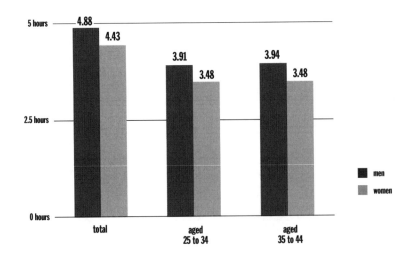

Table 9.2 Time Use of Men by Primary Activity and Age, 2011

(average number of hours per day men aged 15 or older spent in primary activities by age, and index to male average, 2011)

	total men	15–19	20–24	25–34	35–44	45–54	55–64	65–74	75+
Total, all activities (hours)	**24.00**	**24.00**	**24.00**	**24.00**	**24.00**	**24.00**	**24.00**	**24.00**	**24.00**
Personal care	9.23	10.12	9.72	8.95	8.95	8.91	9.03	9.39	9.89
Household activities	1.36	0.56	0.81	1.01	1.30	1.54	1.64	2.19	2.17
Caring for and helping household members	0.27	0.11	0.09	0.45	0.59	0.29	0.10	0.03	0.06
Caring for and helping people in other households	0.13	0.06	0.15	0.13	0.15	0.12	0.12	0.23	0.08
Work and work-related activities	3.89	0.76	3.69	5.53	5.17	4.88	4.10	1.60	0.43
Education	0.46	3.05	0.95	0.40	0.11	–	0.00	0.00	–
Consumer purchases (store, telephone, Internet)	0.31	0.20	0.27	0.26	0.31	0.32	0.34	0.41	0.40
Professional and personal care services	0.05	0.01	0.02	0.03	0.04	0.06	0.05	0.07	0.09
Household services	0.01	–	–	0.01	0.01	0.01	0.02	0.03	0.00
Government services and civic obligations	0.01	0.00	–	0.00	0.00	0.00	0.00	0.00	0.00
Eating and drinking	1.16	0.95	1.05	1.09	1.11	1.17	1.21	1.45	1.37
Socializing, relaxing, and leisure	4.88	5.28	4.86	3.91	3.94	4.47	5.23	6.60	7.56
Sports, exercise, and recreation	0.43	1.11	0.58	0.39	0.37	0.27	0.35	0.39	0.23
Religious and spiritual activities	0.12	0.13	0.14	0.07	0.15	0.11	0.12	0.11	0.22
Volunteer activities	0.13	0.14	0.13	0.06	0.13	0.12	0.14	0.18	–
Telephone calls	0.06	0.10	0.08	0.05	0.07	0.05	0.05	0.07	0.03
Traveling	1.25	1.03	1.27	1.31	1.35	1.43	1.29	1.02	0.86

INDEX OF TIME USE BY AGE TO MALE AVERAGE

Total, all activities	**100**	**100**	**100**	**100**	**100**	**100**	**100**	**100**	**100**
Personal care	100	110	105	97	97	97	98	102	107
Household activities	100	41	60	74	96	113	121	161	160
Caring for and helping household members	100	41	33	167	219	107	37	11	22
Caring for and helping people in other households	100	46	115	100	115	92	92	177	62
Work and work-related activities	100	20	95	142	133	125	105	41	11
Education	100	663	207	87	24	–	0	0	–
Consumer purchases (store, telephone, Internet)	100	65	87	84	100	103	110	132	129
Professional and personal care services	100	20	40	60	80	120	100	140	180
Household services	100	–	–	100	100	100	200	300	0
Government services and civic obligations	100	0	–	0	0	0	0	0	0
Eating and drinking	100	82	91	94	96	101	104	125	118
Socializing, relaxing, and leisure	100	108	100	80	81	92	107	135	155
Sports, exercise, and recreation	100	258	135	91	86	63	81	91	53
Religious and spiritual activities	100	108	117	58	125	92	100	92	183
Volunteer activities	100	108	100	46	100	92	108	138	–
Telephone calls	100	167	133	83	117	83	83	117	50
Traveling	100	82	102	105	108	114	103	82	69

Note: Primary activities are those respondents identified as their main activity. Other activities done simultaneously, such as eating while watching TV, are not included. Numbers do not add to 24.00 because not all activities could be coded due to insufficient detail, respondent could not remember, etc. The index is calculated by dividing time use of men by age by time use of the average man and multiplying by 100. "–" means sample is too small to make a reliable estimate or denominator is zero.
Source: Bureau of Labor Statistics, unpublished tables from the 2011 American Time Use Survey, Internet site http://www.bls.gov/tus/home.htm; calculations by New Strategist

Table 9.3 Time Use of Women by Primary Activity and Age, 2011

(average number of hours per day women aged 15 or older spent in primary activities by age, and index to female average, 2011)

	total women	15–19	20–24	25–34	35–44	45–54	55–64	65–74	75+
Total, all activities (hours)	**24.00**	**24.00**	**24.00**	**24.00**	**24.00**	**24.00**	**24.00**	**24.00**	**24.00**
Personal care	9.71	10.43	10.11	9.61	9.39	9.37	9.51	9.81	10.35
Household activities	2.18	0.81	1.40	1.92	2.52	2.34	2.48	2.50	2.89
Caring for and helping household members	0.58	0.18	0.71	1.35	1.16	0.38	0.12	0.08	0.02
Caring for and helping people in other households	0.16	0.11	0.04	0.07	0.13	0.28	0.29	0.15	0.11
Work and work-related activities	2.73	0.90	3.35	3.60	3.32	3.75	3.01	1.12	0.14
Education	0.42	3.20	0.88	0.25	0.13	0.11	0.04	0.00	0.00
Consumer purchases (store, telephone, Internet)	0.43	0.31	0.41	0.39	0.50	0.48	0.41	0.48	0.38
Professional and personal care services	0.10	0.04	0.09	0.08	0.09	0.13	0.06	0.17	0.17
Household services	0.01	–	0.00	0.01	0.01	0.02	0.01	0.01	0.00
Government services and civic obligations	0.00	0.00	0.00	0.00	0.01	0.00	0.00	0.00	0.00
Eating and drinking	1.09	0.97	1.04	1.06	1.05	1.02	1.14	1.26	1.34
Socializing, relaxing, and leisure	4.43	4.39	3.90	3.48	3.48	4.02	4.90	6.25	6.69
Sports, exercise, and recreation	0.25	0.47	0.33	0.29	0.26	0.20	0.20	0.18	0.15
Religious and spiritual activities	0.19	0.16	0.12	0.12	0.14	0.19	0.21	0.28	0.35
Volunteer activities	0.16	0.13	0.17	0.15	0.14	0.15	0.14	0.23	0.23
Telephone calls	0.13	0.24	0.10	0.10	0.09	0.11	0.15	0.18	0.17
Traveling	1.16	1.31	1.15	1.31	1.31	1.23	1.07	1.03	0.68

INDEX OF TIME USE BY AGE TO FEMALE AVERAGE

	total women	15–19	20–24	25–34	35–44	45–54	55–64	65–74	75+
Total, all activities	**100**	**100**	**100**	**100**	**100**	**100**	**100**	**100**	**100**
Personal care	100	107	104	99	97	96	98	101	107
Household activities	100	37	64	88	116	107	114	115	133
Caring for and helping household members	100	31	122	233	200	66	21	14	3
Caring for and helping people in other households	100	69	25	44	81	175	181	94	69
Work and work-related activities	100	33	123	132	122	137	110	41	5
Education	100	762	210	60	31	26	10	0	0
Consumer purchases store, telephone, Internet)	100	72	95	91	116	112	95	112	88
Professional and personal care services	100	40	90	80	90	130	60	170	170
Household services	100	–	0	100	100	200	100	100	0
Government services and civic obligations	–	–	–	–	–	–	–	–	–
Eating and drinking	100	89	95	97	96	94	105	116	123
Socializing, relaxing, and leisure	100	99	88	79	79	91	111	141	151
Sports, exercise, and recreation	100	188	132	116	104	80	80	72	60
Religious and spiritual activities	100	84	63	63	74	100	111	147	184
Volunteer activities	100	81	106	94	88	94	88	144	144
Telephone calls	100	185	77	77	69	85	115	138	131
Traveling	100	113	99	113	113	106	92	89	59

Note: Primary activities are those respondents identified as their main activity. Other activities done simultaneously, such as eating while watching TV, are not included. Numbers do not add to 24.00 because not all activities could be coded due to insufficient detail, respondent could not remember, etc. The index is calculated by dividing time use of women by age by time use of the average woman and multiplying by 100. "–" means sample is too small to make a reliable estimate or denominator is zero.
Source: Bureau of Labor Statistics, unpublished tables from the 2011 American Time Use Survey, Internet site http://www.bls .gov/tus/home.htm; calculations by New Strategist

In Dual-Income Couples, Husbands Spend More Time Working

Wives spend more time on housework and childcare.

For the nation's dual-income couples with children under age 18, the daily schedule still looks pretty traditional. Husbands spend more time at work. Wives spend more time in the kitchen and caring for kids.

Married fathers who work full-time spend more time at work on an average day than their female counterparts—6.03 hours for men versus 5.24 hours for women (these statistics include both weekdays and weekends). Fathers spend less time than mothers doing housework, caring for children, and driving children around. They spend more time than mothers on only one childcare activity—playing and doing hobbies with children.

Although fathers with full-time jobs spend more time working than mothers with full-time jobs, because fathers do less housework and childcare they have more leisure time. Married fathers with full-time jobs have 3.68 hours of leisure per day compared with 2.91 hours for their female counterparts. They spend most of their leisure time watching television.

■ Married fathers with full-time jobs and preschoolers at home spend more than one hour a day caring for children as the primary activity.

Fathers have more leisure time than mothers

(hours of leisure time per day among married parents employed full-time by age of children, 2007–11)

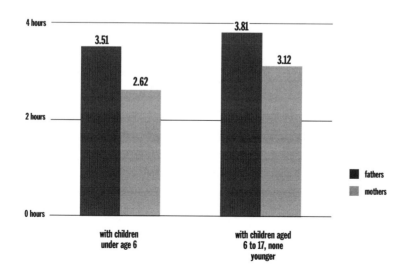

Table 9.4 Primary Activities of Dual-Income Couples with Children under Age 18, 2007–11

(average hours spent and percent participating in primary activities per day for married fathers and mothers employed full-time with children under age 18, and index of women to men, 2007–11)

AVERAGE HOURS PER DAY	husbands employed full-time	wives employed full-time	index of women to men
Total, all activities	**24.00 hrs.**	**24.00 hrs.**	**100**
Personal care activities	8.59	8.96	104
Sleeping	7.98	8.12	102
Household activities	1.34	1.95	146
Housework	0.26	0.82	315
Food preparation and cleanup	0.37	0.79	214
Lawn and garden care	0.23	0.07	30
Purchasing goods and services	0.34	0.55	162
Grocery shopping	0.06	0.13	217
Consumer goods purchases, except grocery shopping	0.22	0.34	155
Caring for and helping household members	0.88	1.29	147
Caring for and helping household children	0.86	1.28	149
Physical care	0.28	0.57	204
Education-related activities	0.09	0.11	122
Reading to/with children	0.03	0.05	167
Playing/doing hobbies with children	0.24	0.22	92
Working and work-related activities	6.07	5.27	87
Working	6.03	5.24	87
Leisure and sports	3.68	2.91	79
Socializing and communicating	0.54	0.60	111
Watching television	2.15	1.53	71
Participating in sports, exercise, and recreation	0.32	0.18	56
Travel	1.41	1.35	96
Travel related to caring for and helping household children	0.16	0.23	144
Other activities, not elsewhere classified	1.70	1.73	102

PERCENT PARTICIPATING ON AVERAGE DAY	husbands employed full-time	wives employed full-time	index of women to men
Total, all activities	**100.0%**	**100.0%**	**100**
Personal care activities	100.0	100.0	100
Sleeping	99.9	99.9	100
Household activities	66.0	87.9	133
Housework	18.3	50.2	274
Food preparation and cleanup	42.9	75.2	175
Lawn and garden care	10.8	4.6	43
Purchasing goods and services	38.5	51.5	134
Grocery shopping	9.5	16.6	175
Consumer goods purchases, except grocery shopping	30.3	38.2	126
Caring for and helping household members	57.3	74.3	130
Caring for and helping household children	55.9	73.3	131
Physical care	34.1	54.7	160
Education-related activities	6.9	12.5	181
Reading to/with children	6.6	10.7	162
Playing/doing hobbies with children	17.5	15.5	89
Working and work-related activities	74.6	70.3	94
Working	73.9	69.9	95
Leisure and sports	94.1	92.2	98
Socializing and communicating	34.2	38.0	111
Watching television	77.8	72.5	93
Participating in sports, exercise, and recreation	17.5	14.4	82
Travel	94.2	94.8	101
Travel related to caring for and helping household children	24.0	41.3	172
Other activities, not elsewhere classified	98.3	98.1	100

Note: Primary activities are those respondents identified as their main activity. Other activities done simultaneously, such as eating while watching TV, are not included. The index is calculated by dividing women's numbers by men's numbers and multiplying by 100.
Source: Bureau of Labor Statistics, American Time Use Survey, Internet site http://www.bls.gov/tus/; calculations by New Strategist

Table 9.5 Primary Activities of Dual-Income Couples with Children Aged 6 to 17, 2007–11

(average hours spent and percent participating in primary activities per day for married fathers and mothers employed full-time with children aged 6 to 17 and none younger, and index of women to men, 2007–11)

AVERAGE HOURS PER DAY	husbands employed full-time	wives employed full-time	index of women to men
Total, all activities	**24.00 hrs.**	**24.00 hrs.**	**100**
Personal care activities	8.56	8.92	104
Sleeping	7.91	8.05	102
Household activities	1.42	2.06	145
Housework	0.25	0.87	348
Food preparation and cleanup	0.35	0.80	229
Lawn and garden care	0.29	0.08	28
Purchasing goods and services	0.32	0.57	178
Grocery shopping	0.06	0.12	200
Consumer goods purchases, except grocery shopping	0.21	0.35	167
Caring for and helping household members	0.54	0.73	135
Caring for and helping household children	0.52	0.72	138
Physical care	0.10	0.20	200
Education-related activities	0.09	0.12	133
Reading to/with children	0.01	0.02	200
Playing/doing hobbies with children	0.09	0.04	44
Working and work-related activities	6.17	5.43	88
Working	6.14	5.40	88
Leisure and sports	3.81	3.12	82
Socializing and communicating	0.51	0.59	116
Watching television	2.27	1.66	73
Participating in sports, exercise, and recreation	0.32	0.18	56
Travel	1.43	1.36	95
Travel related to caring for and helping household children	0.15	0.19	127
Other activities, not elsewhere classified	1.75	1.81	103

The column group heading reads: **couples with children aged 6 to 17, none younger**

PERCENT PARTICIPATING ON AVERAGE DAY	couples with children aged 6 to 17, none younger		
	husbands employed full-time	wives employed full-time	index of women to men
Total, all activities	**100.0%**	**100.0%**	**100**
Personal care activities	100.0	100.0	100
Sleeping	99.8	99.8	100
Household activities	67.6	88.2	130
Housework	18.0	52.3	291
Food preparation and cleanup	42.9	74.7	174
Lawn and garden care	12.7	5.7	45
Purchasing goods and services	37.5	52.0	139
Grocery shopping	8.8	16.5	188
Consumer goods purchases, except grocery shopping	29.8	39.4	132
Caring for and helping household members	45.3	62.3	138
Caring for and helping household children	43.4	60.5	139
Physical care	18.0	34.2	190
Education-related activities	8.2	14.2	173
Reading to/with children	2.2	5.3	241
Playing/doing hobbies with children	6.7	3.7	55
Working and work-related activities	74.9	71.7	96
Working	74.5	71.2	96
Leisure and sports	94.3	93.9	100
Socializing and communicating	33.8	38.8	115
Watching television	79.0	73.5	93
Participating in sports, exercise, and recreation	18.1	14.8	82
Travel	94.2	94.9	101
Travel related to caring for and helping household children	24.0	36.0	150
Other activities, not elsewhere classified	98.3	98.1	100

Note: Primary activities are those respondents identified as their main activity. Other activities done simultaneously, such as eating while watching TV, are not included. The index is calculated by dividing women's numbers by men's numbers and multiplying by 100.
Source: Bureau of Labor Statistics, American Time Use Survey, Internet site http://www.bls.gov/tus/; calculations by New Strategist

Table 9.6 Primary Activities of Dual-Income Couples with Children under Age 6, 2007–11

(average hours spent and percent participating in primary activities per day for married fathers and mothers employed full-time with children under age 6, and index of women to men, 2007–11)

	couples with children under age 6		
AVERAGE HOURS PER DAY	husbands employed full-time	wives employed full-time	index of women to men
Total, all activities	**24.00 hrs.**	**24.00 hrs.**	**100**
Personal care activities	8.63	9.00	104
Sleeping	8.07	8.22	102
Household activities	1.22	1.81	148
Housework	0.27	0.75	278
Food preparation and cleanup	0.39	0.78	200
Lawn and garden care	0.16	0.05	31
Purchasing goods and services	0.37	0.52	141
Grocery shopping	0.07	0.13	186
Consumer goods purchases, except grocery shopping	0.24	0.32	133
Caring for and helping household members	1.35	2.05	152
Caring for and helping household children	1.33	2.04	153
Physical care	0.51	1.06	208
Education-related activities	0.08	0.09	113
Reading to/with children	0.05	0.08	160
Playing/doing hobbies with children	0.46	0.47	102
Working and work-related activities	5.93	5.05	85
Working	5.88	5.02	85
Leisure and sports	3.51	2.62	75
Socializing and communicating	0.58	0.60	103
Watching television	1.98	1.34	68
Participating in sports, exercise, and recreation	0.31	0.19	61
Travel	1.37	1.33	97
Travel related to caring for and helping household children	0.17	0.29	171
Other activities, not elsewhere classified	1.63	1.62	99

PERCENT PARTICIPATING ON AVERAGE DAY	couples with children under age 6		
	husbands employed full-time	wives employed full-time	index of women to men
Total, all activities	**100.0%**	**100.0%**	**100**
Personal care activities	100.0	100.0	100
Sleeping	100.0	100.0	100
Household activities	64.3	87.4	136
Housework	18.6	47.4	255
Food preparation and cleanup	43.0	75.8	176
Lawn and garden care	8.7	3.2	37
Purchasing goods and services	39.6	50.8	128
Grocery shopping	10.2	16.8	165
Consumer goods purchases, except grocery shopping	30.8	36.5	119
Caring for and helping household members	70.4	91.0	129
Caring for and helping household children	69.5	90.8	131
Physical care	51.6	83.0	161
Education-related activities	5.5	10.2	185
Reading to/with children	11.3	18.2	161
Playing/doing hobbies with children	29.3	31.7	108
Working and work-related activities	74.3	68.4	92
Working	73.4	68.2	93
Leisure and sports	93.7	89.8	96
Socializing and communicating	34.7	36.8	106
Watching television	76.5	71.0	93
Participating in sports, exercise, and recreation	16.8	13.9	83
Travel	94.3	94.6	100
Travel related to caring for and helping household children	23.9	48.6	203
Other activities, not elsewhere classified	98.3	98.2	100

Note: Primary activities are those respondents identified as their main activity. Other activities done simultaneously, such as eating while watching TV, are not included. The index is calculated by dividing women's numbers by men's numbers and multiplying by 100.
Source: Bureau of Labor Statistics, American Time Use Survey, Internet site http://www.bls.gov/tus/; calculations by New Strategist

Older Men Watch the Most TV

Women aged 35 to 44 spend the least amount of time watching television.

The average American spends 4.65 hours a day in leisure activities, more than half that time in front of a television. After personal care activities (mostly sleeping), leisure activities take up the largest share of the average person's day including 2.75 hours a day of watching television. Older men and women spend the most time watching TV, men aged 65 or older spending nearly five hours a day watching television as the primary activity.

Socializing and communicating is the second most time-consuming leisure activity after watching television, and women spend more time socializing than men. Teenage girls spend 69 percent more time socializing than the average person. Older men and women spend the most time reading, and men under age 25 spend the most time participating in sports and exercise. Teenage boys spend more time than anyone else playing games (a category that includes computer gaming as well as board and card games).

■ As younger generations age, they may spend less time reading and more time on the computer.

Men aged 65 or older watch the most TV, and women aged 35 to 44 watch the least

(average hours per day people aged 15 or older spend watching television as the primary activity, by sex and selected age group, 2011)

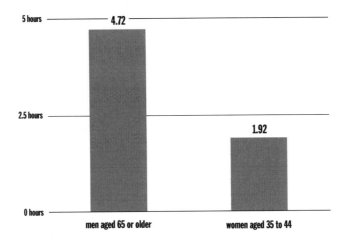

Table 9.7 Time Spent Sleeping by Age and Sex, 2011

(average number of hours per day people aged 15 or older spend sleeping, and index of time use by sex to average, 2011)

	total people	men	women
Aged 15 or older	**8.66 hrs.**	**8.57 hrs.**	**8.75 hrs.**
Aged 15 to 19	9.39	9.44	9.34
Aged 20 to 24	9.18	9.15	9.21
Aged 25 to 34	8.57	8.35	8.80
Aged 35 to 44	8.39	8.31	8.48
Aged 45 to 54	8.32	8.19	8.45
Aged 55 to 64	8.42	8.35	8.48
Aged 65 or older	8.97	8.96	8.98
INDEX OF TIME TO AVERAGE			
Aged 15 or older	**100**	**99**	**101**
Aged 15 to 19	108	109	108
Aged 20 to 24	106	106	106
Aged 25 to 34	99	96	102
Aged 35 to 44	97	96	98
Aged 45 to 54	96	95	98
Aged 55 to 64	97	96	98
Aged 65 or older	104	103	104

Note: Primary activities are those respondents identified as their main activity. Other activities done simultaneously, such as eating while watching TV, are not included. The index is calculated by dividing time use of each age/sex group by time use of the average person and multiplying by 100.
Source: Bureau of Labor Statistics, unpublished tables from the 2011 American Time Use Survey, Internet site http://www.bls .gov/tus/home.htm; calculations by New Strategist

Table 9.8 Time Spent Watching Television by Age and Sex, 2011

(average number of hours per day people aged 15 or older spend watching television as the primary activity and index of time to average, by age and sex, 2011)

	total people	men	women
Aged 15 or older	**2.75 hrs.**	**2.99 hrs.**	**2.52 hrs.**
Aged 15 to 19	2.17	2.29	2.04
Aged 20 to 24	2.24	2.47	2.00
Aged 25 to 34	2.09	2.24	1.95
Aged 35 to 44	2.21	2.52	1.92
Aged 45 to 54	2.71	2.99	2.43
Aged 55 to 64	3.20	3.40	3.02
Aged 65 or older	4.16	4.72	3.72
INDEX OF TIME TO AVERAGE			
Aged 15 or older	**100**	**109**	**92**
Aged 15 to 19	79	83	74
Aged 20 to 24	81	90	73
Aged 25 to 34	76	81	71
Aged 35 to 44	80	92	70
Aged 45 to 54	99	109	88
Aged 55 to 64	116	124	110
Aged 65 or older	151	172	135

Note: Primary activities are those respondents identified as their main activity. Other activities done simultaneously, such as eating while watching TV, are not included. The index is calculated by dividing time use of each age/sex group by time use of the average person and multiplying by 100.
Source: Bureau of Labor Statistics, unpublished tables from the 2011 American Time Use Survey, Internet site http://www.bls .gov/tus/home.htm; calculations by New Strategist

Table 9.9 Time Spent Socializing and Communicating by Age and Sex, 2011

(average number of hours per day people aged 15 or older spend socializing and communicating as the primary activity and index of time to average, by age and sex, 2011)

	total people	men	women
Aged 15 or older	**0.61 hrs.**	**0.57 hrs.**	**0.66 hrs.**
Aged 15 to 19	0.88	0.74	1.03
Aged 20 to 24	0.72	0.72	0.72
Aged 25 to 34	0.60	0.55	0.65
Aged 35 to 44	0.55	0.47	0.64
Aged 45 to 54	0.52	0.48	0.55
Aged 55 to 64	0.56	0.56	0.56
Aged 65 or older	0.64	0.60	0.68
INDEX OF TIME TO AVERAGE			
Aged 15 or older	**100**	**93**	**108**
Aged 15 to 19	144	121	169
Aged 20 to 24	118	118	118
Aged 25 to 34	98	90	107
Aged 35 to 44	90	77	105
Aged 45 to 54	85	79	90
Aged 55 to 64	92	92	92
Aged 65 or older	105	98	111

Note: Primary activities are those respondents identified as their main activity. Other activities done simultaneously, such as eating while watching TV, are not included. The index is calculated by dividing time use of each age/sex group by time use of the average person and multiplying by 100.
Source: Bureau of Labor Statistics, unpublished tables from the 2011 American Time Use Survey, Internet site http://www.bls.gov/tus/home.htm; calculations by New Strategist

Table 9.10 Time Spent Reading by Age and Sex, 2011

(average number of hours per day people aged 15 or older spend reading as the primary activity and index of time to average, by age and sex, 2011)

	total people	men	women
Aged 15 or older	**0.30 hrs.**	**0.24 hrs.**	**0.35 hrs.**
Aged 15 to 19	0.15	0.11	0.19
Aged 20 to 24	0.12	0.12	0.13
Aged 25 to 34	0.15	0.11	0.18
Aged 35 to 44	0.20	0.15	0.24
Aged 45 to 54	0.26	0.24	0.28
Aged 55 to 64	0.38	0.36	0.40
Aged 65 or older	0.69	0.55	0.80
INDEX OF TIME TO AVERAGE			
Aged 15 or older	**100**	**80**	**117**
Aged 15 to 19	50	37	63
Aged 20 to 24	40	40	43
Aged 25 to 34	50	37	60
Aged 35 to 44	67	50	80
Aged 45 to 54	87	80	93
Aged 55 to 64	127	120	133
Aged 65 or older	230	183	267

Note: Primary activities are those respondents identified as their main activity. Other activities done simultaneously, such as eating while watching TV, are not included. The index is calculated by dividing time use of each age/sex group by time use of the average person and multiplying by 100.
Source: Bureau of Labor Statistics, unpublished tables from the 2011 American Time Use Survey, Internet site http://www.bls .gov/tus/home.htm; calculations by New Strategist

Table 9.11 Time Spent Participating in Sports, Exercise, or Recreation by Age and Sex, 2011

(average number of hours per day people aged 15 or older spend participating in sports, exercise, or recreation as the primary activity and index of time to average, by age and sex, 2011)

	total people	men	women
Aged 15 or older	**0.30 hrs.**	**0.39 hrs.**	**0.22 hrs.**
Aged 15 to 19	0.69	0.95	0.41
Aged 20 to 24	0.43	0.55	0.31
Aged 25 to 34	0.31	0.37	0.25
Aged 35 to 44	0.27	0.33	0.22
Aged 45 to 54	0.21	0.26	0.17
Aged 55 to 64	0.25	0.33	0.18
Aged 65 or older	0.21	0.29	0.15
INDEX OF TIME TO AVERAGE			
Aged 15 or older	**100**	**130**	**73**
Aged 15 to 19	230	317	137
Aged 20 to 24	143	183	103
Aged 25 to 34	103	123	83
Aged 35 to 44	90	110	73
Aged 45 to 54	70	87	57
Aged 55 to 64	83	110	60
Aged 65 or older	70	97	50

Note: Primary activities are those respondents identified as their main activity. Other activities done simultaneously, such as eating while watching TV, are not included. The index is calculated by dividing time use of each age/sex group by time use of the average person and multiplying by 100.
Source: Bureau of Labor Statistics, unpublished tables from the 2011 American Time Use Survey, Internet site http://www.bls .gov/tus/home.htm; calculations by New Strategist

Table 9.12 Time Spent Relaxing and Thinking by Age and Sex, 2011

(average number of hours per day people aged 15 or older spend relaxing and thinking as the primary activity and index of time to average, by age and sex, 2011)

	total people	men	women
Aged 15 or older	**0.29 hrs.**	**0.30 hrs.**	**0.29 hsr.**
Aged 15 to 19	0.19	0.19	0.19
Aged 20 to 24	0.24	0.16	0.32
Aged 25 to 34	0.19	0.21	0.17
Aged 35 to 44	0.24	0.28	0.20
Aged 45 to 54	0.26	0.27	0.25
Aged 55 to 64	0.33	0.36	0.30
Aged 65 or older	0.55	0.55	0.54
INDEX OF TIME TO AVERAGE			
Aged 15 or older	**100**	**103**	**100**
Aged 15 to 19	66	66	66
Aged 20 to 24	83	55	110
Aged 25 to 34	66	72	59
Aged 35 to 44	83	97	69
Aged 45 to 54	90	93	86
Aged 55 to 64	114	124	103
Aged 65 or older	190	190	186

Note: Primary activities are those respondents identified as their main activity. Other activities done simultaneously, such as eating while watching TV, are not included. The index is calculated by dividing time use of each age/sex group by time use of the average person and multiplying by 100.
Source: Bureau of Labor Statistics, unpublished tables from the 2011 American Time Use Survey, Internet site http://www.bls.gov/tus/home.htm; calculations by New Strategist

Table 9.13 Time Spent Playing Games and Using the Computer for Leisure by Age and Sex, 2011

(average number of hours per day people aged 15 or older spend playing games and using the computer for leisure as primary activities and index of time to average, by age and sex, 2011)

	playing games			leisure computer use		
	total people	men	women	total people	men	women
Aged 15 or older	**0.22 hrs.**	**0.28 hrs.**	**0.16 hrs.**	**0.22 hrs.**	**0.26 hrs.**	**0.18 hrs.**
Aged 15 to 19	0.68	1.12	0.21	0.39	0.47	0.31
Aged 20 to 24	0.48	0.81	0.15	0.23	0.29	0.18
Aged 25 to 34	0.20	0.29	0.11	0.21	0.27	0.15
Aged 35 to 44	0.09	0.13	0.04	0.21	0.22	0.20
Aged 45 to 54	0.09	0.06	0.11	0.18	0.19	0.17
Aged 55 to 64	0.13	0.06	0.19	0.19	0.22	0.17
Aged 65 or older	0.20	0.08	0.29	0.20	0.25	0.16
INDEX OF TIME TO AVERAGE						
Aged 15 or older	**100**	**127**	**73**	**100**	**118**	**82**
Aged 15 to 19	309	509	95	177	214	141
Aged 20 to 24	218	368	68	105	132	82
Aged 25 to 34	91	132	50	95	123	68
Aged 35 to 44	41	59	18	95	100	91
Aged 45 to 54	41	27	50	82	86	77
Aged 55 to 64	59	27	86	86	100	77
Aged 65 or older	91	36	132	91	114	73

Note: The category "leisure computer use" does not include playing computer games. The category "playing games" includes computer and videogames, board games, and card games. Primary activities are those respondents identified as their main activity. Other activities done simultaneously, such as eating while watching TV, are not included. The index is calculated by dividing time use of each age/sex group by time use of the average person and multiplying by 100.
Source: Bureau of Labor Statistics, unpublished tables from the 2011 American Time Use Survey, Internet site http://www.bls.gov/tus/home.htm; calculations by New Strategist

Women Spend the Most Time Cooking and Cleaning

Men spend the most time caring for their lawns.

Among household activities, food preparation is the most time consuming. The average woman spent 0.61 hours cooking on the average day in 2011, or 37 minutes (this figure includes those who cooked lavish meals as well as those who went out to eat and did not cook at all). The average man spent a much smaller 0.25 hours cooking (15 minutes). Men in every age group spend less than an average amount of time cooking. The story is the same with house cleaning. In nearly every age group, women spend an above-average amount of time cleaning and men spend less. A different pattern emerges with lawn care. Men in nearly every age group spend more time than women in lawn care. Men aged 65 or older tend their lawns three times longer than the average person.

Not surprisingly, time spent caring for household children peaks among women aged 25 to 34, who are likely to have preschoolers. As the demands of children ease, pets take up the slack. The time people spend caring for their pets exceeds the average beginning in the 45-to-54 age group and peaks among women aged 55 to 64.

■ Women spend more time than men doing housework. Men spend more time at work.

Older men spend three times the average amount of time tending their lawns

(indexed average number of hours per day men spend in lawn care, by age, 2011; time spent by the average person = 100)

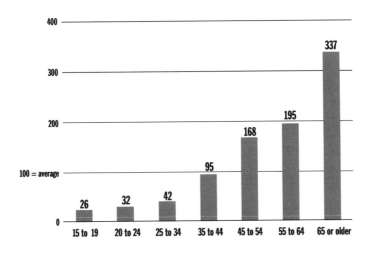

Table 9.14 Time Spent Housecleaning by Age and Sex, 2011

(average number of hours per day people aged 15 or older spend housecleaning as the primary activity and index of time to average, by age and sex, 2011)

	total people	men	women
Aged 15 or older	**0.38 hrs.**	**0.19 hrs.**	**0.56 hrs.**
Aged 15 to 19	0.19	0.14	0.25
Aged 20 to 24	0.34	0.20	0.48
Aged 25 to 34	0.38	0.21	0.55
Aged 35 to 44	0.45	0.18	0.71
Aged 45 to 54	0.38	0.19	0.55
Aged 55 to 64	0.36	0.15	0.55
Aged 65 or older	0.45	0.24	0.61
INDEX OF TIME TO AVERAGE			
Aged 15 or older	**100**	**50**	**147**
Aged 15 to 19	50	37	66
Aged 20 to 24	89	53	126
Aged 25 to 34	100	55	145
Aged 35 to 44	118	47	187
Aged 45 to 54	100	50	145
Aged 55 to 64	95	39	145
Aged 65 or older	118	63	161

Note: Primary activities are those respondents identified as their main activity. Other activities done simultaneously, such as eating while watching TV, are not included. The index is calculated by dividing time use of each age/sex group by time use of the average person and multiplying by 100.
Source: Bureau of Labor Statistics, unpublished tables from the 2011 American Time Use Survey, Internet site http://www.bls .gov/tus/home.htm; calculations by New Strategist

Table 9.15 Time Spent Doing the Laundry by Age and Sex, 2011

(average number of hours per day people aged 15 or older spend doing the laundry as the primary activity and index of time to average, by age and sex, 2011)

	total people	men	women
Aged 15 or older	**0.16 hrs.**	**0.07 hrs.**	**0.25 hrs.**
Aged 15 to 19	0.04	0.03	0.04
Aged 20 to 24	0.08	0.04	0.13
Aged 25 to 34	0.14	0.07	0.21
Aged 35 to 44	0.21	0.08	0.35
Aged 45 to 54	0.18	0.07	0.28
Aged 55 to 64	0.18	0.06	0.29
Aged 65 or older	0.18	0.09	0.26
INDEX OF TIME TO AVERAGE			
Aged 15 or older	**100**	**44**	**156**
Aged 15 to 19	25	19	25
Aged 20 to 24	50	25	81
Aged 25 to 34	88	44	131
Aged 35 to 44	131	50	219
Aged 45 to 54	113	44	175
Aged 55 to 64	113	38	181
Aged 65 or older	113	56	163

Note: Primary activities are those respondents identified as their main activity. Other activities done simultaneously, such as eating while watching TV, are not included. The index is calculated by dividing time use of each age/sex group by time use of the average person and multiplying by 100.
Source: Bureau of Labor Statistics, unpublished tables from the 2011 American Time Use Survey, Internet site http://www.bls.gov/tus/home.htm; calculations by New Strategist

Table 9.16 Time Spent in Food and Drink Preparation by Age and Sex, 2011

(average number of hours per day people aged 15 or older spend in food and drink preparation as the primary activity and index of time to average, by age and sex, 2011)

	total people	men	women
Aged 15 or older	**0.43 hrs.**	**0.25 hrs.**	**0.61 hrs.**
Aged 15 to 19	0.15	0.07	0.23
Aged 20 to 24	0.28	0.18	0.38
Aged 25 to 34	0.41	0.23	0.59
Aged 35 to 44	0.50	0.28	0.72
Aged 45 to 54	0.49	0.29	0.67
Aged 55 to 64	0.47	0.28	0.65
Aged 65 or older	0.53	0.34	0.69
INDEX OF TIME TO AVERAGE			
Aged 15 or older	**100**	**58**	**142**
Aged 15 to 19	35	16	53
Aged 20 to 24	65	42	88
Aged 25 to 34	95	53	137
Aged 35 to 44	116	65	167
Aged 45 to 54	114	67	156
Aged 55 to 64	109	65	151
Aged 65 or older	123	79	160

Note: Primary activities are those respondents identified as their main activity. Other activities done simultaneously, such as eating while watching TV, are not included. The index is calculated by dividing time use of each age/sex group by time use of the average person and multiplying by 100.
Source: Bureau of Labor Statistics, unpublished tables from the 2011 American Time Use Survey, Internet site http://www.bls .gov/tus/home.htm; calculations by New Strategist

Table 9.17 Time Spent Cleaning Up in the Kitchen by Age and Sex, 2011

(average number of hours per day people aged 15 or older spend cleaning up in the kitchen as the primary activity and index of time to average, by age and sex, 2011)

	total people	men	women
Aged 15 or older	**0.12 hrs.**	**0.05 hrs.**	**0.18 hrs.**
Aged 15 to 19	0.04	0.02	0.07
Aged 20 to 24	0.06	0.00	0.09
Aged 25 to 34	0.09	0.04	0.13
Aged 35 to 44	0.15	0.05	0.25
Aged 45 to 54	0.12	0.06	0.19
Aged 55 to 64	0.13	0.05	0.20
Aged 65 or older	0.17	0.08	0.24
INDEX OF TIME TO AVERAGE			
Aged 15 or older	**100**	**42**	**150**
Aged 15 to 19	33	17	58
Aged 20 to 24	50	0	75
Aged 25 to 34	75	33	108
Aged 35 to 44	125	42	208
Aged 45 to 54	100	50	158
Aged 55 to 64	108	42	167
Aged 65 or older	142	67	200

Note: Primary activities are those respondents identified as their main activity. Other activities done simultaneously, such as eating while watching TV, are not included. The index is calculated by dividing time use of each age/sex group by time use of the average person and multiplying by 100.
Source: Bureau of Labor Statistics, unpublished tables from the 2011 American Time Use Survey, Internet site http://www.bls .gov/tus/home.htm; calculations by New Strategist

Table 9.18 Time Spent on Lawn, Garden, and Houseplant Care by Age and Sex, 2011

(average number of hours per day people aged 15 or older spend in lawn, garden, and houseplant care as the primary activity and index of time to average, by age and sex, 2011)

	total people	men	women
Aged 15 or older	**0.19 hrs.**	**0.26 hrs.**	**0.13 hrs.**
Aged 15 to 19	0.03	0.05	0.00
Aged 20 to 24	0.04	0.06	0.00
Aged 25 to 34	0.08	0.08	0.09
Aged 35 to 44	0.13	0.18	0.08
Aged 45 to 54	0.25	0.32	0.18
Aged 55 to 64	0.27	0.37	0.18
Aged 65 or older	0.40	0.64	0.21
INDEX OF TIME TO AVERAGE			
Aged 15 or older	**100**	**137**	**68**
Aged 15 to 19	16	26	0
Aged 20 to 24	21	32	0
Aged 25 to 34	42	42	47
Aged 35 to 44	68	95	42
Aged 45 to 54	132	168	95
Aged 55 to 64	142	195	95
Aged 65 or older	211	337	111

Note: Primary activities are those respondents identified as their main activity. Other activities done simultaneously, such as eating while watching TV, are not included. The index is calculated by dividing time use of each age/sex group by time use of the average person and multiplying by 100.
Source: Bureau of Labor Statistics, unpublished tables from the 2011 American Time Use Survey, Internet site http://www.bls .gov/tus/home.htm; calculations by New Strategist

Table 9.19 Time Spent Caring for Household Children by Age and Sex, 2011

(average number of hours per day people aged 15 or older spend caring for and helping household children as the primary activity and index of time to average, by age and sex, 2011)

	total people	men	women
Aged 15 or older	**0.34 hrs.**	**0.21 hrs.**	**0.47 hrs.**
Aged 15 to 19	0.13	0.09	0.16
Aged 20 to 24	0.36	0.08	0.64
Aged 25 to 34	0.81	0.40	1.22
Aged 35 to 44	0.72	0.49	0.95
Aged 45 to 54	0.22	0.20	0.23
Aged 55 to 64	0.05	0.06	0.04
Aged 65 or older	0.01	0.01	0.01
INDEX OF TIME TO AVERAGE			
Aged 15 or older	**100**	**62**	**138**
Aged 15 to 19	38	26	47
Aged 20 to 24	106	24	188
Aged 25 to 34	238	118	359
Aged 35 to 44	212	144	279
Aged 45 to 54	65	59	68
Aged 55 to 64	15	18	12
Aged 65 or older	3	3	3

Note: Primary activities are those respondents identified as their main activity. Other activities done simultaneously, such as eating while watching TV, are not included. The index is calculated by dividing time use of each age/sex group by time use of the average person and multiplying by 100.
Source: Bureau of Labor Statistics, unpublished tables from the 2011 American Time Use Survey, Internet site http://www.bls .gov/tus/home.htm; calculations by New Strategist

Table 9.20 Time Spent on Pet Care by Age and Sex, 2011

(average number of hours per day people aged 15 or older spend caring for animals and pets as the primary activity and index of time to average, by age and sex, 2011)

	total people	men	women
Aged 15 or older	**0.09 hrs.**	**0.08 hrs.**	**0.10 hrs.**
Aged 15 to 19	0.05	0.04	0.05
Aged 20 to 24	0.04	0.03	0.05
Aged 25 to 34	0.06	0.05	0.07
Aged 35 to 44	0.09	0.10	0.09
Aged 45 to 54	0.11	0.10	0.12
Aged 55 to 64	0.11	0.09	0.14
Aged 65 or older	0.12	0.12	0.12
INDEX OF TIME TO AVERAGE			
Aged 15 or older	**100**	**89**	**111**
Aged 15 to 19	56	44	56
Aged 20 to 24	44	33	56
Aged 25 to 34	67	56	78
Aged 35 to 44	100	111	100
Aged 45 to 54	122	111	133
Aged 55 to 64	122	100	156
Aged 65 or older	133	133	133

Note: Primary activities are those respondents identified as their main activity. Other activities done simultaneously, such as eating while watching TV, are not included. The index is calculated by dividing time use of each age/sex group by time use of the average person and multiplying by 100.
Source: Bureau of Labor Statistics, unpublished tables from the 2011 American Time Use Survey, Internet site http://www.bls .gov/tus/home.htm; calculations by New Strategist

Teenage Girls Spend the Most Time on the Phone

Middle-aged men spend the most time traveling.

The average American travels more than one hour a day, making travel one of the most time-consuming daily activities. Travel time peaks among men aged 45 to 54 at 1.43 hours per day, primarily because of the commute to work.

It is no surprise that teenagers spend the most time on the telephone (including texting) as the primary activity. Teenage girls spend more than twice the average amount of time on the phone. People aged 65 or older spend the most time involved in religious activities, with women aged 65 or older devoting more than twice the average amount of time to religion.

Time spent grocery shopping peaks among older Americans, but only because older men boost their participation in the activity. Time spent grocery shopping is above average for women in most age groups and for men aged 65 or older. Time spent shopping for other items peaks among women aged 35 to 44.

■ Time spent volunteering is highest among men and women aged 65 or older because they have the most free time.

Women aged 65 or older spend the most time in religious activities

(indexed average hours per day women spend in religious activities as the primary activity, by age, 2011; time spent by the average person = 100)

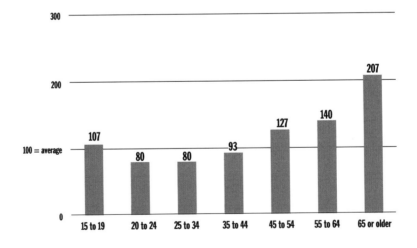

Table 9.21 Time Spent Shopping for Groceries by Age and Sex, 2011

(average number of hours per day people aged 15 or older spend shopping for groceries as the primary activity and index of time to average, by age and sex, 2011)

	total people	men	women
Aged 15 or older	**0.11 hrs.**	**0.08 hrs.**	**0.13 hrs.**
Aged 15 to 19	0.03	0.02	0.05
Aged 20 to 24	0.07	0.05	0.10
Aged 25 to 34	0.11	0.08	0.14
Aged 35 to 44	0.12	0.08	0.16
Aged 45 to 54	0.12	0.09	0.15
Aged 55 to 64	0.11	0.09	0.13
Aged 65 or older	0.14	0.14	0.14

INDEX OF TIME TO AVERAGE

	total people	men	women
Aged 15 or older	**100**	**73**	**118**
Aged 15 to 19	27	18	45
Aged 20 to 24	64	45	91
Aged 25 to 34	100	73	127
Aged 35 to 44	109	73	145
Aged 45 to 54	109	82	136
Aged 55 to 64	100	82	118
Aged 65 or older	127	127	127

Note: Primary activities are those respondents identified as their main activity. Other activities done simultaneously, such as eating while watching TV, are not included. The index is calculated by dividing time use of each age/sex group by time use of the average person and multiplying by 100.
Source: Bureau of Labor Statistics, unpublished tables from the 2011 American Time Use Survey, Internet site http://www.bls.gov/tus/home.htm; calculations by New Strategist

Table 9.22 Time Spent Shopping (except for Food or Gas) by Age and Sex, 2011

(average number of hours per day people aged 15 or older spend shopping for consumer goods except food or gas as the primary activity and index of time to average, by age and sex, 2011)

	total people	men	women
Aged 15 or older	**0.24 hrs.**	**0.20 hrs.**	**0.27 hrs.**
Aged 15 to 19	0.20	0.16	0.24
Aged 20 to 24	0.24	0.20	0.27
Aged 25 to 34	0.19	0.15	0.23
Aged 35 to 44	0.26	0.20	0.32
Aged 45 to 54	0.26	0.20	0.30
Aged 55 to 64	0.24	0.22	0.26
Aged 65 or older	0.26	0.24	0.28
INDEX OF TIME TO AVERAGE			
Aged 15 or older	**100**	**83**	**113**
Aged 15 to 19	83	67	100
Aged 20 to 24	100	83	113
Aged 25 to 34	79	63	96
Aged 35 to 44	108	83	133
Aged 45 to 54	108	83	125
Aged 55 to 64	100	92	108
Aged 65 or older	108	100	117

Note: Primary activities are those respondents identified as their main activity. Other activities done simultaneously, such as eating while watching TV, are not included. The index is calculated by dividing time use of each age/sex group by time use of the average person and multiplying by 100.
Source: Bureau of Labor Statistics, unpublished tables from the 2011 American Time Use Survey, Internet site http://www.bls .gov/tus/home.htm; calculations by New Strategist

Table 9.23 Time Spent Participating in Religious Activities by Age and Sex, 2011

(average number of hours per day people aged 15 or older spend participating in religious activities as the primary activity and index of time to average, by age and sex, 2011)

	total people	men	women
Aged 15 or older	**0.15 hrs.**	**0.12 hrs.**	**0.19 hrs.**
Aged 15 to 19	0.14	0.13	0.16
Aged 20 to 24	0.13	0.14	0.12
Aged 25 to 34	0.09	0.07	0.12
Aged 35 to 44	0.15	0.15	0.14
Aged 45 to 54	0.15	0.11	0.19
Aged 55 to 64	0.16	0.12	0.21
Aged 65 or older	0.24	0.16	0.31

INDEX OF TIME TO AVERAGE

	total people	men	women
Aged 15 or older	**100**	**80**	**127**
Aged 15 to 19	93	87	107
Aged 20 to 24	87	93	80
Aged 25 to 34	60	47	80
Aged 35 to 44	100	100	93
Aged 45 to 54	100	73	127
Aged 55 to 64	107	80	140
Aged 65 or older	160	107	207

Note: Primary activities are those respondents identified as their main activity. Other activities done simultaneously, such as eating while watching TV, are not included. The index is calculated by dividing time use of each age/sex group by time use of the average person and multiplying by 100.
Source: Bureau of Labor Statistics, unpublished tables from the 2011 American Time Use Survey, Internet site http://www.bls .gov/tus/home.htm; calculations by New Strategist

Table 9.24 Time Spent Volunteering by Age and Sex, 2011

(average number of hours per day people aged 15 or older spend volunteering as the primary activity and index of time to average, by age and sex, 2011)

	total people	men	women
Aged 15 or older	**0.15 hrs.**	**0.13 hrs.**	**0.16 hrs.**
Aged 15 to 19	0.14	0.14	0.13
Aged 20 to 24	0.15	0.13	0.17
Aged 25 to 34	0.11	0.06	0.15
Aged 35 to 44	0.13	0.13	0.14
Aged 45 to 54	0.14	0.12	0.15
Aged 55 to 64	0.14	0.14	0.14
Aged 65 or older	0.23	0.24	0.23
INDEX OF TIME TO AVERAGE			
Aged 15 or older	**100**	**87**	**107**
Aged 15 to 19	93	93	87
Aged 20 to 24	100	87	113
Aged 25 to 34	73	40	100
Aged 35 to 44	87	87	93
Aged 45 to 54	93	80	100
Aged 55 to 64	93	93	93
Aged 65 or older	153	160	153

Note: Primary activities are those respondents identified as their main activity. Other activities done simultaneously, such as eating while watching TV, are not included. The index is calculated by dividing time use of each age/sex group by time use of the average person and multiplying by 100.
Source: Bureau of Labor Statistics, unpublished tables from the 2011 American Time Use Survey, Internet site http://www.bls.gov/tus/home.htm; calculations by New Strategist

Table 9.25 Time Spent on the Telephone by Age and Sex, 2011

(average number of hours per day people aged 15 or older spend on the telephone as the primary activity and index of time to average, by age and sex, 2011)

	total people	men	women
Aged 15 or older	**0.10 hrs.**	**0.06 hrs.**	**0.13 hrs.**
Aged 15 to 19	0.17	0.10	0.24
Aged 20 to 24	0.09	0.08	0.10
Aged 25 to 34	0.07	0.05	0.10
Aged 35 to 44	0.08	0.07	0.09
Aged 45 to 54	0.08	0.05	0.11
Aged 55 to 64	0.10	0.05	0.15
Aged 65 or older	0.12	0.05	0.18
INDEX OF TIME TO AVERAGE			
Aged 15 or older	**100**	**60**	**130**
Aged 15 to 19	170	100	240
Aged 20 to 24	90	80	100
Aged 25 to 34	70	50	100
Aged 35 to 44	80	70	90
Aged 45 to 54	80	50	110
Aged 55 to 64	100	50	150
Aged 65 or older	120	50	180

Note: Primary activities are those respondents identified as their main activity. Other activities done simultaneously, such as eating while watching TV, are not included. The index is calculated by dividing time use of each age/sex group by time use of the average person and multiplying by 100.
Source: Bureau of Labor Statistics, unpublished tables from the 2011 American Time Use Survey, Internet site http://www.bls .gov/tus/home.htm; calculations by New Strategist

Table 9.26 Time Spent Traveling by Age and Sex, 2011

(average number of hours per day people aged 15 or older spend traveling as the primary activity and index of time to average, by age and sex, 2011)

	total people	men	women
Aged 15 or older	**1.21 hrs.**	**1.25 hrs.**	**1.16 hrs.**
Aged 15 to 19	1.16	1.03	1.31
Aged 20 to 24	1.21	1.27	1.15
Aged 25 to 34	1.31	1.31	1.31
Aged 35 to 44	1.33	1.35	1.31
Aged 45 to 54	1.33	1.43	1.23
Aged 55 to 64	1.17	1.29	1.07
Aged 65 or older	0.90	0.95	0.86
INDEX OF TIME TO AVERAGE			
Aged 15 or older	**100**	**103**	**96**
Aged 15 to 19	96	85	108
Aged 20 to 24	100	105	95
Aged 25 to 34	108	108	108
Aged 35 to 44	110	112	108
Aged 45 to 54	110	118	102
Aged 55 to 64	97	107	88
Aged 65 or older	74	79	71

Note: Primary activities are those respondents identified as their main activity. Other activities done simultaneously, such as eating while watching TV, are not included. The index is calculated by dividing time use of each age/sex group by time use of the average person and multiplying by 100.
Source: Bureau of Labor Statistics, unpublished tables from the 2011 American Time Use Survey, Internet site http://www.bls .gov/tus/home.htm; calculations by New Strategist

Women Are More Likely to Vote than Men

The 54 percent majority of 2012 voters were women.

Forty years ago in the presidential election of 1972, men were more likely to vote than women. In that year, 64.1 percent of men and 62.0 percent of women voted in the election. Beginning in 1980, women voted at a higher rate than men. In the 2008 presidential election, the gap between women's and men's voting rates peaked—with women 4.7 percentage points more likely than men to vote. In 2012, the gap dropped to 4.1 percentage points.

Because women have a higher voter participation rate than men, and because there are more women than men among adults in the United States, women account for the majority of voters. In 2012, 54 percent of voters were women, and female voters outnumbered male voters by nearly 10 million. The female advantage can be seen in every age group with little variation.

■ Men's voting rate has fallen over the past 40 years, while women's voting rate has been fairly stable.

Female voters outnumbered male voters by nearly 10 million in 2012

(number of voters by sex, 2012)

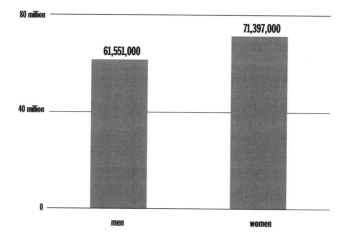

Table 9.27 Voting Rate in Presidential Elections by Sex, 1972 to 2012

(percent of people aged 18 or older who reported voting in presidential elections by sex, and index of voting rate by sex to total, 1972 to 2012)

	total	men	women
2012	56.5%	54.4%	58.5%
2008	58.2	55.7	60.4
2004	58.3	56.3	60.1
2000	54.7	53.1	56.2
1996	54.2	52.8	55.5
1992	61.3	60.2	62.3
1988	57.4	56.4	58.3
1984	59.9	59.0	60.8
1980	59.2	59.1	59.4
1976	59.2	59.6	58.8
1972	63.0	64.1	62.0

INDEX OF MEN AND WOMEN TO TOTAL

	total	men	women
2012	100	96	104
2008	100	96	104
2004	100	97	103
2000	100	97	103
1996	100	97	102
1992	100	98	102
1988	100	98	102
1984	100	98	102
1980	100	100	100
1976	100	101	99
1972	100	102	98

Note: The index is calculated by dividing the voting rate of men and women by the total voting rate and multiplying by 100.
Source: Bureau of the Census, Voting and Registration, Internet site http://www.census.gov/hhes/www/socdemo/voting/index
.html; calculations by New Strategist

Table 9.28 Voters by Age and Sex, 2012

(number and percent distribution of people who reported voting in the presidential election by age and sex, 2012; numbers in thousands)

	total	men	women
Total voters	**132,948**	**61,551**	**71,397**
Aged 18 to 24	11,353	5,198	6,155
Aged 25 to 44	39,942	18,336	21,606
Aged 45 to 64	52,013	24,537	27,476
Aged 65 or older	29,641	13,481	16,160
Total voters	**100.0%**	**46.3%**	**53.7%**
Aged 18 to 24	100.0	45.8	54.2
Aged 25 to 44	100.0	45.9	54.1
Aged 45 to 64	100.0	47.2	52.8
Aged 65 or older	100.0	45.5	54.5

Source: Bureau of the Census, Voting and Registration, Internet site http://www.census.gov/hhes/www/socdemo/voting/index .html; calculations by New Strategist

10

Wealth

Median household net worth peaks at $290,113 among married couples aged 65 or older.

Every household type and almost every age group saw its net worth fall between 2005 and 2011, after adjusting for inflation.

Motor vehicles are the most commonly owned asset.

Median equity in motor vehicles ranged from $4,393 among female-headed families to $8,613 among married couples.

The home is the single most valuable asset owned by the largest share of Americans.

Fully 80 percent of married couples own a home, as do 57 percent of male-headed families and 45 percent of female-headed families.

Most households are in debt.

The median amount owed by debtors ranged from a low of $32,000 among female-headed families to a high of $100,000 among married couples.

Social Security is the most important source of income for older men and women.

Eighty-nine percent of women and 86 percent of men aged 65 or older receive Social Security income.

The expected age of retirement is climbing for both men and women.

Few are "very confident" they will have saved enough for a comfortable retirement, according to the 2013 Retirement Confidence Survey.

Married Couples Have the Greatest Wealth

Male-headed families saw their net worth fall the most.

Married couples had a median net worth (assets minus debts) of $144,559 in 2011, well above the $68,828 median for all households, according to the Census Bureau's Survey of Income and Program Participation. Male-headed families had a net worth of $24,480, and the net worth of female-headed families was just $7,113.

Almost every household type saw its median net worth fall sharply between 2005 and 2011, after adjusting for inflation. For the average household, median net worth fell 36 percent between 2005 and 2011. Married couples saw their net worth fall 28 percent, and the decline was a nearly identical 27 percent for female-headed families. Among male-headed families, however, net worth fell by a larger 43 percent between 2005 and 2011. The only exception to across-the-board declines in net worth occurred among female-headed families with a householder under age 35, but they gained only a few hundred dollars.

Net worth rises with age regardless of household type. It peaks among married couples aged 65 or older at $290,113. Nearly one-third of elderly married couples have a net worth of $500,000 or more. In contrast, more than one-fourth of the youngest married couples have no wealth at all—meaning their liabilities are greater than their assets. Among male- and female-headed family householders under age 35, the percentage with zero or negative net worth was a larger 30 and 43 percent, respectively.

■ Net worth exceeds $100,000 among married couples with a householder aged 35 or older and for male- and female-headed families with a householder aged 65 or older.

The net worth of married couples exceeds $100,000

(median household net worth by type of household, 2011)

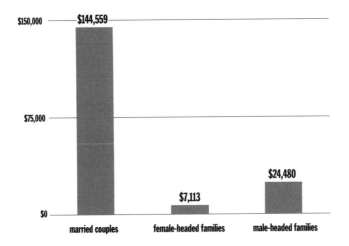

Table 10.1 Median Household Net Worth by Type of Household and Age of Householder, 2005 and 2011

(median household net worth by type of household and age of householder, 2005 and 2011; percent change, 2005–11; in 2011 dollars)

	2011	2005	percent change
Total households	**$68,828**	**$107,344**	**−35.9%**
Married couples	**144,559**	**199,695**	**−27.6**
Under age 35	20,656	38,455	−46.3
Aged 35 to 54	121,845	206,729	−41.1
Aged 55 to 64	244,416	342,822	−28.7
Aged 65 or older	290,113	343,702	−15.6
Female-headed families	**7,113**	**9,681**	**−26.5**
Under age 35	972	576	68.8
Aged 35 to 54	7,113	15,535	−54.2
Aged 55 to 64	59,483	84,251	−29.4
Aged 65 or older	105,218	135,437	−22.3
Male-headed families	**24,480**	**42,596**	**−42.5**
Under age 35	7,113	8,235	−13.6
Aged 35 to 54	26,500	50,816	−47.9
Aged 55 to 64	87,472	141,183	−38.0
Aged 65 or older	122,916	167,005	−26.4

Source: Bureau of the Census, Wealth and Asset Ownership, Survey of Income and Program Participation, Internet site http://www.census.gov/people/wealth/; calculations by New Strategist

Table 10.2 Distribution of Net Worth among Married-Couple Households by Age, 2011

(number of married-couple households, median net worth, and percent distribution of net worth, by age of householder, 2011)

	total couples	under 35	35 to 54	55 to 64	65 or older
Number of married couples	58,041,331	9,198,915	25,747,918	12,321,761	10,772,737
Median net worth	$144,559	$20,656	$121,845	$244,416	$290,113

DISTRIBUTION OF MARRIED-COUPLE HOUSEHOLDS BY NET WORTH

Total married couples	100.0%	100.0%	100.0%	100.0%	100.0%
Zero or negative	12.7	26.0	13.9	8.0	4.1
$1 to $4,999	4.9	10.1	5.0	3.1	2.5
$5,000 to $9,999	3.1	6.0	3.3	2.1	1.3
$10,000 to $24,999	5.5	10.8	5.7	3.5	2.9
$25,000 to $49,999	6.5	10.4	7.4	4.8	3.0
$50,000 to $99,999	9.9	12.5	10.8	7.9	7.7
$100,000 to $249,999	20.3	14.5	20.3	21.4	24.0
$250,000 to $499,999	16.8	6.1	16.8	18.9	23.4
$500,000 or more	20.3	3.6	16.9	30.4	31.1

Source: Bureau of the Census, Wealth and Asset Ownership, Survey of Income and Program Participation, Internet site http://www.census.gov/people/wealth/; calculations by New Strategist

Table 10.3 Distribution of Net Worth among Female-Headed Families by Age, 2011

(number of female-headed families, median net worth, and percent distribution of net worth, by age of householder, 2011)

	total female-headed families	under 35	35 to 54	55 to 64	65 or older
Number of female-headed families	15,333,108	4,078,948	7,361,970	1,974,098	1,918,091
Median net worth	$7,113	$972	$7,113	$59,483	$105,218

DISTRIBUTION OF FEMALE-HEADED HOUSEHOLDS BY NET WORTH

Total female-headed families	100.0%	100.0%	100.0%	100.0%	100.0%
Zero or negative	30.5	42.8	30.8	21.5	12.5
$1 to $4,999	15.4	24.0	14.9	8.4	5.8
$5,000 to $9,999	8.0	12.8	7.6	4.1	3.5
$10,000 to $24,999	6.8	7.4	7.4	4.9	5.3
$25,000 to $49,999	7.2	4.3	8.6	8.9	6.4
$50,000 to $99,999	9.6	3.6	10.3	14.3	15.0
$100,000 to $249,999	11.6	3.2	11.6	17.8	23.3
$250,000 to $499,999	6.3	1.3	5.1	10.6	16.7
$500,000 or more	4.5	0.5	3.6	9.4	11.5

Source: Bureau of the Census, Wealth and Asset Ownership, Survey of Income and Program Participation, Internet site http://www.census.gov/people/wealth/; calculations by New Strategist

Table 10.4 Distribution of Net Worth among Male-Headed Families by Age, 2011

(number of male-headed families, median net worth, and percent distribution of net worth, by age of householder, 2011)

	total male-headed families	under 35	35 to 54	55 to 64	65 or older
Number of male-headed families	5,931,394	1,584,567	2,978,211	738,806	629,811
Median net worth	$24,480	$7,113	$26,500	$87,472	$122,916

DISTRIBUTION OF MALE-HEADED HOUSEHOLDS BY NET WORTH

Total male-headed families	100.0%	100.0%	100.0%	100.0%	100.0%
Zero or negative	21.3	29.6	22.1	12.3	7.2
$1 to $4,999	11.0	14.3	11.1	8.9	4.5
$5,000 to $9,999	8.1	11.6	7.8	4.0	5.9
$10,000 to $24,999	9.9	15.5	8.5	7.6	4.8
$25,000 to $49,999	8.4	5.6	10.2	7.1	8.0
$50,000 to $99,999	11.9	11.7	10.8	13.1	15.9
$100,000 to $249,999	15.1	8.0	15.7	26.9	16.4
$250,000 to $499,999	8.3	2.3	8.4	9.9	21.1
$500,000 or more	6.1	1.3	5.4	10.2	16.2

Source: Bureau of the Census, Wealth and Asset Ownership, Survey of Income and Program Participation, Internet site http://www.census.gov/people/wealth/; calculations by New Strategist

Motor Vehicles Are the Most Commonly Owned Asset

A home is the second most commonly owned asset among married couples.

Most households, regardless of household type, own a motor vehicle. The figure ranges from a high of 94 percent among married couples to a low of 76 percent among female-headed families. Among married couples, a home is the second most common asset, owned by 80 percent. The median equity couples have in their home rises from a low of $20,000 among the youngest couples to a high of $150,000 among couples aged 65 or older.

Among male- and female-headed families, a savings account is the second most common asset, owned by 62 percent of male-headed and 54 percent of female-headed families. In third place is a home, with 57 percent of male-headed families and 45 percent of female-headed families being homeowners.

The majority of married couples have a 401(k) account, and those accounts have a median value of $40,000. A smaller 29 to 36 percent of female- and male-headed families have 401(k) accounts, respectively, with a median value of $12,000 for female-headed families and $22,000 for male-headed families.

■ Among asset owners, the equity held in rental property exceeds the value of all other assets. But few households own rental property—just 8 percent of couples and 2 to 4 percent of female- and male-headed families.

Homeownership is an important asset for many households

(percent of households that own a home by type of household, 2011)

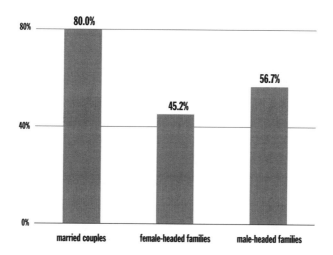

Table 10.5 Asset Ownership of Married-Couple Households by Age, 2011

(percent of total and married-couple households owning selected assets, and median value or equity of asset for owners, by age of married-couple householder, 2011)

	total households	married couples total	under 35	35 to 54	55 to 64	65 or older
PERCENT WITH ASSET						
Interest earning asset at financial institution	69.8%	77.6%	70.8%	76.8%	80.6%	81.8%
Regular checking account	29.0	31.0	32.5	32.8	29.5	26.9
Stocks and mutal fund shares	19.6	26.1	15.0	23.7	31.9	34.3
Own business	13.8	18.6	14.8	21.2	21.7	12.4
Motor vehicles	84.7	93.5	91.9	93.8	94.8	92.7
Own home	65.3	80.0	57.8	79.3	88.3	91.0
Rental property	5.5	7.7	4.0	6.7	10.2	10.3
IRA or KEOGH account	28.9	37.2	21.6	35.5	45.2	45.5
401(k) and thrift savings	42.1	54.3	52.6	63.0	59.0	29.5
MEDIAN VALUE OR EQUITY OF ASSET FOR OWNERS						
Interest earning asset at financial institution	$2,450	$4,100	$2,000	$3,400	$6,000	$8,200
Regular checking account	600	900	700	800	1,000	1,208
Stocks and mutal fund shares	20,000	25,000	6,619	19,000	32,000	65,000
Own business (equity)	8,000	10,000	10,000	10,000	10,000	8,500
Motor vehicles (equity)	6,824	8,613	5,986	8,764	10,302	9,639
Own home (equity)	80,000	86,000	20,000	70,000	118,000	150,000
Rental property (equity)	180,000	200,000	82,000	171,600	220,000	340,000
IRA or KEOGH account	34,000	42,007	11,000	33,000	60,000	75,000
401(k) and thrift savings	30,000	40,000	17,680	40,000	58,500	50,000

Source: Bureau of the Census, Wealth and Asset Ownership, Survey of Income and Program Participation, Internet site http://www.census.gov/people/wealth/; calculations by New Strategist

Table 10.6 Asset Ownership of Female-Headed Families by Age, 2011

(percent of total and female-headed family households owning selected assets, and median value or equity of asset for owners, by age of female-headed family householder, 2011)

	total households	female-headed				
		total	under 35	35 to 54	55 to 64	65 or older
PERCENT WITH ASSET						
Interest earning asset at financial institution	69.8%	53.5%	37.5%	56.8%	66.5%	61.7%
Regular checking account	29.0	29.7	24.1	30.1	39.6	29.9
Stocks and mutal fund shares	19.6	7.9	1.7	8.5	12.8	13.8
Own business	13.8	8.4	6.4	8.9	9.8	9.4
Motor vehicles	84.7	76.1	66.8	78.6	83.4	79.1
Own home	65.3	45.2	19.3	45.4	66.4	77.6
Rental property	5.5	1.9	0.4	1.6	3.3	4.7
IRA or KEOGH account	28.9	14.5	5.2	15.3	25.4	19.7
401(k) and thrift savings	42.1	29.3	16.7	35.7	38.8	21.6
MEDIAN VALUE OR EQUITY OF ASSET FOR OWNERS						
Interest earning asset at financial institution	$2,450	$500	$198	$500	$1,150	$1,800
Regular checking account	600	200	106	200	400	400
Stocks and mutal fund shares	20,000	7,350	–	7,000	7,000	14,000
Own business (equity)	8,000	2,500	2,000	2,000	–	–
Motor vehicles (equity)	6,824	4,393	3,113	4,313	5,447	6,149
Own home (equity)	80,000	56,000	16,000	48,000	73,000	118,000
Rental property (equity)	180,000	157,000	–	–	–	–
IRA or KEOGH account	34,000	15,000	1,900	16,266	24,000	21,000
401(k) and thrift savings	30,000	12,000	4,500	12,000	24,000	20,000

Note: "–" means sample is too small to make a reliable estimate.
Source: Bureau of the Census, Wealth and Asset Ownership, Survey of Income and Program Participation, Internet site http://www.census.gov/people/wealth/; calculations by New Strategist

Table 10.7 Asset Ownership of Male-Headed Families by Age, 2011

(percent of total and male-headed family households owning selected assets, and median value or equity of asset for owners, by age of male-headed family householder, 2011)

	total households	male-headed total	under 35	35 to 54	55 to 64	65 or older
PERCENT WITH ASSET						
Interest earning asset at financial institution	69.8%	62.3%	59.6%	61.1%	63.6%	73.4%
Regular checking account	29.0	32.1	29.9	32.0	39.3	29.2
Stocks and mutal fund shares	19.6	10.8	9.5	9.5	14.4	16.2
Own business	13.8	13.9	8.2	18.4	14.0	6.7
Motor vehicles	84.7	84.0	78.5	86.3	84.4	86.4
Own home	65.3	56.7	35.3	59.4	69.1	84.0
Rental property	5.5	3.6	0.9	4.3	8.0	1.8
IRA or KEOGH account	28.9	18.0	13.3	16.0	31.2	23.9
401(k) and thrift savings	42.1	36.1	29.5	40.2	40.3	28.2
MEDIAN VALUE OR EQUITY OF ASSET FOR OWNERS						
Interest earning asset at financial institution	$2,450	$1,000	$500	$1,000	$1,700	$5,100
Regular checking account	600	400	600	300	690	–
Stocks and mutal fund shares	20,000	6,000	–	4,000	–	–
Own business (equity)	8,000	10,000	–	10,000	–	–
Motor vehicles (equity)	6,824	5,760	5,070	5,549	7,113	6,622
Own home (equity)	80,000	46,000	30,000	30,000	74,000	100,000
Rental property (equity)	180,000	64,000	–	–	–	–
IRA or KEOGH account	34,000	19,000	7,759	19,000	20,000	–
401(k) and thrift savings	30,000	22,000	10,000	30,000	35,000	–

Note: "–" means sample is too small to make a reliable estimate.
Source: Bureau of the Census, Wealth and Asset Ownership, Survey of Income and Program Participation, Internet site http://www.census.gov/people/wealth/; calculations by New Strategist

Most Households Are in Debt

Married couples owe the most.

Most households, regardless of household type, are in debt. The figure ranges from a high of 80 percent among married couples to a low of 64 percent among female-headed families.

Four types of debt are most common: home-secured (mortgage), credit card, vehicle loan, and "other" debt—a category that includes student loans. Home-secured debt is the most common type among married couples (54 percent) and male-headed families (37 percent), followed by credit card debt, vehicle debt, and other debt. Credit card debt is most common among female-headed families (35 percent), followed by home-secured debt, vehicle loans, and other debt.

Married couples with debt owe the most money, a median of $100,000 in 2011. Female-headed families with debt owe a median of $32,000, and male-headed families with debt owe $57,000. Home-secured debt is the largest for the three types of households, and business debt ranks second—but few households own businesses. Other debt (much of it student loans) exceeds vehicle debt among male- and female-headed families.

■ Fewer than half of households have outstanding credit card debt, and the median amount owed by those with credit card debt ranges from $3,000 to $4,000.

Married couples are most likely to be in debt

(percent of households with debt by type of household, 2011)

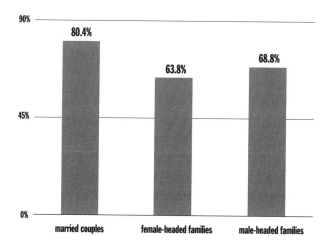

Table 10.8 Debt of Married-Couple Households by Age, 2011

(percent of total and married-couple households with debt, and median amount of debt for debtors, by age of married-couple householder, 2011)

	total households	married couples				
		total	under 35	35 to 54	55 to 64	65 or older
PERCENT WITH DEBT						
Total debt	**69.0%**	**80.4%**	**84.8%**	**88.2%**	**81.4%**	**56.6%**
Secured debt	55.3	69.3	72.0	78.9	70.9	42.2
Home debt	40.5	54.2	51.0	65.5	54.8	29.2
Business debt	4.1	6.0	5.0	7.0	7.2	3.2
Vehicle debt	30.4	39.4	50.6	45.3	36.3	19.3
Unsecured debt	46.2	54.2	61.0	60.3	53.2	35.0
Credit card debt	38.3	45.8	45.9	51.4	46.7	31.3
Loans	6.8	8.6	10.3	9.8	8.2	4.9
Other debt	18.6	21.7	36.6	24.7	17.3	7.0
MEDIAN AMOUNT OF DEBT FOR DEBTORS						
Total debt	**$70,000**	**$100,000**	**$102,750**	**$122,500**	**$86,000**	**$34,000**
Secured debt	91,000	110,000	113,200	128,900	94,000	58,000
Home debt	117,000	128,000	140,000	140,000	100,000	87,000
Business debt	25,000	25,000	25,000	25,000	30,000	25,000
Vehicle debt	10,000	11,000	11,500	12,000	10,700	10,000
Unsecured debt	7,000	8,000	10,000	9,000	6,870	4,002
Credit card debt	3,500	4,000	3,500	4,700	4,000	3,000
Loans	7,000	8,000	7,000	8,000	9,000	7,800
Other debt	10,000	10,000	13,000	11,000	10,000	3,000

Note: "Other debt" includes student loans.
Source: Bureau of the Census, Wealth and Asset Ownership, Survey of Income and Program Participation, Internet site http:// www.census.gov/people/wealth/; calculations by New Strategist

Table 10.9 Debt of Female-Headed Families by Age, 2011

(percent of total and female-headed families with debt, and median amount of debt for debtors, by age of female-headed family householder, 2011)

	total households	female-headed				
		total	under 35	35 to 54	55 to 64	65 or older
PERCENT WITH DEBT						
Total debt	**69.0%**	**63.8%**	**53.8%**	**68.6%**	**74.2%**	**55.9%**
Secured debt	55.3	45.7	34.4	49.6	59.9	39.8
Home debt	40.5	28.8	14.5	33.9	41.6	26.4
Business debt	4.1	2.1	1.7	1.9	3.9	1.7
Vehicle debt	30.4	26.0	25.0	27.1	29.9	20.1
Unsecured debt	46.2	44.6	38.6	47.0	53.1	39.9
Credit card debt	38.3	34.7	25.6	36.3	46.2	35.4
Loans	6.8	5.9	5.3	6.2	5.8	5.8
Other debt	18.6	22.0	23.1	23.6	21.6	13.5
MEDIAN AMOUNT OF DEBT FOR DEBTORS						
Total debt	**$70,000**	**$32,000**	**$15,000**	**$40,000**	**$53,800**	**$29,000**
Secured debt	91,000	54,000	16,000	65,000	71,157	40,000
Home debt	117,000	97,000	103,000	98,500	101,000	67,000
Business debt	25,000	20,500	–	–	–	–
Vehicle debt	10,000	8,000	7,000	8,000	9,000	7,600
Unsecured debt	7,000	7,000	6,000	7,500	7,000	7,000
Credit card debt	3,500	3,000	2,000	3,000	3,500	3,799
Loans	7,000	5,000	3,000	5,000	–	–
Other debt	10,000	10,000	10,000	11,000	10,000	10,000

Note: "Other debt" includes student loans. "–" means sample is too small to make a reliable estimate.
Source: Bureau of the Census, Wealth and Asset Ownership, Survey of Income and Program Participation, Internet site http://www.census.gov/people/wealth/; calculations by New Strategist

Table 10.10 Debt of Male-Headed Families by Age, 2011

(percent of total and male-headed families with debt and median amount of debt for debtors, by age of male-headed family householder, 2011)

	total households	male-headed				
		total	under 35	35 to 54	55 to 64	65 or older
PERCENT WITH DEBT						
Total debt	**69.0%**	**68.8%**	**69.6%**	**70.9%**	**70.8%**	**54.6%**
Secured debt	55.3	54.2	47.9	60.0	61.4	34.5
Home debt	40.5	36.7	26.3	43.3	43.8	23.3
Business debt	4.1	3.6	2.3	5.0	3.2	0.9
Vehicle debt	30.4	30.4	29.7	33.1	32.6	16.6
Unsecured debt	46.2	43.5	49.5	42.4	41.0	36.3
Credit card debt	38.3	34.5	34.7	35.8	34.0	28.4
Loans	6.8	6.9	6.1	7.8	7.2	4.2
Other debt	18.6	19.7	27.7	15.5	21.3	18.0
MEDIAN AMOUNT OF DEBT FOR DEBTORS						
Total debt	**$70,000**	**$57,000**	**$28,000**	**$89,000**	**$61,000**	**$23,100**
Secured debt	91,000	87,000	61,000	101,000	77,000	38,000
Home debt	117,000	118,000	107,000	130,000	100,000	–
Business debt	25,000	62,500	–	–	–	–
Vehicle debt	10,000	9,000	9,200	10,000	8,500	–
Unsecured debt	7,000	8,100	9,000	8,000	8,688	7,700
Credit card debt	3,500	3,800	2,700	4,000	3,500	–
Loans	7,000	6,000	–	7,000	–	–
Other debt	10,000	10,000	10,000	7,500	–	–

Note: "Other debt" includes student loans. "–" means sample is too small to make a reliable estimate.
Source: Bureau of the Census, Wealth and Asset Ownership, Survey of Income and Program Participation, Internet site http://www.census.gov/people/wealth/; calculations by New Strategist

Social Security Is the Top Income Source for Older Men and Women

Among people aged 65 or older, men are more likely than women to receive pension income.

Social Security is by far the most important source of income for people aged 65 or older. Nearly 90 percent of women and 86 percent of men in the age group receive Social Security income. Women received a median of $11,439 from Social Security in 2011, and men received a larger $15,881. Men's Social Security income is higher than women's because it is based on earnings, and on average men earn more than women. The second most common source of income for older Americans is interest—53 percent of men and 47 percent of women aged 65 or older receive interest income, but the median amount received is tiny compared with Social Security.

Forty-three percent of men receive retirement income, and 41 percent pension income. Among women, the figures are smaller—29 and 23 percent, respectively. For those who receive these income streams, the amount is substantial, however: more than $15,000 a year from each source for men and more than $9,000 from each for women. Twenty-seven percent of men and 17 percent of women aged 65 or older have earnings from work, and for those who do the median exceeds that from any other income source—nearly $31,000 for men and $19,000 for women.

■ A growing share of the elderly will receive earnings in the years ahead as labor force participation climbs in the older age groups.

Men are more likely than women to have pension income

(percent of people aged 65 or older receiving Social Security, pension, and earnings income, by sex, 2011)

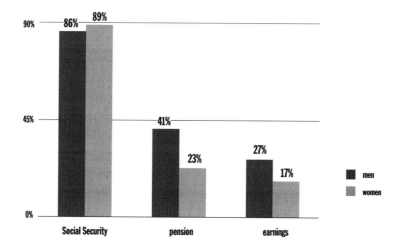

Table 10.11 Source of Income for Women Aged 65 or Older, 2011

(number of total people aged 65 or older receiving income, number and percent of women receiving income, and women's share of total, 2011; ranked by number of total people receiving income; people in thousands as of 2012)

	total people receiving income	women receiving income number	women receiving income percent	women's share of total
Total aged 65 or older	**40,195**	**22,276**	**100.0%**	**55.4%**
Social Security	35,169	19,810	88.9	56.3
Interest	19,862	10,397	46.7	52.3
Retirement income	14,325	6,542	29.4	45.7
Pension income	12,460	5,156	23.1	41.4
Earnings	8,648	3,740	16.8	43.2
Dividends	7,584	3,665	16.5	48.3
Rents, royalties, estates, or trusts	3,103	1,525	6.8	49.1
Survivor benefits	1,859	1,523	6.8	81.9
Veterans benefits	1,299	211	0.9	16.2
SSI (Supplemental Security Income)	1,297	899	4.0	69.3

Source: Bureau of the Census, 2012 Current Population Survey Annual Social and Economic Supplement, Internet site http://www.census.gov/hhes/www/cpstables/032012/perinc/toc.htm; calculations by New Strategist

Table 10.12 Source of Income for Men Aged 65 or Older, 2011

(number of total people aged 65 or older receiving income, number and percent of men receiving income, and men's share of total, 2011; ranked by number of total people receiving income; people in thousands as of 2012)

	total people receiving income	men receiving income number	men receiving income percent	men's share of total
Total aged 65 or older	**40,195**	**17,918**	**100.0%**	**44.6%**
Social Security	35,169	15,360	85.7	43.7
Interest	19,862	9,464	52.8	47.6
Retirement income	14,325	7,783	43.4	54.3
Pension income	12,460	7,304	40.8	58.6
Earnings	8,648	4,908	27.4	56.8
Dividends	7,584	3,919	21.9	51.7
Rents, royalties, estates, or trusts	3,103	1,578	8.8	50.9
Survivor benefits	1,859	336	1.9	18.1
Veterans benefits	1,299	1,089	6.1	83.8
SSI (Supplemental Security Income)	1,297	398	2.2	30.7

Source: Bureau of the Census, 2012 Current Population Survey Annual Social and Economic Supplement, Internet site http://www.census.gov/hhes/www/cpstables/032012/perinc/toc.htm; calculations by New Strategist

Table 10.13 Median Income of People Aged 65 or Older by Source, 2011

(median income received by people aged 65 or older by sex, and women's income as a percent of men's, by type of income, 2011)

	median income for total people receiving income	median income for men receiving income	median income for women receiving income	women's income as a percent of men's
Total aged 65 or older	**$19,939**	**$27,707**	**$15,362**	**77%**
Social Security	13,376	15,881	11,439	86
Interest	1,590	1,620	1,563	98
Retirement income	12,282	15,568	9,193	75
Pension income	12,458	15,515	9,024	72
Earnings	24,893	30,841	19,260	77
Dividends	2,023	2,075	1,969	97
Rents, royalties, estates, or trusts	3,855	3,822	3,881	101
Survivor benefits	7,913	11,508	7,437	94
Veterans' benefits	8,770	7,469	11,733	134
SSI (Supplemental Security Income)	5,322	6,660	4,710	89

Source: Bureau of the Census, 2012 Current Population Survey Annual Social and Economic Supplement, Internet site http://www.census.gov/hhes/www/cpstables/032012/perinc/toc.htm; calculations by New Strategist

Expected Age of Retirement Is Climbing

Many workers lack confidence in having enough money for a comfortable retirement.

Although most working men and women say they have saved for retirement, most are not confident they will have enough saved to live comfortably throughout retirement. Only 17 percent of men and 10 percent of women are "very confident" in their ability to afford a comfortable retirement, according to the 2013 Retirement Confidence Survey of the Employee Benefit Research Institute. Only 18 percent of men and 15 percent of women are "very confident" they are doing a good job of preparing financially for retirement.

Perhaps because of this lack of confidence, most workers expect to postpone retirement until age 65 or older. Sixty-eight percent of workers (69 percent of men and 67 percent of women) say they won't retire until age 65 or older. This figure is up from 57 percent before the Great Recession in 2007.

■ Only 17 percent of men and 11 percent of women are "very confident" in having enough money to take care of medical expenses in retirement.

Few men and women will opt for early retirement

(percent of workers who expect to retire before age 65, by sex, 2013)

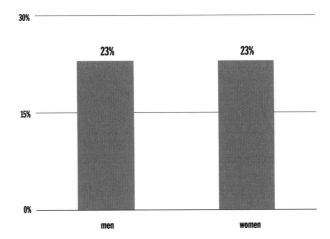

Table 10.14 Retirement Attitudes and Planning by Sex of Worker, 2013

(responses of workers aged 25 or older to selected questions about retirement, by sex, 2013)

	total	men	women
Percentage of workers who have saved for retirement	**66%**	**66%**	**66%**
RETIREMENT SAVINGS INDICATORS			
Currently saving for retirement	57	58	56
Currently offered workplace retirement savings plan	46	48	45
Contribute to workplace retirement savings plan	38	40	36
Have an IRA	47	46	47
PERCENTAGE "VERY CONFIDENT" IN			
Having enough money to live comfortably throughout retirement	13	17	10
Having enough money to take care of basic expenses in retirement	25	30	21
Doing a good job of preparing financially for retirement	17	18	15
Having enough money to take care of medical expenses in retirement	14	17	11
The Social Security system continuing to provide benefits of at least equal value to the benefits received by retirees today	5	5	6
The Medicare system continuing to provide benefits of at least equal value to the benefits received by retirees today	6	7	5

Source: Employee Benefit Research Institute, 2013 Retirement Confidence Survey, Internet site http://www.ebri.org/surveys/rcs/2013/

Table 10.15 Expected Age of Retirement by Sex, 2013

(percent distribution of workers aged 25 or older by expected age of retirement, by sex, 2013)

	total	men	women
Total workers	**100%**	**100%**	**100%**
Before age 60	9	11	7
Aged 60 to 64	14	12	16
Age 65	25	22	28
Aged 66 to 69	10	11	10
Age 70 or older	26	29	23
Never retire	7	7	6
Don't know	8	7	8

Source: Employee Benefit Research Institute, 2013 Retirement Confidence Survey, Internet site http://www.ebri.org/surveys/rcs/2013/

Glossary

adjusted for inflation Income or a change in income that has been adjusted for the rise in the cost of living, or the consumer price index.

age Classification by age is based on the age of the person at his/her last birthday.

American Community Survey The ACS is an on-going nationwide survey of 250,000 households per month, providing detailed demographic data at the community level. Designed to replace the census long-form questionnaire, the ACS includes more than 60 questions that formerly appeared on the long form, such as questions about language spoken at home, income, and education. ACS data are available for areas as small as census tracts.

American Housing Survey The AHS collects national and metropolitan-level data on the nation's housing, including apartments, single-family homes, and mobile homes. The nationally representative survey, with a sample of 55,000 homes, is conducted by the Census Bureau for the Department of Housing and Urban Development every other year.

American Indians American Indians include Alaska Natives unless those groups are shown separately.

American Time Use Survey Under contract with the Bureau of Labor Statistics, the Census Bureau collects ATUS information, revealing how people spend their time. The ATUS sample is drawn from U.S. households completing their final month of interviews for the Current Population Survey. One individual from each selected household is chosen to participate in ATUS. Respondents are interviewed by telephone about their time use during the previous 24 hours.

Asian The term "Asian" includes Native Hawaiians and other Pacific Islanders unless those groups are shown separately.

baby boom Americans born between 1946 and 1964.

baby bust Americans born between 1965 and 1976, also known as Generation X.

Behavioral Risk Factor Surveillance System The BRFSS is a collaborative project of the Centers for

Disease Control and Prevention and U.S. states and territories. It is an ongoing data collection program designed to measure behavioral risk factors in the adult population aged 18 or older. All 50 states, three territories, and the District of Columbia take part in the survey, making the BRFSS the primary source of information on the health-related behaviors of Americans.

black The black racial category includes those who identified themselves as "black" or "African American."

Consumer Expenditure Survey The CEX is an ongoing study of the day-to-day spending of American households administered by the Bureau of Labor Statistics. The CEX includes an interview survey and a diary survey. The average spending figures shown are the integrated data from both the diary and interview components of the survey. Two separate, nationally representative samples are used for the interview and diary surveys. For the interview survey, about 7,500 consumer units are interviewed on a rotating panel basis each quarter for five consecutive quarters. For the diary survey, 7,500 consumer units keep weekly diaries of spending for two consecutive weeks.

consumer unit *(on spending tables only)* For convenience, the term consumer unit and household are used interchangeably in the spending section of this book, although consumer units are somewhat different from the Census Bureau's households. A consumer unit includes all the related members of a household or any financially independent member of a household. A household may include more than one consumer unit.

Current Population Survey The CPS is a nationally representative survey of the civilian noninstitutional population aged 15 or older. It is taken monthly by the Census Bureau for the Bureau of Labor Statistics, collecting information from 60,000 households on employment and unemployment. In March of each year, the survey includes the Annual Social and Economic Supplement, which is the source of most national data on the characteristics of Americans, such as educational attainment, living arrangements, and incomes.

disability The National Health Interview Survey

estimates the number of people aged 18 or older who have difficulty in physical functioning, probing whether respondents could perform nine activities by themselves without using special equipment. The categories are walking a quarter mile; standing for two hours; sitting for two hours; walking up 10 steps without resting; stooping, bending, kneeling; reaching over one's head; grasping or handling small objects; carrying a 10-pound object; and pushing/pulling a large object. Adults who reported that any of these activities was very difficult or they could not do it at all were defined as having physical difficulties.

dual-earner couple A married couple in which both the householder and the householder's spouse are in the labor force.

earnings A type of income, earnings is the amount of money a person receives from his or her job. *See also* Income.

employed All civilians who did any work as a paid employee or farmer/self-employed worker or who worked 15 hours or more as an unpaid farm worker or in a family-owned business during the reference period. All those who have jobs but are temporarily absent from their jobs due to illness, bad weather, vacation, labor management dispute, or personal reasons are considered employed.

expenditure The transaction cost including excise and sales taxes of goods and services acquired during the survey period. The full cost of each purchase is recorded even though full payment may not have been made at the date of purchase. Average expenditure figures may be artificially low for infrequently purchased items such as cars because figures are calculated using all consumer units within a demographic segment rather than just purchasers. Expenditure estimates include money spent on gifts for others.

family A group of two or more people (one of whom is the householder) related by birth, marriage, or adoption and living in the same household.

family household A household maintained by a householder who lives with one or more people related to him or her by blood, marriage, or adoption.

female/male householder A woman or man who maintains a household without a spouse present. May head family or nonfamily household.

foreign-born population People who are not U.S. citizens at birth.

full-time employment Full-time is 35 or more hours of work per week during a majority of the weeks worked.

full-time, year-round Indicates 50 or more weeks of full-time employment during the previous calendar year.

General Social Survey The GSS is a biennial survey of the attitudes of Americans taken by the University of Chicago's National Opinion Research Center. NORC conducts the GSS through face-to-face interviews with an independently drawn, representative sample of 1,500 to 3,000 noninstitutionalized people aged 18 or older who live in the United States.

generation X Americans born between 1965 and 1976, also known as the baby-bust generation.

Hispanic Because Hispanic is an ethnic origin rather than a race, Hispanics may be of any race. While most Hispanics are white, there are black, Asian, American Indian, and even Native Hawaiian Hispanics.

household All the persons who occupy a housing unit. A household includes the related family members and all the unrelated persons, if any, such as lodgers, foster children, wards, or employees who share the housing unit. A person living alone is counted as a household. A group of unrelated people who share a housing unit as roommates or unmarried partners is also counted as a household. Households do not include group quarters such as college dormitories, prisons, or nursing homes.

household, race/ethnicity of Households are categorized according to the race or ethnicity of the householder only.

householder The householder is the person (or one of the persons) in whose name the housing unit is owned or rented or, if there is no such person, any adult member. With married couples, the householder may be either the husband or wife. The householder is the reference person for the household.

householder, age of The age of the householder is used to categorize households into age groups such as those used in this book. Married couples, for example, are classified according to the age of either the husband or wife, depending on which one identified him- or herself as the householder.

housing unit A housing unit is a house, an apartment, a group of rooms, or a single room occupied or intended for occupancy as separate living quarters. Separate living quarters are those in which the occupants do not live and eat with any other persons in the structure and that have direct access from the outside of the building or through a common hall that is used or intended for use by the occupants of another unit or by the general public. The occupants may be a single family, one person living alone, two or more families living together, or any other group of related or unrelated persons who share living arrangements.

Housing Vacancy Survey The HVS is a supplement to the Current Population Survey, providing quarterly and annual data on rental and homeowner vacancy rates, characteristics of units available for occupancy, and homeownership rates by age, household type, region, state, and metropolitan area. The Current Population Survey sample includes 60,000 occupied housing units and about 9,000 vacant units.

housing value The respondent's estimate of how much his or her house and lot would sell for if it were for sale.

iGeneration Americans born between 1995 and 2009.

immigrants Aliens admitted for legal permanent residence in the United States.

income Money received in the preceding calendar year by a person aged 15 or older from any of the following sources: earnings from longest job (or self-employment), earnings from jobs other than longest job, unemployment compensation, workers' compensation, Social Security, Supplemental Security income, public assistance, veterans' payments, survivor benefits, disability benefits, retirement pensions, interest, dividends, rents and royalties or estates and trusts, educational assistance, alimony, child support, financial assistance from outside the household, and other periodic income. Income is reported in several ways in this book. Household income is the combined income of all household members. Income of persons is all income accruing to a person from all sources. Earnings are the money a person receives from his or her job.

industry Refers to the industry in which a person worked longest in the preceding calendar year.

job tenure The length of time a person has been employed continuously by the same employer.

labor force The labor force tables in this book show the civilian labor force only. The labor force includes both the employed and the unemployed (people who are looking for work). People are counted as in the labor force if they were working or looking for work during the reference week in which the Census Bureau fields the Current Population Survey.

labor force participation rate The percent of the civilian noninstitutional population that is in the civilian labor force, which includes both the employed and the unemployed.

male householder *See* Female/Male Householder.

married couples with or without children under age 18 Refers to married couples with or without own children under age 18 living in the same household. Couples without children under age 18 may be parents of grown children who live elsewhere or they could be childless couples.

median The median is the amount that divides the population or households into two equal portions: one below and one above the median. Medians can be calculated for income, age, and many other characteristics.

median income The amount that divides the income distribution into two equal groups, half having incomes above the median, half having incomes below the median. The medians for households or families are based on all households or families. The median for persons are based on all persons aged 15 or older with income.

metropolitan statistical area, or MSA To be defined as an MSA, an area must include a city with 50,000 or more inhabitants, or a Census Bureau–defined urbanized area of at least 50,000 inhabitants and a total metropolitan population of at least 100,000 (75,000 in New England). The county (or counties) that contains the largest city becomes the "central county" (counties), along with any adjacent counties that have at least 50 percent of their population in the urbanized area surrounding the largest city. Additional "outlying counties" are included in the MSA if they meet specified requirements of commuting to the central counties and other selected requirements of metropolitan character (such as population density and percent urban). In New England, MSAs are defined in terms of cities and towns rather than counties. For this reason, the concept of New England County Metropolitan Area is used to define metropolitan areas in the New England division.

millennial generation Americans born between 1977 and 1994.

mobility status People are classified according to their mobility status on the basis of a comparison between their place of residence at the time of the March Current Population Survey and their place of residence in March of the previous year. Nonmovers are people living in the same house at the end of the period as at the beginning of the period. Movers are people living in a different house at the end of the period from that at the beginning of the period. Movers from abroad are either citizens or aliens whose place of residence is outside the United States at the beginning of the period, that is, in an outlying area under the jurisdiction of the United States or in a foreign country. The mobility status for children is fully allocated from the mother if she is in the household; otherwise it is allocated from the householder.

National Health and Nutrition Examination Survey The NHANES is a continuous survey of a representative sample of the United States civilian noninstitutionalized population. Respondents are interviewed at home about their health and nutrition, and the interview is followed up by a physical examination that measures such things as height and weight in mobile examination centers.

National Health Interview Survey The NHIS is a continuing nationwide sample survey of the civilian noninstitutional population of the United States conducted by the Census Bureau for the National Center for Health Statistics. In interviews each year, data are collected from more than 100,000 people about their illnesses, injuries, impairments, chronic and acute conditions, activity limitations, and use of health services.

National Survey of Family Growth Sponsored by the National Center for Health Statistics, the NSFG is a periodic nationally representative survey of the civilian noninstitutionalized population aged 15 to 44. In-person interviews are completed with men and women, collecting data on marriage, divorce, contraception, and infertility. The 2006–10 survey updates previous NSFG surveys taken in 1973, 1976, 1988, and 1995, and 2002.

National Survey on Drug Use and Health The NSDUH is an annual survey of a nationally representative sample of people aged 12 or older living in households, noninstitutional group quarters (such as college dorms), and military bases in the United States. It is the primary source of information about illegal drug use in the United States and has been conducted since 1971. Interviews are held in person and incorporate procedures (such as anonymity and computer-assisted interviewing) that will increase respondents' cooperation and willingness to report honestly about their illicit drug use behavior.

nonfamily household A household maintained by a householder who lives alone or who lives with people to whom he or she is not related.

nonfamily householder A householder who lives alone or with nonrelatives.

non-Hispanic People who do not identify themselves as Hispanic are classified as non-Hispanic. Non-Hispanics may be of any race.

non-Hispanic white People who identify their race as white and who do not indicate a Hispanic origin.

nonmetropolitan area Counties that are not classified as metropolitan areas.

occupation Occupational classification is based on the kind of work a person did at his or her job during the previous calendar year. If a person changed jobs during the year, the data refer to the occupation of the job held the longest during that year.

occupied housing units A housing unit is classified as occupied if a person or group of people is living in it or if the occupants are only temporarily absent—on vacation, for example. By definition, the count of occupied housing units is the same as the count of households.

outside principal city The portion of a metropolitan county or counties that falls outside of the principal city or cities; generally regarded as the suburbs.

own children Own children are sons and daughters, including stepchildren and adopted children, of the householder. The totals include never-married children living away from home in college dormitories.

owner occupied A housing unit is "owner occupied" if the owner lives in the unit, even if it is mortgaged or not fully paid for. A cooperative or condominium unit is "owner occupied" only if the owner lives in it. All other occupied units are classified as "renter occupied."

part-time employment Part-time is less than 35 hours of work per week in a majority of the weeks worked during the year.

percent change The change (either positive or negative) in a measure that is expressed as a proportion of the starting measure. When median income changes from $20,000 to $25,000, for example, this is a 25 percent increase.

percentage point change The change (either positive or negative) in a value that is already expressed as a percentage. When a labor force participation rate changes from 70 percent to 75 percent, for example, this is a 5 percentage point increase.

poverty level The official income threshold below which families and people are classified as living in poverty. The threshold rises each year with inflation and varies depending on family size and age of householder.

principal city The largest city in a metropolitan area is called the principal or central city. The balance of the metropolitan area outside the principal or central city is regarded as the "suburbs."

proportion or share The value of a part expressed as a percentage of the whole. If there are 4 million people aged 25 and 3 million of them are white, then the white proportion is 75 percent.

race Race is self-reported and can be defined in three ways. The "race alone" population comprises people who identify themselves as being of only one race. The "race in combination" population comprises people who identify themselves as being of more than one race, such as white and black. The "race, alone or in combination" population includes both those who identify themselves as being of one race and those who identify themselves as being of more than one race.

recession generation Americans born from 2010 to the present.

regions The four major regions and nine census divisions of the United States are the state groupings as shown below:

Northeast:
—New England: Connecticut, Maine, Massachusetts, New Hampshire, Rhode Island, and Vermont

—Middle Atlantic: New Jersey, New York, and Pennsylvania

Midwest:
—East North Central: Illinois, Indiana, Michigan, Ohio, and Wisconsin

—West North Central: Iowa, Kansas, Minnesota, Missouri, Nebraska, North Dakota, and South Dakota

South:
—South Atlantic: Delaware, District of Columbia, Florida, Georgia, Maryland, North Carolina, South Carolina, Virginia, and West Virginia

—East South Central: Alabama, Kentucky, Mississippi, and Tennessee

—West South Central: Arkansas, Louisiana, Oklahoma, and Texas

West:
—Mountain: Arizona, Colorado, Idaho, Montana, Nevada, New Mexico, Utah, and Wyoming

—Pacific: Alaska, California, Hawaii, Oregon, and Washington

renter occupied *See* Owner Occupied.

Retirement Confidence Survey The RCS—sponsored by the Employee Benefit Research Institute, the American Savings Education Council, and Mathew Greenwald & Associates—is an annual survey of a nationally representative sample of 1,000 people aged 25 or older. Respondents are asked a core set of questions that have been included in the survey since 1996, measuring attitudes and behavior toward retirement. Additional questions are asked about current retirement issues.

rounding Percentages are rounded to the nearest tenth of a percent; therefore, the percentages in a distribution do not always add exactly to 100.0 percent. The totals, however, are always shown as 100.0. Moreover, individual figures are rounded to the nearest thousand without being adjusted to group totals, which are independently rounded; percentages are based on the unrounded numbers.

self-employment A person is categorized as self-employed if he or she was self-employed in the job held longest during the reference period. Persons who report self-employment from a second job are excluded, but those who report wage and salary income from a second job are included. Unpaid workers in family businesses are excluded. Self-employment statistics include only nonagricultural workers and exclude people who work for themselves in incorporated business.

sex ratio The number of men per 100 women.

Survey of Income and Program Participation
The Survey of Income and Program Participation is a continuous, monthly panel survey of up to 36,700 households conducted by the Census Bureau. It is designed to measure the effectiveness of existing federal, state, and local programs and to measure economic well-being, including wealth, asset ownership, and debt.

unemployed Unemployed people are those who, during the survey period, had no employment but were available and looking for work. Those who were laid off from their jobs and were waiting to be recalled are also classified as unemployed.

white The "white" racial category includes many Hispanics (who may be of any race) unless the term "non-Hispanic white" is used.

Youth Risk Behavior Surveillance System The YRBSS was created by the Centers for Disease Control to monitor health risks being taken by young people at the national, state, and local level. The national survey is taken every two years based on a nationally representative sample of 16,000 students in 9th through 12th grade in public and private schools.

Bibliography

Bureau of Labor Statistics
  Internet site http://www.bls.gov/
  —American Time Use Survey, unpublished tables, Internet site http://www.bls.gov/tus/
  —Characteristics of Minimum Wage Workers, 2011, Internet site http://www.bls.gov/cps/minwage2011tbls.htm
  —Consumer Expenditure Survey, Internet site http://www.bls.gov/cex/home.htm
  —Current Population Survey, Internet site http://www.bls.gov/cps/tables.htm#empstat
  —Employee Tenure, Internet site http://www.bls.gov/news.release/tenure.toc.htm
  —Employment Characteristics of Families, Internet site http://www.bls.gov/news.release/famee.toc.htm
  —*Monthly Labor Review*, "Labor Force Projections to 2020: A More Slowly Growing Workforce," January 2012, Internet site http://www.bls.gov/opub/mlr/2012/01/home.htm

Bureau of the Census
  Internet site http://www.census.gov/
  —2000 Census, American Factfinder, Internet site http://factfinder2.census.gov/faces/nav/jsf/pages/index.xhtml
  —2010 Census, American Factfinder, Internet site http://factfinder2.census.gov/faces/nav/jsf/pages/index.xhtml
  —American Community Survey, American Factfinder, Internet site http://factfinder2.census.gov/faces/nav/jsf/pages/index.xhtml
  —Current Population Survey, Annual Social and Economic Supplement, Internet site http://www.census.gov/hhes/www/income/data/
  —Educational Attainment, Annual Social and Economic Supplement, Internet site http://www.census.gov/hhes/socdemo/education/
  —Families and Living Arrangements, Current Population Survey Annual Social and Economic Supplement, Internet site http://www.census.gov/hhes/families/
  —Families and Living Arrangements, Historical Time Series, Internet site http://www.census.gov/hhes/families/data/historical.html
  —Fertility, Historical Time Series Tables, Internet site http://www.census.gov/hhes/fertility/data/cps/historical.html
  —Gender: 2000, Census 2000 Brief, Internet site http://www.census.gov/population/www/cen2000/briefs/
  —Geographic Mobility/Migration, Current Population Survey Annual Social and Economic Supplement, Internet site http://www.census.gov/hhes/migration/
  —Health Insurance, Current Population Survey Annual Social and Economic Supplements, Internet site http://www.census.gov/hhes/www/cpstables/032012/health/toc.htm
  —Historical Income Data, Current Population Survey Annual Social and Economic Supplements, Internet site http://www.census.gov/hhes/www/income/data/historical/index.html

—Historical Poverty Tables, Current Population Survey Annual Social and Economic Supplements, Internet site http://www.census.gov/hhes/www/poverty/data/historical/index.html

—Income, Current Population Survey Annual Social and Economic Supplements, Internet site http://www.census.gov/hhes/www/income/data/index.html

—Number, Timing, and Duration of Marriages and Divorces: 2009, Detailed Tables, Internet site http://www.census.gov/hhes/socdemo/marriage/data/sipp/2009/tables.html

—Population Estimates, Internet site http://www.census.gov/popest/index.html

—Population Projections, Internet site http://www.census.gov/population/projections/

—Poverty, Current Population Survey Annual Social and Economic Supplements, Internet site http://www.census.gov/hhes/www/poverty/index.html

—School Enrollment, CPS Historical Time Series Tables on School Enrollment, Internet site http://www.census.gov/hhes/school/data/cps/historical/index.html

—School Enrollment, CPS October 2011—Detailed Tables, Internet site http://www.census.gov/hhes/school/data/cps/2011/tables.html

—Voting and Registration, Internet site http://www.census.gov/hhes/www/socdemo/voting/index.html

—Wealth and Asset Ownership, Survey of Income and Program Participation, Internet site http://www.census.gov/people/wealth/

Department of Homeland Security

Internet site http://www.dhs.gov/

—Yearbook of Immigration Statistics, Internet site http://www.dhs.gov/yearbook-immigration-statistics

Employee Benefit Research Institute, American Savings Education Council, and Mathew Greenwald & Associates

Internet site http://www.ebri.org/

—2013 Retirement Confidence Survey, Internet site http://www.ebri.org/surveys/rcs/

National Center for Education Statistics

Internet site http://nces.ed.gov/

—Digest of Education Statistics, Internet site http://nces.ed.gov/programs/digest/

—Projections of Education Statistics to 2021, Internet site http://nces.ed.gov/programs/projections/projections2021/

National Center for Health Statistics

Internet site http://www.cdc.gov/nchs/

—*Anthropometric Reference Data for Children and Adults: United States, 2007–2010*, National Health Statistics Reports, Series 11, No. 252, 2012, Internet site http://www.cdc.gov/nchs/nhanes.htm

—*Births: Final Data for 2010*, National Vital Statistics Reports, Vol. 61, No. 1, 2012, Internet site http://www.cdc.gov/nchs/births.htm

—*Births: Preliminary Data for 2011*, National Vital Statistics Reports, Vol. 61, No. 5, 2012, Internet site http://www.cdc.gov/nchs/births.htm

—*Current Contraceptive Use in the United States, 2006–2010, and Changes in Patterns of Use since 1995*, National Health Statistics Reports, No. 60, 2012, Internet site http://www.cdc.gov/nchs/nsfg.htm

—*Deaths: Preliminary Data for 2011*, National Vital Statistics Reports, Vol. 61, No. 6, 2012, Internet site http://www.cdc.gov/nchs/deaths.htm

—*First Marriages in the United States: Data from the 2006–2010 National Survey of Family Growth*, National Health Statistics Reports, No. 49, 2012, Internet site http://www.cdc.gov/nchs/nsfg/new_nsfg.htm

—*Health, United States*, Internet site http://www.cdc.gov/nchs/hus.htm

—*Mean Body Weight, Height, and Body Mass Index, United States 1960–2002*, Advance Data, No. 347, 2004, Internet site http://www.cdc.gov/nchs/pressroom/04news/americans.htm

—*Summary Health Statistics for the U.S. Population: National Health Interview Survey, 2011*, Series 10, No. 255, 2012, Internet site http://www.cdc.gov/nchs/nhis/new_nhis.htm

—*Summary Health Statistics for U.S. Adults: National Health Interview Survey, 2011*, Series 10, No. 256, 2012, Internet site http://www.cdc.gov/nchs/nhis.htm

Survey Documentation and Analysis, Computer-assisted Survey Methods Program, University of California, Berkeley

Internet site http://sda.berkeley.edu/

—General Social Surveys, 1972–2012 Cumulative Data Files, Internet site http://sda.berkeley.edu/cgi-bin/hsda?harcsda+gss12

Index

of parent children live with, 256–257
probability of reaching marital anniversary by, 277–280
marriage
   gay, attitude toward, 20
   happiness of, 27
   median age at first, 245
   probability of reaching anniversary, 277–280
   same-sex, 283
married couples. *See also* Female-headed families, Male-headed families, Single-parent households *and* Single-person households.
   assets of, 408
   by age of householder, 260–261, 267–268, 282–283
   by age of husband and wife, 273
   by education of householder, 282
   by education of husband and wife, 274
   by presence of children, 259–263, 267–268, 282–283
   by race and Hispanic origin of householder, 262–263
   by race and Hispanic origin of husband and wife, 274
   debt of, 412
   dual income, 171, 173, 201–203, 207, 282, 368–373
   employment status of parents, 201–203
   homeownership of, 282–283, 408
   in poverty, 185–187
   income of, 167–168, 170–171, 282–283
   interracial, 274
   net worth of, 403–404
   same-sex, 283
   spending of, 334–342
   time use of, 368–373
   trends, 259
   wives earning more than husbands, 172–173
Medicaid coverage. *See* Health Insurance.
medical care, attitude toward government role in, 40
Medicare, attitude toward, 419. *See also* Health insurance.
middle class identification, 14
Midwest. *See* Region.
migraine headaches, 114–115
military health insurance. *See* Health insurance.
minimum wage workers, 236–238
mobility, geographic, 319–324
mortgage
   debt, 412–414
   interest, 334–360
mothers. *See also* Births.
   in labor force, 201–203, 205
   stay-at-home, 24–25, 271

   time use of, 368–373
   working, 23–25
mutual funds, as asset, 408–410

neighborhood, fear of walking at night, 8
nephritis, as cause of death, 125–126
net worth, 403–406
never-married. *See* Marital status.
news, sources of, 37
newspapers, frequency of reading, 37
Northeast. *See* Region.

obese. *See* Weight status.
occupation, 212–227. *See also* Employment status and Industry.
   earnings by, 160–162
overweight. *See* Weight status.

parents
   biological, step, adoptive, 256–257
   children living with both, 256–257
   spending of, 334–360
   standard of living, 11
   stay at home, 271
   time use of, 368–373
   work status of, 201–205
pension income, 416–417
personal care activities, time spent, 363–373
personal care products and services, spending on, 334–360
personal insurance and pensions, spending on, 334–360
pets, time spent caring for, 389
physical activity, 92
physician visits. *See* Health care visits.
political
   leanings, 39
   party affiliation, 39
poverty status
   by age, 183–184
   by household type, 185–187
   by presence of children, 185–187
   by race and Hispanic origin, 183–184
   trends, 181–182, 185–187
prayer, frequency of, 34
premarital sex, attitude toward, 19
prescription drug use, 120
projections
   of labor force, 240–241
   of population, 291–292, 305–306
property taxes, spending on, 334–360

race. *See* individual race/Hispanic origin groups.